African Theocology

African Theocology

Studies in African Religious Creation Care

Ebenezer Yaw Blasu

Foreword by Allison Mary Howell

WIPF & STOCK · Eugene, Oregon

AFRICAN THEOCOLOGY
Studies in African Religious Creation Care

Copyright © 2020 Ebenezer Yaw Blasu. All rights reserved. Except for brief quotations in critical publications or reviews, no part of this book may be reproduced in any manner without prior written permission from the publisher. Write: Permissions, Wipf and Stock Publishers, 199 W. 8th Ave., Suite 3, Eugene, OR 97401.

Wipf & Stock
An Imprint of Wipf and Stock Publishers
199 W. 8th Ave., Suite 3
Eugene, OR 97401

www.wipfandstock.com

PAPERBACK ISBN: 978-1-5326-8361-9
HARDCOVER ISBN: 978-1-5326-8362-6
EBOOK ISBN: 978-1-5326-8363-3

Manufactured in the U.S.A. FEBRUARY 11, 2020

With great love and admiration, I dedicate this work to the glory of God and to my sister Bernice Peace Amavi Toklo in appreciation of the educational foundation she laid for me. Thank you, sister, for all the sacrifices you made to send me to secondary school against all odds. That was the strong springboard for my educational flights to date. God richly bless you.

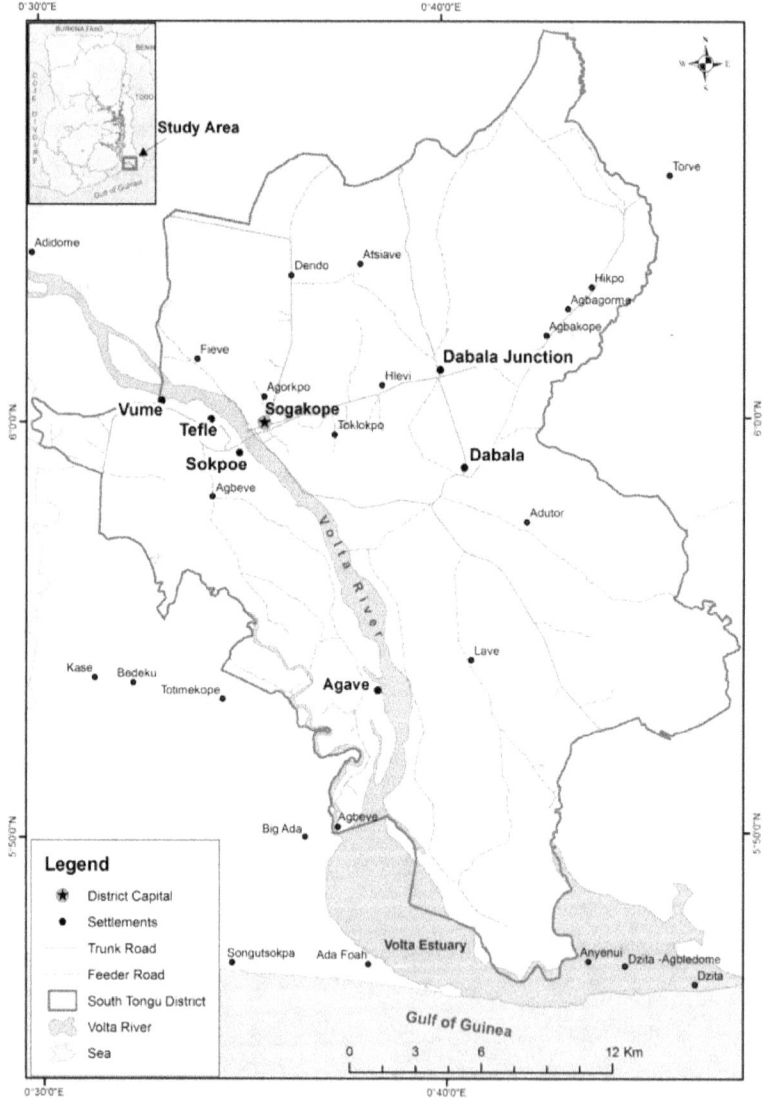

Map 1: South Tɔŋu District showing Study Area: Sokpoe, Sogakɔfe, Dabala Junction and Dabala

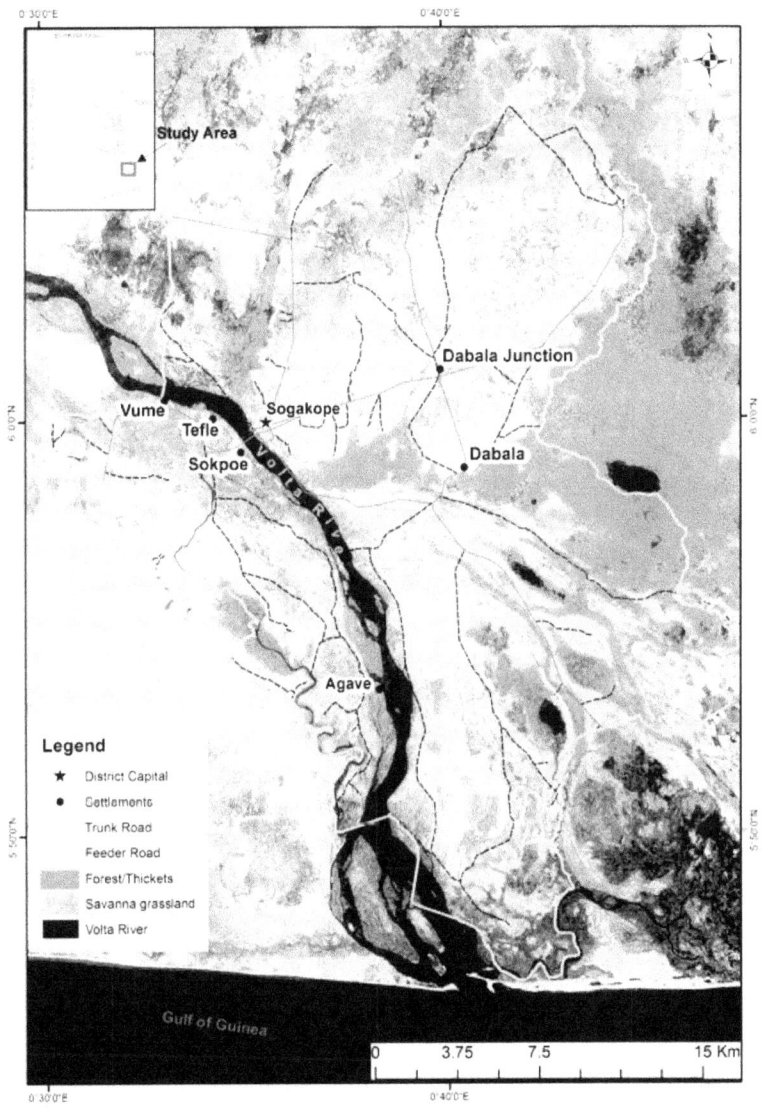

Map 2: Ecological Map (Esri satellite image) of South Tɔŋu

Contents

List of Tables and Figures | x
Abbreviations | xi
Foreword by Allison Mary Howell | xiii
Acknowledgements | xv

Introduction: An African Christian Response to the Global Eco-Crisis | 1

Part 1   Moral Environmentalism | 17
  CHAPTER 1   Learning Environmental Science as Fact and as Faith | 19
  CHAPTER 2   Religious Worldviews and Understanding Ecology | 39
  CHAPTER 3   Creation Care in Religious Traditions of Africa | 70
  CHAPTER 4   Modernity and African Religious Eco-Care Praxis | 103

Part 2   The Sokpoe-Eʋe and Eco-Care | 117
  CHAPTER 5   The Religious Mind-Views of *Xexeme* (Creation) and *Amegbetɔ* (Humanity) | 119
  CHAPTER 6   Religious Eco-Valuing and Ethical Praxis | 143
  CHAPTER 7   Religious Birthing Rites and Ecological Relations | 170
  CHAPTER 8   Eco-Sustainability Associated With Funerary Rites | 195

Part 3   African Theocology | 227
  CHAPTER 9   A Proposed African Alternative to Enviromental Science Curriculum | 229

Appendix: Transcripts of Interview Responses | 241
Glossary | 245
Bibliography | 249
Index | 257

Tables and Figures

Tables

Table 1.1: Human Disturbance of the Natural World | 32

Table 6.1: Eco-Valuing of Primal Religionists Indicated by Order for Rescuing Drowning Creatures | 145

Table 6.2: Sacred Forests and Associated Taboos in Sokpoe | 157

Figures

Figure 2.1: General Structure of African Worldviews | 44

Abbreviations

AACU	Association of American Colleges and Universities
ACI	Akrofi-Christaller Institute of Theology, Mission and Culture
AI	Appreciative Inquiry
AIC	African Indigenous Christianity
ARS	Apostolic Revelation Society
CE	Common Era
CEM	Christ Evangelical Mission
CERSGIS	Centre for Remote Sensing and Geographic Information Services
COP	Church of Pentecost
DHCCC	Divine Healing Church of Christ in Christ
EPA	Environmental Protection Agency
ERMP	Environmental and Rural Management Program
GNSP	General (or Interdisciplinary) Studies/Program
GPA	Grade Point Average
HoD	Head of Department
IAPCHE	International Association for the Promotion of Christian Higher Education
ICT/Maths	Information, Communication and Technology/Mathematics Department
MEST	Ministry of Environment, Science and Technology
MSC	Most Significant Change
NAB	National Accreditation Board

Abbreviations

NCCC	National Climate Change Committee
OM	Outcome Mapping
PIE	Participatory Impact Evaluation
PUCG	Presbyterian University College, Ghana
TD	Transformational Development
UNEP	United Nations Environment Program

Foreword

THE PAST THIRTY YEARS have witnessed an exponential increase in the number of articles and books on climate change and the environmental crisis. Many Christian theologians and writers have also produced a variety of Christian perspectives. In African Christianity, a growing number of authors are addressing issues related to the critical environmental and ecological problems that exist on the continent. The amazing study that follows presents the findings of Rev. Dr. Ebenezer Blasu's search for an African Christian response to the global eco-crisis, with a particular focus on Africa. He has thus documented a significant amount of material produced by Africans. The profound value of his work, however, lies in his examination of the praxis of creation care in the religious traditions of Africa. He introduces us specifically to those of the Sokpoe-Eʋe in the Volta Region of Ghana.

Dr. Blasu's investigations cover the major religious (primal, Islamic and Christian) concepts of creation and the role of the Sokpoe-Eʋe people in eco-care. The remarkable feature of this work is his study of Sokpoe-Eʋe religious worldviews of creation and humanity, their religious eco-valuing and ethical praxis, the use of religious birthing rites as primers for ecological relations and his gleanings about eco-sustainability from their funerary rites. He is well equipped to interpret this material, being a Sokpoe-Eʋe himself, with an in-depth knowledge of both the language and the context, having lived among his own people for extensive periods of his life. In his research on the Sokpoe-Eʋe, Dr. Blasu has discovered within the language words that expand our understanding of ways of explaining the universe.

The author's initial training and experience as an agriculturalist have given him invaluable insight into cultural, land and creation issues that are pertinent to this study. As a Christian pastor and theologian, Rev. Dr. Blasu has chosen to go beyond his own religious tradition to usher us into an understanding of the other major traditions of the Sokpoe-Eʋe, so we can learn from them as well.

There is such a wealth of material here. In fact, the depth of this study shows that a similar research project is possible in other ethnic groups, for Dr. Blasu has gone beyond the superficial task of simply identifying and classifying proverbs and taboos. Rather, he skilfully weaves together his experience, knowledge and insights to argue for an African theocology. He concludes his study by proposing an alternative environmental science curriculum.

Dr. Blasu's research does not only proffer a distinctive voice in the fields of African religious studies, ecological responses and theology. Quite apart from its rich insights, this study also provides us with possible models as Africa's contribution to the world discourse on our endangered environment, for which we are grateful to Dr. Blasu.

—Allison Mary Howell
>Associate Professor and Adjunct Staff, Akrofi-Christaller Institute of Theology, Mission and Culture

May 2019

Acknowledgements

I OFFER PROFOUND GRATITUDE to the Almighty God, who provided the courage, strength, wisdom and patience to me, and to all those who helped in making this project successful since the time of my PhD research study to the production of this book.

I owe special debt of gratitude to Prof. Allison M. Howell, Akrofi-Christaller Institute of Theology, Mission and Culture, Akropong-Akuapem, Ghana, for her consistent encouragement support and invaluable suggestions; and to Prof. Anthony Balcomb of the University of Kwazulu-Natal, South Africa, who readily accepted and proofread the final manuscript.

Prof. John Allen Grim of Yale University, School of Forestry and Environmental Studies, is highly appreciated in this project. He was enthused about my desire to bring an African perspective to religious ecological studies in Christian higher educational institutes. He concretized his wish for my success by donating the book *Islam and Ecology: A Bestowed Trust*, for which he and Evelyn M. Tucker wrote the series foreword. This was one of the books produced from a series of conferences on world religions and ecology from 1996 through 1998 and published by the Center for the Study of World Religions, Harvard Divinity School. This, together with the volume he edited, *Indigenous Religions and Ecology*, were, respectively, the primary resources of literature for the Islamic and indigenous religious aspects of my study. Dr. Maureen Iheanacho, you perfected my writing skills. Thanks.

Similarly, Rev. Dr. Samuel Asiedu-Amoako of Ramseyer Training Centre, Abetifi, Ghana, deserves a big "thank you" for giving me access to most of his personal ecological collections related to the study that resulted in this book.

You cannot be forgotten, Dr. Sandra Kunz of Trinity Theological College, Legon. Your personal interest, encouragement and invaluable suggestions after reading the synopsis of this project at its very beginning not only broadened my horizons, but also kept my focus on working towards a pragmatic outcome. The type of book you anticipated—one that can postulate an African model for practical Christian ecological theology—and gingered me on, is now here.

    I pray God's blessing on my wife, Evelyn Ama Blasu, and our four adult children for standing by me in the difficult times. Evelyn's explanations on birthing phenomena from a midwife's point of view significantly enhanced my interpretation of ecological importance of birthing rites among the Sokpoe-Eʋe. Above all, her supportive and encouraging voice—"God is with you; you will do it"—has been such a great motivational and sustaining sound that I enjoyed hearing throughout the work. Mama Lynn, God bless you. This has become your prayer and song any time I have faced strenuous academic activity at a postgraduate level since 2005. My children could not understand why at this old age I should spend my little energy pursuing not only another masters and PhD degree, but tediously working out the thesis into a book ultimately. Yet they have lent their prayer and financial support, knowing it is of the Lord. Thank you, boys, for paying your sister's school fees so Mum and I could direct our funds to both the study and the book project.

Introduction

An African Christian Response to the Global Eco-Crisis

Background

IN 2010, A FORTY-FIVE-YEAR-OLD woman from Bawku West District in the Upper East Region of Ghana granted an interview to researchers from the Ministry of Environment, Science and Technology (MEST), who were reviewing the extent of the socioeconomic impacts of Ghana's eco-crisis. She responded,

> I have seven children . . . The floods collapsed our three rooms and washed our crops . . . Hunger stared us straight in the face . . . Getting firewood is now very difficult and most times I have to climb trees for dried branches . . . sometimes I do this with my baby on my back . . .[1]

This woman's lamentation and her reference to "getting firewood" points to the wider anthropogenic[2] causes of climate change, which impact both humans and the environment in many parts of Ghana. The results of climate change are reflected in floods, loss of landed property, crop failure, hunger, land degradation, lack of wood energy, vulnerability of women and children to various life-threatening dangers and gradual loss of biodiversity. The Environmental Protection Agency (EPA) of Ghana corroborates this evidence with further instances of difficulties with obtaining potable water, as inland water bodies dry up and water tables fall, and food insecurity resulting from devastation of harvested crops through raised temperatures and plant pathological factors. A section of their 2004 report observes that temperatures in the country are gradually rising and this is affecting

---

1. "Ghana Goes for Green Growth," 28.

2. Curry, *Ecological Ethics*, 201. Curry asserts that "a significant amount of climate change is almost certainly anthropogenic (human-caused)."

agriculture. According to the report a 1° Celsius rise in temperature, for instance, has resulted in a general reduction in production levels of corn and millet. The report shows, furthermore, that while the fast rate of deforestation is creating warmer weather in the cities, high temperatures also destroy the flora and fauna. The resultant effects of all these include the onset of desertification in the Upper East, especially in Bawku area; many perennial rivers in the country are becoming seasonal, and sea levels are rising in coastal areas such as Keta and Ada—areas that already experience the devastating effects of sea erosion. The report states further that as buildings and other properties are destroyed, people and birds are compelled to migrate to other areas. In addition, projections indicate that there will be an increase in certain kinds of pests and diseases.[3]

If climate change in Ghana contributes to a breakdown in human and other-than-human well-being, then it goes against total wellness of all beings (3 John 1:2), which is the divine will, because it denies them their basic essential life needs. Humans and other animals, birds, and fish suffer from food insecurity, ill health, and an unsafe habitat, leading to frequent migrations in search of safer and greener pastures. In addition, plant life is subjected to both the vagaries of the deteriorating climatic conditions and the wanton destructive behaviors of humans. The government of Ghana, declaring climate change as a "developmental challenge" in 2010, appealed to Ghanaians to get involved in a concerted effort to care for creation.[4] In this respect and to this end, educational departments and institutions may design and offer appropriate environmental science curricula, which may stimulate moral environmentalism in the youth and students.

The Presbyterian Church of Ghana (PCG), responding to national and global needs for lasting action in mitigating the eco-crisis, enshrined in her holistic educational philosophy a missional[5] policy for inspiring moral eco-care "discipleship" in students. Stated as the seventh article, the environmental policy of the PCG educational philosophy expects that education should "lead" (transform) individuals "to appreciate the need to maintain the environment and protect the natural resources" (morally care for creation) in order "to avoid their degeneration and consequent destruction of humanity."[6] This policy seems anthropocentric in that it focuses on only the

---

3. Environmental Protection Agency, *Ghana State of Environment Report 2004*, 6.

4. H. E. John Dramani Mahama, Vice-President of Ghana, quoted in "Ghana Goes for Green Growth," 9.

5. Martey, "Foreword" to Presbyterian Church of Ghana, *Policy Document on General Education*, 5 and 13, states that the schools are "mediums of making converts" indirectly through practical faith and study of the Scriptures.

6. Presbyterian Church of Ghana, *Policy Document on General Education*, 14.

Homo sapiens species in the eco-community with the objective to promote sustenance of nature for the sake of and to benefit only human life. Nevertheless, it suggests a theological intention of the church, at least policy-wise, for Presbyterian formal education not only to necessarily include ecological studies in the curricula, but that such studies should actually "lead" (morally transform) the learner to appreciate the need to maintain the environment.[7] That is to say environmental study needs to impact pupils and students of Presbyterian educational institutions to morally and responsibly care for creation.[8]

From the mid-nineteenth century, a mission-oriented philosophy undergirding Presbyterian education in Ghana operated only at pretertiary levels until it was introduced at tertiary level at the beginning of the twenty-first century. Although the praxis of this philosophy and policy has not been "subjected to [systematic] scrutiny,"[9] the obvious influence of Presbyterian training on the spiritual and socioeconomic life of many people in Ghana and Africa has been notable. Kwamena-Poh describes this influence as creating in Presbyterian trained learners a "connection between conversion to Christianity and social well-being through hard work."[10] Now, in the first decade of the twenty-first century, the church has opportunity to apply, in principle, the objective of holistic mission education at the university level. Specifically, the impact of Presbyterian educational philosophy on religious and moral environmentalism is of great concern and the basis for this study.

---

7. Presbyterian Church of Ghana, *Policy Document on General Education*, 14.

8. I am a Presbyterian minister—born, bred, schooled, baptized and confirmed as Presbyterian. I recall in the mid-twentieth century (1960s) as a pupil in Sokpoe Ghana Presbyterian primary school our young minds were already introduced to environmental consciousness and responsibility through lessons in nature study, gardening and hygiene. Pragmatically these subjects encouraged us to enthusiastically plant tree seedlings and responsibly water them until they grew so we could inscribe our names on them. Others were in charge of flowerbeds that beautified the frontage of the school premises; and walking on lawns was highly forbidden. Personal hygiene and cleanliness demanded that our teachers inspected our school uniforms, fingernails, hairdos and teeth every Monday and Friday. The motivation and impulsion for responding to this basic ecological training was in dividing us into "sections" identified by colors: green, red, yellow and blue. The sections competed in the ecological activities, and the lowest-scored section would suffer hooting or given some task during evening closing assembly on Fridays. Every section leader and members therefore worked hard to avoid the Friday shout of "*Namɔ kpe, green kpe*" (a Ga expression for "Who is last, green is last") that crowned the week's school interactions.

9. Martey, "Foreword" to Presbyterian Church of Ghana, *Policy Document on General Education*, 5.

10. Kwamena-Poh, *Vision and Achievement*, xxiii.

For, in my view, the various students exposed to studying environmental science as a mandatory interdisciplinary course (GNSP 101) at PUCG over the first decade have not grasped the essence of the course in forming them as human beings made in the image of God (*imago Dei*).[11] Consequently, they tend to disregard the course, treat it as irrelevant, and simply consider it an "unnecessary burden" to be cursorily completed quickly in a semester, just to satisfy academic requirement. This observation may have one or many root causes: from the attitudes of both the students and teachers, the design (objectives and content) of the course and/or the method of teaching and learning it, among others.[12] In this case we have, perhaps, a problem of non-achievement regarding holistic education as mission and for moral transformation, particularly in the teaching and learning of mandatory environmental science at PUCG, as implied in PCG's educational policy. By extension, it also implies a failure of the church to impart many college-level youths with holistic education, in this case self-motivation for moral environmental responsibility. A more fundamental question, however, is whether the strategy of holistic education as vision and mission is attainable. The Very Rev. Prof. Emmanuel Martey, a past moderator of the General Assembly of PCG, reflecting on PCG's educational philosophy, has said that "the basic motive of employing the schools as mediums of making converts[13] has not yet been subjected to any scrutiny."[14] According to Allan A. Glitthorn, one reason to assess a program or policy is when it "is widely used but has had little systematic evaluation."[15] Thus, an effort to verify, through systematic scrutiny, the observed tendency of students to downplay environmental science as a mandatory course, particularly its concerns for Christian moral creation care impact, is an expedient reason for the study.

Consequently, the study based its purpose and objectives on the presupposition that influencing behavioral change in African Christianity through missional education holds a significant potential in morally

---

11. It is inferable from Myers, *Walking with the Poor*, 202, that being in the image of God implies, among other things, a vocation or mission involving moral responsibility in their human-Earth relations.

12. In short, there appears to be a question or challenge about the understanding and effectiveness of studying the general Environmental Science (GNSP 101) course as part of efforts to fulfil PUCG's Christian mission mandate and strategy in influencing the moral conscience of the students for self-motivation to environmental responsibility.

13. Converts in this case refers to disciplined leaders with moral responsibilities based on integrated Christian faith and praxis in learning.

14. Martey, "Foreword" to Presbyterian Church of Ghana, *Policy Document on General Education*, 5.

15. Glatthorn, *Writing the Winning Dissertation*, 76.

sustainable human-Earth relationships.¹⁶ Hence, it aimed to perform two main tasks:

1. To subject the Environmental Science (GNSP 101) curriculum to scrutiny by analyzing its attainability and potentials in holistic education for moral transformation towards the care of creation, as a mission strategy of PCG, in the first decade of PUCG.
2. To investigate the major religious (primal, Islamic and Christian) concepts of creation and the role of humans in eco-care among the Sokpoe-Eʋe, to inform designing a proposed African theocology curriculum.

This book presents the latter of the two related and subsequential objectives and their research findings corresponding to the two academic fields of Christian higher education as holistic mission and religious ecology as impulsion for creation care, respectively. The first objective and details of its research findings are reported in another book, *Building the Twenty-First Century Christian Academy: Christian Higher Education as Holistic Mission and Moral Transformation*. The relevance of that research for this book is that it pointed to the need for further fieldwork related to the development of a new proposed curriculum called "African theocology."

Proposing African Christian theocology as a religious ecology that may motivate creation care is a response to the search for holistic approaches in combating the global eco-crisis from an African perspective. Ben-Willie Kweku Golo observes that while the Western church responds to eco-crisis, particularly climate change in various forms, African Christianity is yet to engage actively with environmental activism¹⁷ and reconstruction of a creation care theology. Despite M. L. Daneel's uncertainty about African contribution to global environmental ethics in view of Western Christian cosmology, his pragmatism in developing an African (Zimbabwean) religious environmentalism from daily experiences of the people is intriguing and exemplary.¹⁸ The proposed African theocology curriculum would be designed with inputs from daily life experiences from religious ecologies in

---

16. This postulation or thesis of the study enjoys corroboration assertion from the Environmental Protection Agency (EPA) of Ghana that "Education and research holds the key to changing negative habits and behavior patterns, improving on livelihoods systems and focusing on best ways of ensuring sustainable national development." Environmental Protection Agency, *National Program on Sustainable Consumption and Production*, 7.

17. Golo, "Redeemed from the Earth?," 352.

18. The Christians in the projects belonged to sects of African Indigenous Christianity (AIC).

Ghana. This led to the second field research as part of my PhD studies, the findings of which constitute the contents of this book.

To the end of designing the African theocology curriculum by learning from the daily life experiences of religious ecologies in Ghana, I investigated the ecological knowledge systems and praxis of the three main religious traditions—the primal, Islamic and Christian—of the Sokpoe-Eʋe in the South Tɔŋu District of Volta Region, Ghana. It was not strictly a comparative phenomenological study of the ecologies of these religious traditions, however, it sought to and identified three minimum common grounds on which to base constructive understanding, motivating discussion and concerted ecological actions. The three common grounds that were retrieved and re-evaluated were their religious worldviews, religious impulsion for and praxis of creation care, and religious priming for harmonious ecological relationships. Religious resources such as scripture, myth narratives, sacramental rituals, symbols and taboos submitted in interviews by some devotees of the three religious traditions in the ecological area provided the analyzed data. This data, as alluded to earlier, was to inform designing the proposed African theocology curriculum. Conventionally, a discourse on engaging God's eco-values and ethics in creation care is often described as "eco-theology." Why then "African theocology"?

African Theocology and Eco-Theology Contrasted

The idea of "theocology" as an evolving twenty-first-century study is similar in many respects to that of "eco-theology," the conventional way of naming the religious approach to studying ecology. Both are comparative in terms of their ultimate purposes and major thematic contents, because they are conceived as subsets or corollaries of the theology of nature. Like African theocology, eco-theology is an emerging discipline of study,[19] beginning since the second half,[20] but more pronounced in the last decade of the twentieth century.[21] My motivation to inverse the name is in order to let African theocology be perceptible, understood and practiced more as *ecological* study, but starting with grounding in God as the creator of ecosystems.

I have earlier indicated that in his book *African Earthkeepers: Holistic Interfaith Mission*, M. L. Daneel was uncertain how, in view of Western Christian cosmology, African indigenous (primal and Christian) religious consciousness of the environment could contribute anything significant to

19. Grim and Tucker, *Ecology and Religion*, 63.
20. Grim and Tucker, *Ecology and Religion*, 87.
21. Cunningham and Saigo, *Environmental Science*, xv.

the development of global environmental ethics. But he was certain that his publication would challenge and inspire someone "in the common quest of Earth keepers worldwide to heal the Earth."[22] Perhaps I am one such challenged and inspired "disciple" of Daneel—a result of his published experiences in Africa. My interest in this study heightened during the course work for my Master of Theology/Doctor of Philosophy program at Akrofi-Christaller Institute (ACI) in the 2013–14 academic year. Particularly in the Theology, Human Needs and Environment course in October 2013, I learnt that "religion provides strong motivation for human protection of the environment,"[23] with a clear case of Daneel's Zimbabwean Earth-keepers. The Zimbabwean Earth-keeping projects were in response to their deforestation challenges, and were developed based on African indigenous religious cosmologies and ethical regulations—both primal and Christian.[24] Intrigued by their example, I intuitively described their work as "African theocology"—a form of ecological studies that necessarily begins with or is centered on God the creator of the ecosystems—as derived from African Christian theology. I shared the inspiration with some colleagues, emphasizing my hope to explore it further as an alternative to the environmental science course in our African universities, especially Presbyterian University College, Ghana (PUCG). By "African theocology" I envisage and mean the study of the relationships between God (the supreme being) as creator and his creations (human and other-than-human) and the role of humanity in these relationships, from the perspective of God and in the context of African religiosity. As an academic discipline, it is essentially to be a facet of or an approach to doing religious *ecology*. It is, therefore, essentially an *ecological* study, but recognizes that ecological/environmental science "needs to be in dialogue with other disciplines," especially African religions and religious ethics, "in seeking not only comprehensive solutions, 'but moral and missional impulsion to solving' both global and local environmental problems."[25] In other words, African theocology is envisioned as a Christian theistic *ecology*, to be studied by exploring African religious worldviews, eco-regulations and rituals, interpreted as much as possible with biblical texts in order to broaden understanding of and commitment to resolving the complex nature of current environmental concerns.[26] Meanwhile,

22. Daneel, *African Earthkeepers*, 106.

23. Daneel, "Zimbabwe's Earthkeepers," in Tucker, ed., *Nature, Science and Religion*, 202.

24. The Christians in the projects belonged to sects of African Indigenous Christianity (AIC).

25. ' "Forum on Religion and Ecology at Yale."

26. "Forum on Religion and Ecology at Yale."

concurrently and independently (as I found later) Howard Kris Carter also defined "theocology" as "a mix of theology and ecology, the study of God and the study of the ecosystems."[27]

This approach to study ecosystems beginning with God and his creation story is of particular importance. It is because, despite the assertions that religious practices have contributed to eco-degradations,[28] many supporters and contributors of religious ecology argue that science education is simply not enough to inspire the change necessary in our current environmental crisis.[29] It is noticeable in the West, for instance, that since the ideological conception and introduction of religious ecologies in academia from the late 1990s there is an increasing "force for eco-transformation," manifested in "growing religious environmentalism, statements on the importance of ecological protection and emergence of hundreds of grassroots projects by religious traditions."[30] I shall discuss or allude to the need for religion, particularly African religious traditions, in studying African theocology as a missional ecological study further in chapter 3. It is sufficient here to state that though science and technology share many important features of human culture with religion, they leave unexplored essential wellsprings of human motivation and concern that shape the world as we know it.[31] African theocology's ultimate hope is to encourage and provide Christian motivation to morally care for the Earth as a mission of the church. This involves regaining God's perspectives on ecology, through interpreting both the content of ecological science and African religious eco-knowledge with Christian Scriptures, as much as possible.

I later discovered, however, that my idea of "theocology" is similar in many respects to that of "eco-theology," the conventional way of calling the Christian religious approach to studying ecology, with emphasis on Christian *theology*. My motivation to inverse the name was in order to let "African theocology" be perceptible and practiced more as *ecological* study

---

27. It is noteworthy that concurrently, in October 2013, when I conceived the ideas of theocology in Akuapem-Akropong, Ghana, another Presbyterian minister, working independently in Auckland, New Zealand, also coined the same title. Howard Kris Carter called a series of teachings he embarked on to promote Christian environmentalism from study of the Psalms "Theocology." His actual theme was "The Breath Print of God and the Renewal of Care for Creation in the Nature Psalms." He explains "Theocology" as in the text and hoped that "as we look at the nature Psalms that we regain sound theological basis [God's perspective] for the care of creation, which in turn will encourage us to care for the planet that God has gifted us." Carter, "Looking Up."

28. Tucker and Grim, "Series Foreword" to Foltz et al., eds., *Islam and Ecology*, xx.

29. ' "What Is ECOTHEOLOGY?"

30. "Forum on Religion and Ecology at Yale."

31. Sullivan, "Series Preface" to Foltz et al., eds., *Islam and Ecology*, xii.

with grounding in God. Secondly, I believe the inversed name connotes the subject's objective and content as a corollary of theology of nature more than the conventional name.

It is noteworthy that conventional eco-theology itself is an emerging discipline of study,[32] beginning since the second half,[33] but more pronounced in the last decade of the twentieth century.[34] As Jonathan J. Bonk wrote in 2008,

> Only now are Catholic, Protestant, and Orthodox missiologists starting to realize that strategies for saving the world have been framed within a theological cocoon that prevented them from adequately understanding the end result of their civilization's notions of progress, development, and the social material destiny of humankind.[35]

Knowing that the conventionally known Eco-theology is a new and evolving academic discipline further strengthened my desire and motivation to deepen the study towards ultimately contributing an African input to the design of what I envisaged as an "African theocology." The additional urge for an African input in environmental science curriculum was from an experience in teaching environmental science at Presbyterian University College, Ghana. Students tended to be uncomfortable with the integration of theological reasoning in environmental scientific learning on the notion that "fact and faith are not integral." This led me to find how the university could rethink and engage in the holistic education mandated by the founding Presbyterian Church of Ghana (PCG); particularly, the teaching and learning of environmental science as a mission strategy for promoting students' moral responsibility to and for the environment.

Literary Sources for the Study

The secondary literature to support and place the study in a proper perspective for analysis, interpretation and utilization are from the two subfields of ecology: ecology as science of understanding and conserving ecosystems, and ecology as religio-ethical or "theocological" ways of shaping human behavior to sustain ecosystem life.

---

32. Grim and Tucker, *Ecology and Religion*, 63.
33. Grim and Tucker, *Ecology and Religion*, 87.
34. Cunningham and Saigo, *Environmental Science*, xv.
35. Bonk, "Mission and the groaning of Creation," 170.

Chapter 1 analyzes the literary sources that deal with "ecology as scientific fact." This places the ecological problem and objectives of the study in the global and local environmental situations to help explain the findings of the research. Therefore, it considers concepts and ideas relating to our environment as ecosystems, with emphasis on eco-crisis or the threats to life on planet Earth, as well as the development and importance of ecology as a science of ecosystems and their conservation for sustainability. I draw some ideas from *Environmental Science: A Global Concern* by William Cunningham and Barbara Saigo and *Environmental Science: The Way the World Works* by Benard J. Nebel and Richard T. Wright. In these books, the authors present us with an opportunity to repair the damage we have caused to the natural world and to find more efficient and environmentally friendly ways of the goods and services we need, by first understanding the natural world and how it works. Some ideas in these books enable this study to define or explain terms related to the environment and summarize principles of environmental (ecological) science that explain how the natural world functions from scientific perspective. Some publications, especially reports of the Environmental Protection Agency (EPA) of Ghana, are also analyzed to appreciate the nature and level of ecological threat in Ghana and, hence, Africa.[36] The chapter ends with an assertion that studying about the environment as scientific facts only is inadequate in stimulating missional and moral creation care; there is need to integrate religious ecology.

Therefore, chapters 2, 3 and 4 analyze some sources for the theistic ecologies of African primal, Islamic and Christian religions. My interest is to understand not only their theologies of the environment, impulsion for and praxis of ecological care, but also challenges implicit in religious ecological praxis vis-à-vis modernity. This enables me to assess similar parameters in the field data from Sokpoe ecological communities in chapters 5 and 6, respectively. The need for these sources is against the supposition that, as Matthew Clarke observes, not only does 80 percent of the world's population profess religious faith, but generally religious belief is pervasive, profound, persuasive and persistent in influencing social behaviors, yet has long been ignored in mainstream development paradigms.[37] While agreeing, I argue in chapter 5 why sometimes, with evidences from my work among the Sokpoe-Eʋe, the potentials in religion for eco-praxis may be ignored. For the Sokpoe-Eʋe ignoring religion in ecological development agenda is, perhaps, largely a result of ignorance of the religious people themselves about the pragmatic potentials in their religious teachings and praxis for

---

36. Environmental Protection Agency, *Ghana State of Environment Report 2004*, 6.
37. Clarke, *Development and Religion*, 1.

creation care. It may also result from the need for survival at the expense of environmental degradation. For all the religious traditions the analytic review of literature focuses specifically on their worldviews, impulsion for and praxis of ecological ethics.

To this end and with respect to Christians, the research analyzes the works of a number of authors for concepts about religious ecology and how religion, particularly Christianity, may influence environmental responsibility. These include *Ecology and Religion* by John Grim and Mary Evelyn Tucker,[38] Hans Schwarz's *Creation*,[39] Solomon Victus's *Eco-Theology and the Scriptures*,[40] Michael S. Northcott's *A Moral Climate: The Ethics of Global Warming*[41] and Patrick Curry's *Ecological Ethics: An Introduction*.[42] With regard to the perspectives of African Christianity some major works are analyzed. J. O. Y. Mante's *Africa: Theological and Philosophical Roots of Our Ecological Crisis*[43] proposes theories of perichoresis that could apply to explaining religious anthropologies of the Sokpoe-Eʋe in chapter 6. Harvey Sindima's article "Community of Life: Ecological Theology in African Perspective" establishes African understanding of life as bounded to nature, though as I argue in chapter 5, Africans' ethical relations with nature is anthropocentric.[44] Ben-Willie Kwaku Golo's "Redeemed from the Earth? Environmental Change and Salvation Theology in African Christianity" finds a problem with African Christian praxis of saving the human soul devoid of any ecological implications, and sees it as resulting from Western heritage of salvation theology.[45] Another significant source is Birgit Meyer's *Translating the Devil: Religion and Modernity among the Eʋe in Ghana*.[46] Although Meyer describes her ethnographic work as "among the Eʋe in Ghana," she actually investigates Christianity at the grassroots level specifically and mainly among the Peki-Eʋe only. She focuses on the Christian evangelical message of the nineteenth-century German Pietistic missionaries from the Norddeutsche Missionsgesellschaft (NMG), Bremen. Her concern is the factors that affected the response of the Peki-Eʋe primal religious, whom she calls "heathendom" or devotees of "Eʋe religion," to the missionary Christian

---

38. Grim and Tucker, *Ecology and Religion*, 62.
39. Schwarz, *Creation*, 165.
40. Victus, *Eco-Theology and the Scriptures*, 46.
41. Northcott, *Moral Climate*, 16.
42. Curry, *Ecological Ethics*, 8.
43. Mante, *Africa*, 5.
44. Sindima, "Community of Life," 137–47.
45. Golo, "Redeemed from the Earth?," 356.
46. Meyer, *Translating the Devil*, xvii.

message. She realizes that missionaries' mispresentation of the devil as "outmoded superstition" did not only "demonize Eʋe gods and spirits," "draw a boundary between Christianity and Eʋe Religion," but also expected discarding "the image of the Devil in local appropriations of Christianity."[47] But Meyer finds, contrarily, that the devil continues to occupy a significant place, either to be ignored or rather fearfully responded to appropriately, in the religious ecology of Peki-Eʋe Christianity. Her analysis and findings hold to a large extent also for the Sokpoe-Eʋe Christians' ecological attitudes. Most Christians in the Sokpoe ecological area were evangelized, at least initially, by the Basel Missionaries (BM); and, as Meyer explains, both the NMG and the BM were trained in the same school with same Protestant Pietistic theology and praxis. From ecological point of view, both Golo and Meyer imply that Western missionary activity contributed significantly in the tendency of the Eʋe Christians in Ghana, and hence Africa, to demystify and disenchant nature, with possibility of exploiting it without any religious and moral concerns.

In the case of the Islamic tradition, the works analytically reviewed include several articles in *Islam and Ecology*, edited by Richard C. Foltz, Frederick M. Denny and Azizan Baharadddin. In this book, while Ibrahim Özdemir, for instance, presents "Understanding of Environmental Ethics from a Qur'anic Perspective,"[48] Seyyed Hossein Nasr's article "Islam, the Contemporary Islamic World, and the Environmental Crisis" outlines both obstacles to realizing implementing Islamic views of the natural environment and what to be done.[49] *My Neighbour's Faith: Islam Explained for Christians* by John Azumah explains basic Islamic teachings that could foster cooperation between Muslims and other religions for concerted ecological actions in religiously plural contexts.

For analyzed information in African primal religions, Ogbu Kalu's article "The Sacred Egg: Worldview, Ecology and Development in Africa," and others in *Indigenous Traditions and Ecology*, edited by John A. Grim,[50] Andrew F. Walls's "African Christianity in the History of Religions" in *The Cross-Cultural Process in Christian History*, as well as Harry K. Agbanu's unpublished PhD thesis, "Environmental Ethics in the Mafi-Eʋe Indigenous Culture,"[51] are the major works examined. Kalu outlines a phenomenological

---

47. Meyer, *Translating the Devil*, xvii.
48. Özdemir, "Toward an Understanding of Environmental Ethics," 4.
49. Nasr, "Islam, the Contemporary Islamic World," 85.
50. Grim, ed., *Indigenous Traditions and Ecology*, selected chapters.
51. Agbanu, "Environmental Ethics in Mafi-Eʋe Indigenous Culture," 95.

structure and components of primal African religious worldviews.⁵² However, Walls opines that the difference in dominating components challenges a postulation that there can be one, *the* African, worldview.⁵³ Agbanu's observation corroborates that of Kalu that the precarious vision of the world is the major impulsion for primal African eco-ethical praxis.⁵⁴ These works together with Harold Turner's idea of kinship with nature as a feature of primal religions that illustrates human interrelationship with the created world⁵⁵ are helpful in interpreting interview results of the primal eco-ethical thought and knowledge of the Sokpoe-Eʋe eco-community.

The Need for Religious Pluralism in the African Theocology Curriculum

The research employed qualitative methods of analyzing both literary and oral data, which were collected based on the understanding that the cosmologies and ecologies of various religious traditions, particularly primal, Islam and Christian in Africa, are helpful for determining an African theocology curriculum. The need to understand the theological perspectives of religions other than Christianity is because, as Patrick Curry observes, we live in a "pluralistic world" (a world of diverse views on same issues),⁵⁶ which means that values and ethical praxis sometimes conflict, with no ideal (generally accepted absolute) or painless resolution in the pluralistic context. In my view, this implies that pragmatic religious ecologies need to accommodate as many virtuous ideals as possible, especially "where there is real potential common ground on a particular issue,"⁵⁷ although they may possibly not accommodate all. Accommodating other virtuous ideals demands that we first understand them even if we do not agree with them; then we may learn from them and use Scripture to interpret them to determine their relevance for Christian eco-ethics and praxis.⁵⁸ In an article about the theology of religions, David Thang Moe suggests some reasons why Christians can learn or share ideas with other faiths in practical missional endeavors, which can

---

52. Kalu, "Precarious Vision," 43.
53. Walls, *Cross-Cultural Process in Christian History*, 123.
54. Agbanu, "Environmental Ethics in Mafi-Eʋe Indigenous Culture," 95.
55. Turner, "The Primal Religions of the World," in Hayes, ed., *Australian Essays in World Religions*, 31.
56. Curry, *Ecological Ethics*, 156.
57. Curry, *Ecological Ethics*, 156.
58. Curry, *Ecological Ethics*, 156.

hold for missional ecological education.⁵⁹ Moe's suggestions in section 4 of the article imply that in missional ecological education in a pluralistic religious context, we need to:

1. Prioritize humanity over religiosity, seeing them first as also made in the image of God (Gen 1:27), though people cannot be separated from their religions.

2. Appreciate the pointers to gospel in their eco-cultures as *praeparatio evangelica*, having also been made in God's image, and in the process identify how to link the gospel to or insert it into and hope to transform their eco-cultures, rather than destroy them totally by considering them as *tabula rasa*. In this way, "some little truths, lights, values and ethical teachings of their religions," about creation and the role of humans in it, "could help them develop their transforming lives" if they continue them under the power and illumination of the Holy Spirit.

3. Recognize the indispensability of other religious eco-values, their daily ecological experiences and use of signs and symbols, for translating the gospel and engaging them in developing local Christian ecologies. The caution, however, is to maintain the integrity of the gospel and uniqueness of Christ in using the signs and symbols to translate the ecological gospel.

4. Face the fact that despite their theological differences, other faiths may have eco-ethical perspectives that are similar to and from which Christians may learn, or vice versa.⁶⁰

In order to gain the primal theological perspective and praxis of ecology, I analyzed data from written and oral sources from the Tɔŋu Eʋe, specifically the Sokpoe-Eʋe in the South Tɔŋu District in Volta Region, Ghana. I chose this research area just because of my cultural familiarity, which could facilitate the process as well as deepen my understanding of views collated. Moreover, apart from the work of H. K. Agbanu on the Mafi-Eʋe in North Tɔŋu, which itself focused on only the indigenous environmental ethics, there is no known work on the religious ecology *per se* in the whole of the Tɔŋu ecological zone. Significantly, there is no report on the entire Tɔŋu ecological zone indicating all three major religions—primal, Islam and Christianity—involved in a single study, be it comparative or phenomenological, as in the current project.

---

59. Moe, "Trinitarian Theology of Religions," 248.
60. Moe, "Trinitarian Theology of Religions," 248.

The retrieved religious eco-data from the responses—worldviews, impulsion for and praxis of eco-ethics—were evaluated, in the case of Christians, with biblical/Christian theological reflections. The PhD thesis of Harry Lawson Agbanu on "Environmental Ethics in Mafi-Eʋe Indiginous Culture" was significant in providing examples of primal ecological ethics and procedures of retrieving and analyzing the primal data. I have ealier indicated that Birgit Meyer's work among the Peki-Eʋe enhanced deducing some explanations for the Sokpoe-Eʋe Christians' ecological attitudes, particularly based on the fear of the devil in their ecosystems. Similarly, the Qur'an and other related literary sources enabled drawing inferences on the Islamic perspectives of the data about the environment.

Structure of the Book

The book follows a three-part structure of discourse. Part 1 is Moral Environmentalism. It presents the critical literary study on how both scientific and the three religious ecologies motivate moral eco-praxis. These have been captured in chapters 2–5 as mentioned earlier above. Part 2 is the field study on the "Sokpoe-Eʋe and Eco-Care" and is discussed in chapters 6–9. The third part, the proposed African theocology, concludes the book in chapters 10 and 11 based on the findings of both the literary study and field research in parts 1 and 2, respectively.

Part 1

Moral Environmentalism

CHAPTER 1

Learning Environmental Science as Fact and as Faith

Introduction

THE OPENING CHAPTER SETS the ultimate objective of this book as proposing African theocology to be an alternative but hopefully more effective curriculum for promoting moral and missional environmentalism than the traditional environmental science. However, it defined African theocology as essentially an environmental science, which necessarily needs to be in dialogue with other disciplines, particularly African religions and religious ethics. This chapter explores the understanding and concepts of environmental science as used in this book. More relevantly for the purpose of this book, it also discourses the potential of environmental science to motivate moral responsibility of students for creation care, particularly when studied within a holistic Christian framework. The definition of environmental science thus used is based on a personal experience of teaching the course at Presbyterian University College, Ghana as a mandatory undergraduate science subject in a general or an interdisciplinary study.

The Notion of Environmental Science (GNSP 101) as an Interdisciplinary Course at PUCG

Clearly, by its nomenclature, environmental science is from a two-term expression: environment and science. The *Oxford Advanced Learner's Dictionary*, defines "environment" as the natural world in which people, animals and plants live.[1] In their *Environmental Science: A Global Concern* textbook for undergraduate education, William Cunningham and Barbara Saigo define "environment" (from the French *environner*, to encircle or surround) as the circumstances or conditions that surround an organism or group of organisms.[2] By these definitions, "the environment" connotes the idea that our *surrounding* is the space, time and other creatures around and amidst which we humans are, but minus us—at micro or macro levels. For Cunningham and Saigo it is the world (space and time) we inhabit, consisting of the natural world and the human-built world. The natural world or environment comprises the flora, fauna, soils, air, and water of the ecosphere (the Earth and the regions around it) that preceded us by billions of years and of which we are part.[3] Brian Thomas Swimme and Mary Evelyn Tucker, authors of *Journey of the Universe*, inform us that the observable universe emerged 13.8 billion years ago, and we now live on a planet orbiting our sun, one of the trillions of stars in one of the billions of galaxies in an unfolding universe that is profoundly creative and interconnected.[4] The human-built world, on the other hand, includes the sociocultural institutions and artifacts that we create for ourselves using science, technology and political organizations.[5]

Science is a way of knowing. Many scientists claim it is a systematic, precise, objective way to study the natural world, employing creativity, skill and insight.[6] The insistence on objectivity is because Francis Bacon, who was highly instrumental in developing modern science, stipulated that we are directly aware of reality (and he means scientifically) in only physical things.[7] Science takes many different forms and is done in assorted ways by widely diverse people. But they have only one aim: to gain a neutral and unbiased comprehension of the natural world and the universality of its

---

1. *Oxford Advanced Learner's Dictionary*, 8th ed.

2. Cunningham and Saigo, *Environmental Science*, 17. This is one of the primary textbooks used for the Environmental Science course (GNSP 101) at Okwahu Campus of PUCG.

3. Cunningham and Saigo, *Environmental Science*, 17.

4. Swimme and Tucker, *Journey of the Universe*, 2.

5. Cunningham and Saigo, *Environmental Science*, 17.

6. Cunningham and Saigo, *Environmental Science*, 48.

7. Henry, *Scientific Revolution and the Origins of Modern Science*. According to Holmes, *Building the Christian Academy*, 75, Descartes' theory of indirect or representative perception had not yet taken over. Moreover, this was the time when the Reformation had created a vacuum of authority in matters on which Scripture is silent, and Protestantism was torn by differing interpretations of the Bible. Everywhere there was obvious need for an objective, universally assured system of acquiring knowledge independent of divisive beliefs.

phenomena.[8] The hope is to ultimately employ the knowledge gained in enhancing the estate of humanity, as Francis Bacon explained.[9]

Ideally, scientific learning follows a series of logical, orderly steps. It begins with observing objects and phenomena in the natural world and formulating a provisional explanation or assumption called a hypothesis. Testing the hypothesis experimentally leads to collecting data (hard facts) that may be analyzed and interpreted, often by consulting the previous knowledge or hypotheses to draw conclusions or inferences of possibilities about the reality. Eventually, with evidence from a group of related investigations, scientists create a theory to explain a set of general principles.[10] This is called positivist inductive or experimental learning by examining the parts to conclude on the whole—that is, from the specific to the general.

It is significant to notice some limitations in scientific learning. The positivist inductive science is sometimes rejected because some academics argue against objectivity claims in science. For them, there is no such thing as an objective, uninvolved observer, drawing experiences from uncertainties in quantum physics. They claim that anytime we make an observation we affect the observed, and subdividing objects or processes into constituent parts loses salient characteristics of the whole.[11] According to Cunningham and Saigo, such critics prefer a holistic or an interpretive approach to science. In doing this they recognize inherent biases and describe or interpret subjects faithfully and as accurately as possible, deducing specifics from generalities. Moreover, it is a common misconception to say that science proves theories, because scientific interpretations are always conditional. Conclusions favoring or contradicting a hypothesis may be modified in the wake of new evidence.[12] For instance, in her discussion on values in ecological science Celia Deane-Drummond argues that the shift from the concept of ecological balance to ecological flux illustrates the difficulties of using ecological science as a basis for values, for as further research is conducted other values appear that call into question the previous notions.[13] With these explanations of the terms "environment" and "science" we may look etymologically at what environmental science is.

8. Cunningham and Saigo, *Environmental Science*, 48.

9. Henry, *Scientific Revolution and the Origins of Modern Science*. See also Curry, *Ecological Ethics*, 37.

10. Cunningham and Saigo, *Environmental Science*, 49.

11. Cunningham and Saigo, *Environmental Science*, 49.

12. Cunningham and Saigo, *Environmental Science*, 49.

13. Deane-Drummond, *Eco-Theology*, 12.

Environmental science as an academic subject is the systematic study of our environment (surroundings, both natural and human-built) and our place in it.[14] It is a highly interdisciplinary academic field that integrates natural sciences, social sciences and humanities in a broad, holistic study of the *world around us*.[15] It is relatively a new field that emerged from natural history and medicine during the Enlightenment, but gathered momentum in the 1960s, particularly with outcries against anthropogenic environmental hazards.[16] One such prominent outcry was the publishing of *Silent Spring* by biologist Rachael Carson in 1962, on pollution and toxicity threats to life. She observed, for instance, how in 1959 aldrin, "a dangerous chlorinated hydrocarbon" dusted from the air over 27,000 acres in southern Michigan against the Japan beetle "caused shocking destruction of animal life and have exposed human beings to undeniable hazard."[17]

William Cunningham in his preface to their text book *Environmental Science: A Global Concern* indicates that this subject may be studied by both science-major and non-science-major students, with the latter exposed to it in the first year at university[18] as part of a general or an interdisciplinary study. Bernard J. Nebel and Richard T. Wright explain why non-science-major students also need to mandatorily study environmental science as

---

14. Cunningham and Saigo, *Environmental Science—A Global Concern*, 17.

15. Cunningham and Saigo, *Environmental Science—A Global Concern*, 17 (italics added).

16. Nebel and Wright, *Environmental Science*, 7.

17. Carson, *Silent Spring*, 87–88. However, fifty years after *Silent Spring*'s eco-alarm, Meiners et al., eds., *Silent Spring at 50*, 95, accused Carson of raising a "false crisis" and substituting sensationalism for fact based on an outward work of popular science. My own response is that it is not difficult to infer that *Silent Spring at 50* sounds more an anti- than pro-environmentalism. The arguments made by authors and editors, who themselves are distinguished professors in property-business-environmental interactions, are not objectivized to necessarily correct Carson's alleged "significant errors and sins of omission," but highly tended to rewin public interests in reflourishing environmental-related business and economic enterprises that *Silent Spring* silenced in the 1970s. Perhaps the current American president, Donald Trump, is pursuing a similar politico-economic-environmental agenda in reducing governmental concerns about the environment. I contend that irrespective of whatever arguments against her, Rachael Carson remains a historically and necessarily bold and fearless ecological "whistle-blower," who not only alerted the public about global anthropogenic eco-crisis but caused conscious efforts at promoting necessary ecological actions. For her publication "triggered repercussions that resonate to this day—from creating the modern environmental movement to spawning federal laws governing air and water quality, protection of endangered species, worker safety, and much more." See Larry Katzenstein, "The Precautionary Principle: *Silent Spring*'s Toxic Legacy," Meiners et al., eds, *Silent Spring at 50*, 245.

18. Cunningham, "Preface" in Cunningham and Saigo, *Environmental Science*, xv.

an interdisciplinary course. They believe that environmental science is appropriate for even non-majors because it is important that people entering virtually every professional area have understanding of the factors underlying environmental issues so that they can have environmental concerns and bearings in their future decision-making processes.[19] Mark Stewart of the University of Maryland, writing in 2010, observed that in North America, as an example, sustainability has exploded onto the higher education scene in the previous few years as a response to calls from local, national, and international realizations of our global ecological predicament becoming clearer.[20]

In Stewart's view, the exponential growth of human population and the insatiable and unsustainable consumption of finite resources are causing profound damage to our global ecosystem. Government, industry, aid organizations, and other groups of people around the world are looking to institutions of higher education to create sustainable solutions to environmental, societal and economic challenges.[21] According to him, between December 2006 and April 2010, more than 680 American colleges and universities answered that call by pledging to "green" their operations and set goals for eliminating their contributions of global warming emissions through the American College and University Presidents' Climate Commitment. Some institutions, including Arizona State University, the University of Georgia, and the University of Maryland, have made significant efforts—such as developing new academic programs, creating graduation requirements, and training faculty on how to integrate sustainability across the curriculum—to educate all their students about sustainability and prepare graduates to be thoughtful citizens of a planet in peril.[22]

In 2017, barely a little under seven years after Stewart's article, his observed and reported positive zeal for environmental education in the USA came under serious threat with a change of government. The new president, Donald Trump, appointed a new head for the Environmental Protection Agency, Scott Pruitt, a climate change skeptic with close ties to the oil and gas industry, to undo automobile emissions regulations. Then he cut environmental protection grant by 30 percent[23] and threatened to withdraw the USA from the 2015 Paris Climate Agreement, aimed at ensuring a

19. Nebel and Wright, *Environmental Science*, xvii.
20. Stewart, "Transforming Higher Education," 1.
21. Stewart, "Transforming Higher Education," 1.
22. Stewart, "Transforming Higher Education," 1.
23. Marans, "Obama EPA Head Savages Donald Trump's Environmental Policies."

low-carbon world, on purely economic and political grounds.[24] However, I believe that one country's political denial of occurrence of, and the subsequent objection to the need for moral ecological education and actions to combat climate change, does not mean creation care efforts have to cease in all other global cultures.[25]

For instance, large expanses of tropical moist forests such as in West Africa are disappearing at a rapid rate,[26] and in Ghana the Environmental Protection Agency (EPA) fears unchecked deforestation threatens desertification conditions and loss of biodiversity due to migration of some species, particularly the avian.[27] Thus there are great efforts towards environmental science education and actions in Ghana, particularly among the public universities and some private Christian university colleges, such as Valley View University (VVU) and Presbyterian University College, Ghana (PUCG). The Ghana government in 2010 declared climate change a developmental challenge with a call for each of us "from every sector and group" including the academia to contribute to solving the problem.[28] Consequently, the Ministry of Education committed itself to promoting environmental education and awareness creation from basic to tertiary level of schooling by, *inter alia*, developing curricula around environmental sustainability.[29]

The PUCG from its inception in 2003 had this concern factored in its institutional concept to integrate environmental sustainability education across programs with environmental science as one of the subjects in a general or an interdisciplinary study. The lecturer who designed and

---

24. Stokols, "Trump to Pull U.S. Out of Paris Climate Accord."

25. Personally, I see these developments as potent with great retardation to global efforts in mitigating eco-crisis and its devastating implications for life on the Earth. Particularly the attempts, such as in this current study, to call for moral and missional ecology in the academia may suffer significant discouragement, if the USA, an influential country in global decision making, does not appropriately resolve this political-environmental tension. Clearly and ontologically it indicates how political factors, especially the sustenance of political will and decisions over time, are very crucial in the prospects of promoting moral ecological education and praxis. However, I am encouraged that a political denial of the reality of anthropological climate change and eco-crisis in general in a country does not by itself factually deny the existential experiences of eco-crisis in that country or other parts of the globe. There are enough significant footprints of eco-crisis in many parts of the world, even if experienced at different dimensions and levels, to support global environmentalism.

26. Cunningham and Saigo, *Environmental Science*, 113.

27. Environmental Protection Agency, *Ghana State of Environment Report 2004*, 6.

28. H. E. John Dramani Mahama, Vice-President of Ghana, message to National Climate Change Committee (NCCC), 1.

29. Naana Jane Opoku-Agyeman, quoted in Asante, "Environmental Education Integrated in School Syllabi."

lectured the first general Environmental Science (GNSP 101) course in 2003 explained that the reason for including it across the curricula of the university was to mitigate "the problem with sanitation in Ghana and misuse of resources, contrary to God's injunction for mankind to take care of His creation."[30] Therefore, the educational purpose was "for students in all programs of study at PUCG to be environmentally literate and conscious of the fact that God expects us to take care of the environment and sustain creation."[31] Mark Stewart similarly explains that, since environmental sustainability offers a conceptual framework for addressing today's problems, students in *every* discipline must be engaged in conversation about it with action to help reshape society toward ecological sustenance. Therefore, in his view, educating all students to be literate in environmental sustainability should not be a goal of only a few select colleges and universities that have strong environmental traditions. Rather, comprehensive eco-sustainability education is an essential pursuit for any college or university that desires to be relevant in the twenty-first century.[32]

It is to this end that Cunningham and Saigo suggest that universities design appropriate environmental science action plans including environmental science curricula, which could contrast with theoretic disciplines by being "mission oriented." That is, the curriculum needs to enable students to seek new, valid, contextual knowledge about the natural world and our impacts on it, but obtaining this information could create in them a responsibility to get involved in trying to do something about the problems we have created.[33] In other words, meaningful responsibility for creation goes beyond academic facts and beliefs in environmental science and touches our personal lives, our lifestyles, and how we personally affect the environment. The study of environmental science, as factual learning, may have to engender moral commitment to concrete or practical ecological actions.[34] Text-based learning needs "to challenge students and those around them to begin making a difference" by taking sustainable ecological actions.[35] The implication is that in addition to scientific knowledge or facts of how the natural world works, studying environmental science as a general and "mission-oriented" subject requires also ecological ethics—the moral (right and

---

30. L-AB001, interview, emailed questionnaire, retrieved 8 November 2014.
31. L-AB001, interview, emailed questionnaire, retrieved 8 November 2014.
32. Stewart, "Transforming Higher Education," 2.
33. Cunningham and Saigo, *Environmental Science*, 17.
34. Nebel and Wright, *Environmental Science*, 13.
35. Nebel and Wright, *Environmental Science*, xviii.

wrong) relationships between humans and the world around us,[36] which directs how we ought to live and act to sustain our ecological community.[37]

In view of this Cunningham and Saigo propose some goals for teaching general and missional environmental science, including (1) awareness and appreciation of the natural and built environment, (2) knowledge of natural systems and ecological concepts, (3) understanding of current environmental issues, (4) and the ability to use critical-thinking and problem-solving skills (with resources such as Scripture as hermeneutic)[38] for environmental issues.[39] In my view these are plausible goals and the first three may be considered as "environmental science as fact" and the last one "ecology as religious faith." Environmental science as fact is the scientific understanding of the natural environment and how it works through natural ecological systems (ecosystems)—the units for ecological actions. It analyzes the complex interactions within and between ecosystems. Ecology as faith, contrarily, as explained by Grim and Tucker, examines cultural awareness of and beliefs about these interactions as to urge or create moral impulsion for action to ensure the continuity of ecosystem life. Whereas the former has given us methods of conservation and management of ecosystems and species, the latter represents an important lens whereby humans can think critically, understand and re-envision their roles as participants in the dynamic processes of life[40] from the perspective of God, the creator of our Earth and its ecosystems.

Natural Ecosystem Function as Principles of Sustainability or Conservation.

Implicit in the study of environmental science is the presupposition that it is when we gain understanding of how our world works through natural ecosystems that we may understand "what is necessary for their conservation"[41] or sustainability. Although the Earth, our planetary home, and its regions (ecosphere) is an environment on its own, it is embedded in another environment, the cosmos or universe, since our planet and its sun are just one of the trillions of planets and stars in one of the billions of galaxies

---

36. Cunningham and Saigo, *Environmental Science*, 37.
37. Curry, *Ecological Ethics*, 3.
38. K. Bediako, "Scripture as the Hermeneutic," 2.
39. Cunningham and Saigo, *Environmental Science*, 17.
40. Grim and Tucker, *Ecology and Religion*, 63.
41. Nebel and Wright, *Environmental Science*, 23.

Learning Environmental Science as Fact and as Faith 27

in an unfolding universe.[42] Environmental scientists limit their studies to the observable ecosphere, and even here define an arbitrary unit for practical purposes of studying and practicing sustainability as the ecosystem. Ecosystems[43] as units for studying environmental science are thus neither necessarily distinct boundaries nor totally isolated from one another.[44] Basically, an ecosystem is a grouping of plants, animals and microbes (biotic community) interacting with each other and with their environment (the surrounding abiotic factors) in such a way as to perpetuate the grouping.[45] Similar or related ecosystems are often grouped together to form major kinds of ecosystems called biomes, particularly on terrestrial environments. Tropical rainforests, grasslands and desserts are examples.[46] Then all the species of living things on Earth, along with all their environments, are grouped as one "super" ecosystem, which is called the biosphere.[47] In this systems approach of studying the environment, the focus is more on roles played by various species of the biotic community than on the uniqueness of individual members.[48] However, valuable insights into how the system works can be obtained from looking at its organization and function.

One basic insight from looking at the organization and function of ecosystems is that energy and materials are obtained, processed, stored or cycled between components of the ecosystem.[49] From the perspective of evolutionary philosophy, the universe is made up of space, mass (matter) and energy. Evolutionists claim it began as a single point that was trillions of degrees hot and instantly rushed out apart in a continuous cosmic unfolding trajectory[50] for about fourteen billion years now.[51] Matter is anything that occupies space and has mass—all gases, liquids and solids in both living and non-living systems. Energy is the ability to move mass; hence it affects matter by causing changes in its position or its state. Because energy does not have mass or occupy space, it cannot be measured in units of weight

42. Swimme and Tucker, *Journey of the Universe*, 2.

43. "Ecosystem" is originally a scientific word, but it has become overused and applied to many other fields, especially in the business world. It has been totally taken out of context and defined in general usage as a complex network or interconnected system, e.g., "Silicon Valley's entrepreneurial ecosystem."

44. Nebel and Wright, *Environmental Science*, 25.

45. Nebel and Wright, *Environmental Science*, 24.

46. Nebel and Wright, *Environmental Science*, 26.

47. Nebel and Wright, *Environmental Science*, 27.

48. Cunningham and Saigo, *Environmental Science*, 62.

49. Cunningham and Saigo, *Environmental Science*, 62.

50. Swimme and Tucker, *Journey of the Universe*, 5.

51. Swimme and Tucker, *Journey of the Universe*, 10.

or volume, but in other kinds of units such as calories or joules.[52] In the ecosystem mass and energy changes occur as producers (autotrophic green plants) make high-potential-energy organic molecules for their bodies from low-potential-energy raw inorganic materials with the help of light energy in the process of photosynthesis.[53] Then the photosynthetic products become food and oxygen that sustain consumers and other heterotrophs.

Generally from the observations of mass-energy interactions four characteristics seem to underlie natural ecosystem function and sustainability: (1) there is disposing of wastes and replenishing nutrients by recycling of all elements; (2) nature uses sunlight as basic energy source, which is both "non-polluting and non-depletable"; (3) and the size of consumer populations is maintained such that overgrazing or other over use does not occur.[54] The fourth characteristic, which is related to and may be an extension of the third, is how ecosystems check the overgrazing and remain in ecological balance. Overgrazing is curbed through balances among the populations of different species and further balances between each species and the abiotic environment. In short, ecosystem balance is essentially population balance by controlling the birth and death rates of each species with both biotic and abiotic factors, which together are known as environmental resistance.[55] The process is referred to as maintenance of biodiversity and is the fourth principle underlying ecosystem function.

From a scientific point of view, environmental issues almost always include an interaction of physical, chemical, and biological processes toward ecological balance.[56] However, in these dynamic processes there are phenomena that are constantly observed as fundamental and described as natural laws. These include the observation that mass in its basic unit as atom remains unchanged during chemical reactions, but can be transformed into another set of mass by either absorbing or releasing energy.[57] Perhaps it is because from the very beginning of the universe mass has the

52. Nebel and Wright, *Environmental Science*, 55.
53. Nebel and Wright, *Environmental Science*, 60.
54. Nebel and Wright, *Environmental Science*, 66.
55. Nebel and Wright, *Environmental Science*, 82.
56. Deane-Drummond, *Eco-Theology*, 12, notes that contemporary ecologists are less attuned to the concept of ecological balance because of the notion of flux, unstable equilibrium, openness to external influences, disturbance from internal and external forces, including humanity. However, she argues that the concept of balance cannot be dispensed with altogether, since knowing that ecosystems are in fragile balance, subject to disturbance, is important to inform the way humanity thinks about ethical conduct in relation to the environment—that is, we need to be aware that this is the case, though not a value term for ethical behavior (how we ought to behave).
57. Nebel and Wright, *Environmental Science*, 56.

quality of transforming into light (energy) or bonding into another mass[58] due to atomic attraction.[59] Similarly, the energy absorbed or released by mass during reactions is neither newly created nor destroyed, but may be just a conversion from one form to another.[60]

For scientists, then, the basic natural environmental law is the law of self-sustainability through conservation of mass and energy, perhaps to sustain life on Earth. In that case it implies that God has no role in the sustainability of the Earth, contrary to Christian cosmology, as I shall later adduce in this chapter. The scientific phenomenon of self-conservation and to support life is implied in what Swimme and Tucker refer to as the "self-organization dynamics" in nature to maintain the delicate conditions of life on Earth. In their view the Earth has adapted itself so as to maintain the narrow band that enables life to flourish. By drawing carbon dioxide out of the atmosphere via photosynthesis, Earth altered the composition of its atmosphere to keep itself cool as the sun grew hotter. Thus, the Earth is not just a big ball upon which living beings exist; Earth is a creative community of beings that reorganizes itself age after age so that it can perpetuate and even deepen its vibrant existence.[61]

That nature scientifically reorganizes and rebuilds itself may be exemplified by the regeneration of a fresh ecosystem on the demilitarized zone between North and South Korea after their war ended in 1953. With no human disturbances, the scarred slopes became reclothed with a dense hardwood forest for wild animals. A similar example of the regenerative power of nature occurred on the political no-man's-land between East and West Berlin when they were separated for forty years.[62]

Now in view of our assumption about environmental science as "fact" at the beginning of this section, to what extent does our knowledge of these underlying principles—natural biogeochemical processes for the "self-organizing" or "self-conservation" or "self-sustainability" of ecosystems—enable or induce us to apply them in our effort to care for creation?

---

58. Swimme and Tucker, *Journey of the Universe*, 9.
59. Swimme and Tucker, *Journey of the Universe*, 12.
60. Nebel and Wright, *Environmental Science*, 59.
61. Swimme and Tucker, *Journey of the Universe*, 56.
62. Cunningham and Saigo, *Environmental Science*, 118.

Natural Ecosystem Conservation and Motivation for Creation Care

A significant outcome of the study of environmental science is conservation knowledge, which is a discipline of ecosystem management, with divided opinion on its relevance. Cunningham and Saigo describe it as the attempt to integrate ecological, economic and social goals in a unified systems approach. It recognizes that we cannot have sustained progress toward social goals in a deteriorating environment or economy, and vice versa. Each of these domains affects, and is affected by, others.[63] Ecosystem management as a science has many ideas drawn from the practical experiences and stipulations of ecologists like Aldo Leopold, who attempted to restore his Sandy County farm to ecological health and beauty.[64] The most common goals of ecosystem management include (1) maintaining visible populations of native species *in situ*; (2) representing, within protected areas, all native ecosystem types across their natural range of variation; (3) protecting essential ecological processes such as nutrient cycles, succession, hydrologic processes, etc. (4); managing over long enough time periods to sustain the evolutionary potential of species and ecosystems; and (5) accommodating human use and occupancy within these constraints.[65] These objectives have been criticized from many angles. Some ecologists see the concept of ecosystem management as mere arrogance of humans in claiming understanding of the dynamic unpredictable qualities of nature to imagine we can manage it. Social developers fear poverty and human needs may not ensure adherence to environmental protection laws.[66] For ethicists like Patrick Curry, arguing from an ecocentric point of view, "stewardship" and "managerialism" are both paternalistic relations with the Earth, though the Earth does not need us as we need it. He shudders why, given the overall historical record for unsuccessfully managing even ourselves, we believe we have the right and ability to manage the natural world.[67] And with practical eyes as environmental scientists Cunningham and Saigo decry how many of our management policies, while well meaning, have not made matters worse rather than better.[68] They see vision statements and organizational plans,

---

63. Cunningham and Saigo, *Environmental Science*, 121.
64. Cunningham and Saigo, *Environmental Science*, 121.
65. Cunningham and Saigo, *Environmental Science*, 123.
66. Cunningham and Saigo, *Environmental Science*, 123.
67. Curry, *Ecological Ethics*, 35.
68. Cunningham and Saigo, *Environmental Science*, 121.

based on science, for ecosystem management as little more than empty slogans, while nothing really changes.[69]

This, however, is far from saying that environmental, and hence, conservation science and practice are of no use. In discussing issues about environmental impact and biodiversity loss, for instance, Celia Deane-Drummond catalogued some benefits of environmental science. At least ecological knowledge helps us define biological diversity, though the species that have so far been identified represent only a small fraction of the actual diversity, especially in areas such as the tropical forests. In addition, conservation science and practice is, at best, a safety measure for known species, as others disappear before they can be notified.[70] The point then is that conservation science and practice is not without significant challenges, particularly the moral commitment to practice it as expected. Said differently, it appears that, contrary to expectation, in spite of the elucidation of the principles of conservation from observing the facts about functioning of discrete natural ecosystems, humanity have by and large failed to morally and strictly abide by them, and this may "have significantly contributed to our current environmental crisis."[71] As Cunningham and Saigo observe, humans have become dominant organisms over most of the Earth, damaging or disturbing half of the world's terrestrial ecosystems' productivity to some extent. This they do through direct consumption, interfering with its production or use, or by altering the species composition or physical processes of human-dominated ecosystems.[72] Table 1.1 presents data on a study that mapped the extent of human disturbance of the natural world in 1995 by Conservation International as reported by Hannah Lee et al. The greatest impacts tended to be in human-dominated ecosystems, particularly the forested and grass lands, including the tropical dry forests.

69. Cunningham and Saigo, *Environmental Science*, 123.
70. Deane-Drummond, *Eco-Theology*, 8.
71. Nebel and Wright, *Environmental Science*, 73.
72. Cunningham and Saigo, *Environmental Science*, 113.

Table 1.1: Human Disturbance of the Natural World[73]

BIOME	TOTAL AREA ($10^6 KM^2$)	PERCENT UNDISTURBED HABITAT	PERCENT HUMAN DOMINATED
Temperate broad-leaved forests	9.5	6.1	81.9
Chaparral and thorn scrub	6.6	6.4	67.8
Temperate grasslands	12.1	27.6	40.4
Temperate rainforests	4.2	33.0	46.1
Tropical dry forests	19.5	30.5	45.9
Mixed mountain systems	12.1	29.3	25.6
Mixed island systems	3.2	46.6	41.8
Cold deserts/semi deserts	10.9	45.4	8.5
Warm deserts/semi deserts	29.2	55.8	12.2
Moist tropical forests	11.8	63.2	24.9
Tropical grasslands	4.8	74.0	4.7
Temperate conifer forests	18.8	81.7	11.8
Tundra and arctic desert	20.6	99.3	0.3

What it means is that human impacts through their intrusion into ecosystems often contrast the four characteristics undergirding natural ecosystem function and sustainability. For instance, Nebel and Wright observe that while nature recycles materials we have, with scientific knowledge, constructed our human systems largely on one-directional flow of elements. It creates problems of depletion at one end and pollution at the other. Meanwhile ecosystems have comparatively low capacities for absorbing waste even when

---

73. Cunningham and Saigo, *Environmental Science*, 114. Original data from Lee et al., "Human Disturbance and Natural Habitat." Note: Where undisturbed and human-dominated areas do not add up to 100 percent, the difference represents partially disturbed lands.

Learning Environmental Science as Fact and as Faith   33

undisturbed. Such is the case, for instance, of fertilizer nutrient phosphate, which is mined from deposits but ends up in waterways with effluents from sewage treatment.[74] About the second principle of sustainability, our heavy dependence on fossil fuel rather than the "nonpolluting and nondepletable" solar energy results in pollution beyond the ecosystem's absorbing capacity. For the third principle, overfishing of the oceans and rivers, overgrazing of range land and deforestation are examples of our shortfall of this principle.[75] As I indicated earlier, large expanses of tropical moist forests such as in West Africa are disappearing at a rapid rate,[76] and in Ghana the Environmental Protection Agency (EPA) fears that unchecked deforestation threatens desertification conditions and loss of biodiversity due to migration of some species, particularly the avian.[77] In addition, related to the fourth principle, Nebel and Wright suggest that as humans unwittingly change basic abiotic parameters, especially excess carbon dioxide resulting in global warming, ecosystems may be upset with loss of biodiversity.[78] Based on some field data gathered by the Ministry of Environment, Science and Technology (MEST) in the Upper East Region of Ghana in 2010, I have argued similarly elsewhere that anthropogenic climate change may lead to biodiversity loss.[79] For Cunningham and Saigo, conversion of natural habitat to human uses is the largest single cause of biodiversity loss.[80] Yet the value of conserving biodiversity is not simply related to ecosystem function: it directly provides instrumental benefits to humans, and indirectly ensures biogeochemical cycling necessary for maintaining global ecology and climate stability.[81]

As argued above, opinions are divided in environmental science, depending on worldviews, about the effectiveness of employing ecosystem management concepts which have been based on scientific facts. Is it the case that we simply have to accept limits on what we can do and have and free ourselves from the illusion that science and technology (alone), as factual learning, can provide solutions to our environmental and social problems?[82] At least, there is the suggestion that not only is there some pessimism about effectiveness of conservation science alone in resolving our

---

74. Nebel and Wright, *Environmental Science*, 73.
75. Nebel and Wright, *Environmental Science*, 73.
76. Cunningham and Saigo, *Environmental Science*, 113.
77. Environmental Protection Agency, *Ghana State of Environment Report 2004*, 6.
78. Nebel and Wright, *Environmental Science*, 104.
79. Blasu, "Compensated Reduction," 19.
80. Cunningham and Saigo, *Environmental Science*, 113.
81. Deane-Drummond, *Eco-Theology*, 10.
82. Cunningham and Saigo, *Environmental Science*. 123.

ecocrisis, but also it may not by itself adequately motivate us to even do what it teaches, with moral commitment. Nebel and Wright suggest we may have to go beyond being "smart to recognize the critical need to establish a balance between our human system and the rest of the biosphere, but also wise enough to *do so*."[83] Deane-Drummond also wrote about and expects "ecological wisdom," arising out of a perceived sense of the interrelationships and integrity of biological nature, to stimulate us for a similar sense of sustaining ecosystem interrelationships and integrity. In other words, for Deane-Drummond the way creatures marvelously attune to their environment and converge into patterns during the course of evolution is a kind of nature's wisdom. She adopts Jeffrey Schloss's definition of wisdom as "living in a way that corresponds to how things are."[84] Then she explains that the way things are could helpfully include ecological insights and knowledge. Wisdom, then, would be living in accordance with our knowledge of such sciences, but in such a way that gave meaning to existence.[85]

Natural wisdom is intriguing, but from the perspective of the Christian faith it is contentious that it may, from mere observation of nature, influence sustained human action of keeping the integrity of creation, unless it points beyond nature itself to its creator. An affirmation of a creator immediately calls into question any scientific notion of a universe that evolved with a biogeophysical clock for self-regulation and sustenance, observable as natural wisdom. As I shall later point out in more detail, Christian faith sees natural law, or what scientists indicate as rejuvenation without human interference, as evidence of God at work in sustaining his Earth. Thus an affirmation of a creator, rather than just observing natural law or wisdom, leads to a theocentric wisdom, one undergirded by and which points to doing the ethical thing—ecological action for integrity of creation—out of faith in and honor of God (Heb 11:6; Prov 1:7).

My position, from the perspective argued above is that, studying environmental science only as fact is inadequate to invoke moral eco-actions or mission orientation. Dianne Bergant strongly argues that lack of ethical impetus in a scientific worldview accounts for the inability to replenish the depleting material resources, or desisting from procuring prosperity at the expense of the basic rights of others.[86] She bases her argument on the observation that although science and technology provide a pattern of growth and prosperity, the resulting benefits of material comfort can no longer be

---

83. Nebel and Wright, *Environmental Science*, 105 (italics original).
84. Schloss, "Wisdom Traditions as Mechanisms," 156.
85. Deane-Drummond, *Eco-Theology*, 13.
86. Bergant, *Earth Is the Lord's*, 10.

sustained at the same rate or for the same number of people.[87] The implication is that studying environmental science only as facts, as it is, for instance, at PUCG, is inadequate to invoke moral eco-care praxis or missional ecological orientation. How then may it become holistic and missional?

Moral Deficiency of Environmental Science as Fact: Need for Ecology as Faith

It is expedient to explain further why studying environmental science as only fact may have difficulty in being mission oriented. As argued above, factual learning of environmental science is largely only a matter of gaining knowledge, but it lacks sufficient motivation for necessary moral ecological actions toward creation care. Two basic reasons come to mind, namely, the cosmic exclusivity implicit in the name of the subject, and the apparent insufficiency and ethical impotence of the knowledge it provides. By "cosmic exclusivity" I mean the possible lack of a sense of belonging to and affection that may induce moral concern or attitude and behavioral action for sustaining the ecosystem place we inhabit. From my earlier etymological definition of environmental science at the beginning of this chapter, we noticed that the term "environment" may literally mean our surroundings, minus us. The key expression is "around or surround," which may connote non-inclusion of humans in the scientific understanding of environment in the study of environmental science. Noting that "environment" is widely understood literally as "that which surrounds," Patrick Curry considers the term as denoting passiveness in setting.[88] Thus, by extension, it is not only difficult to assume but also not surprising to observe a plausible propensity for students, as it was at PUCG, to be passive or lack motivation for proactive eco-praxis in studying environmental science, itself defined as "a study of the world around us."[89]

From an ethical point of view, Patrick Curry argues that the concept of "around us" makes the term lend itself far too readily to two anthropocentric assumptions that contribute massively to ecological crisis. They are that ultimately only "we" (humans) matter and that the value, and indeed reality, of everything else only matters to the extent it enables us to get on with our own show.[90] Such anthropocentric understanding characterizing the study of environmental science as a secular subject may leave a student with a

---

87. Bergant, *Earth Is the Lord's*, 10.
88. Curry, *Ecological Ethics*, 8.
89. Cunningham and Saigo, *Environmental Science*, 17.
90. Curry, *Ecological Ethics*, 8.

sense of being apart from and not part of nature. That is, they are cosmically excluded, at least, relationally. Yet in order to counter our destructive attitudes to the environment we humans need to understand ourselves as contingently embedded in a network of relationships, as Michael Northcott correctly identifies.[91]

Perhaps the sense of cosmic exclusivity is related to inability of the scientific facts alone to stimulate the sense of ecological embedding—what I call "religio-ethical impotence" in the learned facts. For as Dianne Bergant implies in her *The Earth Is the Lord's*, scientific and technological facts lead us to believe that we can step outside of our environment to examine it and control it.[92] From her perspective, science and technology tend to give us a false sense of being apart from and not part of the environment, as if "we merely live within the environment as we live within a building."[93] I reiterate my argument that "notwithstanding the good that science entails for development, teaching [environmental science] without a mind-set to induce moral transformation and responsibility for preserving our Earth is a mission only half accomplished."[94] Commenting on the book *EcoSpirit: Religious and Philosophies for the Earth*, Deane-Drummond consents to the author's recognition that scientific "facts alone about environmental issues are not enough; what is needed is something more elemental, that probes the background assumptions pervading modern thought."[95] She means that learning that provides information anterior to scientific assumptions of the observable universe, and points to origins of the universe, must be added or even be fundamental to scientific learning for the latter to be morally influential.

Swimme and Tucker speak of a celebrated physicist and cosmologist, Freeman Dyson, who, reflecting on and trying to make sense of the origin of the universe, particularly the scientific discovery of its steady evolutionary expansion, realized that he had come to feel at home in the universe in a new way. He was quoted as saying: "The more I examine the universe and study the details of its architecture, the more evidence I find that the universe in some sense must have known that we are coming."[96] In a comment, Swimme and Tucker admit that humans were not present in any explicit sense at the beginning, but Dyson suggests that we are now learning ways

---

91. Northcott, *Moral Climate*, 16.
92. Bergant, *Earth Is the Lord's*, 10.
93. Bergant, *Earth Is the Lord's*, 10.
94. Blasu, "Our Earth, Our Responsibility," 267.
95. Deane-Drummond, *Eco-Theology*, xi.
96. Swimme and Tucker, *Journey of the Universe*, 11.

in which life was implicitly present in the very dynamics themselves, from the very first moment.[97]

It is indicative from Deane-Drummond's suggestion that a fundamental learning in environmental science that may affect environmental attitudes may be through myth and symbol making. For her, "'myth' is not intended to imply the lack of truth, but rather shows its capacity to reach beyond the rational to include other dimensions of knowing."[98] This is the dimension of spirituality or religion or theology, which enables us to disentangle the roots of such myths and their impact, negative or positive, on human relationships with the Earth. She indicates also rightly that though religious thinking and practices are part of the problem they also are part of the potential way forward for creation care, because they seek to recover our sense of place on the Earth, a reminder that the Earth is our common home, and that the story of the Earth and that of humans are one. This they do by uncovering the basis for our proper relationship between the origin of the Earth (God), ourselves (humanity) and the environment (cosmos).[99]

Thus, in studying the world of nature from a religious, particularly a Christian perspective, John Grim and Mary Tucker in their *Ecology and Religion* prefer to use the term "ecology." Defined as the study of the interrelationships of organisms and their surroundings,[100] Grim and Tucker think, rightly in my view, ecology describes the dynamic interactions of humans with nature more specifically than the term *environment*, which can suggest that nature is something apart from humans.[101] They explain that in a Christian worldview of nature or cosmology, the idea of ecology locates humans within the horizon of emergent, interdependent life and does not view humanity as the vanguard of evolution, nor as the exclusive fabricator of technology, nor as a species apart from nature.[102]

Invariably the religious reflections include ethics as that which needs to be practiced reordering vertical and horizontal relationships. In Africa and, hence, Ghana the major religious domains for such ecological reflections

---

97. Swimme and Tucker, *Journey of the Universe*, 12.

98. Deane-Drummond, *Eco-Theology*, xi.

99. Deane-Drummond, *Eco-Theology*, xi.

100. Grim and Tucker, *Ecology and Religion*, 178.

101. Grim and Tucker, *Ecology and Religion*, 62. They define environment as "the natural setting and conditions in which a biological entity lives [and that it] can refer to smaller ecological niches or larger bioregions or used broadly to the entire natural world on which life depends" (179). I recall that I had that feeling of humans not being part of nature according to the definitions of "environment" in the textbooks, when teaching Environmental Science (GNSP 101) in 2009 at Okwahu campus of PUCG.

102. Grim and Tucker, *Ecology and Religion*, 62.

are the primal, Christian and Islamic traditions, which are all theistic, faith-based religions. It is in this sense that I call the additional or fundamental learning suggested by Deane-Drummond to make the study of environmental science holistic "ecology as faith." I have earlier explained that the scientific study of ecology as fact analyzes the complex interactions within and between ecosystems, but ecology as faith examines cultural awareness of and beliefs about these interactions as creative, generative and normative for the continuity of life. The former is about methods of conservation and management of ecosystems and species; the latter helps humans to understand and re-envision their roles as morally responsible participants in the dynamic processes of life.[103]

Therefore, I propose that integrating ecology as faith and as fact promises a hope for providing a more effective impetus in the subject to stimulate creation care. Particularly in Ghana, and hence Africa, emphasis on religious ethics is highly commendable. Although economic survival and theistic spirituality are crucial in influencing ecological responsibilities of most Africans, I argue from my work among the Sokpoe-Eʋe that our theistic cultural self-understanding of life, if interpreted by the gospel, will contain a motivation that is anterior to the motivation of economic gains.[104] Birgit Meyer's findings among the Peki-Eʋe suggest that their Christian ecologies and motivation for ecological actions in most cases are based on enchantment of ecosystems and fear of spiritual entities.[105] In the article "Discerning Moral Status in the African Environment," Fainos Mangena challenged "the criteria used to confer moral status in the Western environment, namely, reason and sentience."[106] She introduced *"the state of creation* as the only criterion that recognizes and respects the moral agency of both human beings and non-human animals" from the perspectives of African worldviews. She argues that it is because "African existence depends to a larger extent on the existence of other-than-human beings—animate and inanimate—since they have both a physical and spiritual mode of existence."[107] I, therefore, proceed next to study the religious worldviews of the primal, Christian and Islamic traditions in Africa, which underpin their moral praxis of creation care.

---

103. Grim and Tucker, *Ecology and Religion*, 63.
104. Blasu, "Compensated Reduction," 24.
105. Meyer, *Translating the Devil*, xvii.
106. Mangena, "Discerning Moral Status in the African Environment," 25
107. Mangena, "Discerning Moral Status in the African Environment," 25.

CHAPTER 2

Religious Worldviews and Understanding Ecology

Introduction: Worldviews and Their Importance in Religious Ecology

THIS CHAPTER EXAMINES THE worldviews, religio-ethical impulses and modes of eco-care praxis of the three major religious traditions in Ghana (and hence Africa): Primal, Christianity, and Islam. The aim, borrowing the words of Normanul Haq, an Islamic environmentalist, is to recover material from these religious traditions that might serve to illuminate how their cultures regard our current global environmental concerns and guide their thinking about them.[1] Ultimately the information recovered will be a critical intellectual framework for comparatively assessing similar parameters in the religious worldviews of the Sokpoe-Eʋe as part of the research in this study. In addition, it is to be factored as shared data from the religious ecologies of these traditions in designing a missional and morally transformative African theocology curriculum for undergraduates in institutions with religiously plural contexts. Curry argues that "Pluralism has important implications for any project to bring about a more ecological society."[2] What then are worldviews, and particularly African worldviews? How do African worldviews affect our relationships to and with the ecological communities or ecosystems in Africa?

A worldview is both a story of origin of the cosmos and mental perception of cosmic phenomena. Andrew Walls calls it a mental "map of the

---

1. Haq, "Islam and Ecology," 125.
2. Curry, *Ecological Ethics*, 25.

universe"³ from which, according to Ogbu Kalu, "people construct how and why things are the way they are"⁴ in the environment of which they are part and live in. He calls it "mind-world" and explains it as a mental picture that empowers people's actions and endows both rhythm and meaning to life processes.⁵ It is the foundation of customs, social norms and laws, being embedded in people's experience and then expressed or re-enacted in their cultures.⁶ From Kwame Bediako we may infer that the culture of a substantial social grouping of persons, which give them identity in relation to other social groupings or communities, has two fundamental characteristics or qualities. The first is an internal disposition of the people to envision life within a certain perspective. This is foundational to all that there is about and in culture and explains why "culture begins internally"⁷ with the mind. The second is that there is a resultant external behavior from the envisioning of the persons of culture.⁸ Bediako's reference to "culture begins internally" fits in with the understanding of "worldview" and hence answers the questions "Who are we?" and "How do we interpret our existence?" when "dealing with culture."⁹

Explaining the term "worldview," the ethnologist Edward Sapir noted some of its contents. He includes things like the "patterns of thought, attitudes toward life, conceptions of time, a mental picture of what ought to be, a people's understanding of their relationship to unseen things and to the order of things, and their view of self and others."¹⁰ John Grim puts it as "a story of the world which informs all aspects of life among a people, giving substance to practices, artistic creation, ritual play and military endeavor a significant content."¹¹ From a more ecological perspective Ogbu Kalu defines worldview as "the unified picture of the cosmos explained by a system of concepts which order the natural and social rhythms and the place of individuals and communities in them."¹² In other words, as I understand it, a worldview is a people's perception of and, hence, inner disposition about reality of the "gecosphere" (the earth, its regions and things in it), which

---

3. Walls, *Cross-Cultural Process in Christian History*, 122.
4. Kalu, "Sacred Egg," 228.
5. Kalu, "Sacred Egg," 228.
6. Kalu, "Sacred Egg," 228.
7. K. Bediako, "Gospel and Culture," 8.
8. K. Bediako, "Gospel and Culture," 8.
9. K. Bediako, "Gospel and Culture," 8.
10. Sapir, *Selected Writings*, 548.
11. Tucker and Grim, eds., *Worldviews and Ecology*, 42.
12. Kalu, "Precarious Vision," 39.

informs their outer behavior in their ecological communities (ecosystems). It is embedded in and interprets their experiences, and so influences their outward behavior in terms of symbolic expressions, re-enacted cultural beliefs and events, customs and traditions, social norms, values and laws.[13]

It is significant to note that central to both worldview and culture is a "personal element" so that the enacted cultural behaviors and artifacts are "all manifestations and signs of the personal elements at the heart of culture."[14] Said differently, culture and worldview are essentially attributes of persons; it is the responses of human persons to their internal perceptions of the ecosystem that we refer to as eco-cultural behaviors or ethos. The eco-cultural behaviors of people may affect their ecosystems positively or negatively. Since it underpins culture, worldview, like culture, can be "learnt unconsciously but deliberately transmitted,"[15] suggesting that it is not static but responds dynamically as impacted by other cultures/worldviews. Kalu believes that the impact of Western worldviews, through their cultural influences on Africa, erode the salient values of the African indigenous worldviews and cultural ethos without providing adequate replacements. Andrew Walls sees it as changing the conventionally identified components of religious systems in Africa under the pressure of internal or external forces.[16] The result is cultural tension and lack of discipline,[17] particularly regarding moral care for the African environment.

The tension appears also in research difficulties in retrieving relevant and reliable information from Africans to "remove the slurs and misconceptions created by foreign scholars,"[18] what Nwosu and Kalu blame on

13. In their article "The Study of African Culture," H. N. Nwosu and O. U. Kalu observe that the most common cultural symbol is language, being the major instrument for expressing ideas, thoughts, feelings and sentiments as realities about and in the ecological community. The mass of detailed standard behaviors and principles or various shared components of life transmitted over the years in the community are the traditional customs. But customary behaviors and lifestyles are themselves guided by values and norms. The values are widely held beliefs or sentiments about which activities, relationships, feelings or goals are important for the well-being of the ecological community. Norms stem from values and prescribe specific rules, blueprints and procedures to guide conduct in specific situations. Nwosu and Kalu, "Study of African Culture," in Kalu, ed., *Readings in African Humanities*, 4.

14. K. Bediako, "Gospel and Culture," 8.

15. Kalu, "Sacred Egg," 230.

16. Walls, *Cross-Cultural Process in Christian History*, 124.

17. Kalu, "Sacred Egg," 231.

18. Nwosu and Kalu, "Study of African Culture," in Kalu, ed., *Readings in African Humanities*, 14. In other words, it is not easy for African scholars now seeking to evolve more critical literature to solicit unadulterated African cultural, and hence worldviews, data from Africans themselves, be it from oral or existing literature. This is partly

"years of acculturation in Western culture and the current system of education in Africa."[19]

Nevertheless, worldviews display substantial durability, while accepting external influences. This may be because human beings, who are central to worldview and culture, can be "conservative and resistant to change."[20] Gillian M. Bediako, comparing the tenacity of primal religion to worldview, believes that it is very rare for a worldview to be entirely destroyed and replaced; rather people tend to modify their maps of reality, correcting, adapting, and altering the sizes of items on it.[21]

Despite internal and external influences, African cultures are not necessarily left without any retrievable indigenous environmental principles, values and ethos from their myths of origin (cosmology), and hence, worldviews. In African cultures there are many myths of origin, outlining myriads of corresponding worldviews, which are religious in nature and largely ethnocentric. For instance, Andrew Walls observes that there are conventionally four component entities identified in the religious systems in Africa, and hence their underpinning worldviews: God, divinities, ancestors, and objects of power, yet they vary as to which component is the dominating one.[22] Thus it is over generalization to speak of *the* African worldview by identifying broad features that unify our myriad worldviews to be representatively *the* African. However, from Andrew Walls we may note, at least, that the "conventionally identified common components"[23] may be distinct from the worldviews of other "cultural areas"[24] such as the Global North. Ogbu Kalu observes that "underlying the varieties of cultures in Africa is a core worldview structure"[25] and they share a deep-seated meaning.[26] With this in mind and concerning myths of origin in particular, Kalu concludes that

because some Africans and African scholars tend to be defensive and romantic about the African past, while others, seek to be authentically African, yet employ European theories uncritically in producing literature of tutelage." See Nwosu and Kalu, "Study of African Culture," in Kalu, ed., *Readings in African Humanities*, 14.

19. Nwosu and Kalu, "Study of African Culture," in Kalu, ed., *Readings in African Humanities*, 14.

20. K. Bediako, "Gospel and Culture," 8.

21. G. Bediako, Editorial to "Primal Religion as the Substructure of Christianity," 1.

22. Walls, *Cross-Cultural Process in Christian History*, 124.

23. Walls, *Cross-Cultural Process in Christian History*, 124.

24. Nwosu and Kalu define "A cultural area" as "a geographical area occupied by peoples whose culture exhibit a significant degree of similarity with each other as well as a significant dissimilarity with cultures of others." Nwosu and Kalu, "Study of African Culture," in Kalu, ed., *Readings in African Humanities*, 6.

25. Kalu, "Sacred Egg," 231.

26. Kalu, "Sacred Egg," 228.

from "the myriads of cosmologies a model can be constructed representing the basic and common features in Africa."[27] He observes, however, that each myth of origin is couched in religious, numinous terms: creation was the act of a Supreme Being utilizing the services of subaltern deities. The divine origin confers a sacred shroud on the created beings and the social order.[28] This suggests a theistic religious mind-view of the world (creation, creator and humanity) in the religious traditions in Africa, which underpin their ecological attitudes and behaviors.

Creation, Creator and Humanity in African Primal Worldviews

Two authors have made illuminating contributions to understanding a phenomenological structure for the religious worldviews of Africa. Harold Turner developed in 1977 a six-feature structure for analyzing the primal religions of indigenous ecological communities in the world.[29] Ogbu U. Kalu in 1978 contributed to understanding a phenomenological structure for African worldviews from the many ethnocentric myths of origin through his studies on "The African Perception of His World."[30] His diagrammatic presentation summarizes his conception and description of a structure that is a depiction of African worldviews (figure 2.1).

---

27. Kalu, "Precarious Vision," 39. Kalu considers "cosmology" as the "impressive term for worldview." However, I contend that worldview is a broader concept than cosmology (the scientific study of the universe and its origin). The latter is just one element of a people's worldview, which is their entire mind-picture or intellectual ordering of reality of life in space-time continuum.

28. Kalu, "Sacred Egg," 228.

29. Turner, "The Primal Religions of the World," in Hayes, ed., *Australian Essays in World Religions*, 31.

30. Kalu, "Sacred Egg," 231.

44 PART 1—MORAL ENVIRONMENTALISM

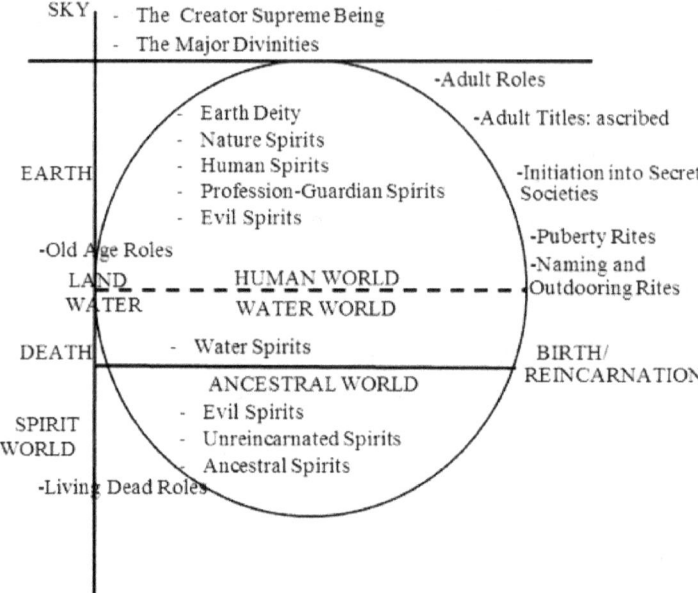

Figure 2.1: A General Structure of African Worldviews

I propose to use Kalu's diagram in analyzing the structure of African primal worldviews. Nevertheless, it is important to observe here a problem with Kalu's diagram: it is a perceived structure of African worldviews but may wrongly imply all these features are present within every cultural group in Africa. Not all African societies display all these features.[31] In reality within it are multiple worldviews or multiple maps of reality. Kalu himself rightly noted that "details may vary, even within an ethnic group."[32]

Like Kalu, my interest here is not in mining the depths of these worldviews, but in focusing on their structure, with its predominantly religious character,[33] and particularly on its implications for shaping the moral attitudes and behaviors of Africans as they relate to and with creation in their ecological communities. For primal Africans' attitude and behaviors toward creation are informed by the understanding that their survival and identity as a people depend on their "bonded" view of and relationship with the structured natural environment.[34]

31. Walls, *Cross-Cultural Process in Christian History*, 123.
32. Kalu, "Sacred Egg," 231.
33. Kalu, "Sacred Egg," 234.
34. Sindima, "Community of Life," 137.

A Structure of the Primal Worldviews in Africa

In formulating a phenomenological structure of African worldviews Kalu bases his diagram on the time-space concept, because of the perception that space and time encapsulate most other experiences.³⁵ He does so not unaware of problems with the concept in Africa. For instance, in the cosmic structure of the Mafi-Eʋe, among the Tɔŋu-Eʋe in Volta Region of Ghana, Agbanu observes that their "environment is more than . . . a matter of quantified period of time or spread of space."³⁶ He does not explain what he means exactly, but it suggests that the African concepts of time and space are problematic. Kalu points out how scholars still debate the concept of time among Africans. The argument is over whether the African mind perceives distant future or not, since we tend to reckon time not in a linear continuum (*chronos*), but based on cyclical events (*kairos*). So also is the African conception of space. We end up pointing to the sky, Earth and underground when questioned about the universe (*cosmos*), implying there are three existential dimensions of space.³⁷

Creation as Space and Other-than-human Creatures in Primal Religious Worldview

With regards to African spatial conceptions in Figure 2.1, three horizontal rectangular boxes represent three united dimensions of space: the sky is at the top, in the middle is the Earth (made up of land and water) and beneath the Earth is the spirit world (i.e., spirits other than the Supreme Spirit Being). According to Kalu the sky is the abode of the Supreme Spiritual Being as the creator and, Kwame Bediako may add for indigenous cosmologies, "the Sustainer of the universe."³⁸ The sky is also occupied by the major divinities: sun, lightening, thunder and the like. The sky divinities are usually males and serve as judges, so people swear by them, particularly in verifying ecological moral conduct. I am aware that the adherents of *yeʋe* cult in Sokpoe ecological area in Volta region, Ghana swear by lightning and thunder as Kalu notes. In Kalu's diagram the moon, on the other hand, is a female deity whose light inspires environmental aesthetics, creativity, songs and dances.³⁹ This may not be the case in every African culture.

---

35. Kalu, "Precarious Vision," 39.
36. Agbanu, "Environmental Ethics in Mafi-Eʋe Indigenous Culture," 95.
37. Kalu, "Precarious Vision," 39.
38. K. Bediako, *Jesus in Africa*, 22.
39. Kalu, "Sacred Egg," 234.

The second dimension of space, the earthly space, is occupied by both human and other-than-human creatures—rocks, mountains, water bodies, flora and fauna—that are features of land and water ecosystems. Most of these earthly features are sacralized, because some African mythologies hold it that they had been inhabited by the divinities that formed land out of the anthill in the marsh.[40] For instance, as Kalu notes, some common trees in West Africa reverenced as being imbued with spirits include: those with massive trunks and buttresses such as silk-cotton tree (*Eriodendron orientale*), iroko (*Chlorophora excels*), or baobab (*Adansonia digitata*). African satinwood (*Cordia milleni*) is inhabited by a musically inclined spirit which renders it useful for making drums. Also, abnormal trees attract dread, e.g., a palm tree with seven trunks or sixteen branches, and mystic trees like one in Gbarnga, Liberia, which re-erected itself on its stump after being axed down for firewood even with the axe wounds still present. In addition, trees or shrubs at cross-junctions or forked roads at the entrance to a village or center of market are sacred.[41] Similarly, Harry Agbanu notes that the Mafi-Eʋe ascribes "very high magico-religious value to some individual trees and animal species." These include: Klɔ (*Piliostigma thonningii*), Logblovi (*Tipananthus species*), Fefeti (*Locaniodiscus cupanoides*), Mango (*Magnifera indica*), Fɔti (*Vitex domiana*), Akukɔti (*Spondias mombin*), Deti (*Elaeis guieneensis*), Yɔkuti (*Vitellaria paradoxa*), Adidoti (*Adansonia digitata*), Wɔti (*Parkia biglobosa*) and Uuti (*Ceiba pentandra*).[42]

While "people in savannah zones tend to use hills as shrines for sending messages to God,"[43] the Mafi-Eʋe "conceive of the land—the living environment—as sacred" and "regards the earth/land as a [deity]" who is mentioned first before other divinities in traditional prayers.[44] For instance, the *Kpɔdoave* forest at Mafi Dugame is sacred because it is the abode of their arch-divinity *Kasaŋgblɛ*, who provides security and general welfare to the community members home and abroad.[45] My own Zoyi clan of Sokpoe sacralize *Alɔlɔdzove* and prohibit menstruating women entering it, because their *Alɔlɔdzo* deity inhabits it and provides a security function for them. In some African worldviews, the Earth as a female divinity not only nurtures the communities with her agro-fertility, but makes land so sacred that

---

40. According to Kalu, "Sacred Egg," 235.
41. Kalu, "Sacred Egg," 235.
42. Agbanu, "Environmental Ethics in Mafi-Eʋe Indigenous Culture," 108.
43. Kalu, "Sacred Egg," 235.
44. Agbanu, "Environmental Ethics in Mafi-Eʋe Indigenous Culture," 98.
45. Agbanu, "Environmental Ethics in Mafi-Eʋe Indigenous Culture," 104.

people swear by her.⁴⁶ Among the Mafi-Eʋe people believed that the Earth is able to impose punishment on anyone accursed with her.⁴⁷

The third dimension of space in Kalu's diagram, described as "spirit world," occurs beneath the Earth. It contains the human ancestral spirits, non-reincarnated spirits and evil spirits. Kwame Bediako refers to it as the "spiritual environment" which although is the realm of the invisible, yet is affirmed by many Africans as real.⁴⁸ In Kalu's diagram both the sky and spirit world rectangles are open at the upper and lower ends, respectively, suggesting a seamless or continues communication between them since "all the spaces are united."⁴⁹ He does not categorically point this out, but the openness into each other of the sky (above the Earth) and spirit world (beneath the Earth) may suggest that in African views of the earthly space (the human world) we perceive only one other real "space," part of which is above and the other part is under the Earth. The spirit world is the space for spiritual entities: ancestors, divinities and the supreme being.⁵⁰ Kwame Bediako underscores the concept of one "spirit space" juxtaposed to "human space" in the ecosphere when he observes about Akan cosmology only one "spirit world on which human [world of] existence is believed to depend."⁵¹ He sees in this spirit world not only "God, the Supreme Spirit Being (*Onyame*), Creator and Sustainer of the universe," but also that "Subordinate to God, with delegated authority from God, are the 'gods' (*abosom*) sometimes referred to as children of God (*Nyamemma*), and the ancestors or 'spirit fathers' (*Nsamanfo*)."⁵² It is also significant to note that in Kalu's diagram both the human world and the entire spirit world are existentially contiguous as evidenced by the presence of spirit entities—Earth deity, nature spirits, human spirits, guardian spirits and evil spirits—located in the human world also. So, spirit entities have their loci in all three dimensions of space, implying, in the worldviews of Africans, that spirit existence is not necessarily spatially limited. Kalu points out that although there are three dimensions of space, they are all united and that in the people's consciousness each space is imbued with powerful forces.⁵³

---

46. Kalu, "Sacred Egg," 235.
47. Agbanu, "Environmental Ethics in Mafi-Eʋe Indigenous Culture," 98.
48. K. Bediako, "Gospel and Culture," 8.
49. Kalu, "Sacred Egg," 234.
50. Kalu, "Sacred Egg," 234.
51. K. Bediako, *Jesus in Africa*, 22.
52. K. Bediako, *Jesus in Africa*, 22.
53. Kalu, "Sacred Egg," 234.

I consider that the prevalence of various spiritual entities through all three dimensions of space underscores the conception of African worldviews as not only religious, but specifically theistic. Kalu describes it as "the sacralization of the environment."[54] When John S. Mbiti asserts that the daily life of the African people are notoriously religious and that religion permeates into all the departments of life so that it is not easy or possible to isolate it,[55] he reinforces that African worldviews, which underpin African religiosity as a cultural phenomenon,[56] are characteristically religious and theistic.

Yet it appears that in ordinary life experiences primal African worldviews are not necessarily theocentric, particularly since not all cultures have God-dominant worldviews. But even in God-dominant religious systems, the Supreme Being or God is not necessarily central, pivotal or the frontline power that people focused attention on for immediate and direct reach; subordinate divinities and ancestors may even be more paramount. It is not God, but either deities (such as at Sokpoe) or both deities and ancestors (such as at Mafi) who are feared in connection with environmental taboos. Discussing environmental management from indigenous resources among the Kikiyu of Kenya, Julius Gathogo premised his argument that the indigenous Kikuyu people were encouraged to preserve the environment by their belief in the sacredness of nature. "Therefore, the ecological concern for people in Mutira . . . was tantamount to co-working *with* [not because of or for] God."[57] They practice an environmental management based on religious but not theocentric cosmology. As noted earlier, Andrew Walls asserts that the identified dominant components of a "primal map" or worldview could be altered by differing circumstances and cultures. He calls it "the reordering of African worldviews."[58] In that case God or the Supreme Being may not always remain central in all life circumstances in the ecosystems.

---

54. Kalu, "Sacred Egg," 240.

55. Mbiti, *African Religions and Philosophy*, 1. See also Mbiti, *Introduction to African Religion*, 30.

56. Kalu, "Sacred Egg," 229.

57. Gathogo, "Environmental Management and African Indigenous Resources," 1 (emphasis added).

58. Walls, *Cross-Cultural Process in Christian History*, 123. See also G. Bediako, Editorial to "Primal Religion as the Substructure of Christianity," 2.

Humanity in Creation and the Phenomenon of Time in Primal Religion

Another concept palpable from Ogbu Kalu's diagrammatic construction of African worldviews is depicted by the other (apart from the rectangles) major geometric shape on the diagram, a circle. Kalu seems to use the space occupied by the circle to illustrate interrelations in the ecosphere while the circumference depicts the cyclic concept of time and hence life, particularly human life. Tumai Nyajeka concludes that "Life is an organic web. The living and the dead are united. The spiritual and the manifest worlds flow together in a circle."[59] How the span of human life flows cyclically between the physical and spiritual spaces in the ecosphere is understood and explained with the conception of time. In other words, to speak of the African's life span during which we engage in various ecological practices and relations in an ecosystem is to invite the concept of time in the African cosmology.

In timing life, Kalu agrees with Mircea Eliade, who argues that traditional societies construct the concept of time around the movement of the agricultural season—a repetitive eternal cycle from planting to harvesting[60] crops or raising to disposal of animals. Kalu likens human life to the cyclic pattern of the other-than-human creation. It moves from "birth, through accession to various stages . . . until death"[61] only to begin a new stage of living as "the personality soul of the individual journeys through the spirit world until reincarnation"[62] in cultures that so believe. Therefore, his diagram shows human life moving anticlockwise, perhaps illustrating the diminishing of the span in the physical/human world with time, to death at the left—end of the diameter, within the earthly space.

Humanity is created by God, the supreme being. As Samuel Agboklu put it in an interview:

> The primal religionist knows that *Mawu* (God) the Most High is the creator of humanity and everything on Earth. Thus, he is called *Sogbolisa*, *Okitikata* (the unchallengeable creator), the Craftsman, and Worker of the good. He created hand and foot, the Earth and all in it. He used clay to create human and breathed breath/spirit into it.[63]

---

59. Nyajeka, "Shona Women and the Mutupo Principle," in Ruether, ed, *Women Healing Earth*, 135. See also Kalu, "Sacred Egg," 234.

60. Eliade, *Sacred and the Profane*. See also Kalu, "Sacred Egg," 231.

61. Kalu, "Sacred Egg," 232.

62. Kalu, "Sacred Egg," 232.

63. Samuel Agboklu, interview at Sokpoe, 2 March 2016. See appendix, A1, for transcription. The same understanding and names of God were expressed by Geoffrey

God, however, gifted humanity the ability to continue procreating its kind.[64] In an interview, Enyi Avenɔgbo is certain that *"amegbetɔ la ŋutsu kple nyɔnu yee dzie"* (human is born of a man and a woman).[65] The human body is consitituted of three things: *ŋutilã* (flesh), *ʋu* (blood)—both of which are essentially from and of soil and water—and *gbɔgbɔ* (spirit), released by God into the human creature.[66] Explaining his views in another interview, Kɔwu Yɔhokpɔ believes that *gbɔgbɔ* as a third constituent of the human body is the invisible aspect of human being; it is like *yafofo* (wind/breath) from God. This explains why a dying person *"nɔa amamu dzi"* (gasps for breath), because *"efe gbɔgbɔ le tsitsim"* (the available air in it diminishes toward an end).[67] But after the physical exit life then journeys through the ancestral world, with "living-dead roles," until, in some cultures, it returns to human world through reincarnation at the right end of the diameter. African worldviews of life, then, denote a contiguous phenomenon; it is also not clearly hierarchical.[68]

The Purpose of Creation and Humanity in Primal Religious Worldview

Although neither Ogbu Kalu nor other scholars spell out categorically what primal reliogionists in Africa see as the purpose of creation and especially humanity, some ideas may be gleaned from my research among the primal Sokpoe-Eʋe. One such basic idea is the anthropocentric conception of creation as being there just to support human life, and that humanity is to procreate while depending on creation's resourcefulness. They were unable to tell clearly the role of humanity on Earth apart from procreation as continuation of God's creative activity. Amega Enyi Avenɔgbo does not know humans' purpose, except that humans perpetuate their kind through sexual reproduction.[69] Atiglo Avinyo mentions procreation and fending for one's family even though ultimately it is God, through the deities "who cares for all of us," where "all of us" means "both human and other-than-human

---

Siame, interview at Sokpoe, 17 February 2016.

64. Geoffrey Siame, telephone interview, 6 April 2017.

65. Enyi Avenɔgbo, interview, Elavanyo, 2 February 2016. See also Kofi Avinyo Atiglo, interview, Elavanyo, 15 February 2016.

66. Geoffrey Siame, interview at Sogakɔfe, 17 February 2016.

67. Kofi Avinyo Atiglo, interview, Elavanyo, 15 February 2016.

68. Kalu, "Sacred Egg," 234.

69. Enyi Avenɔgbo, interview, Elavanyo, 2 February 2016.

creation on the Earth."⁷⁰ In a telephone interview, Geoffrey Siame implies that the main purpose or role of humanity is for us "to represent God" in all that God does in the world.

> In the understanding of our ancestors God created humans to represent him. So he made us in his image. But since he is invisible we craft *legbawo* (images) like humans or other creatures, which act as messengers between us and God. If there is any other role it is procreation. As creator he gave us opportunity to also procreate, and provided all things to enable us perform these duties in the environment for our use.⁷¹

Perhaps Geoffrey Siame might have been influenced by his basic education in Christian school in stating that God created humans in his own image and as his representatives. However, rationalizing his and all the other responses, it is deducible that in the Sokpoe-Eʋe primal religious thought of participants, God creates and gave humanity ability to procreate; God cares for all creation and enables humanity to care for its family. In a sense then humanity images God, at least, in his creation and caring activities. But God's caring activity is through the deities, and eventually humanity, as Avinyo explains; wherefore humanity represents God or participates in God's creation care activity on Earth. But other-than-human creation remains to only instrumentally provide for the well-being of humanity in a precarious environment.

Perhaps the holistic and abiding interconnected nature of primal religious views of the world contributes to the difficulty in identifying categorical and distinctive purposes for creation and humanity. Kwame Bediako argues that the primal religious worldview is not only "decidedly *this-worldly*," but also that "this *this-worldliness* encompasses God and [humanity] in abiding relationship with God—which is the destiny of humanity, and the purpose and goal of the universe."⁷² By "universe" Bediako implies both human and other-than-human creation, and that their destiny or ultimate purpose is to work mutually toward sustaining the abiding interconnectivity. In other words, in the primal religious worldview there is no transcendent "spiritual world separate from the realm of regular human existence" where also are the other-than-human creatures. Theoretically, the purpose, then, of "human existence is to participate in the constant interplay of the divine-human

---

70. Kofi Avinyo Atiglo, interview, Elavanyo, 15 February 2016

71. Geoffrey Siame, telephone interview, 6 April 2017. See appendix, A2, for transcript.

72. K. Bediako, *Jesus in Africa*, 92.

encounter"[73] to sustain all creation. Yet in practice, at least, from observations among the Sokpoe-Eʋe, human-nature relations are anthropocentric.

Expectedly, these conceptions of the universe have shaped and underpinned African primal religiosity and the subsequent attitudes and behaviors to creation. But Allison Howell bemoans that the spiritual engagement with land and water, once part of the fabric of African spirituality, seems to have become unraveled in our time, especially with relationship to illegal gold mining and also in other ecological areas as well.[74] Or could this engagement be more observable from the other religious traditions—Islam and Christianity?

Creation, Creator and Humanity in Islamic Worldviews

By Islamic[75] as an adjective I imply discovering the meaning of nature and humankind's relationship with it from the perspectives of the Qur'an and prophetic traditions[76] rather than from any one Islamic sect or movement. Writing the introduction to his coedited *Islam and Ecology*, Richard C. Foltz indicates that from its origin fourteen centuries ago Islam offers a basis for ecological understanding and stewardship from the Qur'an, *Sunna* (prophetic deeds of Muhammad) and *hadiths* (prophetic words of Muhammad). These sources provide the principles for Islamic way of life or law, the *sharīʾa*,[77] and so are the main sources of Islamic ecological knowledge in which Muslims look for authoritative answers to the questions about the natural environment.[78] Yet the articulation of Islamic ethics to guide human-natural environment relations in contemporary terms—recognizing the urgency of the global crisis now facing us all—is quite new. It started with American-trained Iranian Shiʾite philosopher Seyyed Hossein Nasr in 1966.[79] In other words, Islamic environmental law, with its undergirding worldview, is not yet recognized as an independent discipline within the

---

73. K. Bediako, *Jesus in Africa*, 92.

74. Howell, "African Spirituality and Christian Ministry," 12.

75. I use "Islamic" to stand for mainstream or classical Islam or "Islam in its intended form" as Saadia Khawar Khan Chishti calls it. He prefers to use "Qur'anic" instead of "Islamic" because there are "un-Islamic practices today, which are misinterpretations or misrepresentations of the pristine intents of al-Qur'an." Chishti, *"Fitra,"* 81 note 3.

76. Özdemir, "Toward an Understanding of Environmental Ethics," 5.

77. Foltz, "Introduction" to Foltz et al., eds., *Islam and Ecology*, xxxvii.

78. Dutton, "Environmental Crisis of Our Time," 325.

79. Foltz, "Introduction" to Foltz et al., eds., *Islam and Ecology*, xxxviii.

Islamic *sharīʾa*.⁸⁰ Nevertheless, as S. Normanul Haq contends, given the durability of classical Islamic civilization, one may legitimately seek ideas from Islam to guide the struggle against the environmental problems that threaten our globe today.⁸¹

Qur'anic worldview is about *God* and how *humans* can comprehend his existence and presence through the *natural world*.⁸² S. Nomanul Haq observes that concerning the cosmos and its relationship to human beings, the Qur'an moves at three simultaneous levels—the metaphysical, human and naturalistic. Yet all three dimensions or levels turn out to interrelate with no ontological separation between the divine and the natural environment, generating a particular conscious human attitude to the world as a whole.⁸³ In other words, there is a sacred dimension of nature as a creation of God that is in Islam but missing in modern scientific worldviews, and human beings are not separate from or above nature, but rather are part of the web of life.⁸⁴ There is then an Islamic theocology—belief in relationships between God, humans and other-than-human creation—which may be comprehended at these three dimensions.

The Creator of Our Home (Earth) in Islamic Understanding

At the metaphysical dimension, which comes first and precedes the other dimensions,⁸⁵ "God, according to the Qur'an, is the real Creator, Owner, and Sustainer of all reality (Qur'an 2:29)."⁸⁶ The Qur'anic revelations that particularly awaken instinctual Islamic worldviews are within the eighty-six *suras* (chapters)⁸⁷ the Prophet of Islam received in the cave of Hira on Mount Jabal al-Nur during his Meccan mission period.⁸⁸ One such text is Qur'an 96:1, "Read in the name of your Lord and Sustainer who created..." From this text Ibrahim Özdemir argues that at the very beginning it is taught that God gives existence and meaning to everything else.⁸⁹ He debunks

80. Llewellyn, "Basis for a Discipline of Islamic Environmental Law," 186.
81. Haq, "Islam and Ecology," 145.
82. Özdemir, "Toward an Understanding of Environmental Ethics," 6 (italics added).
83. Haq, "Islam and Ecology," 125.
84. Özdemir, "Toward an Understanding of Environmental Ethics," 4.
85. Özdemir, "Toward an Understanding of Environmental Ethics," 10.
86. Özdemir, "Toward an Understanding of Environmental Ethics," 7.
87. Azumah, *My Neighbour's Faith*, 48.
88. Özdemir, "Toward an Understanding of Environmental Ethics," 6.
89. Özdemir, "Toward an Understanding of Environmental Ethics," 7.

from Islamic theological perspectives the scientific notion that nature is the result of accidental evolution or chaotic configurations, without meaning or purpose.[90] Perhaps Özdemir is referring to the fact that scientific evolution theories try to arrange a systematic and chronological outbirthing of the complex cosmos.[91] The scientific fact may be convincing to many, but still limited to only the "observable universe" and significantly unable to explain the source of the already existing "single point" mixture of visible "luminous matter" and the invisible "dark matter" that "was trillions of degrees hot and that instantly rushed apart" to become "all of space and time and mass and energy."[92] To the Muslim, just as the Christian, the source of even that single point of matter that may have evolved into the cosmos over billions of years in scientific assertions is still God.[93] Yet it is not also the case that certain things and phenomena in the created order, particularly in connection with the physical world, cannot be explained by and with science. The invention of modern medical practices, and any impacts—positive or negative—on animal (human and other-than-human) life, for instance, might not have been possible without knowledge of the natural sciences—biology, chemistry and physics. Nonetheless, to the theistic religious person like the Muslim, both the knowledge and substances employed in medical science are ultimately the works and provisions of the creator God. He created all things and did so with and for a deliberate purpose.

Creation and Its Purpose in Islamic View

The Muslim participants in this study in the Sokpoe ecological area consist mostly of long-term settlers from West African Islamic countries and a few indigenes converted to Islam. Their responses suggest, for instance, that they, like both the traditionalists and Christians, have a twofold view of *xexeme* (creation). On one hand it is the spatially structured cosmic place for life now in temporality on Earth, stretching from the Earth's surface through the atmosphere up to and including the sky. As a place for temporal life, *xexeme* consists structurally of the first of seven or eight Earths, its atmosphere and the sky, which is the first of seven or eight heavens. The

---

90. Özdemir, "Toward an Understanding of Environmental Ethics," 8.
91. Swimme and Tucker, *Journey of the Universe*, 2.
92. Swimme and Tucker, *Journey of the Universe*, 5.
93. Bookless, *Planetwise*, 20, points out that the difference between biblical cosmology and those of others is that only God creates out of nothing, while other accounts either have an already existing material from which the world is shaped or the world just emanated from a creator.

Qur'an, and hence Islamic cosmology, however, mentions "seven heavens and the earth" in the universe (Qur'an 17:44). For Muslims in the Sokpoe eco-area only the first heaven and first Earth constitute *xexeme*, because they are perceptible and knowable. Both human and other-than-human creatures as well as non-living creations occupy *xexeme*.

The Qur'an emphasizes why creation exists and what it means, bestowing a transcendental significance on it as ậya (sign or pointer) to God. Creation is an emblem of God, a means through which God speaks to humanity[94] about himself as "a Creator who is All-Powerful, All-Knowing and All-Merciful."[95] Nature is then a "book" just like the Qur'an, with the same author, God.[96] Seeyed Hossein Nasr calls them "Cosmic Qur'an and Recorded Qur'an," respectively.[97] Muslims, therefore, regard both creation and the Qur'anic verses as ậyat, signs or pointers to God.[98] A further inference is that as God reveals and manifests himself through his creation, this gives humans the impression that God is within us.[99] In other words, Muslims do not think that God abandoned his creation, but is ever concerned with and involved in its sustenance—providing food, water, crops etc. (Qur'an 80:24–32). Thus, in Islam "nature is sacred but not divine, for divinity belongs to God alone," who being "All-Sacred" cannot but create only a sacred cosmos that reflects his wisdom.[100]

In addition, Qur'an speaks of the cosmos as an integral system governed by a set of immutable laws, the natural laws, which embody God's command (*amr*, plural ậwamir). Since nature cannot but strictly submit to its *amr*, resulting in its observed coherent interconnectivity, order and regularity,[101] Qur'an regards nature's obedience to manifest God's glory as submission. This makes nature an imperative *Muslim* (submissive). Qur'an 22:18 states: "Don't you see that to God bow down in worship all things that are in the heavens and on Earth the sun, the moon, the stars; the hills, the trees, the animals; and a great number among mankind . . . ?" As Özdemir explains, the only difference between other-than-human creation and humankind is that the former is *Muslim* without free will, implying that only

---

94. Haq, "Islam and Ecology," 126.
95. Özdemir, "Toward an Understanding of Environmental Ethics," 8.
96. Özdemir, "Toward an Understanding of Environmental Ethics," 9.
97. Nasr, "Islam, the Contemporary Islamic World," 95.
98. Haq, "Islam and Ecology," 126.
99. Özdemir, "Toward an Understanding of Environmental Ethics," 12.
100. Nasr, "Islam, the Contemporary Islamic World," 96.
101. Haq, "Islam and Ecology," 132.

humankind can be Muslim through free choice morally.[102] Thus, in Islamic theocology biogeophysical cycles, for instance, natural processes that ensure eco-balance are regarded not as mere self-sustaining attributes of nature as may be argued in Gaia theory; they are commands of God, which nature, a good *Muslim*, only obeys.

Moreover, as part of its natural-law-abiding function, other-than-human creation is presented by Qur'an as existing to nourish, support and sustain all life and human life in particular. However, there is a moral and religious system to control the centrality of human life and, hence, human relations with nature.[103] This may be described as guided or regulated anthropocentric self-understanding of human and other-than-human relationships. Patrick Curry may term it "light green or shallow" ecology in so much as it limits direct value (and *raison d'être* of nature) to human beings.[104] Haq thinks that, unlike Christianity, the Islamic view does not present any concept that humanity may understand rightly or wrongly "'to subdue the earth' and seek to establish 'dominion' over the natural world."[105] For Qur'an 24:42 makes it clear that "to only God belongs the dominion of the heavens and the earth." Contrarily, in practice, as I point out in chapter 4, Muslims also misapply the concept of *khalifacy* to subdue creation.

Another important ecological observation Qur'an points at in nature is the principle of measure and balance. Qur'an 54:49, which reads, "Verily We have created all things in proportion and measure," is explained as depicting that in the cosmos only "God is absolute and infinite, every creature is finite."[106] By implication the resourcefulness of creation is not only limited, but, significantly, it is God who limits it. Qur'an 15:21 states it as: "And there is not a thing, but with Us are the stores thereof. And we send it not down except in a known measure." Closely related to the concept of "measured out" (*qadar, qadr, taqdir*) is that of "cosmic balance" (*mīzān*), which is expressed to mean that "God intends no injustice to any of His creatures . . . " (Qur'an 3:108–9). To this end God gives each cosmic entity its *amr* (divine command) as a natural law, which guides its being and function in a healthy relation to the larger cosmic whole.[107] The suggestion here is that Islamic worldviews perceive inherent regulatory mechanisms in nature—divinely predetermined limitations and principles of balanced cosmic

---

102. Özdemir, "Toward an Understanding of Environmental Ethics," 16.
103. Haq, "Islam and Ecology," 126.
104. Curry, *Ecological Ethics*, 61.
105. Haq, "Islam and Ecology," 133.
106. Özdemir, "Toward an Understanding of Environmental Ethics," 12.
107. Haq, "Islam and Ecology," 132.

existence—which ensure ecological morality or eco-justice and cosmological or material self-conservation. I shall return to this point in chapter 3.

Humanity in Islamic Worldview

Humanity occupies the third dimension of Islamic worldview. The Qur'an presents human beings as cosmic entities created "out of baked clay" (Qur'an 23:13–14; 15:26) from and for the Earth, to be earthlings.[108] The human image is the "best of forms" (*fi ahsāni taqwim*) and so humans are considered the noblest of creatures (*Ashraf al-makhluqat*).[109] Humans are both servants of God (*'abd-Allah*) and vicegerents of God (*khalīfa Allah*).[110] In this capacity they are theomorphic, treated as if possessing some God-qualities. For they alone, among all creation, accepted a divine call to carry the moral burden of being custodians of the Earth.[111] They reflect the way God "dominates" over his creation and cares for it as servants in submission to God's control.[112] In short, as vicegerents, humanity, theoretically, can be stewards of creation on the condition that they submit to only directions of God in taking ecological actions. For they, and not any other creatures, are accountable to God for their acts.[113] In this respect the Qur'an humbles humanity by declaring other-than-human creation greater than them (Qur'an 40:57), although many do not know.[114] Inferably, in Islamic worldviews humans are to relate to and with the other-than-human creation as managers or stewards, and this relationship is expected to be theocentric—very antithetical to eco-centrism. In Christianity, as an Abrahamic tradition like Islam, such a theocentric ecology implies that ultimate authority remains with God the creator; human ecological actions need to be a matter of "because of God" or "to the glory of God," being the believer's "commitment to the love of God and neighbor."[115] Patrick Curry notes, "humanity can use the natural world but only with due regard for the fact that God created it and gave us responsibility for its well-being."[116] The stewardship or managerial ideology

---

108. Haq, "Islam and Ecology," 126.
109. Haq, "Islam and Ecology," 133.
110. Nasr, "Islam, the Contemporary Islamic World," 97.
111. Haq, "Islam and Ecology," 133.
112. Nasr, "Islam, the Contemporary Islamic World," 97.
113. Haq, "Islam and Ecology," 133.
114. Haq, "Islam and Ecology," 133.
115. Blasu, "Compensated Reduction," 22.
116. Curry, *Ecological Ethics*, 34.

is religiously laudable, but Curry rightly doubts its practical reality, given the historical record of not successfully managing ourselves.[117]

To conclude, it is not difficult to deduce that the relationship that the Qur'an enjoins between humans and other-than-humans is for a Muslim to "love creation for the sake of its Creator," as Ibrahim Özdemir puts it.[118] This is a similar understanding to Christian worldviews.

Creation, Creator and Humanity in Christian Worldviews

As in Islam, a Christian theology of creation and the articulation of a Christian environmental ethics in contemporary terms are quite new. It is a new dimension of theology with a cause.[119] In other words, it is partly in response to, or at least prompted by, agitations against the reigning evolutionism ideology prior to the 1960s in the West, which held a "worldview in which God does not exist and does not participate in the events of the world."[120] But more significantly it responded to criticisms from environmentalists that the Judeo-Christian heritage, with its traditional teachings of human dominion over creation, bore a serious degree of responsibility for the ecological crisis.[121]

David Hallman believes that Christian theocologizing began in the 1960s and in the early 1970s when a growing number of theologians and ethicists in some denominations and theological institutions began to reflect on creation and the place of humans within it. But in Africa, though this was also the period of the genesis of African Christian theology,[122] the ecological dimension did not feature significantly in the works of the early African theologians.[123] All the same, the less evidence of emphasis on ecology in African Christian thought at the time was not a "*refusal* to engage the natural world in its theology," as Ben-Willie Golo,[124] following J. O. Y.

---

117. Curry, *Ecological Ethics*, 35.

118. Özdemir, "Toward an Understanding of Environmental Ethics," 29.

119. Victus, *Eco-Theology and the Scriptures*, 46.

120. Schwarz, *Creation*, 165.

121. Hallman, ed., *Ecotheology*, 397. See also Victus, *Eco-Theology and the Scriptures*, 46.

122. Mante, *Africa*, 5, suggests in a footnote that Muzorewa, *Origins and Development of African Theology*, 3, cited in Fueter, "Theological Education in Africa," was the first to use the term "African theology."

123. Mante, *Africa*, 23.

124. Golo, "Redeemed from the Earth?," 350.

Mante,¹²⁵ seems to imply; rather it was because they were preoccupied with "the problem of deculturation, which the Western church has posed for the ordinary African Christian"¹²⁶ and which was the contextual necessity at the time for the first generation of Christian scholars—the question of "Identity as a Key to understanding the concerns [including ecology] of Christian Theology in modern Africa."¹²⁷

A second remark is that although the salvation message is the core message and mission of the Christian church, the (redeemable and/or) redeemed person lives, moves and has his/her being within a material space (the ecosystem).¹²⁸ Indeed, it is in and with the ecosystem that the salvific faith of the Christian encounters cultural dimensions of the divine-human relations. Then the Christian Bible needs to be central in interpreting how the Christian culture engages with such relationships in the ecosystem.¹²⁹ However, wondering in his *Eco-Theology and the Scriptures* how far the Bible can be treated as a book of science to deal with ecology, Solomon Victus observes, rightly, that despite lots of scientific principles noticeable in it, the Bible is basically neither a scientific nor an ecological book. Nevertheless, as long as the total message of the Bible can meaningfully link with reality, it finds relevance in all cultures and all situations. Therefore, Christians still hold on to the Bible as a good source book for modern ecological questions too, being "the light of the world."¹³⁰

The Creator of Our Home, Earth, in Christian Understanding

Like Kwame Bediako, Hans Schwarz does not only affirm the Scriptures for discerning the biblical view of creation, but also suggests close attention to the first two chapters of Genesis, since they focus on creation and may well set the tone for everything else said about creation in the Bible.¹³¹ The Genesis accounts—the Priestly or P (Gen 1:1—2:4a) and Yahwist or J (2:4b–24)

---

125. Mante, *Africa*, 23.
126. Mante, *Africa*, 23.
127. K. Bediako, *Theology and Identity*, 1.
128. Golo, "Redeemed from the Earth?," 350.
129. K. Bediako, "Scripture as the Hermeneutic," 2.
130. Victus, *Eco-Theology and the Scriptures*, 45.
131. Schwarz, *Creation*, 166. Paul House similarly observes that these two chapters are the most crucial passages in the Law concerning creation; the text does not include everything the Law, let alone the Bible, has to say about creation, but it does provide the framework for all that follows. See House, "Creation in Old Testament Theology."

narratives[132]—link the existence of the world (heaven and Earth) and all that is in it, including human and other-than-human creatures, to God. From the Old Testament both Paul House[133] and Hans Schwarz explain that the Hebrew term *bara*, and from the New Testament Schwarz adds the Greek *ktizo* (which means to create), are theologically significant, because they are used exclusively for only divine activity, especially creativity.[134] To the Christian believer the idea of creation is an article of faith.[135] None of us existed when the world began. To say that God created is to presuppose his existence primus. This is unequivocally a declaration of faith based on God's revelation (Heb 11:3), the credibility of which "does not depend on natural science,"[136] although "some things in it are open to scientific explanation."[137] Based on Hebrews 11:3 Victus contends that by faith we know God created the Earth *ex nihilo*,[138] as Schwarz also implies from Romans 4:17 that there was no pre-existent matter (substance); everything is created (Eph 3:9).[139] To be sure, R. J. Williams defines creation as "the bringing of the universe into existence by God. It is a calling into being that which did not exist before."[140] Then, soon after the emergence of the primordial ecosphere God involved it to participate in his ongoing creative activity: the Earth, responding to God's call, put forth vegetation (Gen 1:11) and the waters and the air produced swarms of living creatures (Gen 1:20).[141]

Victus suggests that this definition "is the Hebrew biblical understanding" and is "quite contrary to the evolution concept."[142] This is because mod-

132. Schwarz, *Creation*, 169.
133. House, "Creation in Old Testament Theology."
134. Schwarz, *Creation*, 166 and 168.
135. MacArthur, "Theology of Creation."
136. MacArthur, "Theology of Creation."
137. C. Westermann, *Genesis*, 13.
138. Victus, *Eco-Theology and the Scriptures*, 49.
139. Schwarz, *Creation*, 168.
140. Williams, *Renewal Theology*, 98. See Golo, "Redeemed from the Earth?," 356.
141. Schwarz, *Creation*, 170.

142. Victus, *Eco-Theology and the Scriptures*, 49. Victus does not indicate what the contradiction is between biblical and evolution concepts of the world. But it is noteworthy that one effect of Enlightenment and the subsequent scientific revolution on Christian higher education, particularly in the West, is divided Christian cosmologies related to debates that have raged around evolution and creation. The scientific account asserts from the works of Nicolaus Copernicus (1473–1543) and Isaac Newton (1642–1727) that the physical universe (unfolds by) and obeys laws of nature that account for the movement of planets as well as physical phenomena on Earth (Edwards, *God of Evolution*, 4). Thus, contrary to what some Christians uphold as biblical, especially OT cosmology, scientists claim that the Earth, along with the rest of our solar system,

ern scientific evolution philosophy and theories arrange a systematic and chronological outbirthing of the complex cosmos.[143] I reiterate that while this may be convincing to many, it is not only limited to the "observable universe," but significantly unable to explain the source of the already existing "single point" mixture of visible "luminous matter" and the invisible "dark matter" that "was trillions of degrees hot and that instantly rushed apart" to become "all of space and time and mass and energy."[144] I have also argued already that to the Abrahamic religions the source of even that single point of matter that may have evolved into the cosmos in scientific assertions is still God.[145] In Deutero-Isaiah (e.g., Isa 40:25-26) and the Wisdom books

---

emerged (not necessarily created) about 4.5 billion years ago (Edwards, *God of Evolution*, 4). Concerning life on the Earth, scientists use evidence from a number of disciplines to explain its evolution. They begin with discovery of bacterial life and microbial communities in rock formations as the first ecosystems more than three billion years ago and conclude that the whole pattern of life on Earth has evolved from these early communities of simple cells (Edwards, *God of Evolution*, 4). The theories of adaptation, natural selection and genetic inheritance by Jean Baptiste de Lamarck (1744-1829), Charles Darwin (1809-1882) and Gregor Mendel, respectively, in the nineteenth century further consolidated the evolutionary cosmology; and the discovery of the structure and function of deoxyribonucleic acid (DNA) by James Watson and Francis Crick in the twentieth century enabled studying evolution at molecular level (Edwards, *God of Evolution*, 4-6). Moreover, Hans Schwarz observes that while Reformers such as Martin Luther (1483-1546) and John Calvin (1509-64) emphasized the sovereignty of God, they did so to declare God not as Creator but rather as the Lord of history (Schwarz, *Creation*, 4). He concludes that science could then continue its course relatively unhampered by the salvation concerns of theology (Schwarz, *Creation*, 4). As a result, now not only is it a taboo to mention the possibility of creation in most institutions of higher education in the West, but "arguments over evolution and creationism have divided Christians for many years" (Bookless, *Planetwise*, 19). Yet at the same time, as Schwarz observes, it is also "now that scientific knowledge has led us not only to new heights but also to existential threats to life" (Schwarz, *Creation*, 20). Although I am aware of both the evolution-creation debate and its consequences, particularly the tendency of Western Christianity to expunge creationism in academia, I argue for the need to develop ecological theology that synthesizes the positives in both ideologies, so as to plausibly regain Christian faith in creation. This responds to the suggestions of both Denis Edwards and David Bookless. Edwards suggests that it is not the role of theology to enter into debates about the intricacies of evolutionary theory, but into a critical dialogue with the broad picture offered by contemporary biology (Edwards, *God of Evolution*, 7). David Bookless puts it as avoiding the how and concentrate on the why of the genesis of the Earth (Bookless, *Planetwise*, 20). My position remains, however, that both the why and how need be engaged if we are to hold fast and even deepen our faith in the face of scientific evidence (Blasu, "Our Earth, Our Responsibility," 256).

143. Swimme and Tucker, *Journey of the Universe*, 2.

144. Swimme and Tucker, *Journey of the Universe*, 5.

145. Bookless, *Planetwise*, 20, points out that the difference between biblical cosmology and those of others is that only God creates out of nothing, while other accounts either have an already existing material from which the world is shaped, or the

God did not mince words but categorically declared his authorship of and sovereignty over the Earth and the heavens and all that there is in them, including darkness and light. In particular, Job 38–39 demonstrates that other-than-human creation can exist and thrive without the intervention of human beings. In Christian worldviews creation and created beings exist and are there because of God's power and sustaining hand.

There are, however, indications also in both the OT (e.g., Isa 65:17–25) and NT (e.g., Rom 8:21–25) that creation in the beginning has to be connected with the new creation in the end, since creation in its present state does not correspond to the glory of God.[146] Thus, Schwarz suggests we understand creation not only in its historical context, as if a singular fact that occurred in the beginning; it contains a dynamic element.[147] In a study on "The World in the Bible," Christopher J. H. Wright argues that the English expression "the world" as used in the Bible rarely translates one Hebrew or Greek word. It may translate "heaven and earth," *erets, adamah, ge, cosmos, ktisis* and *aiōn*.[148] It is noteworthy that the English word in the Letter to the Hebrews 11:3 is "worlds," translating the Greek *aiōn*. This means "universe or ages." Suggestively, God's acts of creating spaces have been occurring over long periods of time, in different epochs as Kwame Bediako avers.[149] For Bediako, while the English usage of *aiōn* implies that creation is related to the "world" as a one-time act of one spatial arena, the meaning of this verse from the Greek sense is that it is God who has been creating and is still creating. It refers to a long period of time without reference to beginning or end, and suggests spaces other than the earthly space alone that we tend to imagine when reading the Bible.[150] Moreover, the dynamic element in the process of creation continues as and in the salvation act of God into the new world. In Deutero-Isaiah (Isa 40–55), which offers abundant statements about the creator God,[151] the verb *bara* is associated with salvation also, suggesting that implicit in the doctrine of creation is the doctrine of

---

world just emanated from a creator.

146. Schwarz, *Creation*, 168.
147. Schwarz, *Creation*, 169.
148. Wright, "World in the Bible," 208.
149. K. Bediako, "Christian Faith and African Culture," 47. Kwame Bediako argues that the Twi translation for aeon (*mresantee*) as in Hebrews 1:2 is closer to the Greek meaning than the English word "worlds." This verse specifically refers to the role of Jesus as creator but the meaning both in Twi and Greek specifically refers to the ongoing act of creation through every age.
150. K. Bediako, "Christian Faith and African Culture," 47.
151. Keitzar, "Creation and Restoration," 53.

salvation.[152] In short, creation is good because of a good creator,[153] but the good creation is temporal and will inevitably decay, requiring salvation into eternal entity as in the mind and will of the creator. Golo believes that the salvation of our corrupt and fallen universe is built into the fabric of creation as a process of re-creation or renewal to culminate in the new world just as happens to a Christian believer (2 Cor 5:17).[154]

What Creation and Its Purposes Are in Christian Understanding

J. H. Wright suggests that for purposes of effective mission (including keeping integrity of creation) we need to be certain about what we mean by "the whole world" or "cosmos,"[155] and hence "all creation." An understanding of what we mean by "all creation" will inform what action and where we act ecologically to be effective Earth-keepers. When the OT uses the expression "heavens and earth" Wright understands it as the whole created universe (the cosmosphere)—"all that exists which is not God."[156] Or in the NT "cosmos" is "the world or universe considered as an ordered whole, or ordered in opposition to God."[157] In reading the Bible we often perceive the cosmos as structurally consisting of two distinct places, heavens and Earth, with "the heavens" perhaps consisting of three hierachical levels, the highest being the abode of God (Deut 10:14). Michael Dowd illustrates this view and labels it as "pre-evolutionary (old) cosmology," which is a picture that shows heaven as located structurally far above the Earth, where God is transcendantly.[158] Humans live *on* the Earth, but relate with God and fellow humanity, and only regard the "Earth as the stage upon which this drama played out."[159] The result, particularly in the West, is that out of this reality function anthropocentric valuing and morality, as well as otherworldly

---

152. Schwarz, *Creation*, 167.

153. House, "Creation in Old Testament Theology."

154. Golo, "Redeemed from the Earth?," 355 and 357. This sense of renewal is also reflected in the Greek term for "new" (*kainos*) used in Revelation 21 and in other places, rather than "new" as in *neos*, i. e., new as in completely new.

K. Bediako, "Scripture as the Hermeneutic of Culture and Tradition," 2.

155. Wright, "World in the Bible," 208.

156. Wright, "World in the Bible," 208.

157. Wright, "World in the Bible," 208.

158. Dowd, *Thank God for Evolution*, 227.

159. Dowd, *Thank God for Evolution*, 227.

behaviors toward an invisible God and toward one another. What happens to the Earth and other-than-human creation is of no moral concern.[160]

For this research I investigated the Sokpoe-Eʋe Christians' understanding of *xexeme* as a possible translation of the ecological terms "environment," "world" and "creation." Their biblical worldview seem to follow Dowd's "pre-evolutionary" cosmology description, though with a slight difference. Like Dowd's description, the Sokpoe-Eʋe Christian pictures *xexeme* as comprising two existential places, *dzifo kple anyigba* (the heavens and the Earth). Unlike Dowd's premodern science illustration, however, these two places in the mind of the Sokpoe-Eʋe Christian are contiguous through atmosphere and open into each other to form a united whole containing every created thing and separated by only time. There is *dzifoxexeme* (the heavenly world), which exists and is experiential to humanity only at death, though it opens into *anyigbaxexeme* (the earthly world) in which we now live and have experiences. Human activities have ecological implications in both, although *xexeme* in daily experience is limited simply to *anyigba kple edzinuwo* (gecosphere, or the Earth and things in it—human and other-than-human, physical and spiritual).[161]

It is noteworthy also that C. H. Wright makes dualistic deductions after his study of biblical concepts of the world or the cosmos. He notes that the cosmos as creation gives the sense of both the physical creation where we live and the place of rebellion and opposition to God—resulting in sin, suffering, poverty, pain and judgement.[162] Similarly, the Sokpoe-Eʋe Christian not only sees the gecosphere as the physical arena for ecological action, but also as both the depiction of ecological valuing and moral conduct. People who do not organize life around biblical and Christian ethical doctrines are called *xexemetɔwo* or *egodotɔwo* (those outside Christian world).[163] What it means is that humanity corrupts the *xexeme* (creation) that God created as good.

God's purpose for creation is not easily apprehended by humanity, yet creation in diverse ways glorifies God and is indicative of his divine attributes. Hans Schwarz thinks creation was neither a necessity nor an accident with God. God wanted and did create[164] for his own purposes, something impossible for humans to rationalize in minute details.[165] Solomon Victus

---

160. Dowd, *Thank God for Evolution*, 227.
161. See *xexeme*, definition 3, in the glossary.
162. Wright, "World in the Bible," 209.
163. Gladys Ahado, interview at Sokpoe, 26 June 2016.
164. Schwarz, *Creation*, 173.
165. Victus, *Eco-Theology and the Scriptures*, 65.

ponders, for instance, "why does God pour rain on the desert where no humans live (Job 38:25–27)?" He further muses how in Job 38–39 God engages Job on the ecology of the world from which Job must have learnt that "the creative breath of God is inspired by beauty, joy, freedom and identity in nature," portraying God's wonders and glory in creation.[166] Bryant Myers, a development theologian, discussing the implications of the creation account in development, construes what Genesis 2 says of "trees pleasing to the eye" to mean aesthetics is part of created order, and that "beauty of creation is itself a witness to God and reveals God's glory (Ps 19:1–4)."[167] God's love, faithfulness, righteousness and justice are compared with those of natural elements (Ps 36:5–6).[168]

The explanations of Hans Schwarz on the P-narrative of Genesis 1 in the OT[169] and of Renthy Keitzar on the prologue to John's Gospel (1:1–3) in the NT[170] suggest that biblical creation references may be theological apologetics aimed at pointing out God's glory to humanity in the face of other cosmologies. The OT texts are assertions against Babylonian myths of origin, and the NT is against the Greek Gnostic understanding that matter is essentially evil and spirit is essentially good, hence the good God cannot be creator of an evil material world. In both cases the intention is to let all the Earth fear the Lord; let all the inhabitants of the world stand in awe of him (Ps 33:8).[171] Similarly, in the Yawistic account of creation the Earth is symbolized as *'oikos*, an ecosystem in which the different biota and abiota coexist symbiotically, fulfilling God's plan and purpose for which they are created.[172] The Good News Bible rendition of Psalm 19:1–4 suggests creation's revelation of God's glory is not just a passive implication, but also an active declaration or announcement albeit in a language not intelligibly perceptible to our human ears: "No speech or words are used, no sound is heard; yet their message goes out to all the world and it is heard to the ends of the earth." In the New Testament, Paul succinctly avers the singular truth is that creation plainly reveals God's invisible attributes, namely, his eternal power and divine nature, in the things that have been made (Rom 1:18–20). In short, creation manifests the incontestable and non-comparative awful greatness, might and wisdom of God (Isa 40:25–26).

166. Victus, *Eco-Theology and the Scriptures*, 65.
167. Myers, *Walking with the Poor*, 62.
168. Victus, *Eco-Theology and the Scriptures*, 66.
169. Schwarz, *Creation*, 170.
170. Keitzar, "Creation and Restoration," 57.
171. Schwarz, *Creation*, 170.
172. Keitzar, "Creation and Restoration," 56.

We can even learn wisdom from creation: tiny creatures like ants, for instance, are biblically commended to be such teachers of social organizational skills and food security planning (Prov 6:6) in the ecosystem. Birds in the air and lilies of the field may remind us, a people of faith, not to be anxious but trust God for daily divine providence (Matt 6:25–34). In the beginning of the seventeenth century, Francis Bacon, a scholastic Christian, challenged his scholars to shift focus from "God's revelation" (the Bible) to and learn from "God's other book" (nature). Implying this in his *The New Organon and Related Writings*, Fulton A. Anderson explains that Bacon insisted on this shift because he believed nature is the better of the two books of God's revelation and provides more concrete and hardcore knowledge to enhance improving the estate of humanity.[173] Bryant Myers observes that the result of that shift is a stunning variety of human inventions and the emergence of modern science in the West: modern medicine, modern agriculture etc.[174] Although Bacon must have awakened Christians to particularly value nature as God's source of empirical knowledge, it is now well known that the extremes of the shift and the resultant development of science and technology has also been accompanied with philosophies and practices of dualism that eventually separated the spiritual from the physical and secularized Christian thought and praxis by the nineteenth century, particularly in the West.[175] The theocological consequence is "a powerfully held view of the other-than-human natural world as a set of inert raw resources to be mastered and exploited by human reason—in other words, ethically negligible."[176] And in this denial of the divine ordering of creation to God and to all God's creatures, and not just to humans, we may identify the true root of our current environmental crisis.[177]

All the same, God created the Earth as both home—the 'oikos—and means to nurture life. Bryant Myers says, "Creation is not a stage, but a living home" that "supports . . . life and well-being with its air, water, trees, fruits, animals."[178] The physicist and cosmologist Freeman Dyson, reflecting on the origin of the universe, particularly the scientific discovery of its steady evolutionary expansion, became convinced that "the universe in some sense

---

173. Anderson, *New Organon and Related Writings*, 23, 78. See also Myers, *Walking with the Poor*, 25.

174. Myers, *Walking with the Poor*, 25.

175. Holmes, *Building the Christian Academy*, 102.

176. Curry, "Ecological Ethics," 37.

177. Northcott, "Christians, Environment and Society," 106.

178. Myers, *Walking with the Poor*, 86.

must have known that we are coming."[179] In other words, Freeman Dyson affirms that biblical cosmology anticipates life; the creator God, having a foreplan of creating both human and other-than-human creatures, created the Earth to suit their life.[180] Schwarz argues from the "Noachic blessing in Genesis 8:22" that God decided to create life other than himself, but this life requires an appropriate arena where there is temporality and order or rhythm of time for existence. For, "not forever, not in eternity, but as long as the Earth exists will there be seedtime and harvest, cold and heat, summer and winter, day and night."[181] The reason, in God's creative wisdom, is that life needs the cyclic changes of day and night for its supporting food to grow, and God decidedly granted and sanctioned it.[182] So God prepared an environment for life before creating even humanity[183] as the last creature of the biblical creation story.[184] Who or what are human beings in the story of creation?

Christian Worldviews of Humanity and Our Place in Creation

According to Hans Schwarz, the biblical P-narratives of creation put humanity in the last group of the creatures or animals (beasts, birds and fishes) that God created on the sixth day. Humanity is, therefore, closely associated with animals, being of same earthly substance and sharing same food materials. However, while P-narrative informs that other animals came forth at God's command from the land, atmosphere (air) and waters, humans, according to J-narrative, were exclusively the work of God; he "formed the man [sic] of the dust from the ground" (Gen 2:7a). Schwarz adds that the human (*adam*) is taken from the earth (*adamah*) and to the earth it shall return (Gen 3:19). Anthropologically, "there is nothing divine in humanity, since it is closely associated with matter."[185] But then God "breathed into the human's nostrils the breath of life, and the human became a living being (*nephesh haya*)" (Gen 2:7b).[186] An aspect of the very being of God, his life-breath or spirit, is now in human nature; it is that by which human beings

---

179. Cited by Swimme and Tucker, *Journey of the Universe*, 11.
180. Swimme and Tucker, *Journey of the Universe*, 11.
181. Schwarz, *Creation*, 172.
182. Schwarz, *Creation*, 172.
183. Keitzar, "Creation and Restoration," 55.
184. Victus, *Eco-Theology and the Scriptures*, 52.
185. Schwarz, *Creation*, 176.
186. Keitzar, "Creation and Restoration," 55. It is noteworthy that animals are also *nephesh haya*—living creatures (Gen 1:24). It is the same term used in 2:7b.

live, and if taken away humanity returns to soil again.[187] So biblically, "[w]e receive our human existence by participating in God's life-giving spirit."[188]

What this means theocologically is that humanity occupies a special niche and so fulfills a unique purpose in God's created order. For, since God took much pain in creating the universe and especially humans (Ps 8:4),[189] and only into humans it appears God breathed his own life-spirit directly, humanity assumes a unity of both *something* divine" and something material, described as "created in the image of God [*imago Dei*] and after his likeness (Gen 1:26) or as the Psalmist says in 8:5 a little lower than God."[190] Humanity seems, then, theomorphic and treated as if possessing some God-qualities (Ps 82:6; John 10:34–36a). In this capacity humans enter a functional relationship with God, being his "vice-gerents on earth"[191] with extended authority to be responsible stewards for the Earth (Gen 2:15).

In addition, creation of humanity demonstrates God's nature and idea of community in the ecosystem. The Hebrew word denoting human being, *adam*, is a collective word, meaning humankind. Hence the narrative adds a qualification that God created "them, male and female" (Gen 1:27). And the creation of the woman not only concluded the creative process of humanity but established the "personal community of humans in the broadest sense,"[192] evidenced in marital companionship, spiritual fellowship and social relations, sustainable by the attribute of love. Schwarz observes that not only did Adam recognize and declare Eve as bone of his bone, but even the bond with the parental home would not be able to stop a man from clinging to his wife for as long as they live (Gen 2:23–24). Thus in OT thought humanity (and a human being) is perceived as a unity even if the narratives distinguish between body and soul.[193] For the creator of all humanity is at the same time the creator of each individual human being (Isa 17:7; Ps 10:8–9), through the procreative process of injecting semen (milk) into female organism to fertilize (curdle like cheese) into a solid embryonic body (flesh) as Job teaches us (Job 10:8–12).[194]

To reiterate, I set out in this chapter to examine the worldviews of the three major religious traditions in Ghana (and hence, Africa). The aim

187. Keitzar, "Creation and Restoration," 55.
188. Schwarz, *Creation*, 177.
189. Victus, *Eco-Theology and the Scriptures*, 52.
190. Keitzar, "Creation and Restoration," 55.
191. Vriezen, *Outline of Old Testament Theology*, 208.
192. Schwarz, *Creation*, 179.
193. Schwarz, *Creation*, 176.
194. Schwarz, *Creation*, 177.

has been to recover religious materials that illuminate their cultural understandings of our current global environmental concerns. But it has also been to appreciate how this eco-cultural understanding guides their ecological thinking and actions, posing the question, "How do these religious worldviews influence the praxis of their respective religious ecologies?" This question is what I wish to answer in the next chapter.

CHAPTER 3

Creation Care in Religious Traditions of Africa

Introduction: Ecological Ethics and Values

FOR THE PRACTICE OF creation care to be meaningful it may have to go beyond academic knowledge and impact our personal lives, our lifestyles, and how we personally affect the environment. This requires ecological ethics—the right and wrong or moral relationships between humans and the world around us[1]—that can engender commitment to concrete or practical ecological actions.[2] This is because the ecological community forms the ethical community,[3] implying that in the ecological community humans need to know how they *ought* to live and act, or relate with other-than-humans also as subjects in one or the other way, to sustain the existence of the entire eco-community of both humans and other-than-humans.[4] Environmental law is the means by which human hands may be restrained from diminishing the capacity of the Earth to support life.[5] But fundamental to eco-ethics and laws is the need for eco-values.

Ecological values are "the ultimate worth of actions or things"[6] that underpin eco-ethical behaviors. They may be either individualist or holist,

---

1. Cunningham and Saigo, *Environmental Science*, 37.
2. Nebel and Wright, *Environmental Science*, 13.
3. Sylvan and Bennett, *Greening of Ethics*, 91, cited by Curry, *Ecological Ethics*, 3.
4. Curry, *Ecological Ethics*, 3.
5. Llewellyn, "Basis for a Discipline of Islamic Environmental Law," 185.
6. Cunningham and Saigo, *Environmental Science*, 37.

on one hand, and on the other, either intrinsic or instrumental.⁷ Defending ecocentric against anthropocentric valuing of nature, Patrick Curry states that "nature—which certainly includes humanity—is the *ultimate* source of all value."⁸ He implies that nature's value is not only intrinsic but a self-endowed quality through evolution. Contrarily, in Africa, both the primal and Abrahamic (Islam and Judeo-Christian) religious traditions affirm from their worldviews that creation is God's handiwork. Creation thus has both intrinsic and instrumental values⁹ conferred by God, not by itself or humans. In primal religion, for instance, God is *Nunyuiwɔla* (creator of the good or value);¹⁰ for Christians "the heavens declare the glory [shining goodness] of God"; in Islam, Allah gave to each (created) thing its form and nature (sura 20:50).¹¹ Suggestively, there are common ideas in both the primal and Christian worldviews that correspond with the Islamic understanding that "every individual creature or being has its own ontological existence as a sign (*aya*) of God and, by its very being, manifests and reveals His majestic and merciful values."¹² The religious eco-ethical point implied here is that the all-valuable and good creator is the only authoritative source and imputer of value and goodness to his creation, both human and other-than-human. It is not possible for any creature, if it is recognized as creation, to have value and moral status (goodness or otherwise) without reference to God's valuing of it.

Ecological values function by being transposed into ethical codes or norms (specific rules and regulations such as taboos) and ritual procedures, which are supposed to guide conduct on specific situations. For ethics, as Patrick Curry explains, concerns the realization of values, both in the sense of "realizing what they are and of making them real." Thus it refers to the moral principles and defined ways of how people *ought* to live and act in their relationships with one another in an ecological community or ecosystem.¹³ In this chapter I examine the specific eco-ethical principles that stimulate or give impulsion for ecological actions and instances of such actions in caring for creation based on the major religious worldviews in Ghana.

---

7. Curry, *Ecological Ethics*, 52. Italics emphasis is in the original text.
8. Curry, *Ecological Ethics*, 2. [italics my emphasis].
9. Llewellyn, "Basis for a Discipline of Islamic Environmental Law," 189.
10. Samuel Agboklu, interview at Sokpoe, 2 March 2016.
11. Özdemir, "Toward an Understanding of Environmental Ethics," 11.
12. Özdemir, "Toward an Understanding of Environmental Ethics," 11.
13. Curry, *Ecological Ethics*," 28.

The Impulsion for and Eco-Care Praxis in Primal Religion

I draw four related inferences from the analytic review of the structure of the African primal worldviews in chapter 2 that may motivate creation care: anthropocentric worldviews, fear of eco-deities, eco-character development and ritualistic priming for eco-relations.

Anthropocentrism and Fear of Deity as Primal Religious Impulsions for Eco-praxis

From my research among the Sokpoe-Eʋe I observed that their worldview is conceptually biocentric but practically anthropocentric. This corroborates observations that the worldviews of Africans are anthropocentric.[14] Thus the consciousness of and motivation for eco-care is generally more skewed to human benefitting than other-than-human creatures' wellness, if the latter are even thought of at all. This is the first inference from the structural analysis of the African worldviews earlier in chapter 2. We have seen that in African worldviews there are also other-than-human creations, especially ubiquitous malevolent and benevolent spiritual entities more powerful than humans. Yet they tend to direct ecological actions to the wellness of only human life, whether living or dead, existing spatially in either the physical or spiritual worlds. Human life is the "*sommum bonum*" (the greatest good), and communal interest overrides individual interest.[15] Harvey Sindima succinctly underscores this conception of biocentrism but praxis of anthropocentrism in the African primal religious cosmology and ecology. He writes:

> The African understanding of the world is life centered. For the African, life is the primary category for self-understanding and provides the basic framework for any interpretation of the world, persons, nature, or divinity.[16]

Sindima thus suggests biocentrism for African primal worldviews, which underscores our interpretation of creation, and hence, ecological phenomena. But in the end, it is specifically the life of humans that matters, rendering ecological relations and actions anthropocentric. For, as is suggestive in his submission, the need for humans to relate with other life forms harmoniously or ethically on Earth is because humans can then experience

---

14. Kalu, "Precarious Vision," 41.
15. Agbanu, "Environmental Ethics in Mafi-Eʋe Indigenous Culture," 96.
16. Sindima, "Community of Life," 137.

fullness or meaning to their own life. As he puts it: "In the human sphere the process of life achieves fullness when humans are richly connected to other people, to other creatures, and to the Earth itself. Humans realize their own fullness by realizing the bondedness of life."[17] The need for human fullness then underpins African eco-ethical praxis.

The second observation and inferred impulsion for eco-praxis is the fear of deities and ancestral spirits rather than the Supreme Being, even in cultures where the worldview has the God component. This I refer to as a theistic but not theocentric worldview and eco-ethics, subsequently. I mean that generally the Supreme Being is not necessarily the reason for ecological relations, actions or inactions in many African cultures. For instance, in the case of the ancestor-dominated worldview of the Akan, the Supreme Being, though revered as creator of the ecosphere, is not bothered with daily life ecological challenges in any practical sense.[18] Similarly, among the Sokpoe-Eυe and the Mafi-Eυe in the Volta Region of Ghana, *Mawu* (the Supreme Being) is creator, but, unlike the Akan, the dominant components in their worldviews are the *trɔ̃wo* (deities). Thus, it is the *trɔ̃wo* that are ultimately encountered and feared for committing environmental crimes in daily life experiences. This second observation—the sense of fear and vulnerability to spiritual entities other than God in the precarious ecosystems—in my view is the key to the import of African worldviews in primal religious eco-praxis. For it is the main reason why our ancestors establish both elaborate religious procedures (e.g. rituals) to manipulate the spirit forces and ethical rules (e.g., taboos) for prohibiting and inhibiting human conduct in the holistic eco-community. In this respect, Kofi Asare Opoku rightly critiqued A. B. Ellis as "certainly wrong" in the latter's assessing that African divinities "can view with equanimity" the most atrocious crimes committed in the eco-community.[19]

In primal Africa, the principles undergirding ecological ethics and ethos are derived from personal religious experiences of rudimentary agricultural practices and other close relations with and in the holistic ecosystem.[20] They are presented in their own genre, often, orally in cultural symbols such as folklores, proverbs, socioreligious taboos, as well as beliefs in totems, sacredness of life and ecosystem places.[21] They are not necessarily written philosophical formulations in Western terminologies like the

17. Sindima, "Community of Life," 137.
18. K. Bediako, *Jesus in Africa*, 25.
19. Asare-Opoku, *West African Traditional Religion*, 157.
20. Agbanu, "Environmental Ethics in Mafi-Eυe Indigenous Culture," 2.
21. Agbanu, "Environmental Ethics in Mafi-Eυe Indigenous Culture," 123.

deontological, consequential or utilitarian and virtue or teleological schools of ethics.[22] Nevertheless, as John Opoku contends, they constitute "a cultural philosophy that authenticates the African standard of [the ethical] humanity, both in perspective and content."[23] Some "may be universally shared" or correspond with the Western formulations in content since ethical codes may be "widespread in human society."[24] The aim of African primal religious eco-ethics is eco-virtuous character cultivation and practice towards harmonious relationships, and hence, abundant life in the ecosystem.[25]

Eco-Regulations and Development of Eco-Character as Life-long Eco-Praxis

The third inference extending from the second is that ultimately eco-culture and ethos are sustained among primal African ecological communities by developing and practicing virtuous ecological relationships or eco-character as a life-long experience. Eco-character development itself results indirectly from enforcing religious ecological regulations and performing rituals that ensure restoration of ecological harmony and just relations. In other words, obeying environmental taboos and performing prescribed rituals to appease the ecological deities are a means of mitigating the vulnerability of human life and/or ensuring harmonious relationships in the ecosphere. However, the religious ecological regulations and rituals go beyond being mere ecological actions to impacting practitioners with internal dispositions that engender harmonious ecological relations in the eco-community.[26]

For instance, in both Sokpoe and Akan ecological areas in Ghana, performing the rites and rituals that either prevent or erase the effects of *busubɔbɔ/mmusu* (ecological crimes) seem to be a hard way of learning from experience to develop some ecological character traits. Kofi Asare Opoku describes *mmusu* among the Akan of Ghana as "acts that bring disaster or cause misfortune."[27] That *mmusu* as ecological sin is implied in the fact that its consequences go beyond the offender and threatens the entire eco-community; it concerns the state and the divinities, and dealing with

---

22. Curry, *Ecological Ethics*," 39.

23. J. Opoku, "African Traditional Ethics," 286.

24. Nwosu and Kalu, "Study of African Culture," in Kalu, ed., *Readings in African Humanities*, 3.

25. Kalu, "Precarious Vision," 44.

26. Curry, *Ecological Ethics*, 49.

27. K. Opoku, *West African Traditional Religion*, 157.

mmusu always requires libation prayer and blood sacrifices.[28] Examples of *busu* among the Mafi-Eʋe, for instance, include flouting taboos regulating the use of land, water and other natural resources, or desecrating the land by having sexual intercourse in the bush or on bare ground, and disregarding sacredness of designated ecosystem places and objects—all of which may result in drought unless the culprits offer expiatory sacrifices.[29] As it were, undergoing the expiatory ritual as sanction may be an ethical learning experience that impacts change in ecological attitude and relational behaviors: ecological repentance, respect for nature, the fear of flouting land deity's ecological taboos and self-discipline in sexual matters. Native Americans describe such responsive spiritual actions of the offenders as "walk[ing] in the beauty way" or following "the good red road"[30]—implying turning eventually onto the right way or developing the right ecological attitude out of experience, by looking into oneself. In the process a moral order is necessarily established, because purity and obedience to ecological rules block the anger of the deities and ruin the intent of evil spirits; it is also required for the efficacy of ecological rituals. Carelessness and immorality may not only render the ritual useless, but also endanger the life of the celebrants.[31]

Ogbu Kalu thinks that eco-character or moral ecological uprightness is required to maintain peace with deities and with creation for abundant ecosystem life.[32] Thus, when the environment poses a challenge, the community probes its inner experience and mental construct of the universe to address and reflect the specific nature of the challenge.[33] We see this also among Native Americans. To counter ecological threats in their holistically perceived ecosystems, Native Americans "look into ourselves" and ask, "Are we participating in creation in a harmonious way? Are we honoring our ancestors? Are we nourishing our Mother Earth as she has nourished us, so that she will continue to nourish future generations?"[34] The result of such self-assessing reflections, even though somewhat anthropocentric, may be associated with eco-ethical lessons.

The pursuance of eco-character development, however, may not be a conscious or intentionally planned and implemented eco-practice. From a

---

28. K. Opoku, *West African Traditional Religion*, 157.

29. Agbanu, "Environmental Ethics in Mafi-Eʋe Indigenous Culture," 145. It is similar among the Sokpoe-Eʋe also as I found in this study.

30. Gonzales and Nelson, "Contemporary Native American Responses," 497.

31. Kalu, "Precarious Vision," 43.

32. Kalu, "Precarious Vision," 42.

33. Kalu, "Sacred Egg," 229.

34. Gonzales and Nelson, "Contemporary Native American Responses," 497.

Western cultural understanding, Patrick Curry calls eco-character "Green Virtue Ethic" (GVE). In his opinion, a Green Virtue Ethic, as an eco-character trait, agreeably, is developed and practiced in the course of a life-long process of learning in communities (human and other-than-human) that "haven't been entirely colonized by modernity."[35] Apparently there are other rituals to initiate, fortify and prime a new human entrant into the eco-community for its life-long development of ecological character at the start of each phase of the life continuum—birth, growth and death.

Ecological Rituals as Grounding and Priming for Creation Care

Apart from performing rituals of expiation as sanctions meted out for ecological crimes, there are others for priming the individuals ecologically by grounding and orienting them. Ecological grounding or orienting in religious traditions refers to the initiation, formally or informally, of a human being into and to identify with the ecological community. It is a means of making humans aware of being not only immersed in nature, but also being inexorably woven into profound relationships that constitute life on Earth and beyond. Ecological grounding gives the sense of self-embedding in an expansive cosmic community.[36] It opens the universe as an ever-present and all-embracing reality, and provides a sense of direction and purpose to situate humans in a larger cosmological reality, in the present and through the span of existence (life) into an unknown future.[37] Thus the cyclic timing of life in the African primal worldviews is a significant factor that directs the African's cultural practices denoting ecological *ethoi*. Each stage of the earthly sojourn of the cyclic life is celebrated with a rite of passage as an expression of the responsible relationship between the individual, the creator and other beings in the gecosphere. In other words, primal people follow the natural laws of their creation stories and perform ceremonies

---

35. Curry, *Ecological Ethics*, 50.

36. From Grim and Tucker, *Ecology and Religion* we learn that Confucianism illustrates this grounding by seeing the individual as embedded in or at the center of a series of concentric, overlapping circles including both humans and nature. Human's responsibility is to cultivate (i.e., morally transform) the self by learning to be sincere and sustain the integrity of nature's ecosystems with careful management (92). Confucian education thus leads one to recognizing one's deeper identity with reality as forming one body with all things (121). This mind of filial relatedness to others in the cosmos makes humans anthropocosmic rather than anthropocentric (121), and so motivates care for the Earth community or biosphere (115).

37. Grim and Tucker, *Ecology and Religion*, 96.

to maintain balance between people, place and spirits.[38] The major rites in earthly life with ecological connotations of orienting and grounding include natal (birthing), empowering (responsibility initiation) and transition (funerary) rites.

Concerning birth, the creation myths and outdooring rites reinforce the relationship between the child and the ecosystem. When the child is born, the outdooring rite seeks to ground it into the ecosystem. In southern Ghana, according to Robert Clobus, the newly born child is laid on the bare Earth[39] perhaps to signify that it is made essentially of clay and so "expected to revere and cooperate with it."[40] Christian ethicist Joshua Kudadjie undertook a pastoral study among the Ada (Dangme) of Ghana to integrate traditional practices and values with Christian outdooring and naming ceremony in the Methodist Church of Ghana. He notes that the traditional ceremony literally introduces the child formally to "the wider world of Earth [and] sky."[41] The outdooring rite may also symbolize formal integration of the child into the community of both the living and the living dead, qualifying it as a potential inheritor of the family land. Clobus observes that most Ghanaian traditions see land as belonging to the family as a sanctuary and a trust of ancestors. This concept makes the living temporary possessors of a heritage that is destined to pass to generations yet unborn,[42] and theoretically could underscore land ethics, economy and preservation of some Ghanaian cultures. Kalu observes that among some Africans eight days after birth the child's umbilical cord is put in a calabash, sprinkled with herbs and, after pronouncements, buried into the soil under a tree at the back of the house. In this way the child is rooted to the land with which it shares an everlasting bond.[43]

Similar birthing rites are observable among the Ada (Dangme) and Sokpoe-Eve of southern Ghana. The Ada, for instance, lay the eight-day-old baby on the bare ground and sprinkle cold water from roof eaves to

---

38. Gonzales and Nelson, "Contemporary Native American Responses," 497.

39. Clobus, "Ecofarming and Land Ownership," 70. Though Clobus did not specify which Ghanaian cultural tribe, yet the Eve and Ada, among whom he was working in the Afram Plains of Ghana at the time of writing, may not be ruled out. The Eve, like the Ga-Dangme of Ghana, outdoors babies by putting them on the bare ground. The Akan, for instance, do not include such ritual in their ceremony.

40. K. Opoku, "Cooking on Two Stones of the Hearth?," 5.

41. Kudadjie, "Researching Morals and Rituals," 35.

42. Clobus, "Ecofarming and Land Ownership," 71. Clobus supported his argument with the Ashanti proverb that "The farm is mine, but the soil belongs to the stool," and the stool symbolizes the office of the chief or family head.

43. Kalu, "Sacred Egg," 233.

cleanse it. Kudadjie could not elicit any explanation for the practice, but was worried of the child's vulnerability to possible infection and, inadvertently, expunged it from his proposed Christian outdooring liturgical order.[44] The Sokpoe-Eʋe, whose outdooring rite resembles that of the Ada, provide explanations for this ritual, which bear significant ecological priming implications. For them the baby being put on bare ground reminds it of its earthiness and establishes filial relationships with the Earth. Rationally the ritual primes the baby to perceive and respect the Earth anthropomorphically as a nurturing mother.[45] Perhaps because in the African primal worldview the ecological community is holistic, B.Y. Quarshie believes that the outdooring ceremonies among the Ga in Ghana symbolize the merging of the spiritual and physical (or sacramental) phenomena of the ecosystem for the child. Laying emphasis on the reality and seriousness of curses in the African context, he sees the rite as occasion not only to invoke material blessings to the baby, but also to teach, encourage and guide how to deal with malevolent forces that may overturn the blessings, by cursing them.[46]

The details of outdooring rites then differ among cultures, but for Kalu the rite not only "provides an opportunity to declare who has returned to the family," it also "covenants the individual to the land and the [ecological] community."[47] The African child expectedly can be ecologically responsible as it grows, having been potentiated ritually to develop eco-character with which to know and be committed to caring for the environment into which it has been oriented and grounded until it exits the human world at death.

However, death is only a passage into the other plane of the continuum of life, a journey in and through the spirit world until a return to human world, which for some eco-cultures, is through reincarnation.[48] As Opoku puts it, "In effect, it is death and birth that are opposites, while life is constant; and birth can be regarded as the entry gate and death as the exit gate through which life passes, only to return again."[49] Kalu claims that for cultures with ancestor-dominated worldviews reincarnation is "reserved for those who lived honest lives and did not die from inexplicable diseases or from lightening—a punishment from the gods for a secret offence."[50] By

---

44. Kudadjie, "Researching Morals and Rituals," 35.

45. This is part of my findings in this research. I shall return to it later with details in chapter 7.

46. Quarshie, "Paul and the Primal Substructure of Christianity," 12.

47. Kalu, "Sacred Egg," 232.

48. Kalu, "Sacred Egg," 234.

49. K. Opoku, "Cooking on Two Stones of the Hearth?," 5.

50. Kalu, "Sacred Egg," 234.

implication, in such cultures ancestors must have been individuals who developed and practiced ecological virtues or character during earthly sojourn. However, for the Sokpoe-Eυe, where the ancestral component is less emphasized in their worldview, reincarnation is the return not of only good people, but also as a second chance for some fortunate individuals to correct their previous incongruous ecosystem life.

The unity of the visible and invisible worlds becomes clear in the funerary rites.[51] Generally the exited (deceased) person is interred *in* the Earth, the very Earth *of which* it was made, and *on* which it was laid at the entrance (birth) into life in the human world. Not every corpse is, however, buried; some that lived unethically in the ecosystem are cremated, as happens among the Mafi-Eυe.[52] Furthermore, the attachment to the land and people of birth, and hence understanding that the dead continue to live but must live among its people, may underlie the practice of ensuring "the departed are buried on their own land, within the homestead" or ecosystem. For the cultural insight that "the deceased remain present" is "physically demonstrated by the form, pattern and location of burial."[53]

These rituals then may signify the ecological importance of the Earth in the continuum of life. The Earth is recognized at the entrance, sojourn and exit of life: it supplies the physical substance (material) for the living body at birth, nurtures it all through earthly life and receives its earthy corpse back at death when the individual is ritually entrusted to it by interment or cremation. Expectedly, the primal natal and funerary rituals are all eventually about preparing or priming individuals to be pragmatically integrated harmoniously and without a blemished eco-character in the cosmic existence on the Earth and beyond it, respectively. Eco-care praxis in Islam too has its own religious motivations.

The Impulsion for and Praxis of Creation Care in Islam

At least three theoretical or reconstructed factors are identifiable from the Islamic worldviews as impulsion or motivators for Islamic participation in

---

51. Kalu, "Sacred Egg," 233.

52. Among the Mafi-Eυe not every corpse is buried in the Earth. According to Agbanu, "Environmental Ethics in Mafi-Eυe Indigenous Culture," 118, a person believed to have taken human life through malevolent spirit means such as witchcraft and sorcery is subjected to *amememe* (disgraceful cremation) ritual. He explains that this ritual is regarded the severest punishment meted to human beings.

53. K. Bediako, "Gospel and Culture," 8.

current global concerns about the environment. First, is the theocentric worldview, second is the concept of cosmic balance and third is the theomorphic status of humanity as *khalifa* (vicegerent of God).

Theocentric Worldview and Taqwa (Reverence) for God

The first source of impulsion for a Muslim to be concerned about the environment and hence participate in creation care relationships and actions is the *taqwa* (reverence) of and gratitude to the creator for his creation, of which humanity is part. The Muslim's entire way of life is historically and inspirationally founded and maintained on one major belief—the belief in God. As John Azumah writes,

> Belief in God (*Allah*) is the first and central belief in Islam. He is depicted as sovereign, king, ruler, and master who is utterly other than his creation. His transcendent status is encapsulated in the familiar Muslim expression, *Allahu akbar* (God is great).[54]

Theocologically the import of "belief in God" in Islamic worldview is the metaphysical affirmation of the Muslim that the cosmos belongs to God. God, according to the Qur'an, is the real creator, owner, and sustainer of all reality (Qur'an 2:29). It suggests that all reality should be seen and read with the point of view in mind that nature originates from God and has an inherent purpose to impel creation's (both human and other-than-human's) submission to God. The strength of a Muslim's claim of Qur'anic cosmology lies in the Islamic understanding that "both the author of Qur'an and creator of nature are the same, God."[55] Thus what the Qur'an ultimately reveals and what nature is ordered to manifest—divine glory in these two books of God—are the same and obliges Muslims to submit to God.[56] Implicit in this affirmation is that the Qur'an enjoins Muslims to "love creation for the sake of its Creator."[57] Commenting ecologically on Qur'an 49:13 ("Most noble of you in the sight of God is he who is most reverent"), Llewellyn thinks Muslims need to revere God in everything, because he is Lord and will try humanity concerning his creatures.[58]

Taqwa as impulsion for eco-praxis receives further strength from another affirmation that Islamic worldviews are "comprehensive, integrated,

54. Azumah, *My Neighbours' Faith*, 28.
55. Özdemir, "Toward an Understanding of Environmental Ethics," 9.
56. Özdemir, "Toward an Understanding of Environmental Ethics," 7.
57. Özdemir, "Toward an Understanding of Environmental Ethics," 29.
58. Llewellyn, "Basis for a Discipline of Islamic Environmental Law," 189.

and holistic," and center on "the unity of reality (*tawhīd*)."[59] Özdemir, explains that *tawhīd* in Qur'anic cosmology refers to the belief and affirmation that God is the very meaning of reality; a meaning manifested, clarified and brought home by the universe, developed further by humans. God is the dimension that makes other dimensions possible.[60] Known as the "cosmological evidence of God's existence" in Islamic theological philosophy (*kalām*), *tawhīd* obliges humanity to morally respond by grateful submission[61] as well as being reverent (to God) and compassionate (to all creatures).[62]

A significant theoretical inference is that if and when Muslims understand the ecological import of *tawhīd* as a Qur'anic teaching, they most likely will submit by taking ecological actions that care for creation and sustain the unity of God. For, a fundamental ethical argument implied in religious ecology as motivator for moral environmental responsibility is the assumption or belief of Curry that "people will naturally do the right thing(s) when they apprehend the natural world correctly," identifying oneself with that world and its fellow inhabitants.[63] The practical challenge, however, is with the right interpretation of Qur'anic texts. The Qur'an, according to Haq, as the source of these teachings, is not a systematic treatise meant to convey ethical doctrines or principles. If this text is to yield a concrete system, it requires an imaginative reconstruction on the part of the reader.[64] Since huge numbers of Muslims, particularly in Africa, are not literate in Arabic, the official language of the Holy Script, imaginative reconstruction that stimulates ecological action in caring for creation may be a non-starter. Even if Arabic literacy is not a challenge, classical Islam recognizes epistemological difficulties in the finality of the reconstruction, unless there is "overwhelming community consensus."[65] Notwithstanding these problems, the Qur'an remains a valuably rich and subtle stimulus to religious *imagination*,[66] perhaps particularly for only Muslims who see themselves as "*khalifas*."[67]

---

59. Özdemir, "Toward an Understanding of Environmental Ethics," 4.
60. Özdemir, "Toward an Understanding of Environmental Ethics," 9.
61. Özdemir, "Toward an Understanding of Environmental Ethics," 9.
62. Llewellyn, "Basis for a Discipline of Islamic Environmental Law," 189.
63. Curry, *Ecological Ethic*, 106.
64. Haq, "Islam and Ecology," 125.
65. Haq, "Islam and Ecology," 125.
66. Haq, "Islam and Ecology," 125 (italics in original).
67. Dien, "Islam and the Environment," in Foltz et al., eds., *Islam and Ecology*, 110.

The Concept of Khalifa (Theomorphic Vicegerent)

The second source of impulsion for Islamic Earth-keeping is from their belief that God has made humans his *khalifas* (vicegerents, stewards) in the world.[68] As I have earlier indicated, in Islam the Qur'an shows that humanity occupies a special functional position in the cosmos, the *khalīfa* or vicegerent of God, by virtue of being theomorphic and a covenant or "trust they have taken upon themselves in pre-eternity."[69] In this position, human beings qualify to become stewards of God on Earth.

> He it is Who made you stewards on the earth, and raised some of you by degrees above others, so that He might try you by means of what He has bestowed upon you. (Qur'an 6:165)

> Thus we have made you to succeed one another's stewards on the earth, that We might behold how you acquit yourselves. (Qur'an 10:14)[70]

Although the concept of *khalīfa* suggests a privilege and honor, yet it is more of a trust, a responsibility and a trial. Among all creatures, only humankind agreed to bear a trust or moral responsibility (Qur'an 33:72) for the Earth. According to Islamic theology it is a responsibility to "be a shepherd over all the lives on Earth that he may touch for good or ill," for which he shall be accountable to God on the day of resurrection[71]—the day "when the earth throws out its burdens" (Qur'an 99:2). As Llewellyn explains, a *khalīfa* acts not for himself/herself, but for his/her Lord and according to his/her Lord's purpose. He shall "be asked about his flock" since all human beings "shall be asked regarding every atom's weight of good that he or she has caused, and every atom's weight of harm" (Qur'an 99:7–8).[72]

As a concept, *khalīfacy* suggests also a trial of the integrity of humanity in managing the things Allah "has bestowed upon you." According to Llewellyn, in a rigorously authenticated *hadith* of Abu Sa'id al-Khudri, the Prophet Muhammad explained that God has made humans his stewards in the world and "He sees how you acquit [prove] yourselves." All the same, it appears God had already foreknown humankind's inability to keep the trust since the Qur'an (33:72) indicates that humanity "was unjust and foolish" and for which reason the Prophet strongly admonished "whatever we do,

---

68. Llewellyn, "Basis for a Discipline of Islamic Environmental Law," 191.
69. Haq, "Islam and Ecology," 127.
70. Llewellyn, "Basis for a Discipline of Islamic Environmental Law," 190.
71. Llewellyn, "Basis for a Discipline of Islamic Environmental Law," 190.
72. Llewellyn, "Basis for a Discipline of Islamic Environmental Law," 190.

we will not leave this world unchanged. We must take heed, then, that we leave it for the better."[73]

The implication, it seems, is that the *khalīfa* position in Islamic thought is gracious and rewarding, but it is also a fearful one, likely to determine the eternal fate and abode of humanity. It is a willful choice of humanity on whom it behooves to do as Allah requires in being faithful stewards of creation or else justly faces his wrath in the end for disobedience. A good understanding and affirmation of this religious concept could (or rather should) be a strong moral impulsion for keeping integrity of creation. Yet, in practice, contrary to the Islamic belief in *khalīfacy*, but true to the Qur'an's prediction (Qur'an 33:72) concerning humans' managing the Earth, Llewellyn observes that "we have proven ourselves thoroughly unjust and foolish."[74]

The observed failure of humanity, as Muslims see it, to be faithful *khalīfas* of the Earth may be because of misrepresentation of the concept by overemphasizing the privilege and honor implied in the term as a mandate to exploit nature.[75] This excuse, however, seems to beg the question about the practical reality and stands out more as intellectual defense by Islamic writers regarding Islam's valuing of human beings. For Llewellyn observes that the position of each human being as a *Khalifah* on the Earth has received considerable attention by Muslim writers in the twentieth century, and its misrepresentation (and misapplication) perhaps is because,

> Under the influence of European Humanism, and in response to allegations that Islam gives too little value to human being, Muslim writers have felt the need to prove that man (sic) has exalted status. As enthusiasm for "progress'" and "development" swept the poorer countries of the world, some reformist thinkers even interpreted the concept of *khalīfa* as a mandate to exploit and develop the earth on behalf of God.[76]

It may thus be argued from a practical ecological point of view that most practicing Islamists, particularly at grassroots levels, likely do not have a thorough and persuasive understanding of the *khalīfa* concept in relation to Earth-keeping. Ibrahim Özdemir blames the loss of many animal species on "our unawareness of Qur'anic values, which regulate . . . humankind's relations with other living species."[77] Or the concept as a religious belief

---

73. Llewellyn, "Basis for a Discipline of Islamic Environmental Law," 191.
74. Llewellyn, "Basis for a Discipline of Islamic Environmental Law," 191.
75. Llewellyn, "Basis for a Discipline of Islamic Environmental Law," 190.
76. Llewellyn, "Basis for a Discipline of Islamic Environmental Law," 190.
77. Özdemir, "Toward an Understanding of Environmental Ethics," 22.

lacks the pervasive influence of a religious ecology that Mathew Clarke describes.[78] I have earlier pointed out that *khalīfacy* or stewardship/managerial ideology is religiously laudable, but may require discipline of adhering to the concept of *qādr* or limits both of the ecosystem and the human managers, to be successful.[79] Moreover, since they serve not themselves but their Lord and his purpose as trustees,[80] *khalīfats* necessarily need be in tune with the eco-ethical and religious caring instructions of their Lord (God) from his books, the Qur'an and the natural world. A significantly known and promoted concept of such eco-information in Islam is "*mīzān*, balance in nature."[81]

The Concepts of Fitra (Instinct) and *Mīzān* (Cosmic Balance)

The third reason for Islamic eco-praxis arises from their self-understanding that humans have instinctual consciousness of our manifold but balanced relations with God and the rest of creation; creation care ought to be a matter of course to humanity. In Islamic ecological reconstruction, ecological crisis is merely a symptom of the broader calamity that human societies are not living in accordance with God's will,[82] which is diligently and purposefully demonstrated in the ordered and just world (cosmos) that he created. Muslim scholars argue that a careful search into and comprehension of the book of nature, like the Qur'an, will awaken human instinctual consciousness of our manifold relations with God and the rest of creation. The reason is that Islam is *din al-fitra*, a religion that reminds that instinctual knowledge is true and primordial (original nature) of humanity by which we live in accordance with the environment. Therefore, environmental consciousness is something that needs not be taught, but merely awakened from observational knowledge of nature and/or reflecting on the Qur'an.[83] This sounds like the Akan proverb "*Obi nkyere abofra Onyame*" (no one points out God to a child), implying the Akan (and hence the African child) knows God instinctively from historical intimate experiences with and in the indigenous environment. In addition, it connotes also the idea that the

---

78. Clarke, *Development and Religion*, 1.
79. Curry, *Ecological Ethics*, 35.
80. Llewellyn, "Basis for a Discipline of Islamic Environmental Law," 190.
81. Amin, "Preface" to Foltz et al., eds., *Islam and Ecology*, xxxiii.
82. Foltz, "Introduction" to Foltz et al., eds., *Islam and Ecology*, xxxix.
83. Chishti, "*Fitra*," 67.

indigenous African child is culturally endowed with the potential for right and wrong about the environment in its consciousness.[84]

Patrick Curry suggests that any ecological ethic reconstruction today is only a "reawakening of something very old" that we have forgotten from our intuitive experience of indigenous culture.[85] This affirms the Islamic assertion that eco-praxis arises from instinctual consciousness of our manifold but balanced relations with God and the rest of creation.[86] Muslims thus believe that by carefully examining the heavens, the Earth all creaturely things and natural phenomena in the environment, one cannot but marvel and praise God as the creator. The learner would necessarily conclude: "Our Lord! Not for nothing have You created (all) this! Glory to You (Qur'an 3:191)."[87] This is natural theology—affirming faith in God from his creation through doxological contemplation. Arthur Holmes refers to this type of learning by doxological contemplation in the early centuries of Christianity, and observes that it moulds a religious moral consciousness.[88] Similarly, Muslims believe such experience changes the searcher's worldview, self-image, attitude, feelings and the patterns of relationships with reality.[89] For the Muslim, the aim of nature is then to point to humanity not only God's ownership of creation, but also his established laws of nature that ensure *mīzān* (cosmic and ecological harmony or balance).

Talking about balance in the ecosystem, Fazlur Rahman, in his *Major Themes of the Qur'an*, explains that "when God creates anything, He places within it its powers or laws of behavior called in the Qur'an 'guidance', 'command', or 'measure' whereby it fits into the rest of the universe."[90] He implies that God potentiates creation to fulfill its purpose without fail as *ayā* by obeying (submitting to) the functional laws to ensure ecological balance (material sustenance) and justice (ethical relations) in the universe. The importance of ecological balance in Qur'anic discourse is further emphasized by Qur'an 55:5–9. It reads:

> The sun and the moon follow courses (exactly) computed; And the herbs and the trees—both (alike) bow in adoration. And the firmament has He raised high, and He has set up the balance (of

---

84. K. Opoku, "Cooking on Two Stones of the Hearth?," 5.

85. Curry, *Ecological Ethics*, 12.

86. Chishti, "*Fitra*," 67.

87. Özdemir, "Toward an Understanding of Environmental Ethics," 7.

88. Holmes, *Building the Christian Academy*, 2.

89. Özdemir, "Toward an Understanding of Environmental Ethics," 6.

90. Rahman, *Major Themes of the Qur'an*, 67. See also Özdemir, "Toward an Understanding of Environmental Ethics," 13.

Justice), In order that you may not transgress (due) balance. So, establish weight with justice and fall not short in the balance.[91]

It is deducible from Muslims' explanations of this verse that it portrays how the firmament keeps its given height and the heavenly bodies, like sun and moon, also stick to their given orbits to sustain balance (rightful relativity) in the cosmos (universe) without fail. That these cosmic bodies keep rightful relations is a warning sign for humans "not to transgress balance" (ethical relations) in all aspects of life. This includes "how [people] *ought* to live and act"[92] ecologically. The phenomenon of cosmic and/or material balance or self-conservation in Islamic worldview corresponds with observations in cosmological and ecological sciences, except with the difference that observable self-conservation in nature is a doing of God. Arguing with evolutionary philosophy regarding the origin of the Earth, Swimme and Tucker refer to "self-organization dynamics" in nature as a process to maintain the delicate conditions of life on Earth. They see the Earth as a creative community of beings that reorganizes itself age after age so that it can perpetuate and even deepen its vibrant existence.[93] Ecologically the Qur'anic worldview suggests that the other-than-human creation, adhering to the *ăwamir* or natural laws, cannot cause perturbations of ecosystems if not interrupted by human beings. Rather, due to the divine *ăwamir* ordained by God, eco-balancing processes such as "biogeochemical cycles"[94] exist in ecosystems. Nomanul Haq asserts that there is a due measure (*qădr*) to things, and a balance (*mīzān*) in the cosmos that humanity must not disturb but fulfill,[95] looking unto the *amr* as self-sustaining law of nature.[96] In other words, since the "natural law *is* never violated as things run their customary course, moral law *ought not* to be violated."[97]

Thus it is reasonably arguable that these Qur'anic texts alone could be enough for developing an environmental ethic of respecting and preserving just and balanced ecological relations by all humanity.[98] The Muslim, in

---

91. Özdemir, "Toward an Understanding of Environmental Ethics," 13.
92. Curry, *Ecological Ethics*, 28.
93. Swimme and Tucker, *Journey of the Universe*, 56.
94. Cunningham and Saigo, *Environmental Science*, 595, define "biogeochemical cycles" as "movement of matter between or within ecosystems; caused by living organisms, geological forces, or chemical reactions. The cycling of nitrogen, carbon, sulfur, oxygen, phosphorus, and water are examples."
95. Haq, "Islam and Ecology," 127.
96. Haq, "Islam and Ecology," 137.
97. Haq, "Islam and Ecology," 132 (italics original).
98. Özdemir, "Toward an Understanding of Environmental Ethics," 13.

particular, is thus expected to live in "better harmony with his surroundings than any other type of man [sic],"⁹⁹ perhaps because of the strong theocological inferences in Islam. Yet, as Özdemir laments, Muslim jurists have lagged behind in contributing solutions to the intensifying environmental problems afflicting Islamic lands. It is because they lack (or are yet rediscovering and formulating) well-articulated Islamic environmental ethics and laws,¹⁰⁰ but at the same time reject those borrowed from industrial West, which are seen as having been derived from alien beliefs.¹⁰¹ At the local front in Ghana, a similar attitude is noticed from my unpublished research into the motivation for and praxis of ecological ethics among Muslims in Sokpoe riverine ecological area in South Tɔŋu, Volta Region. Muslims participating in this study seem to have no distinctively Islamic eco-ethics. Yet they vehemently oppose the primal religious eco-regulations and rituals in order not to compromise the purity of their Islamic faith and fate while sharing the same riverine ecosystem with the traditionalists and Christians.

The seemingly lack of practical Islamic ecological values, ethics and norms may be due partly to the observation that though the Sokpoe-Moslem's life and living is highly determined by the teachings of Qur'an, they, like "the majority of Muslims in the Islamic world," are unaware of the "powerful and persuasive spiritual teachings of Islam about the natural world and the relations of human beings to it."¹⁰² Idris Ibrahim, son of the Zamarama *sarechi* of Sogakɔfe zongo, laments how the imams do not teach "these things; they have only one message instead of addressing pertinent issues in our lives."¹⁰³ Idrisu was virtually echoing the same feelings of Seyyed Hossein Nasr, who, writing on "Islam and the Environmental Crisis," decried that even the *ulamā* (traditional guardians of Islamic knowledge in its various dimensions) do not teach or preach the Islamic views on the environment.¹⁰⁴ And maybe the imams do not address environmental issues because generally the exceedingly rich contributions that Islamic law and ethics have to offer in addressing environmental concerns in the Islamic world as a whole remain largely unarticulated (not promoted) and unrealized.¹⁰⁵ Chief Imam Mahmud Abu Bakr of Sogakɔfe zongo admitted with humility that "it is not everything that I know because of the level of my

99. Özdemir, "Toward an Understanding of Environmental Ethics," 16.
100. Özdemir, "Toward an Understanding of Environmental Ethics," 28.
101. Llewellyn, "Basis for a Discipline of Islamic Environmental Law," 186.
102. Nasr, "Islam, the Contemporary Islamic World," 85.
103. Idrisu Ibrahim, interview at Sogakɔfe, 23 April 2016.
104. Nasr, "Islam, the Contemporary Islamic World," 87.
105. Llewellyn, "Basis for a Discipline of Islamic Environmental Law," 186.

education."¹⁰⁶ Despite not being well informed ecologically, he and other Muslims in this study detest any ecological regulations not specifically attributable to Qur'an, and for that matter, Allah. All these notwithstanding, it is encouraging to know that Islamic eco-ethic is being reconstructed and practiced "today, at the dawn of the twenty-first century and in a time of worldwide environmental crisis."¹⁰⁷

Islamic Eco-Valuing, Ethical Principles and Praxis

In Islam ecological values and ethics are together reconstructed from the Qur'an and Hadith as part of the legal and moral principles in the *fiqh*-law. For Islam in its essence is a religion of law—the *shari'a*, which literally means the guided way to life.¹⁰⁸ According to Nomanul Haq, "*Fiqh*, or the Islamic science of jurisprudence, is a systematic and fully structured theoretical search for God's *sharia*, or Way [of life], that had to be gleaned from and constructed out of the myriad of *adilla* (here, legal indicators) provided for reflection throughout God's āyāt."¹⁰⁹ Practically, *fiqh* includes axiological and ethical principles for understanding or determining the legal status of an act, "a determination arrived at through the application of *correct*, though not epistemologically certain, procedural rules."¹¹⁰

The ultimate ethical and legal objective of *fiqh* is the welfare of God's creation on Earth and beyond, known as "Masālih al-khalq: *the universal common good*."¹¹¹ Other guiding principles derived from this include "Masālih" and "mafāsid," the law of benefits and detriments. This law operates through emphasis on maximizing ecological benefits and minimizing detriments; universal versus individual welfare, which encourages preserving eco-community interest over the individual interest; or the greater preferred to lesser ecological needs. The rest of the ethical principles include choosing the lesser of two ecological evils, the interest of the powerless over

---

106. Imam Mahmud Abu Bakar, interview at Sogakɔfe, 5 April 2016.

107. Özdemir, "Toward an Understanding of Environmental Ethics," 29.

108. Llewellyn, "Basis for a Discipline of Islamic Environmental Law," 186.

109. Haq, "Islam and Ecology," 142.

110. Haq, "Islam and Ecology," 142 (italics original). According to Llewellyn, "Basis for a Discipline of Islamic Environmental Law," 187, acts are evaluated with a five-tier scale: an act may be obligatory, recommended, permitted, reprehended or prohibited. Thus, it provides prohibitive, injunctive and prescriptive ethics enforceable by individual and social conscience in addition to imperatives enforced by the courts.

111. Llewellyn, "Basis for a Discipline of Islamic Environmental Law," 193 (italics original).

the powerful in eco-justice, and averting detriments by taking precaution to prevent ecological harm rather than insist on benefit.[112]

These principles are not without challenges. They are highly anthropocentric and, at best, what Curry calls "moral extensionism" to describe "mid-green or intermediate" ecological ethics.[113] That is to say, what has been thought of first as human values are considered also true of other-than-humans and is the easiest way in retrieval and reconstruction in an eco-ethical project. The challenge, however, may be that with moral extensionism other-than-human creation remains vulnerable to anthropocentric treatment: "the land, air, water and other animals will always in the crunch take second place to the perceived welfare of self, family and friends."[114] For instance, in applying "the benefits and detriments" principle, "how does one measure total benefits and costs, material and nonmaterial, for humans and other creatures?"[115] Or since in Islam known interests supersede conjectural or probable interests, will there be the political will to "approve a project of which the economic benefits are known, while scientific information regarding harmful impacts to human health and ecosystems is incomplete or inconclusive?"[116]

Apparently, practical environmental ethics tend to be articulated more from the Hadith than the other āyāt of God. As Haq notes, in the Hadith there are several concerns expressed with a degree of urgency pertaining to the natural environment, its status, its relation to human life and, hence, what may be termed environmental ethics.[117] They include, *inter alia*, concerns about animal sacrifice, agriculture and land cultivation, medicine, hunting, use of water and irrigation.[118] The importance of Hadith in retrieving and reconstructing Islamic ecological ethics is because the Hadith is regarded as a translation of broad Qur'anic eco-principles into specific rules for the actual practice of the eco-community. Moreover, being the established tradition from the life of the Prophet, Hadith is a model all Muslims are *required* to emulate and follow.[119]

Among many others, two pertinent creation care or practical ecological models in the Hadith include the institutions of *himā* and *harām*. They

---

112. Llewellyn, "Basis for a Discipline of Islamic Environmental Law," 194.
113. Curry, *Ecological Ethics*, 72.
114. Curry, *Ecological Ethics*, 72.
115. Llewellyn, "Basis for a Discipline of Islamic Environmental Law," 195.
116. Llewellyn, "Basis for a Discipline of Islamic Environmental Law," 197.
117. Haq, "Islam and Ecology," 141.
118. Haq, "Islam and Ecology," 142.
119. Haq, "Islam and Ecology," 141 (italics original).

had a long history of pre-Islamic abuse of land exploitation and dispossession. But Muslims claim they were transformed by the Prophet to become environmental and ethical policies. *Himā* literally means protected or forbidden place for natural life[120] and may be considered the Islamic equivalent of contemporary reserved forested land, natural parks and nature conservancy.[121] Four conditions determine declaring *himā*: need and fairness ensured by the community, ecological proportionality relative to total land area of community, resisting commercialized development and envisaged economic gains to be in interest of societal welfare.[122] Similarly, *harām* as sacred territory is often associated with wells, natural springs, rivers and forests on waste land (*mawāt*).[123]

Daily prayers are also considered an important Islamic ecological praxis; they make humans be identified with and integrated in other-than-human creation as both obey the call to pray by standing up, bending and prostrating.[124]

Like Muslims, Christians also have reasons or motivators for participating in global search of pragmatic resolution of the eco-crisis.

The Impulsion for and Praxis of Creation Care in Christianity

From the Christian worldviews examined in the previous chapter, I notice three sources to draw undergirding motivation for Christian participation in current global concerns about the environment. These are the theocentric worldviews of creation, humanity's kinship with creation and the theomorphic status of humanity as *imago Dei* and vicegerent.

---

120. Haq, "Islam and Ecology," 144.
121. Nasr, "Islam, the Contemporary Islamic World," 98.
122. Haq, "Islam and Ecology," 144.
123. Haq, "Islam and Ecology," 144.
124. Özdemir, "Toward an Understanding of Environmental Ethics," 18, makes this point upon agreeing with Muhammad Hamidullah that "mountains stand immobile like Muslims stand before Allah devoutly" (Qur'an 2:238); animals remain perpetually bent as Muslims are commanded to do (Qur'an 2:43) and trees remain prostrate as Muslims are ordered to do (Qur'an 53:62).

The Christian Theocentric Worldview as Impulsion for Eco-Praxis

A primary motivation for Christians to care for creation may be inferred from the teaching that Christians are to obey and please God as well as seek his righteousness as their love for God in all their relationships in the ecosystem. This implies a theocentric worldview. Theocentrism is basically a Judeo-Christian ideology, connected to theocracy.[125] Author Richard A. Young rightly points out that a Christian theocentric worldview teaches that God is the center of the universe, the source and upholder of meaning, purpose, values and ethics as well as the unifying principle of the cosmos. Everything exists for the sake of God and to serve his purposes.[126] Christian theology affirms that there is only one God, whom the Christian must not only love with all the soul, heart and might (Deut 6:4–6), but also look up to for help in all situations, because he is the creator, owner, sustainer, protector and redeemer of the Earth and all in it (Ps 121:1–8). A consequence of this theocentric affirmation is the Christian's urge to love God (John 14:24) by obeying and pleasing him in all things, including ecological responsibilities. The urge to love God in all things becomes the motivation in theocentric cosmology for ecological actions, including ensuring ecological relations that reflect the righteousness of God in the eco-community (Matt 6:33).

There are significant ecological implications for promoting Christian theocentrism. Richard Young argues that it encourages us to put faith and trust in God for the ultimate solution to our eco-crisis, provides a reason for the existence of every creature and produces a holistic view of life, since everything is related by virtue of its being created by God. Simon Victus opines, and it is practically a considerable view, that Christian theocentrism may be an ultimate solution to the present divergent views for tackling the ecocrisis. This is because it encompasses the concerns of the other views such as anthropocentrism, biocentrism, ecocentrism, etc. without doing injustice to any of them and without acquiescing in their shortcomings. I believe that a paradigm shift towards theocentrism will influence environmental vicegerency, which is our human responsibility to the environment

---

125. Victus, *Eco-Theology and the Scriptures*, 119.

126. Young, *Healing the Earth*, 128. The ecological implications listed by Richard Young (p. 128) include: Theocentrism resolves the ethical dilemma without giving humanity absolute rights; preserves the uniqueness of humanity without yielding to anthropocentric arrogance; provides basis for true stewardship; provides direction in resolving environmental problems (divine intention in creation); encourages us to put faith and trust in God for the ultimate solution to our eco-crisis; provides a reason for the existence of every creature; and because it produces a holistic view of life, since everything is related by virtue of its being created by God.

and expression of faith that the whole cosmos is a living revelation of God. But our environmental vicegerency may be moved also by the fact that we share materiality with nature as ecological kin and kith.

Human Kinship with the Earth as Reason for Creation Care

Another reason or motivator for Christian participation in creation care praxis may be found in the reconstructed idea of our kinship with the Earth. Kinship with nature is a biblical truth presented in both the Old and New Testaments stories or teachings about creation, its sustenance and hopeful redemption. Gillian Bediako claims it was "abandoned inadvertently due to erroneous and ignorant Western Christian theology, but recoverable in African primal spirituality."[127] An example of strong African primal religious belief in kinship with nature, which can be reconstructed for Christian theocology, is observable in the birthing rites of the Sokpoe-Eʋe as found in chapter 7 of this book. The ceremony involves burying the umbilical cord and placenta in the soil, placing the baby nakedly on bare soil, and ensuring he or she urinates onto the soil. All these symbols are to inform and ground the baby as an earthling, which primes it for creation care as the child grows into responsible status. Bryant Myers observes, "while in no way the same, the worldview of the Bible is closer to the worldview of traditional cultures," such as in Africa, "than it is to the modern worldview"[128] of the West. They are both not only holistic but also suggest strong bond between humanity and the materiality of Earth, particularly as demonstrated when Christ—"the creator, sustainer, and redeemer of creation"—"became flesh" or earthling.[129]

That both humankind and other-than-human creatures are kin is noticeable in the Christian views and teachings on creation and salvation. From creation stories it is obvious that both humans and other-than-human creatures are products of the same material substance, elements of Earth. We saw earlier that soon after their emergence the primordial Earth and its waters were involved by God to participate in his ongoing creative activity. The Earth responded to God's call and put forth vegetation and various kinds of beasts (Gen 1:11, 24), and the waters and air (atmosphere) produced swarms of aquatic living creatures and birds, respectively (Gen 1:20).[130] Then towards the end God formed humanity (*adam*) of the dust

---

127. G. Bediako, "Primal Religion and Christian Faith," 14.
128. Myers, *Walking with the Poor*, 8.
129. Myers, *Walking with the Poor*, 8.
130. Schwarz, *Creation*, 170.

from the ground *(adamah)* (Gen 2:7a). Thus, all are created by the same God from the same materials, and by virtue of divinely endowed function they all serve in mutual or symbiotic vocation to sustain all life on Earth. In Ghana concerning forests, for example, it is commonly said, "When the last tree dies the last man dies." But to emphasize the fact that the only possible breach of this mutual function is anthropogenic, American Indians of the Cree tribe formulated this statement more fittingly: "Only when the last tree has been cut, the last river is poisoned, and the last fish is caught, one will realize that one cannot eat money."[131]

As in creation, so also is the doctrine of salvation. Humanity's kinship with nature is so apparent in Africa that we need to emphasize not only a personal but also a cosmic view of salvation. From a theocological point of view, Golo decries how that traditionally Christian salvation theology emphasizes only individual encounter with Jesus Christ leading to repentance and redemption from sin, the transformation into a new person and empowerment through the Holy Spirit to live a new life. "Salvation" in that sense "is understood spiritually and heavenwards and pictured as an eschatological blissful state in which Christians participate."[132] Yet ecologically this means removing humanity from this creation, regarded as corrupted by sin from its goodness, into the "transformed and sanctified state through the sacrifice of Jesus Christ."[133] The result is that the cosmic shape of salvation is minimized or even entirely overlooked in Western Christianity.

Golo continues that the otherworldliness concept of Christian salvation theology spilled over to Africa through Western missionaries and did not only find home but was even radicalized due to the holistic but precarious African cosmology. In this cosmology multifarious spirits vivify the cosmos, but malevolent ones may discourage belief in Christ and living fulfilled Christian life. Hence salvation is understood as redemption from sin and evil forces, transformation into a new person and turning away from creation by waging war against the evil forces within it.[134] Birgit Meyer observes among the Peki-Eʋe in Ghana that the Pietistic salvation message of the Norddeutsche Missionsgesellschaft (NMG) did not only "demonize" the "Eʋe gods and spirits," but also drew a "boundary between Christianity and Eʋe religion"[135] and hence cultural self-understanding. It is not surprising, for instance, that despite the strong kinship belief exhibited in primal

---

131. Nehring, ed., *Ecology*, 254. See also Victus, *Ecotheology and the Scriptures*, 6.
132. Golo, "Redeemed from the Earth?," 356.
133. Golo, "Redeemed from the Earth?," 356.
134. Golo, "Redeemed from the Earth?," 351.
135. Meyer, *Translating the Devil*, xvii.

religious birthing rites at Sokpoe ecological area in Ghana, the Christians there, also nurtured mostly with Western Pietistic Protestant theology by the Basel missionaries (BM), expunged the symbolic grounding rituals from the outdooring liturgy because they are "*egodotɔwo tɔ*" (for non-Christians).[136]

Furthermore, the mercantilist manner of presenting the salvation message in Africa resulted in an anthropocentric utilitarian notion of salvation that has reduced the Earth to commoditization, with no spiritual significance, save an abode of demonic spirits which must be overcome if humans would live in material prosperity—a sign of salvation especially in neo-Pentecostalism. In her analysis of the Peki-Eʋe's reasons for converting to Christianity, Birgit Meyer believes that "Christian religion was attractive because it offered the material means to achieve a prosperous and relatively high position in colonial society."[137]

In a nutshell, a missionary dualistic worldview and otherworldly salvation theology in contemporary Africa has not succeeded in sustaining the way the primal African conceives of creation.[138] Yet, neither did it succeed also in completely unraveling the African Christian's holistic but precarious cosmology. Birgit Meyer concludes, "demonization by no means implies that the former gods and spirits [in Eʋe cosmology] will disappear out of people's lives," including Christians.[139] Thus the Eʋe Christian is left in a religious dilemma of how the Christian salvation theology pragmatically reconciles monotheism with Africans' ontological experiences of other spiritual forces vivifying the gecosphere.

Yet Jesus' death and resurrection brings humans into a state of reconciliation with God and also open the way for the reconciliation of all things to God. The Earth does not only suffer God's curse on and destruction of humanity due to the latter's disobedience or sinfulness (Gen 3:17–19; 6–8), but also co-enjoys God's promise of no destructive deluge again (Gen 9:7–17) and hopeful redemption (Rom 8:19–23). Saint Paul teaches that creation waits in eager expectation for the children of God to be revealed. For the creation was subjected to frustration, not by its own choice, but in hope that it will be liberated from its bondage to decay and brought into the glorious kingdom of the children of God by the same redeemer, who had permitted the subjection.

So, the redemption of the Earth for eternal existence is also linked with that of humanity—to have full life (John 10:10). Before the consummation

---

136. James Cudjoe, Church of Pentecost, interview at Sokpoe, 26 June 2016.
137. Meyer, *Translating the Devil*, 11.
138. Golo, "Redeemed from the Earth?," 352.
139. Meyer, *Translating the Devil*, xvii.

of redemption, both humanity and creation groan from the consequences of "their"[140] sin, which threaten destruction of their life, painfully, to decay. However, to the Christian, biogeophysical cyclic processes that ensure equilibrium of the ecosphere for life are divine provisions for healing. Christian doctrine asserts that God the Father heals his people and the land (all creation, 2 Chr 7:14–15), and that Christ as the perfect human (Son of God), who is identified with and so represents the whole creation (Col 1:15–20); met the required conditions, when strengthened by the Holy Spirit (Luke 22:43), and atoned for the sins of creation with his blood on the cross (Isa 53:4–5). Ernest Lucas believes that Jesus' healing miracles should not be seen in a purely human-centered perspective. They are signs of the coming renewal of the whole created order.[141]

Thus, despite threatening devastations of terrestrial life as consequences of sin, all creation hopes for the triune God's active sustenance and working towards consummation of redemption for eternal fullness of life. In this way, Christ the second Adam is "keeper" of the Earth more perfectly than the first Adam since in him "all things hold together" (Col 1:17).[142] Perhaps the first Adam (fallen humanity) became ecologically bankrupt due to misinterpretation of its cultural self-understanding as the image of God.

Human Self-understanding as Imago Dei and Vicegerent as Impulsion for Creation Care

Two Christian teachings that are controversial and yet truly underscore and mandate Christians to practice creation care are the theomorphism and vicegerency of humanity. Biblical texts such as Genesis 1:26–28 and Psalm 8:4 describe humanity as a being in the image of God or after his likeness (*imago Dei*) or a little lower than God and given dominion over God's handiworks. But ecologically these passages have been problematic. Often they are interpretively reduced to the anthropocentric "*imago Dei*" and "dominion" theses, which have been the cause of many debates, accusations and labeling of Christianity as anti-ecological religion and great contributor to the current eco-crisis.[143] However, it is arguable that the problematic

---

140. As we discussed earlier the sin of humanity was imputed for creation also and both started suffering its consequences of varied painful' experiences since the time of Adam (Gen 3:16–19)

141. Lucas, "New Testament Teaching on the Environment," 94.

142. Daneel, *African Earthkeepers*, 215.

143. White, "Historical Roots of Our Ecological Crisis," 1203, is the most noted accuser of Christianity's ecological heritage based on this passage. See also Curry,

nature of this doctrine in itself suggests its potency also as an impulsion for Christian eco-care praxis. Thus, it is important that we discern what it means to be created in God's image[144] particularly in reconstructing Christian theocology with regards to the place or role of humanity in creation.

According to Solomon Victus, in the OT, two Hebrew words *tzelm* (image) and *demut* (likeness) are used for the expression "created as *imago Dei* (God's image)." The former refers to physical form like an image or idol, which cannot be conceived in Hebrew thought, given their strict adherence to the Decalogue, and the latter is simply a similitude. Therefore, Victus argues that in the Priestly text of Genesis these words are just a "synonymous parallelistic statement" being a literary genre of Hebrew poetry though some try to differentiate between them.[145] In any case, since in the biblical creation stories only humanity was created in and designated as *imago Dei* it is not difficult to conclude humans "are very close to God"[146] and have an elevated position over against other creatures.[147] For instance, humans, by virtue of their genetic programming and neurobiological possibilities, have been endowed with unique capabilities, with which they shape the Earth for good or bad, and hence, are co-creators with God,[148] but also, unlike God, are destroyers of creation. As John Chryssavgis argues, "the human person is characterized by paradoxical dualities: . . . created yet creative."[149]

But this is not to be understood as deifying humans or making them domestic servants of the gods as in Mesopotamian and Babylonian mythologies, respectively,[150] despite such a suggestion in Psalm 82:6a "You are gods, sons of the Most High, all of you." Leonardo Boff argues from an Eastern Orthodox Christian understanding that when viewed in God's perspective and light, all things are sacraments, and "the word, human beings, and things are signs and symbols of the transcendent."[151] Boff implies, agreeably, that the meaning of *imago Dei* and humanity being given "dominion" need to be viewed and interpreted in the perspective and light of God in reconstructing Christian theocology, for instance. Doing so brings out that both

---

Ecological Ethics, 33.

144. Schwarz, *Creation*, 179.
145. Victus, *Eco-Theology and the Scriptures*, 83.
146. Victus, *Eco-Theology and the Scriptures*, 83.
147. Schwarz, *Creation*, 181.
148. Schwarz, *Creation*, 175.
149. Chryssavgis, "World of the Icon and Creation," 87.
150. Schwarz, *Creation*, p 181.
151. Boff, *Sacraments of Life*, 49. See also Hessel and Ruether, eds. *Christianity and Ecology*, 90.

humans and other-than-human creation (things) are both matter with same moral and sacramental value; both then matter in the sight of their maker, God.

In other words, human needs and desires are not to be considered in any sense higher than those of the rest of nature (without reference to God), for the human is nothing more than a part of nature before God.[152] Thus even if humans are given the special status of image of God we do not have the mandate to be arrogant, dominant and oppressive.[153] Rather the OT text means to be God's vicegerent; "to act [graciously] in God's place, as his administrator and representative" of the ecosphere; and, from the NT, it is "to be ethically shaped in conformity with God and to act in a manner for which God serves as the prototype [ecologist] (Phil 2:5; Rom 15:5)"[154] As Schwarz explains, being in God's image and having dominion does not imply a special ontological quality, but an assertion about the ecological function of humanity. It is a role that contains authority but at the same time humility to represent and model God's loving and caring nature, which then makes us truly creatures and also co-creators.[155] That humanity's "dominion authority" demands humility and moral accountability is because it is derived; only God wields actual dominion over creation as Peter succinctly spells out: "To God be dominion forever and ever" (1 Pet 5:11).

It is also a role with moral responsibility. The first Adam was thus given functional instruction to "work" (use) and yet "keep" (care for or sustain) the land (Gen 2:15), but he cannot have full freedom to do whatever he wants to do, being limited and forbidden to eat of the fruit of the tree of the knowledge of good and evil (Gen 2:17). So he can function only within the limits of and according to God's ecological ethics such as sustainable use of resources (Gen 2:15) and Sabbath rest (Gen 2:2). His authority is derived from God and is "not a license to anthropocentrically exploit creation and subjugate it to his desires."[156] Norman L. Geisler discusses the materialistic, pantheistic and Christian worldviews in his chapter on ecology. He concludes that in Christianity God is the creator and humans are the keeper of God's glorious world. It is our duty to keep and not corrupt, to preserve and not pollute.[157] Doing otherwise is ecological sin.[158] Yet, as I see it, that

---

152. Victus, *Eco-Theology and the Scriptures*, 103.
153. Victus, *Eco-Theology and the Scriptures*, 83.
154. Schwarz, *Creation*, 182.
155. Schwarz, *Creation*, 183.
156. Schwarz, *Creation*, 182.
157. Geisler, *African Christian Ethics*, 333.
158. Zizioulas, "Comment on Pope Francis' Encyclical *Laudato Si*."

is the fate which exactly befell the first *Adam* (the fallen humanity); he has historically exhibited success in "working" but failed woefully in "keeping" the land. It would be left for Christ, the second *Adam*, as Daneel says, to prove a "keeper" of the Earth more perfectly than the first Adam since in him "all things hold together" (Col 1:17).[159]

The theocological implication is that just as the first Adam represents fallen humanity so Christ, the second Adam, is a figure of the regenerated humanity (Rom 5:18–19), the head of the new creation (2 Cor 5:17). Jesus, unlike sinful Adam, is the exact imprint of God's nature (Heb 1:3). He then demonstrates the true picture of being in God's image, vicegerent and, therefore, the one with the perfect creation care disposition. Jesus the Word as the creator is also the Word become flesh (John 1:14);[160] and in the flesh he is the one who truly reveals God, the image of the invisible God, the firstborn of all creation (Col 1:15).[161] He then is the one in whom the image of God (*imago Dei*) is restored, and consequently he makes believers "a new creation" (2 Cor 5:17).[162] What it means is that as in Christ we are being reconstituted with the true *imago Dei* nature, it is imperative that we are motivated as vicegerents to care for creation in Christ's way. We are created in Christ Jesus for good works (beginning with creation care, Gen 2:15), which God prepared beforehand so that we should walk in them (Eph 2:10b).

Thus, in practice we must care for creation because humans are immersed in nature, inexorably woven into profound relationships that constitute life on Earth.[163] Humans are called to a priestly role of responsibility and vicegerency toward creation. This sense of a call to responsible Earthcare, made the Ecumenical Patriarch Bartholomew to speak of human degradation of the environment as ecological sin.[164] We sin against God who created to reveal himself and provide a good place for us to live; we sin against the environment and ourselves by blocking the environment from

---

159. Daneel, *African Earthkeepers*, 215.

160. Keitzar, "Creation and Restoration," 59.

161. Keitzar, "Creation and Restoration," 60.

162. Keitzar, "Creation and Restoration," 61.

163. Bauckham, "New Testament Teaching on the Environment," 100.

164. Zizioulas, "Comment on Pope Francis' Encyclical *Laudato Si*." See also Grim and Tucker, *Ecology and Religion*, 166, who report their experience with the Ecumenical Patriarch Bartholomew during expedition to Greenland for a symposium titled 'The Arctic: Mirror of Life' in September 2007. As they (150 international participants) realized how human activities are melting the Greenland ice sheets into the Arctic Ocean, the Eastern Orthodox Church leader outraged "this is ecological sin and crime against creation."

nurturing us.¹⁶⁵ However, in obeying the call, as Curry warns, we must recognize creation's limited carrying capacities and the limits of our caring ¹⁶⁶ by adhering strictly to God's eco-values and eco-ethics. For, only humans in all creation will be held accountable for the way(s) in which we have exercised our responsibility.¹⁶⁷

Christian Eco-Valuing and Practice of Eco-Ethical Principles

Reconstructing Christian eco-values, ethics and regulations is a formulation of principles based on our theocentric worldview. These principles are reflected in and may be gleaned from the Christian Bible, but particularly the Genesis stories of creation and OT in general, which lay the foundation for our Christian theocentric eco-ethics. Norman Geisler contends that Christians may not be bound by all OT environmental laws, particularly the ceremonial and sacrificial regulations already fulfilled by Christ. However, he finds that the OT provides good and basic eco-ethical instructions and examples, especially the fundamental law of rest.¹⁶⁸ In other words, most Christian eco-ethics and praxis are derived from God's crown in creation, which is the Sabbath and not humanity.

Solomon Victus thinks that humans claim, wrongly, with anthropocentric self-understanding "supremacy and crownship for being created at the last."¹⁶⁹ The error in the claim is because, with that self-understanding, we misinterpret the "dominion" and "*imago Dei*" concepts¹⁷⁰ to mean have the right to do whatever we want to the Earth and all its inhabitants without ethical constraints.¹⁷¹ It is also palpable from Islamic ecology that only when human hands are restrained with environmental laws that we can desist from diminishing the capacity of the Earth to support life.¹⁷² With eco-theological concern Jürgen Moltmann rightly reverses the concept of the "crown of creation" from humanity to Sabbath;¹⁷³ in my view, that is what the nar-

165. Geisler, *African Christian Ethics*, 333.
166. Curry, *Ecological Ethics: Introduction*, 35.
167. Berry, "Christian Approach to the Environment," 73.
168. Geisler, *African Christian Ethics*, 325.
169. Victus, *Eco-Theology and the Scriptures*, 52.
170. Curry, "Ecological Ethics," 33.
171. White, "Historical Roots of Our Ecological Crisis," 1203. See also Curry, *Ecological Ethics*, 33.
172. Llewellyn, "Basis for a Discipline of Islamic Environmental Law," 185.
173. Moltmann, *God in Creation*, 31. See also Victus, *Eco-Theology and the Scriptures*, 50.

ratives actually present. Hans Schwarz holds the same view arguing that it is rather "the seventh day as day of rest" and not humanity that was mentioned at the end of creation.[174] Even though Robert W. Godfrey doubts if God being eternal, immutable and impassable can ever tire of creative work,[175] Moltmann believes that creation out of nothing suggests it happened out of God's energy.[176] This means that God necessarily dispensed and invested but not necessarily exhausted energy nor was exhausted of energy himself in creation, as Godfrey imagines. Instead it is a primordial announcing and pointing to an existential fact and truth about ecosystem life: that energy dissipation and a consequential need for a system of refreshing through rest is ontological and inevitable. This then is a fundamental biblical principle for eco-ethics.

In other words, the rightful shift in creation crownship from humanity to Sabbath (day of rest) draws significant moral ecological implications. At least, it reminds us to reread and rethink through the biblical narrative of creation with ecological eyes, thereby realizing a scriptural basis for the phenomenon of "rest" or giving a period of respite in ecosystem life as a fundamental divine moral ecological establishment to be observed in creation care praxis. It paves the way for ecological ethics, taboos and regulations that ensure rejuvenation and regeneration or re-energizing of the ecosystem as against the modern anthropocentric economic view of continuous exploitative usage. This is significant in that the creator himself observes it, giving further credence to a Christian theocentric worldview in addressing the eco-crisis since it teaches that God is not only the source of Christian values and ethics, but also the good exemplar of praxis. He created, owns and sustains cosmic life by establishing and personally, in Jesus Christ, showing us the aim and right way of observing the principle of sabbatical rest (Matt 12:1–14; Heb 4:9). Moreover, observing sabbatical rest acknowledges the holiness of God in creation (Exod 31:14); thus, not complying desecrates God's establishment, an act imputable as doing evil (Isa 56:2). It is ecological sin.

Norman Geisler outlines a few biblical ecological regulations and their purposes derived from the "rest" principle, as follows: the law of Sabbath rest for one day out of seven—it refreshes and increase productivity of both life and land (Exod 23:12); the law of land resting, one out of seven years for fallowing and rejuvenating of land—it prevents overuse and replenishes

---

174. Schwarz, *Creation*, 169.

175. Godfrey, *God's Pattern For Creation*, 61.

176. Moltmann, *God in Creation*, 31. See also Victus, *Eco-Theology and the Scriptures*, 51.

the land's carrying capacity, that is, leaves plenty for both humans and animals (Exod 23:10-11); the law of Jubilee returns land to original owners every fifty years—it ensures justice in land possession and avoids exploitation (Lev 25:23-28); and the law of harvesting, intentionally discriminate reaping so as to leave some for the poor, alien and animals—it prevents the greedy tendency to rob the land of all its resources, and also cares for the needy humans and animals in the eco-community. This demonstrates God's loving care for creation (Lev 19:9; Exod 23:11).[177]

Other eco-ethical principles from the Bible include the laws of sanitation—for cleansing food, hands, and utensils (Lev 13-14)—quarantine of those with infectious diseases (Lev 13:9-11), incinerating infectious clothing (Lev 13:52) and covering excrement (Deut 23:13). All were to ensure holiness and environmental health by preventing pollution. Then there is the law of warfare: even in the exigencies of war, the life-preserving environment must not be disturbed; trees may be felled only for essential military services such as building a siege (Deut 20:19-29). And there is the law against land greed, since land greed destroys productivity of the land (Ps 24:1-10), perhaps because it disregards God's ownership of the land.[178] Michael Northcott explains, for instance, that in Hebrew law and in the New Testament the right to property is not an absolute right but a right derived from God's gift of creation to humans and, in the case of the Israelites, God's gift of the Promised Land to the former Hebrew slaves. Limits on the rights and freedoms of property holders, such as the Sabbath and Jubilee laws, were an expression of the fact that the property holders were not absolute owners of the land but stewards or tenants who held it in trust on behalf of God who gave it to them.[179]

Concluding this chapter, I surmise that the religious eco-ethics and impulsions for praxis of creation care analytically reviewed in it suggest that religious ecologies have great potential to contribute to local and global efforts in resolving the eco-crisis if well reconstructed and practiced where appropriate. For instance, the fear of deities and ancestral spirits associated with the precarious worldviews of primal religionists underpins establishing ecological taboos and rituals that restrain human hands against ecological damage. Other practices such as birthing rites have potential of priming even infants for creation care. For Islam and Christianity, their theocentric worldviews and theomorphic self-understandings as vicegerents are crucial in their praxis of eco-ethics, which are derived from their holy scriptures.

177. Geisler, *African Christian Ethics*, 326.
178. Geisler, *African Christian Ethics*, 327.
179. Northcott, "Christians, Environment and Society," 106.

Generally, the insight of this chapter corroborates Matthew Clarke's observation that "religious belief is pervasive, profound, persuasive and persistent in influencing social behaviors."[180]

However, a relevant question is whether the insights from the review and Clarke's observation can stand modern scientific worldviews and anthropocentric ecological challenges. The next chapter examines how realistic and effective religious eco-ethics can be in the face of modernity.

---

180. Clarke, *Development and Religion*, 1.

CHAPTER 4

Modernity and African Religious Eco-Care Praxis

Thinking through Limitations of Religious Ecology

JOHN GRIM AND MARY Evelyn Tucker argue that because religious ecology "in the past sustained individuals and cultures in the face of internal and external ecological threats" there is "a growing consensus that religions may play significant role now also."[1] In Ghana, for instance, Howell called on both government and religious bodies, especially Christians, to return to religious engagement with the environment. This call was a response to her observation that "the spiritual engagement with land and water, once part of the fabric of African spirituality, seems to have become unraveled in our time."[2] However, Agrawal and Gibson, in an article, express concern that the implications of turning to community practices in eco-preservation amongst people of primal beliefs in the face of modernity are little analyzed in most writings on community-based conservation.[3] Implicit in their observation and concern is that there might be significant challenges with employing primal religious ecological ethics, good as they are in themselves, in contemporary times. By extension a similar concern may be raised against the other religious traditions too, and needs to be attended to in our quest for a holistic approach to resolving eco-crisis.

---

1. Tucker and Grim, "Series Foreword" to Grim, ed., *Indigenous Traditions and Ecology*, xx.
2. Howell, "African Spirituality and Christian Ministry," 12.
3. Agrawal and Gibson, "Enchantment and Disenchantment," 649.

In this chapter I examine some proposed answers to the pragmatic question: In the face of modern anthropocentric worldviews, economically oriented policies of organizations and scientism in developmental approaches, how realistic are the various religious eco-ethical principles in maintaining impulsion for and effectiveness in caring for creation? This is more so since there is increasing tendency in many African and Islamic cultures to succumb to Western population's characteristic consumerist attitude and high dependence on science and technology to provide humanity's insatiable needs.[4] The situation is made more serious as developing nations are often compelled by human and economic needs to enforce policies that obviously and grossly lack or are less emphatic about environmental considerations and, rather, anthropocentrically focus on economic growth models.[5]

Some Deficiencies in Primal Religious Eco-Praxis in the Face of Modernity

In chapter 3, I emphasized that the primal African religious eco-praxis is highly influenced by socialization of the environment. This in itself is based on Africans' precarious visions of the ecosphere. Hence, ecological actions for harmony in the ecosystem involve mainly elaborate rituals and taboos to control human ecological conduct[6] and various deities and ancestral cults are believed to control how resources must be used.[7] But Ogbu Kalu sincerely doubts if primal religious ethics, although at heart environmentally friendly, can promote a healthy ecological balance. This is because they are weak in or even lack the sustainability suited to modern pressures.[8] Kalu sees veneration of deities associated with ecological entities, for instance, which is a primal cultural ecological coping mechanism, as a vulnerable response. Its ethic is inadequate for replenishment required in modern resource management demanded by population and land use pressures.[9]

---

4. Nasr, "Islam, the Contemporary Islamic World," 88.
5. Avenɔgbo, "Aesthetic Impact of Ghanaian Socio-Cultural Practices," 7.
6. Kalu, "Precarious Vision," 44.
7. Kalu, "Sacred Egg," 236.
8. Kalu, "Sacred Egg," 241.
9. Kalu, "Sacred Egg," 240. Kalu gives an example of ecological veneration as when one placates a spirit inhabiting a tree to descend for palm wine only to fell the tree behind it. Yet there is no cult to replant; rather it is left unto the god. Kalu considers this practice as one lacking the ethic of ecological replenishment, which cannot cope with modernity.

Another obstacle is that the absence of any visible retribution of humans who violate eco-rules by deities and ancestral spirits demystifies the deities and nullifies the fear-impulsion for creation care. Many community members may become unwilling to cooperate with locally initiated eco-projects[10] because the impulsion factor—fear of the deities—is no longer there. Demystifying environmental deities may explain why, despite growing interest in traditional knowledge systems as means of conserving the environment throughout the world, much of the literature on primal societies and their roles as conservationists cast doubt on the existence of environmental ethics in these societies.[11] Agrawal and Gibson, for instance, observe that scholars of social evolutionary change and modernization theorists in the nineteenth and twentieth centuries envisioned the disappearance of traditions, religious beliefs and ethics in primal communities. They believed these communities would be replaced by societies characterized by modernity, scientific technologies and a market economy. However, Agrawal and Gibson contend, rightly, that these are merely views to despoil primal communities as being out of balance with nature, and based on new anthropological and historical research, to suggest that primal communities may not, after all, be practically as friendly to the environment.[12] Evelyn Tucker and John Grim admit that there is "the dark side" of all religious (and hence primal) ecology and a "disjunction between theory and practice," but they quickly add that it is not peculiar to religion; it occurs in all philosophies.[13] They mean that sensitive ideas in religions, including ecological ones, are not always evident in environmental practices, even in cultures sympathetic to the environment.[14] However, they believe that the disjunction should not automatically invalidate the complex worldviews and rich cosmologies embedded in primal religions.[15]

Admittedly, primal religious eco-praxis has some potential, at least in terms of past lessons to guide the present, but it cannot address all the complicated global eco-crises in our generation. In her Melanesian experience Mary N. MacDonald is certain that their primal cosmology and ecology

10. Kalu, "Sacred Egg," 241.

11. Agbanu, "Environmental Ethics in Mafi-Eve Indigenous Culture," iii.

12. Agrawal and Gibson, "Enchantment and Disenchantment," 629 (abstract). See also Agbanu, "Environmental Ethics in Mafi-Eve Indigenous Culture," 2.

13. Tucker and Grim, "Series Foreword" to Grim, ed., *Indigenous Traditions and Ecology*, xx.

14. Tucker and Grim, "Emerging Alliance of World Religions and Ecology," 3 see also 1.

15. Tucker and Grim, "Series Foreword" to Grim, ed., *Indigenous Traditions and Ecology*, xx.

inform managing ecological challenges, which may offer insight into our present global predicament. However, she avers also that they have limitations; we can look to them for suggestions, but not expect them to give easy answers to complicated global questions today.[16] Similarly, Tirso Gonzales and Melissa Nelson opine, primal religious eco-ethics may still serve as sources of learning since their ecological ethoi emerged as principles and specific codes, often couched in mythological stories and rules, from past ecologically harmful decisions and experiences.[17] Ogbu Kalu's story about the Amanuke from Nigeria may be insightful here.

In "The Sacred Egg" Ogbu Kalu narrates a story about how the Amanuke primal community vehemently protested a World Bank-loan-supported irrigation project undertaken by the Nigerian government in 1996 without their cultural input. The project would improve agriculture by enabling cropping the year round. But the villagers complained that the forest adjoining the farmland housed their epical ancestral shrine. "Besides," they argued, "if the ancestral progenitors had wanted them to harvest crops year-round, they would have caused the springs which coursed underground to burst to the surface. Ancestors are very loving and usually careful about such things."[18] I reinterpret and reconstruct some conservation lessons from this. That it is not the practice of their ancestors to provide year-round water may represent Amanuke's conservation philosophy for regulating the agricultural production frequency or limiting intensive production to the season when water is available. In this way they would ensure that only subsistence needs were supplied by and in the ecosystem in the right season. The overall eco-effect would include land fallow and the soil regaining nutrients during the off-season period, conservation of food crops by avoiding tendencies for unnecessary overproduction and overconsumerism, and, hence, prevention of wastage and food insecurity. It might also influence the development of the eco-ethic of hard work since laziness during the season in which water is available might result in crop failure and hunger. This was a religious eco-belief and practice of ancestral veneration, born out of close local association with nature. It does not provide a modern scientific means, but points to plausible explanation and motivation for moral conservation praxis, resolving human food need and promoting hard work as an eco-ethic. Suggestively, global eco-ethical knowledge and praxis necessarily requires local roots, and not the other way around. For eco-ethics cannot be successfully imposed by diktat or policy; it must be encouraged on the basis

16. MacDonald, "Changing Habits, Changing Habitats," 592.
17. Gonzales and Nelson, "Contemporary Native American Responses," 498.
18. Kalu, "Sacred Egg," 225.

of what is ecological and ethical in what people already value, know and do where they are.[19] As Agbanu puts it with regards to teaching environmental science in academia, a student needs local sociocultural interaction to provide understanding of the environment and how it functions in historical and traditional context as a foundation for any meaningful scientific ecological knowledge.[20] This means encouraging and engaging students to be practically interested and involved in their local ecologies.

Challenges of Implementing Islamic Religious Ecology in the Face of Modernity

Seyyed Hossein Nasr discusses many obstacles to practice Islamic environmental ethics in the modern world and goes on to suggest ways in which these obstacles might be overcome. His fears may be sorted and categorized into global and local factors. There are the envisaged strong influences on the Islamic world of science and technology, Western value setting in socioeconomic agenda affecting the environment, and both modern and fundamental Muslims preferring and promoting Western science against Islamic science, at the global level. Local level factors include governments opposed to Islamic environmentalism, Islamic revivalists not emphasizing environmental concerns, lack of ecological awareness and preparation of the *ulamă* or traditional scholars, who are custodians and preachers of Islam to the masses, as well as migration and urbanization. In the latter case he explains that the city immigrants tend to lose their premigration rural ecological instincts due to urgency of urban survival matters.[21]

This is not different from observations in Ghana, especially at the Sokpoe ecological area. Asked why rural Muslims tend to drop their environmental ethos when immigrated to city *zongos* (Islamic eco-communities), Hajia Sanni Fatti from Sogakɔfe zongo blames it on lack of an adequate ecologically minded upbringing, daily busyness for survival that leaves no time for personal and environmental care and sheer laziness.[22] On her part, in a separate interview, Hajia Hawusatu Eleas, who had witnessed such a situation in Nima, a suburb of Accra, believes that it also results from eco-cultural influence, due to the conglomeration of different ethnic migrants with cultures that lack good ecological ethos rather being more influential.[23]

19. Curry, *Ecological Ethics*, 174.
20. Agbanu, interview, University of Ghana, Legon, 23 November 2015.
21. Nasr, "Islam, the Contemporary Islamic World," 87.
22. Hajia Sanni Fatti, interview at Sogakɔfe, 14 April 2016.
23. Hajia Hawusatu Elias, interview at Sogakɔfe, 12 April 2016.

The characteristics of cultural heterogeneity in zongo eco-communities presents another significant challenge to Islamic eco-ethical praxis as observed in rural zongo eco-communities in the Sokpoe area, and which perhaps is intensified in city zongos. It is the question of a possible psychosocial effect on Muslims' self-understanding of belonging to a "zongo." According to the Sogakɔfe zongo chief, Alhaji Abdullah Muhammad, the Hausa word "zongo" connotes the idea of a resting place for Muslim strangers on a continuous migratory journey, particularly by trekking. This makes members of a zongo community tend to perceive themselves as strangers, mere visitors, passers-by who are not necessarily part of the town of settlement. Thus, irrespective of duration of stay they tend to distance themselves from the indigenes culturally by referring to them as *dutɔwo* (owners of the town), a people to whom the Muslims do not belong by their way of life.[24] Meanwhile, Imam Ali of Dabala-Junction-zongo observes that apart from the Islamic religious link, there is a high propensity for the different ethnic groups and even individuals not to integrate but to insistently maintain the culture and ecological ethos of their home of origin. As he puts it:

> In a zongo, people from different places come with their home cultural mind-sets and converge at one place. Each tends to behave according to his/her cultural self-understanding, creating very little room for cultural integration or compromises and mutual respect. The lingual differences of Hausa, Frafra, Dagati and Zamramra further worsen the weak mutuality situation in the zongo.[25]

In short, there is a high tendency to resist feeling inferior to another eco-cultural group. My contention is that the result of the seemingly sense of "not belonging to the land of the indigenes" and "tendency for cultural independence" and "resisting social inferiority" is an indictment for having an ecologically passive attitude and behavior. And the situation worsens in city zongos because, as Hajia Hawusatu Eleas laments, it poses challenges for mobilizing and depending on communal spirit in cleaning the environment compared with that of village zongos.[26] David Bookless argues that unless we feel grounded in a land of birth or domicile it is difficult to be motivated to involve oneself in creation care praxis.[27]

---

24. Alhaji Abdullah Muhammad (zongo *sarachi*), interview at Sogakɔfe, 5 April 2016.

25. Imam Alhaji Ali, interview at Dabala Junction, 17 May 2016. See appendix, A3, for transcript.

26. Hajia Hawusatu Elias, interview at Sogakɔfe, 12 April 2016.

27. Bookless, *Planetwise*, 50.

Muslims are enjoined by the Qur'an to rely on natural instinct to care for creation.[28] However, the apparent prevalent psychosocial problems—lack of cultural cohesion and non-cooperation—in zongo life analyzed above may render this expected primordial environmental endowment less effective. Sharing of positive eco-praxis is weak, and the situation is worsened by the fact that pragmatic efforts to raise serious Islamic ecological concerns among Muslims have been generally insufficient in the Muslim world since the 1980s.[29] The same reason that Islam started raising serious eco-concerns only lately could be advanced for the poverty in the eco-education of *ulamas*. Yet Nasr blames it on Islam's attention and energy being directed in defending the religion against Christian and secular intrusions during the past two centuries.[30]

Nasr's suggestions for the way forward emphasize both formal and informal ecological education at all levels and academic disciplines. This includes the *madāris* or traditional training institutes for religious leaders. The eco-educational curricula or sermons of *imāms* in his view should have objectives and contents that can erase and replace the modern scientific worldview with the Islamic worldview.[31] Nasr hopes that in the end Muslims at all levels who are committed practically to promoting Islamic ecology may be motivated with local, national and international awards.[32] This underscores my proposal for an African Theocology curriculum to serve missional purposes in higher educational institutes in Ghana, drawing on shared experiences from primal, Islamic and Christian religions.

Some Limitations of Christianity for Eco-Praxis in Modern Times

The emphasis running through this book is what Simon Victus opines: that Christian theocentrism may be an all-inclusive ideology to address the ecological concerns of and questions arising from other views.[33] Yet such an assertion raises pragmatic questions about Christian eco-heritage and conflicts in the relation between modern scientific and religious views in ecological studies. Mary Tucker and John Grim's caution becomes

---

28. Chishti, "*Fitra*," 67.
29. Nasr, "Islam, the Contemporary Islamic World," 86.
30. Nasr, "Islam, the Contemporary Islamic World," 86.
31. Nasr, "Islam, the Contemporary Islamic World," 100.
32. Nasr, "Islam, the Contemporary Islamic World," 103.
33. Victus, *Eco-Theology and the Scriptures*, 120.

instructive: that we do not underplay the negative shadow side or claim too much of religion's potential for ethical persuasiveness.[34]

Indeed, in the literature, Christianity's ecological heritage, especially from the West, casts a negative shadow on its potential as a religion for promoting progressive creation care praxis in the (post)modern world. For instance, Lynn White's labeling of Christianity in the mid-twentieth century as the most anthropocentric religion and the primary historical cause of ecological crisis, based on Genesis 1:26–28, has been variously criticized.[35] However, Patrick Curry observes that up to now what Hitzhusen calls the "White Thesis"[36] has "so far been *commonly and influentially understood* by those who want to understand it that way."[37] Moreover, it appears the first or most common reference in literature any time the negative Christian ecological heritage is mentioned. Thus, the notion of the "White Thesis" may pose pragmatic challenges to applying Christian ideas to resolving ecological issues in the modern secularized world. This calls for Christian responses without denying but appropriately identifying causal sources of the accusations for attention in the quest for effective creation care praxis.

To White's conviction that Genesis 1:26–28 gives humans the right to do whatever they want to the Earth, Patrick Curry echoes the Christian response that "other very different interpretations of the Bible are possible."[38] Christian theocological reconstruction is occurring extensively across the globe.[39] The theocological reconstruction process admittedly recognizes the earlier inaccurate interpretations of biblical texts and themes, particularly with modern scientific discoveries about the physical universe. The process involves retrieving, re-evaluating and reconstructing new contextual understandings that suggest theocentrism rather than anthropocentrism being the actual biblical presentation of the God-creation-human relations.

---

34. Tucker and Grim, "Series Foreword" to Foltz et al., eds., *Islam and Ecology*, xx.

35. For criticisms on Lynn White's thesis see the following works: Hitzhusen, "Judeo-Christian Theology and the Environment"; Wendell Berry, "God and country," in Berry, *What Are People For?*; Ester and Seuren, "Religious Beliefs and Environmental Attitudes"; Foley, "Who Cut Down the Sacred Tree"; Moncrief, "Cultural Basis for Our Environmental Crisis"; Tuan, "Our Treatment of the Environment"; Curry, *Ecological Ethics*, 33.

36. Hitzhusen, "Judeo-Christian Theology and the Environment," 58.

37. Curry, *Ecological Ethics*," 34 (italics original).

38. Curry, *Ecological Ethics*," 33.

39. See, for example, the works of Grim and Tucker, *Ecology and Religion*; Victus, *Eco-Theology and the Scriptures*; Craig, "Christ, Creation, Stewardship and Missions," 137; Deane-Drummond, *Eco-Theology*; Bookless, *Planetwise*; Bonk, "Mission and the Groaning of Creation"; Northcutt, *Moral Climate*; Wright, "Theology and Ethics of the Land"; Young, *Healing the Earth*; Moltman, *God in Creation*; Carson, *Silent Spring*.

Grim and Tucker report, for instance, on "The Harvard Project," a "ten-part conference series on World Religions and Ecology" organized from 1996 to 1998 at the Harvard Centre for the Study of World religions.[40] These conferences and the volumes of books resulting from them acknowledge both the problems and promises of religion, and hence, Christianity in caring for creation.[41]

Generally, the reconstructed Christian worldviews are promoting change in the role of humanity in creation from masters and managers to morally responsible participant vicegerents, in the manner of the second Adam, Jesus Christ. The current study itself is an example. It is set out to contribute an African contextual aspect of reconstructing Christian theocology, but with the shared perspective of both the primal and Islamic religious traditions in Africa. In addition, writing in the late twentieth century, Gordon Wenham observed that Western Christian theological books and ethics said hardly anything about the environment.[42] Now in the early twenty-first century, volumes of Christian theocological books are being produced in the West as a result of scores of studies, conferences and projects of pro-creation care.[43] Even Lynn White pointed out that Judeo-Christian culture has a tradition of caring for nature. He recommends St. Francis of Assisi as an inspiration and patron of all environmentalists[44] and so "has sought a solution within the Christian tradition itself."[45]

Furthermore, though Lynn White blames Christians alone for the anthropocentric approaches that have created the ecological crisis,[46] Curry's response is that "pre-Christian humanity also engaged in many bouts of ecological destructiveness—mass felling of forests, the hunting of some megafauna to extinction, etc." Additionally, he says "non-Christian people also have done the same" destruction of creation.[47] Richard Young agrees that the degradation of the environment began long before Christian era. He mentions various examples including Native Americans, not influenced by Christianity, who killed eagles and herds of buffalo merely to respectively

---

40. Grim and Tucker, *Ecology and Religion*, 6.
41. Grim and Tucker, *Ecology and Religion*, 8.
42. Wenham, "Old Testament and the Environment," 86.
43. As examples of Western Christian theocological works in the twenty-first century see Grim and Tucker, *Ecology and Religion*; Sorely, "Christ, Creation, Stewardship and Missions"; Bookless, *Planetwise*; Bonk, "Mission and the Groaning of Creation"; Northcutt, *Moral Climate*.
44. Cunningham and Saigo, *Environmental Science*, 41.
45. White, "Historical Roots of Our Ecological Crisis," 1203.
46. Victus, *Eco-Theology and the Scriptures*, 18.
47. Curry *Ecological Ethics*, 33.

make their traditional headdresses and eat their tongues.[48] Young then concludes that "it is obvious that the root cause of eco-crisis lie elsewhere."[49] Could the "elsewhere" be a cultural deficiency in fallen humanity and only magnified with inaccurate interpretation of the Bible by the nineteenth-century Christians in the West? Norman Geisler argues, rightly, that the root of eco-injustice, for instance, is not lack of education but moral bankruptcy,[50] which I believe can be dealt with more effectively with religion, especially faith in Christ.

Curry further alludes that "the eco-crisis didn't really gather pace until the industrial revolution in the nineteenth century."[51] He means that the church's contribution to eco-crisis may not be denied, yet not the church *per se*, but rather the industrial revolution maximized the rate into existential significance, at a time when the West was secularized.

Another negative label on the Christian eco-heritage is what Richard Young notices as the attitude of some Christians he calls "reframers" rather than "reformers." The former rejoices over eco-crisis and the decaying of the Earth, because to them it fulfils apocalyptic parts of the Bible in their own time as a "sign" that Christ's second coming is at hand. For them eco-crisis is thus not a bother, nor should it be, because God has enough resources for the church to use in propagating the gospel to the end of the age according to Matthew 24, Mark 13 and Luke 21.[52] However, it may be argued that even if cosmic cataclysms fulfill prophesies about the Lord's Second Advent, that fact is not itself a biblical injunction to humans not to fulfill their vicegerency vocation as *imago Dei*. As much as cosmic perturbations will signal the Second Advent, there is nothing in Scripture suggesting that Christians could not remain faithful in their role as ecological vicegerents (1 Cor 4:1–2). Biblically, no matter what anthropogenic damage and desecration is caused to it, creation is looked and seen as good by (the Son of) God who sustains and cares for it. Scripture indicates that it is the decaying creation, just like the decaying sinful humanity, that the Lord died for and is recreating through his redeeming work on the cross alongside the redemption of the causers of the decay, humanity (Rom 5:8; 8:21). If humans choose to be faithless, he remains faithful to his good creation. He initiated steps to save all creation—human and other-than-human (Ps 36:6b).

48. Young, *Healing the Earth*, 31.
49. Young, *Healing the Earth*, 31.
50. Geisler, *African Christian Ethics*, 317.
51. Curry *Ecological Ethics*, 33.
52. Young, *Healing the Earth*, 18.

I perceive yet another major challenge to Christian creation care praxis in modern times; it is what I call "the fact-faith conflict," being the argument of some students against inclusion of some biblical texts in an undergraduate environmental science class in Presbyterian University College, Ghana in 2010. As earlier indicated in the Introduction of this book, the students regarded the environmental science as purely a science subject for which they had paid, and did not want to be interrupted with religious morals for which they did not pay. Their notion that fact and faith do not agree implies science and religion are incongruous and not integral. The students' reaction appears to be like a materialistic worldview that undergirds modern scientific approaches to ecology, seen as conflicting with a Christian theocentric worldview. Norman Geisler sums up the materialistic worldview with these words: "after denying a Creator and a distinctive spiritual aspect in human beings, it affirms unbounded optimism in humans' ability to solve their own problems."[53] Specifically, the materialists or scientists see the physical world as eternal, uncreated and its resources unlimited, based on the first thermodynamic law that energy can neither be created nor destroyed. Geisler answers that this first law is not about the origin, but the constancy of energy in the universe. However, the second thermodynamic law implies a creator for creation since it acknowledges that usable energy in a closed, isolated system such as the universe is decreasing. That which decreases cannot be eternal, it must have first increased from some origin—God, in Christian theocentrism. Then in that vein physical resources are also limited.[54]

Additionally, a materialistic or scientific worldview insists that with "technoscience" humans can solve almost any problem (ecological ones included), and that global education can correct economic "maldistribution" to ensure eco-justice.[55] Geisler rightly objects to these assertions, because even with technoscience we cannot predict *all* relevant information to solve *all* our life problems, nor can we completely eliminate errorless deductions from what we know. Moreover, the root of eco-injustice is not lack of education but moral bankruptcy.[56] Without underrating the value of education, especially in addressing the eco-crisis, Cephas Narh implies from historical fact that knowing the good does not necessarily end in doing the good. With several examples globally, he asserts most of the men and women who

---

53. Geisler, *African Christian Ethics*, 315.
54. Geisler, *African Christian Ethics*, 316 and 318.
55. Geisler, *African Christian Ethics*, 316.
56. Geisler, *African Christian Ethics*, 317.

have caused untold hardship to society in our earthly home are very well educated and learned.[57]

I agree with Curry's perspective that the Christian theocentric worldview and ecology do not "deny that science can supply us with very important truths, nor that it has a rightful place in our ongoing [eco-]cultural conversation." It is not "anti-science," rather "anti-*scientism*: the modern cult of science, according to which science is not one way of being among many but the *only* valid or true one.[58] Perhaps *scientism* is what the students meant in thinking that "fact" and "faith" are incongruous, cannot and must not be integrated. Yet Geisler rightly concludes that "Our ecological system will not be transformed until our ethical system is changed for the better. After all, it is people who are abusing the environment. Hence, we must transform people before we can hope to transform our environment for the better."[59]

I have contended earlier that teaching science without a mindset to induce moral transformation and responsibility for keeping our Earth is only a half-accomplished mission,[60] and a dangerous one at that, because of possible negative effects on the student. Each student as a human in higher education is either a potential conserver or a threat to our environment, perhaps more than the lower educated or non-educated, dependent on the responsiveness in using the higher knowledge gained. The tension between being a threat to and conserver of Earth at higher educational levels is perhaps more pronounced in the case of science students. As an illustration, computer science graduates from Christian higher institutions managing computer hardware firms, having learnt from environmental science that the Earth is the sink for waste products, may be the first to pollute the environment indiscriminately with their dangerous computer wastes. Or young Ghanaian chemical engineers who operate *galamsay* (illegal small-scale mining) with their expertise are a threat to polluting our water bodies. The agricultural scientist, who out of the impoverishment of soil and inland water for food and fish production uses uncontrolled or improperly regulated inorganic substances, is a threat.

Data analyzed in my current research reveals a possible danger of infertility looming over the heads of women in the research area if they continue drinking water from the river in which also tilapia farming is in progress. The reason is that, as I am told, the farmers use a certain hormone

---

57. Narh, *Moral Linkage in Learning*, 2, 4, 6.
58. Curry *Ecological Ethics*, 25 (italics original).
59. Geisler, *African Christian Ethics*, 319.
60. Blasu, "Our Earth, Our Responsibility," 254.

(an androgen called 17α-methyl-testosterone) to "unisex" the fryers so as to gain earlier market weight at lower cost.[61] I surmise that logically a hormone that turns female fish to male may likely render a woman infertile as an accumulated residual effect. Some of the participating farmers in the study seem to be aware of such possible danger.[62] They protect themselves from possible impotency by wearing rubber hand gloves and strict attention to hand washing with carbolic soap.[63] But the unsuspecting girls living downstream drink and wash with that water unawares and without any protection. On June 7, 2017, Prof. Frimpong Boateng, the Ghanaian Minister of Environment, Science and Technology, in response to the "Kwame Bediako Memorial Lecture" indicated that he similarly feared possible residual effects of agro-toxins on both human and other-than-human life in most of the Ghanaian ecological areas. He noted particularly the gradual reduction in vulture populations in Ghana as a possible consequence of residual agro-toxins.

Thus, although in practice there are some limitations with religious ecology, yet there are also significant reasons for its engagement in creation care praxis. Both Christian environmentalists and holistic institutions, therefore, need to advocate for this engagement at all plausible levels of the population and vocations. The people of Sokpoe ecological area in the Volta Region of Ghana provide some instances of religious creation care praxis that I consider worthy of consideration in designing an African theocology curriculum. In the next four chapters, which constitute Part 2 of this book, I propose to analyze their religious worldviews, eco-ethical knowledge and praxis as well as glean eco-sustainable factors implicit in their birthing and funerary rites.

61. Edem Agbatɔ, interview at Sokpoe-Vogɔme, 24 February 2016.
62. Mathew Agbatɔ, interview at Sokpoe-Vogɔme, 24 February 2016.
63. Wisdom Kwame Blasu, interview at Sokpoe Bodzodife, 28 March 2016.

Part 2

The Sokpoe-Eʋe and Eco-Care

CHAPTER 5

The Religious Mind-Views of *Xexeme* (Creation) and *Amegbetɔ* (Humanity)

African Theocology as a Paradigm

IN SCIENCE AND PHILOSOPHY, a paradigm is a distinct set of concepts or thought patterns, including theories, research methods, postulates, and standards for what constitutes legitimate contributions to a field. The African theocology curriculum that I refer to in the previous chapter is a paradigm in that apart from integrating both scientific and religious ecologies, it specifically insists on theocentric approaches derived from African religious consciousness, eco-praxis and sociocultural self-understanding and tolerance as eco-communal beings. Presbyterian University College, Ghana (PUCG) is a Christian institution, but, like many African cultures today, is also a religiously plural academic eco-community. The proposed African Theology curriculum thus hopes to motivate environmental morality relatively more effectively than the current Environmental Science (GNSP 101) as studied at PUCG. This is because it aims at promoting African communalism and religious tolerance for concerted effort in taking ecological actions. This will then help fulfill PCG's purpose of missional environmentalism at PUCG. African theocology as a paradigm then requires sharing common experiences on pertinent issues from religious cosmologies and ecological ethics in Ghana.

The aim of this chapter is to retrieve, re-evaluate and, where possible, reconstruct the Sokpoe-Eʋe religious cosmologies—their concepts of the origin of planet Earth and all its human and other-than-human occupants. The primal, Christian and Islamic cosmologies thus analyzed will be practical instances of what undergird real daily experiences of religious ecological relationships in a Ghanaian, and hence African context. The issue/area interrogated is participants' concepts of *xexeme* (creation or the cosmic environment); it is to appreciate what they understand and refer to in daily ecosystem life experience as *xexeme*—its origin, structure and occupants. Particularly, the chapter seeks to know their religious anthropologies and how humans' nature predisposes them to relate with and in an ecosystem as they do.

Creator and Creation in Primal, Islamic and Christian Religious Traditions

From everyday experience the study presumed *xexeme* as the ecological term that readily translates the English words "creation" or "world" as "environment." The Sokpoe-Eʋe, however, have challenges in explaining *xexeme* because it has more than one usage. When asked, "what is *xexeme*?," Enyi Avenɔgbo, a primal religionist, responded: "*nye mateŋu atsɔ asi aɖo xexeme dzi tutu o*" (I cannot put fingers on what *xexeme* is exactly).[1] A similar observation is reported by Agbanu from his studies of the cosmic structure in the view of the Mafi-Eʋe in North Tɔŋu.[2] Nevertheless, in the current study the Sokpoe-Eʋe use the term in daily life in both cultural and geographical contexts. Culturally, *xexeme* is *agbebaɖanɔnɔ*, meaning detestable human ways of life or behavioral responses to situations in an eco-community. Geographically it is *agbenɔƒe*, meaning the habitat or place of life.[3]

That *xexeme* connotes an eco-cultural ethos in the minds of respondents interviewed from the three religions in the Sokpoe-Eʋe eco-area may be evidenced in some of their Eʋe literary expressions. Amega Enyi Avenɔgbo illustrated it with the expression "*xexeme gblẽ evɔ xexeme mele dzedzem mía kpɔ o.*" That is, *xexeme* is deteriorating though it is not visible to us.[4] He explains the statement as referring to one's discontentment and discouraging feelings about peoples' negative relational attitudes to and/or behaviors that suggest things are not as good as before in the eco-community. Muslims like Adiza Garba, Memuna Kudi, and Idrisu Ibrahim in separate interviews also perceive *xexeme* as our way or conduct of life that

---

1. Enyi Avenɔgbo, interview at Elavanyo, 2 February 2016. He said, "*Nye mateŋu atɔ asi nusi xexeme nye la dzi koŋ o*," that is, "I cannot put fingers on what exactly *xexeme* stands for at a go." In short, it is not easy to define *xexeme* with only one idea.

2. Agbanu, "Environmental Ethics in Mafi-Eʋe Indigenous Culture," 95.

3. Abdullah Muhammad, interview at Sogakɔƒe, 5 April 2016. He is the zongo *sarachi* (chief).

4. Enyi Avenɔgbo, interview at Elavanyo, 2 February 2016.

can determine future destiny to be either desirous or objectionable. Adiza Garba, for instance, explains it saying that *xexeme* means being careful how we live and taking steps to ensure a good future for us,[5] which, according to Ibrahim Idrisu, will result from complying with all that *Mawunya* (God's word) teaches us.[6] In other words, unless one is careful to live according to God's laws of life, the resultant lifestyle is that of *xexeme*, and hence detestable. So at death our *xexeme* ends and we go into God's judgment thereafter[7] in the Last Day with eternal consequences in either "*janna* (heaven) or *jahanna* (hell)."[8] Similarly, the Christian participants explain *xexeme* as the lifestyles of people, ways considered usually contrary to those expected of Christians, and so negative enough to be rejected or avoided in preferrence to going to *dzifo* (heaven), the holy abode of *Mawu* (God).[9] Using an etymological approach, Rev. M. K. Adikpe, a retired Presbyterian minister, explains it as: that manner of living which makes one feel spiritually *xixa* (narrowed or hemmed in) even in the open vast physical arena,[10] because one is out of tune with God's moral laws of ordered life and consequently awaits eschatological judgement.[11] People who do not organize life around biblical and Christian ethical doctrines are called *xexemetɔwo* or *egodotɔwo* (those outside Christianity).[12] In addition to negative lifestyle, *xexeme* also connotes discomforting environmental situations. I remember a close relative, an asthmatic, who when suffering from an attack after a respite from a previous bout would lament, "*nye xexemee ga vlu*" (literally, "my *xexeme* [asthmatic condition] has gone wild again"). Thus, both the deterioration of behaviors and worsening human life conditions as issues pertaining to eco-cultural life of a people are referred to as *xexeme*, implying cultural phenomena that are unacceptable or unwanted.

In the early twentieth century, Westermann Dietrich, a German missionary working among the Eʋe ecological communities in West Africa, made a similar observation in his *Gbefiala* (*Eʋe-English Dictionary*).[13] On

5. Adizah Garba, interview at Sogakɔfe, 12 April 2016. Others holding similar views at Sogakɔfe include Idrisu Ibrahim, 23 April 2016; Memuna Kudi, 13 April 2016; and Abdullah Mahmud, interview at Dabala, 25 May 2016.

6. Idrisu Ibrahim, interview at Sogakɔfe, 23 April 2016.

7. Imam Mahmud Abu Bakar, interview at Sogakɔfe, 5 April 2016.

8. Azumah, *My Neighbour's Faith*, 33.

9. James Cudjo (COP), interview at Sokpoe, 26 June 2016.

10. M. K. Adikpe (PCG) interview at Mefe, 2 June 2016.

11. Matthew Agbatɔ (DHC), interview at Sokpoe-Bodzoɖife (Vogɔme), 24 February 2016.

12. Gladys Ahado, interview at Sokpoe, 26 June 2016.

13. D. Westermann, *Gbefiala or Eʋe-English Dictionary*.

one hand, *xexeme* is culturally the ways and/or conditions of human life on Earth under the sky that are more or less undesirable. He noted that when life presents abnormal occurrences that are either existentially threatening or are relationally disgusting to society it is because *xexeme le gbegblẽm* (*xexeme* is getting bad or spoilt). Westermann translates *xexeme* in this sense as "fate" or life situations that are *tɔtrɔm* (changing with the times) in the direction of *xexeme gbegblẽ* (spoiling world).[14] Thus, the first ecological usage of *xexeme* in the Sokpoe-Eʋe religious worldviews is any culturally unacceptable or detestable life situations in the eco-community.

On the other hand, *xexeme* is ecologically considered by the primal people in the study as *agbenɔfe* (Eʋe) or *dunia* (Hausa), the space made by *Mawu Sogbolisa* (God/Allah) for inhabitation by humans.[15] The Muslim and Christian participants also affirm the same and that God/Allah is creator of *xexeme*. Memuna Kudi, a Muslim, answering a question about the origin of *xexeme*, replied in Hausa: "*Awusatɔwo gblɔ be Allah ne dunia muke chiki' alo Allah shine dunia*," which means, "the Muslim says God created the world and we are in it" or simply "the world is God's."[16] Her views correspond with those of Islamic theologian Özdemir, who debunks, rightly from Islamic theological perspectives, the notion that nature is the result of accidental evolution or chaotic configurations.[17] The Christians in this study had no different views; the origin of *xexeme* is *Mawu* (God), as submitted, for instance, by Mercy Akafo.[18]

The respondents from all three religions showed that God himself is not created, and lives high above *xexeme*. He has power, however, over and relates to and communicates with the Earth. For the primalists, God's ecological concerns are mediated and eco-ethical regulations enforced through his *trɔ̃wo* and *trɔ̃nuawo* (deities and their agents).[19] Kwame Bediako asserts that for primal cosmologies "the Supreme Being appears alienated from earthly phenomena, but is the Sustainer of the universe,"[20] perhaps doing so through what Kalu calls the "minor divinities."[21] On their part, the

---

14. D. Westermann, *Gbefiala or Eʋe-English Dictionary*, "spoilt world" in the original. *Xexeme le gbegblẽm* actually refers to living conditions, socially, religiously and ecologically not in tandem with how the creator purposes it to be, at least per their worldview.

15. Geoffrey Siame, interview at Sogakɔfe, 17 February 2016.

16. Memuna Kudi, interview at Sogakɔfe, 13 April 2016.

17. Özdemir, "Toward an Understanding of Environmental Ethics," 8.

18. Mercy Awo Akafo (PCG), interview at Elavanyo, 28 December 2015.

19. Geoffrey Siame, interview at Sogakɔfe, 17 February 2016.

20. K. Bediako, *Jesus in Africa*, 22.

21. Kalu, "Sacred Egg," 234. A similar view of God's alienation but non-disconnection

Muslim respondents believe that God reaches out to the *xexeme* through the Qur'an, prophets, pastors and imams to guide human relations with creation.[22] Thus Idrisu Ibrahim bemoans that it is by "our refusal to be Muslims" (that is, to submit to God's laws about life in the eco-community) that we suffer challenges in the environment.[23] This corroborates the Islamic theocological notion that environmental degradation is merely a symptom of the broader calamity that human societies are not living in accordance with the will of God in the ecosphere.[24]

Xexeme as *agbenɔfe* (living habitat), is the open vast geographical arena (huge ecosystem) where, according to Kofi Avinyo Atiglo, a traditionalist, we experience alternation of day/light and night/darkness.[25] Structurally it extends from *dzifo* (the sky), where we can see and point to above us, down through *yame* (atmosphere) to *anyigbadzi* (Earth's surface), where humans live and put their feet.[26] Both Muslim and Christian participants affirm this structure. Hajia Fatti Sanni, Hajia Hawusatu Eleas and Memuna Kudi in separate interviews explained the Eʋe word *xexeme* etymologically as a place that gives the sense of being physically *xixa* (narrowed or hemmed in) on the Earth's surface by both the sky above and the underground below us. This is why it is called *xexeme*,[27] being a corruption of *xixame* (where one is physically narrowed). As I indicated earlier some Christians hold the same notion of *xixa*, but in a spiritual sense (narrowed by ungodliness) rather than a physical sense (narrowed by structures). For the Christians, *xexeme* as space is *anyigba kple edzinuwo* (the Earth and its occupants),[28]

---

from the human world is observable in the primal worldview of the Mizo people of India as noted by Lalsangkima Pachuau. The Mizo believe in the existence of *Pathian*, the supreme being, as well as souls, ancestors and other ambivalent spirit beings. But "in the primal religion of the Mizo, *Pathian* was viewed as a distant being whom the final fate of every human being rested, but as remote from the day-to-day life of the people." Pachuau, "Primal Spirituality as the Substructure," 11.

22. Idrisu Ibrahim, interview at Sogakɔfe, 23 April 2016; Hajia Fati Sanni, interview at Sogakɔfe, 14 April 2016.

23. Idrisu Ibrahim, interview at Sogakɔfe, 23 April 2016.

24. Foltz, "Introduction" to Foltz et al., eds., *Islam and Ecology*, xxxix.

25. Kofi Avinyo Atiglo, interview at Elavanyo, 15 February 2016.

26. Enyi Avenɔgbo, interview at Elavanyo, 2 February 2016.

27. Hajia Hawusatu Eleas, interview at Sogakɔfe, 12 April 2016; Memuna Kudi, interview at Sogakɔfe, 13 April 2016; Hajia Fati Sanni, interview at Sogakɔfe, 14 April 2016.

28. These include the responses from participants in separate interviews, such as: Evelyn Blasu, Abetifi, 16 January 2016; Winner Eworyi, Sokpoe, 3 February 2016; Andrews Ahado, Sokpoe, 5 February 2016; Francis Hordo, 11 February 2016; and Edward Kattah, Sokpoe, 11 March 2016.

being the place for life (*kodzogbe*); it does not include *avlime* or *tsĩefe* (the subterrenian abode of the living dead).²⁹ *Anyigbadzi* (Earth's surface) is distinct from *dzifo si míkpɔa* (the observable sky, heaven) and separated from but contiguous with it by *yame gbadzaa* (vast open atmosphere).³⁰ Ogbu U. Kalu points out how that the African conception of space is problematic, because we end up pointing to the sky and, beyond it, the Earth and the underground when questioned about the "world,"³¹ implying we conceive three dimensions of one cosmic space. Perhaps the difficulty and hence varied ways in which the sense of vastness of *xexeme* was expressed by the Eʋe is what Westermann recorded in his explanatory statement, "*Xexeme: nugã wònye; elolo, ele megbe, ele ŋgɔgbe* (The world: is a great thing, it is large, it is behind you and before you)."³²

Considering C. H. Wright's explanations, the structural descriptions above suggest that *xexeme* may translate the Hebrew *erets* (the Earth as a whole) or the Greek *ge* (the Earth as the place of human habitation and distinct from the sea or sky).³³ However, to the Sokpoe-Eʋe, *xexeme* is not limited to only *anyigbadzi* (Earth's surface, i.e., *eret* or *ge*); *xexeme* (Eʋe) or *dunia* (Hausa) is actually *anyigbadzi* (Earth's surface), where we live, but extends up through *yame* (the atmosphere) to *dzifo* (first heaven or sky/firmament/stratosphere), where we see above our head.³⁴

Unlike the primal religionists, both Muslims and Christians perceive multiple *dzifowo* (heavens). They talk about *Dzifoʋii* (highest heaven, the third for Christians and seventh for Muslims) as not only the abode of God, but also the aspired eschatological and post mortem destination for good Muslims³⁵ and Christians.³⁶ Although the Qur'an, in sura 17:44, speaks about "The seven heavens and the earth . . ." constituting the cosmos, Muslims in this study conceive the world made up of seven heavens and seven Earths, but assert only the first heaven and first Earth constitute *xexeme*, because they are perceptible and knowable.

In terms of ecological timing of life in the ecosystem, some Christians and Muslims recognize two *xexemewo* (worlds) as *Anyigbadzi xexeme* or

---

29. Winner Eworyi (PCG), interview at Sokpoe, 3 February 2016; Hordo Francis, interview at Sokpoe, 11 February 2016.

30. Edward Klu Kattah (PCG), interview at Sokpoe, 11 March 2016.

31. Kalu, "Precarious Vision," 39.

32. D. Westermann, *Gbefiala or Eʋe-English Dictionary*.

33. Wright, "World in the Bible," 208.

34. Imam Mahmud Abu Bakar, interview at Sogakɔfe, 5 April 2016. He is the chief imam of Sogakɔfe.

35. Abdul Aziz Muhammad, interview at Sogakɔfe, 13 April 2016.

36. Gladys Ahado (COP), interview at Sokpoe, 26 June 2016.

The Religious Mind-Views of Creation and Humanity 125

kodzogbe (human world), where we live now temporarily on the Earth, and *Dzifovii* or *Dzifoxexeme* (celestial world), where believers will spend eternity. Temporality is experiential then on Earth and transitions at death into eternity in heaven.[37] The primal religious participants, contrarily, speak of only *avlime* as the habitat of the dead, although some are not certain where *ŋɔlĩwo* (the souls/spirits of the dead) dwell permanently.[38] In that case Kwame Bediako's commentary on Mulago's studies among the Bantu that in the African's experiences of daily ecosystem life "the primal worldview is decidedly *this-worldly*"[39] may be true among the primal Sokpoe-Eʋe. By "this-worldly" Bediako means "limited to the here-and-now and the perceptible." In this sense, though Bediako uses the expression "this-worldly" for primal worldview of the Bantu, in this study it is applicable also for the Christian and Islamic worldviews of the Sokpoe-Eʋe.

For all three religions in the Sokpoe ecological area, especially the primal religionists and the Christians, *xexeme* (the Earth's surface and atmosphere), *avlime* (the subterrenian abode of the living dead) and *dzifo* (heaven) as places for life are distinct but spatially contiguous and open inexorably into each other. I therefore coin the terms "gecosphere," "celesphere" and "subterresphere" to distinguish them respectively, and also because they aptly describe their cosmologies, in my view, literally. I shall explain more about these terms later in this chapter, but suffice it now to know that it is inferable from the responses that each of these spheres has its own spatial dimensions. As analyzed above in this chapter, the gecosphere consists of the Earth's surface, atmosphere and sky/firmament/stratosphere; the celesphere, particularly from Christian responses, is the space for hell as second heaven and the third or highest heaven as well as other planets; while the subterresphere locates the abodes and gateways for the souls/spirits of the living dead.

Regarding the components of *xexeme*, all three religions in the Sokpoe eco-area perceive creation as consisting of both human and other-than-human creatures, which are either physical or spiritual, located throughout the three spatial dimensions of the "gecosphere." For Siame Geoffrey and Francis Hordo, speaking as a primal religionist and a Christian, respectively, the top-most end of *xexeme* is *dzifo* (the sky or stratosphere), where the sun, moon, stars and rain are located.[40] To these things Abdullah Mu-

37. Mercy Awo Akafo (PCG), interview at Elavanyo, 28 December 2015.

38. Kwame Grey and Klayi Avi, in seperate interviews at Sokpoe, 2 February 2016; Samuel Agboklu, interview at Sokpoe, 2 March 2016.

39. K. Bediako, *Jesus in Africa*, 92.

40. Geoffrey Siame, interview at Sogakɔfe, 17 February 2016; Francis Hordo, interview at Sokpoe, 11 February 2016.

hammed, a Muslim, adds lightening, clouds and thunder.[41] Kwame Grey and Klayi Avi see with primal religious eyes things in *xexeme* (the Earth's surface and atmosphere) as including a mass of air surrounding us, forests and animals, water bodies and fish, mountains and valleys, birds and flies. There are also spiritual entities including *trɔ̃wo* (Earth deities as messengers of *Mawu Sogbolisa*) with their *trɔ̃nuawo* (agents/priests of the deities),[42] multifarious *gbɔgbɔvɔ̃wo* (evil spirits/forces) that often threaten human life, *ŋɔlĩwo* (ghosts) of living-dead humans.[43] The Muslim and Christian counterparts add to these things pastors, imams, chapels, mosques *abosam* (satan), shrines[44] and *azizawo* (dwarfs);[45] then *adzewo* (flesh-eating spirits such as witches)[46] and *ŋɔlĩvɔ̃ɖiwo kple kɔkɔewo* (ghosts of evil and righteous people) awaiting hell and highest heaven, respectively, but now roaming in the air mass or atmosphere.[47]

It is significant to note that most of the Muslim participants do not believe in ghosts. According to John Azumah the second pillar of faith in Islam is belief in supernatural beings, who fall into three categories: "angels, jinns, and the devil."[48] No ghosts are mentioned, suggesting they do not fall into any of the categorized supernatural beings.[49] Nevertheless, Idrisu Ibrahim thinks the ghost-concept among the indigenous Sokpoe-Eʋe is like *jinns* in Islam since *jinns* are human but in spirit forms, with some being

---

41. Chief Abdullah Muhammad, interview at Sogakɔfe, 5 April 2016. He is the zongo *sarachi* (chief).

42. Geoffrey Siame, interview at Sogakɔfe, 17 February 2016.

43. Kwame Grey and Klayi Avi, interview at Sokpoe, 2 February 2016.

44. Hajia Fati Sanni, interview at Sogakɔfe, 14 April 2016.

45. Adizah Garba, interview at Sogakɔfe, 12 April 2016. Although Muslims generally do not believe in ghosts, she does due to the testimonies of the Eʋe. For dwarfs, Muslims believe they exist, and she has had personal experience of encounter with them. Hajia Hawusatu Eleas, interview, 12 April 2016, also had similar experience with dwarfs in corroboration.

46. Edinam Kisseh, interview at Sokpoe, 1 March 2016; Dickson Blasu, interview at Sokpoe, 3 February 2015.

47. Jacob Azuma, interview at Sokpoe, 5 February 2016; Edward Klu Kattah, interview at Sokpoe, 11 March 2016.

48. Azumah, *My Neighbour's Faith*, 30.

49. It is noteworthy, however, that those Muslims in the study who are proselytes from Southern Ghana ethnic extractions or grew up in Tɔŋu cultural milieu tend to believe in ghosts, at least because of what pertains in the cultural area. See the responses of Adizza Garba, interview at Sogakɔfe, 12 April 2016. She was born and bred in typical Tɔŋu villages like Alɔyi, Tɔdzienu and Atiteti. She has never seen a ghost but believes in the concept of ghosts because the Tɔŋu neighbors often speak about it.

good and others bad just like ghosts.⁵⁰ Qur'an (sura 72:11) speaks of *jinns* being either "righteous or contrary."

Generally, in terms of its components as denoted by the religious traditions in Sokpoe, *xexeme* may translate the Greek *ta panta*, which as Chris Wright explains signifies the whole of God's creation, visible and invisible, material and spiritual.⁵¹ Similarly, considering components, Samuel Agboklu defines *xexeme* as *dzɔdzɔme petee* (all creation or nature or entities other than God).⁵² This sounds like Wright's Christian view that "'heaven and Earth' in the OT or 'cosmos' in the NT describes the space that includes the whole created universe—all that exists that is not God."⁵³ However, in the mind of Agboklu and others in this study, "all creation" is limited to the perceptible aspect of the cosmos, from the Earth's surface through atmosphere to the sky, making up the "gecosphere."

Some of the primal religionists and Muslims in this study think that things above *xexeme* (gecosphere) are unknowable. In separate interviews, Enyi Avenɔgbo explains that "beyond the sky (i.e., in the celesphere) no-one has been there to tell us what there is,"⁵⁴ and as Hajia Sanni puts it, "The things in the other heavens and Earths are not known, because no-one has been to them."⁵⁵ However, other traditionalists such as Geoffrey Siame and Samuel Agboklu conjecture, *Mawu* (God) and *mawudɔlawo* (God's angels) must be at *dzifovii* (highest heaven), because they want to avoid the solar heat in *dzifo* (the sky, stratosphere).⁵⁶ Similarly, some other Muslims also believe God and *malayikum* (angels, in Hausa)⁵⁷ are in the seventh heaven,⁵⁸ called *fidaus* (paradise) in the Qur'an.⁵⁹ All the prophets, including Isa (Jesus) and Mohammed, as well as the righteous Muslims shall be taken to stay

---

50. Idrisu Ibrahim, interview at Sogakɔfe, 23 April 2016.

51. Wright, "World in the Bible," 209.

52. Samuel Agboklu, interview, Sokpoe, 2 March 2016.

53. Wright, "World in the Bible," 208.

54. Enyi Avenɔgbo, interview at Elavanyo, 2 February 2016.

55. Hajia Fati Sanni, interview at Sogakɔfe, 14 April 2016.

56. Geoffrey Siame, interview at Sogakɔfe, 17 February 2016; Samuel Agboklu, interview at Sokpoe, 2 March 2016. Their idea of God and angels in the highest heaven might be borrowed from their exposure to Christian thoughts around them. At least Samuel Agboklu has no doubt about God and angels being in the highest heaven.

57. Hajia Hawusatu Eleas, interview at Sogakɔfe, 12 April 2016.

58. Chief Abdullah Muhammad, interview at Sogakɔfe, 5 April 2016. He is the zongo *sarachi* (chief). Other Muslim participants believe there are seven Earths and seven heavens, but only the first Earth and heaven form *dunia* or *xexeme* (the human environment).

59. Abdul Aziz Muhammad, interview at Sogakɔfe, 13 April 2016.

in *fidaus* after their judgements at the close of the world.[60] This Islamic view varied slightly with those of the Christian participants only in specification of places and people. Andrews Ahado, for instance, believes that beyond *dzifo* (sky) is a second *dzifo* where is located *dzomavɔme* (hell) and *anyigba bubuwo* (other planets) not occupied by any living things.[61] For Edward Kattah *Dzifovii* (the third or highest heaven) is where God, Jesus Christ, the Holy Spirit, angels and *amekɔkɔewo fe luvɔwo* (souls of the saints, i.e., righteous Christians) dwell.[62] With regards to *anyigbate* (the space below the gecosphere) the three religious traditions perceive it cosmologically as the place where we have underground air, minerals and water, as well as *avlime* (the abode for living dead). Respondents such as Samuel Agboklu, a primal religionist;[63] Idrisu Ibrahim, a Muslim;[64] and Evelyn Blasu, a Christian,[65] for instance, expressed this same view in separate interviews.

Generally, all participants from the three religious traditions in the study see the purpose of *xexeme*, particularly the other-than-human creation, anthropocentrically. Other-than-human creation exists to serve humanity instrumentally. From a primal religious angle, Klayi Avi,[66] George Grey[67] and Christiana Agboklu[68] in separate interviews see *xexeme* as the God-gifted home for living humanity. Geoffrey Siame thinks *xexeme* provides us with all the things that enable us perform the duties of procreation and family care in the eco-community.[69] The Muslim counterparts explain that *xexeme* is a cosmic place for life now temporarily on Earth, though it hems us in between the sky and the underground.[70] For Abu Bakar we live in *xexeme* because it is where we can get food to eat and grass for our animals—even air.[71] According to Islamic theologian Nomanul S. Haqq,

60. Abdul Aziz Muhammad, interview at Sogakɔfe, 13 April 2016.

61. Andrews Ahado (PCG), interview at Sokpoe, 5 February 2016. This idea of a second heaven is, however, only assumed by Mr. Ahado as a logical conclusion from biblical talks about the third heaven. It is doubted, yet not very clear or certain in the minds of other participants or in my own mind, particularly his locating of hell in the second heaven.

62. Edward Kattah (PCG), interview at Sokpoe, 11 March 2016.

63. Samuel Agboklu, interview at Sokpoe, 2 March 2016.

64. Idrisu Ibrahim, interview at Sogakɔfe, 23 April 2016.

65. Evelyn Blasu, interview at Abetifi, 16 January 2016.

66. Klayi Avi, interview at Sokpoe, 2 February 2016.

67. Kwame Grey, interview at Sokpoe, 2 February 2016.

68. Christiana Agboklu, interview at Sokpoe, 2 March 2016.

69. Geoffrey Siame, telephone interview, 6 April 2017.

70. Hajia Fati Sanni, interview at Sogakɔfe, 14 April 2016.

71. Imam Mahmud Abu Bakar, interview at Sogakɔfe, 5 April 2016. He is the chief

the Qur'an presents other-than-human creation as a "muslim" that submits to God by performing its function to nourish, support and sustain all life and human life in particular. But more importantly creation exists as an *ậya* (sign or pointer) to God; it is an emblem of God, a means through which God speaks to humanity.[72] This second purpose of other-than-human creation, however, did not occur to the Muslims in this study. The Christian participants were no different. In separate interviews, Evelyn Blasu,[73] Mercy Akafo[74] and Mary Awusi Blasu[75] were very certain that God did not want us to suffer and so created *anyigba kple edzinuwo kata* (the Earth and all in it) for our use before we came.[76] Thus all the participants understand *xexeme* as existing to secure human habitation and nurturing. From a Christian point of view, it appears that their view is limited. Although Keitzar agrees that truly "God prepared an environment for life before creating even humanity",[77] in Scripture, other-than-human creation exists first and foremost to glorify God (Ps 19:1–4), even by the nurturing of humanity.[78] What then are the religious views about humanity?

Primal, Islamic and Christian Views of Humanity and Its Role in Creation

In the religious cosmology of the Sokpoe-Eυe there are differences in details but also commonalities in their religious anthropologies related to the creation, constitution and purpose of humanity. The interviewees were asked the question: "*Le wò gɔmesese nu aleke amegbetɔ va dzɔ ɖe xexeame?*" (In your opinion how did humankind originate in the world?). All the respondents from the three religious traditions agreed it was from *Mawu/Allah*. However, some of the primal religionists, while affirming it, have difficulty in reconciling with the process of realisation. Amega Enyi Avenɔgbo, a

---

imam of Sogakɔfe.

72. Haq, "Islam and Ecology," 126.
73. Evelyn Blasu, interview at Abetifi, 16 January 2016.
74. Mercy Awo Akafo, interview at Sokpoe-Elavanyo, 28 December 2015.
75. Mary Awusi Blasu, interview at Sokpoe-Elavanyo, 2 February 2016.
76. To an extent they echo the celebrated physicist and cosmologist Freeman Dyson, who exclaimed, "The more I examine the universe and study the details of its architecture, the more evidence I find that the universe in some sense must have known that we are coming!" Quoted in Swimme and Tucker, *Journey of the Universe*, 11.
77. Keitzar, "Creation and Restoration," 55.
78. Keitzar, "Creation and Restoration," 56. The same is argued in Islam also (Qur'an 17:44).

primal religionist, responded: "*le nyatefe me la nyemenya o*" (in sincerity I do not know). He does not know the origin or the real purpose of humanity on Earth, but he knows the human species perpetuates itself through sexual reproduction.[79] He knows and believes the common saying that we originate from God, but cannot explain how God made us. What is certain for him is that "*Amegbetɔ la ŋutsu kple nyɔnu yee dzie*" (Human is born of a man and a woman).[80] In the views of Samuel Agboklu and Kofi Avinyo Atiglo, on the other hand, *Mawu* (God) is the originator of humanity; he created us with soil and put spirit or breath into us.[81] In his Islamic view Idrisu Ibrahim was not very certain about the origin of humans except that a person enters the world through procreation. On his part, Alhassan Ibrahim believes *Mawu* (Allah) is the origin of humanity. Humans are created from and with clay.[82] Alhassan's views were not different from those of all the Christian participants, including Maxwell Agbewɔvi, a pastor of Apostolic Revelation Society (ARS).[83]

The question of what constitutes humanity and, hence, makes us think and behave ecologically in one way or the other does not easily find common grounds among the religious traditions. The differences were, however, only in terms of details. For instance, some of the primal religious respondents considered that humans are constituted of two components, *ŋutilā* (body) and *gbɔgbɔ* (spirit/soul). I recall Samuel Agboklu's view reported earlier in chapter 2, because apart from pointing to *Mawu* as creator it provides also some insight into the primal ideas of human constitution.

> *Trɔ̃subɔlawo* (primal religionists) know that *Mawu* (God) the Most High is the creator of humanity and everything on Earth. Thus, he is called *Sogbolisa*, *Okitikata* (the unchallengeable creator), *Aɖaŋu wɔtɔ* (the Craftsman), and *Dɔnyuiwɔtɔ* (Worker of the good). He created hand and foot, the Earth and all in it. He used clay to create human and breathed breath/spirit into it.[84]

79. Enyi Avenɔgbo, interview at Elavanyo, 2 February 2016.

80. Avenɔgbo, interview at Elavanyo, 2 February 2016. See also Kofi Avinyo Atiglo, interview at Elavanyo, 15 February 2016.

81. Agboklu, interview at Sokpoe, 2 March 2016; Kofi Avinyo Atiglo, interview at Elavanyo, 15 February 2016.

82. Alhassan Ibrahim, interview at Sogakɔfe, 14 April 2016. See appendix, A4, for transcript.

83. Maxwell Agbewɔvi, interview at Sokpoe, 26 February 2016.

84. Agboklu, interview at Sokpoe, 2 March 2016. See appendix, A1, for transcript. The same understanding and names of God were expressed by Geoffrey Siame, interview at Sokpoe, 17 February 2016.

The Religious Mind-Views of Creation and Humanity   131

In Agboklu's view, the human is made up of two things: *ŋutilā* (body), which essentially is from and of the soil, and *gbɔgbɔ* (spirit), which is *eya* (wind or breath). Other primal views as from Kɔwu Yɔhokpɔ[85] emphasize *evu* (blood) as a significant component though it is part of the body. Thus *ŋutilā* (body) is made up of *lākusi* (flesh) and *evu* (blood), which are essentially from and of soil, and together with *gbɔgbɔ* (spirit/breath) make humanity a three-component entity. *Gbɔgbɔ*, released into the human creature by *Mawu* (God),[86] is the invisible aspect of the human being; it is like *yafofo* (wind/breath) from God.[87] This explains why a dying person "*nɔa amamu dzi*" (gasps for breath), because "*efe gbɔgbɔ le tsitsim*" (the available air in it diminishes toward an end).[88]

For Avinyo Atiglo, though God created human beings, both blood and flesh enter them through nutrients. Agboklu does not know how blood attains its functional nature in the body as we know it. However, he and others like Avinyo Atiglo and Geoffrey Siame, in separate interviews, hold the same views that functionally blood couples breath/spirit and only with this togetherness do they enliven the body. As individual constituents neither on its own can make the body experience *agbe* (enlivening).[89] In other words, the life-giving spirit or breath can exist in the human only in confluence with and so necessarily requires blood to function,[90] perhaps because there is a special *kadodo* (bond or affinity) between blood and the life-spirit/breath that God put in us.[91]

Answering the same questions about the human constitution from an Islamic view point, Alhassan Ibrahim responded as follows:

> First of all, Qur'an teaches that through an angel, *Mawu* (Allah) sent for clay with which he created *ame* (creature) and kept it to dry for forty years. Thence after, *Mawu* breathed life spirit into it; that became Adam. Later *Mawu* used one of Adam's ribs to create *Hawa* (Eve) and placed them both in the garden of paradise.[92]

---

85. Kɔwu Yɔhokpɔ, interview at Sogakɔfe 17 February 2016.

86. Geoffrey Siame, interview at Sogakɔfe, 17 February 2016.

87. Kɔwu Yɔhokpɔ, interview at Sogakɔfe, 17 February 2016.

88. Kofi Atiglo, interview at Elavanyo, 15 February 2016.

89. Kofi Atiglo, interview at Elavanyo, 15 February 2016; Siame, interview at Sokpoe, 17 February 2016; Agboklu, interview at Sokpoe, 2 March 2016.

90. Siame, interview at Sokpoe, 17 February 2016.

91. Kofi Atiglo, interview atElavanyo, 15 February 2016.

92. Alhassan Ibrahim, interview at Sogakɔfe, 14 April 2016. See appendix, A4, for transcript.

In this view Adam as human was created from and with clay. The *amee* (created thing), which is also known as *ŋutilā* (body), only became enlivened when after forty years God breathed *agbegbɔgbɔ* (enlivening spirit) and it became a living human person called Adam. *Hawa* (Eva), the next human to Adam, on the other hand, was created out of Adam's *axafu* (rib) by God, suggesting she has the same origin and constitutional components as Adam. Asked what exactly these components are, Alhassan Ibrahim answered, "*Anyi kple gbɔgbɔ ye wɔ ame*" (Human is composed of *anyi* [clay] and *gbɔgbɔ* [spirit/breath]).[93] But in a separate interview Idrisu Ibrahim provides further details that *Mawu* creates *lākusi* (flesh) and *evu* (blood) from clay and puts *gbɔgbɔ* into the flesh during procreation. That is why death occurs when *gbɔgbɔ* exits *ŋutilā*.[94] In the same vein the zongo *sarechi* (chief) of Sogakɔfe, Abdullah Muhammad, did not state it categorically, but his response implied that God is both creator of the first humans and procreator of the rest of humanity thereafter. He espoused the Islamic understanding of reproduction and expounded on it as follows:

> Everyone is born of woman and man. In pregnancy the *etsi* (semen) poured into the uterus by a man turns *evu* (blood) after forty days. The blood turns *lākusi* (flesh) in forty days, and then in the next forty days, which is the end of fourth month, God puts *gbɔgbɔ* (spirit/breath) into and turns flesh to *amegbetɔ* to be birthed later.[95]

Abdullah Muhammad thus points out that in procreation the potency in human semen to develop into an individual through a blood clot is not possible without God's *gbɔgbɔ* (enlivening spirit) in the process. He explains further that the role of *gbɔgbɔ* in *amegbetɔ* may be likened to the *"ingini"* (engine) of *lɔli* (lorry). It is *gbɔgbɔ* that chooses a person's *kadira* (destiny) upon God's instruction and makes him/her able to move about in the ecosystem, particularly towards its destiny. There are four contrasting destinies, namely, either *dzɔgbenyuie* (fortune) or *dzɔgbevɔ̃e* (misfortune), *vidzidzi* (fertility) or *konɔ* (barrenness), and *sedziwɔwɔ* (obedience) or *aglādzedze* (rebellion).[96] No human or power can alter a person's chosen destiny. Thus if, for instance, a person's *gbɔgbɔ* chooses obedient *kadira* yet he/she begins to live a rebellious life, the *kadira* will necessarily change him/her to become

---

93. Alhassan Ibrahim, interview at Sogakɔfe, 14 April 2016.

94. Idrisu Ibrahim, interview at Sogakɔfe, 23 April 2016.

95. Abdullah Muhammad (zongo *sarachi*), interview at Sogakɔfe, 5 April 2016. See appendix, A5, for transcript.

96. Even though he said there are four destinies, he could remember only three.

obedient before dying.[97] Perhaps it is in line with Islamic belief in predestination that whatever God decrees about a thing or person is unchangeable since it is preserved on a tablet in heaven.[98]

The Islamic worldview about the making of humans from the responses of the Muslim participants in this study suggests that God is not only the origin of humanity but also continues his original creation pattern in the procreation of humans by humans. Anthropologically, humans consist essentially of created earthy material and a God-endowed immaterial life-breath/spirit. Since the beginning God continues to be involved in creation by ensuring his creation pattern perpetuates in procreativity of humans by humans.

Responding to the question about the constitution of a human being from the Christian perspective, Dickson Blasu, an elder in the Apostolic Revelation Society (ARS), identified three basic constituents in the making of humans: *ŋutilā* (body/flesh), *gbɔgbɔ* (spirit/breath) and *evu* (blood). In his view the spirit is alive, but flesh and blood on themselves are not living.[99] The same three-component formula was noted in the views of other respondents like Evelyn Blasu, Edward Kattah, Winner Eworyi, Martin Doade (all Presbyterians), Jacob Azuma (of Church of Pentecost) and Mathew Agbatɔ of the Divine Healing Church of Christ in Christ (DHCCC), in separate interviews, but with a difference in the third component. Unlike Dickson Blasu, the other interviewees name the third component as *luvɔ* (soul)[100] instead of *evu* (blood). While *ŋutilā* is physical and is made out of soil, both *gbɔgbɔ* and *luvɔ* proceed from God and are in form of spirit. On the contrary, Maxwell Agbewɔvi, a pastor of ARS, thinks of only two constituents, *ŋutilā* and *gbɔgbɔ*, because *gbɔgbɔ* is also called *luvɔ* (soul) or *ŋɔlī* (ghost), and *evu* is essentially part of *ŋutilā*. Because *ŋutilā* is of Earth, visible material and mortal, it differs from *gbɔgbɔ*, which is immaterial, invisible and the immortal life-breath of God.[101] Similarly, retired Rev. M. K. Adikpe[102] and Presbyter Andrews Ahado, both of the Presbyterian Church of Ghana, perceive categorically only two constituents: *ŋutilā* (body/flesh) and *gbɔgbɔ* (spirit/breath). Andrews Ahado, for instance, had this to say:

97. Abdullah Muhammad (zongo *sarachi*), interview at Sogakɔfe, 5 April 2016.
98. Azumah, *My Neighbour's Faith*, 33.
99. Dickson Blasu, interview at Sokpoe, 3 February 2016.
100. Evelyn Blasu, interview at Abetifi, 16 January 2016; Edward Kattah, interview at Sokpoe, 11 March 2016; Winner Eworyi, interview at Sokpoe, 3 February 2016; Jacob Azuma, interview at Sokpoe, 5 February 2016; Mathew Agbatɔ, interview at Sokpoe-Bodzodjfe, 24 February 2016.
101. Maxwell Agbewɔvi, interview at Sokpoe, 26 February 2016.
102. Rev. M. K. Adikpe (retired), interview at Mepe, 2 June 2016.

> Human is made up of ŋutilā (body/flesh) and gbɔgbɔ (breath/spirit), which God breathed into it. God calls it luvɔ gbagbe (living soul). Thus, when a human being dies it is no longer called with a name; it is referred to simply as ameε (the lifeless created thing). In gbɔgbɔ is located the ability of thinking, heart desiring and having emotions. When the Bible talks about the luvɔ that sins shall be the same that dies, it is amegbetɔ (human being) who hears or thinks that Bible refers to as luvɔ gbagbe (living soul).[103]

For Andrews Ahado and many others in this study, there are only two basic constituents in the structural making of human beings: ŋutilā (the flesh) and gbɔgbɔ (the spirit). The flesh comprises the solid muscular body and a fluid aspect of blood. It is created by God from or with soil, being physical, tangible and observable, but lifeless. The spirit on the other hand is a life-giving breath of or from God directly, and contains the personal qualities of thinking, desiring and feeling. Conjoining both flesh and spirit constituents together results in a sentient, moral and living entity with disposition to be either mortal or immortal. It is called luvɔ gbagbe (living soul) or amegbetɔ (enlivened created thing), what we commonly imply when we refer to a human being or a person as an "individual." Responding to further questions investigating distinctiveness of the structural constituents of the human being, Ahado argues that since by saying "the luvɔ that sins the luvɔ shall die," God refers to amegbetɔ then amegbetɔ is luvɔ, being a short form of luvɔ gbagbe. But luvɔ gbagbe implies enlivened luvɔ, that is, luvɔ into which God inspired his spirit or life-giving breath.

In another sense, amegbetɔ also means enlivened created thing or that creation into which life breath is inspired. Then ame corresponds with but is not equal to luvɔ, in that both can be enlivened when gbɔgbɔ as the spirit or the life-breath is present in them; but in daily life experience ame is a tangible and visible material entity, while luvɔ is understood as a non-observable, intangible and immaterial entity. Therefore, ame and luvɔ differ by their substantial nature yet are similar in having the quality to be enlivened by the spirit.

Ahado resolves the difficulties in making clear distinction of the constituents that make humans by summarizing that humanity is both material and immaterial at the same time, with the latter being the real person. In a separate interview, Francis Hordo, whose views corroborate Ahado's in

---

103. Andrews Ahado, interview at Sokpoe, 5 February 2016.

many respects, calls our immaterial aspect *amenyenye ŋutɔ* (the real being of a human person).[104]

An anthropological inference and rationalization from the various responses suggest that *amenyenye ŋutɔ* (the real being of human) is invisible. It is a never-dying entity called *luvɔ gbagbe* (living soul) or *luvɔ* (soul) for short. *Luvɔgbagbe* is an infusion of *luvɔ* and *gbɔgbɔ* at the creation of humanity. The fusion makes both entities such a unity that none can be distinguished from the other.[105] However, only *gbɔgbɔ* has the qualities of being full of *agbe* (life),[106] *makumaku* (immortality),[107] *hea susu* (thinks or rationalizes) and *sena nu* (feels or is sentient).[108] Furthermore, unlike the immaterial *gbɔgbɔ*, which proceeds directly from God, *luvɔ* despite being immaterial yet is created concurrently as a mirror image or shadow[109] of the material *ame* created with *anyi* (clay).[110] Because they are creations, neither *luvɔ* (soul) nor *ame* (also called *ŋutilā*, body) are self-living, though either can be enlivened.[111] Meanwhile *luvɔ*, being immaterial, is the more predisposed to being fused with another immaterial entity, *gbɔgbɔ*, resulting in *luvɔgbɔagbe* (enlivened soul), which assumes the immortality of *gbɔgbɔ*.[112]

This is what J. O. Y. Mante means when he says, "The soul should be seen as that part of the body which is open to God (or heaven) and the body as that part of the soul, which is open to God's earth."[113] In other words, *ame-agbetɔ* (human being) is the enlivened created thing or being, which

---

104. Francis Hordo, interview at Sokpoe, 11 February 2016.

105. Francis Eworyi, interview at Sokpoe-Elavanyo, 3 March 2016.

106. Mercy Akafo, interview at Sokpoe-Elavanyo, 28 December 2015.

107. Francis Hordo, interview at Sokpoe, 11 February 2016.

108. Andrews Ahado, interview at Sokpoe, 5 February 2016.

109. Mama Mary Amɛ Azuma, interview at Sokpoe, 1 March 2016. She illustrates this thought of *luvɔ* (soul) being the immaterial mirror image of the materialistic *ame* (human), with the shadow or dark figure cast on a surface such as the ground, outlining the form or shape of a person, when we are in between light and the surface. She believes that the real being of a human is such a virtual lifeless shadow at creation, but becomes enlivened when infused with the life-breath or spirit from God. For her this explains why the Eʋe call a human shadow cast on a surface *luvɔ*, while that of other solid objects is differently described as *vɔvɔli*. In other words, only humans have *luvɔ*.

110. Mercy Akafo, interview at Sokpoe-Elavanyo, 28 December 2015.

111. Francis Hordo, interview at Sokpoe, 11 February 2016.

112. Francis Hordo, interview at Sokpoe, 11 February 2016. My own reflection upon listening to these interview responses is that Heb 4:12 seems to suggest that two items were conjoined into inseparable living soul. The text suggests that once a living soul is formed it cannot be separated into its spirit and soul constituents except if God, who conjoined them, wants to and can do so by his word. For it is written, "the word of God . . . penetrates to dividing soul and spirit."

113. Mante, *Africa*, 157.

is a psychosomatic conjoining of *luvɔ gbagbe* (living soul) with *ame/ŋutilā/ anyi kuku* (lifeless flesh/clay/earth); it is not an embodied soul or a "soulfull" body. The blood appears the confluence of the conjoining[114] and explains why spillage of human blood results in death even as God warns us against it.[115] *Ame-agbetɔ* takes on the combined characteristics of its constituents to become sentient, rational, moral and living, but capable of lifelessness or mortality too.

This then may explain why *amegbetɔ* (human being) and *luvɔ gbagbe* (living soul) or just *luvɔ* (soul), for short, are interchangeable. For "a soul has a body and the body has a soul."[116] It is also essentially the reason why some think of human as constituted of three items. On one hand, it is *ŋutilā* (body, which is flesh/muscle), *evu* (blood) and *gbɔgbɔ* (spirit);[117] on the other, *ŋutilā* (body, which is flesh/muscle and blood together), *luvɔ* (soul) and *gbɔgbɔ* (spirit).[118] Yet others simply see only two constituents: *ŋutilā* (body, which is flesh/muscle and blood) and *gbɔgbɔ* (immaterial life breath of God conjoined to soul, which is created but immaterial).[119] Thus ordinarily the word *gbɔgbɔ* translates "spirit" or "breath," but when it describes the immaterial component of humanity it stands for *luvɔ gbɔagbe* (breathing or living soul) in the mind of the Sokpoe-Eʋe Christian. It also stands to reason that neither *ŋutilā* nor *gbɔgbɔ* (or *luvɔ*) as a single entity is human until there is a confluence between them. Conjoining the two parts is part of the process by which God creates humans.

This worldview of the Sokpoe-Eʋe Christian then suggests that existentially humanity is not a dualism, but a holism, being at once earthling flesh and divine breath/spirit, with material body and immaterial soul. But the difficulty of perceiving, in reality, how materialism and immaterialism can constitute a being at once may be explained with J. O. Y. Mante's postulation of applying perichoresis to explain Christian anthropology. He asserts from a Christian theological angle that to have a clearer perception of the constitution of human being in our generation "it is important to affirm afresh" that "the soul is not the body nor is the body the soul."[120] Rather, body and soul are inseparably connected and they exist in perichorectic

---

114. Dickson Blasu, interview at Sokpoe, 2 February 2016.
115. Rev. Maxwell K. Adikpe, interview at Mefe, 2 June 2016.
116. Mante, *Africa*, 157.
117. Dickson Blasu, interview at Sokpoe, 3 February 2016.
118. Daniel Agbota, interview at Sokpoe, 11 February 2016.
119. Mercy Akafo, interview at Sokpoe-Elavanyo, 28 December 2015; M. K. Adikpe, interview at Mefe, 2 June 2016; Andrews Ahado, interview at Sokpoe, 5 February 2016.
120. Mante, *Africa*, 156–57.

The Religious Mind-Views of Creation and Humanity 137

unity, that is, they mutually interpenetrate each other and thereby bring each other to glory[121]—the glorious image of the perichorectic creator God. Mante believes that this "perichoretic understanding of body and soul has the advantage of solving the soul/body dualism created by Cartesianism."[122] But why did God create human beings?

The primal religious interviewees are unable to tell clearly the role of humanity on Earth apart from procreation as continuation of God's creative activity.[123] Samuel Agboklu believes that God endowed humanity with procreation to continue his creation activity.[124] Atiglo Avinyo mentions procreation and fending for one's family even though ultimately it is God, through the deities, "who cares for all of us," where "all of us" means "both human and other-than-human creation on the Earth," as he explains.[125] Geoffrey Siame's views on humanity's role on Earth may be another point analyzable from his response that I alluded to earlier:

> In the understanding of our ancestors God created humans to represent him. So he made us in his image. But since he is invisible we craft *legbawo* (images/statutes) like humans or other creatures, which act as messengers between us and God. If there is any other role it is procreation. As creator he gave us opportunity to also procreate, and provided all things to enable us perform these duties in the environment for our use.[126]

It is difficult to decipher whether the background of basic education in a Christian school has any influence on the worldview of Geoffrey Siame in stating that God created humans in his own image and as his representatives. However, rationalizing all the responses collated from the interviewees, it is deducible that in the Sokpoe-Eʋe primal religious thought, God creates and gives humanity the ability to procreate; God cares for all creation and enables humanity to care for its family. In a sense then humanity images God, at least in his creation and caring activities. But God's caring activity is through the deities and eventually humanity, as Avinyo explains; wherefore humanity represents God. But this seems more of a theoretic deduction. What is more probable is rather the antropocentric and instrumental view that the other-than-human creation is "to be used" by humans

---

121. Mante, *Africa*, 157.

122. Mante, *Africa*, 157.

123. Avenorgbo, interview at Elavanyo, 2 February 2016, does not know humans' purpose, except that humans perpetuate their kind through sexual reproduction.

124. Samuel Agboklu, interview at Sokpoe, 2 March 2016.

125. Kofi Atiglo, interview at Elavanyo, 15 February 2016.

126. Siame, telephone interview, 6 April 2017. See appendix, A2, for transcript.

in performing their God-given duties of procreating and caring for families, as Geoffrey Siame explains. The anthropocentric view of humans is further significantly demonstrated, from an ecological point of view, with the fact that only humans are formally welcomed into or sent off from the physical earthly eco-communtiy with birthing and funerary rites, respectively. I shall, however, discuss these rites in chapters 7 and 8, respectively, as actions that prime for sustainable ecological relations in the "gecosphere."

On the question of the Islamic understanding of humanity's purpose on Earth or why we are created, the responses suggest that Muslims in the Sokpoe ecological area understand our primary role on Earth is to "worship" or "submit" to God as a Muslim. In separate telephone interviews Malam Alhassan Ibrahim of Sogakɔfe[127] and Imam Alhaji Ali of Dabala Junction[128] stressed this point. They explained that both humans and *jinns* are the only creatures to be judged regarding their worship of God. All other creatures—such as trees and animals—are to service humanity to live well and perform the duty of being a Muslim. But according to Imam Ali humans have a responsibility to care for these other-than-human creatures, particularly animals; failure to do so is sin and is punishable by God. What appears as a second role of humanity in the responses is procreation. In this regard, malam Alhassan Ibrahim sees humanity as "*khalifa* or representative of God to continue creation activity." On his part, Imam Alhaji Ali believes procreation is ultimately God's *dɔdeasi* (assignment), yet it was effectuated through Satan's deception of Adam and Eve to "eat the forbidden fruit (sexual intercourse)." He does not know why God would allow this important intention for humanity to be realized through Satan, but he asserts that God wants humans to represent him (*khalifa*) in perpetuating his creativity.

On Christian views of why humanity was created, Rev. Adikpe, a retired Presbyterian minister at Mepe, explains: "*Mawu wɔ ame be wòaɖi ye. Mawu nye lɔlɔ̃, eye wò di be ame naɖe yefe lɔlɔ̃ afia*" (God is love and created humans to be a means of demonstrating his loving nature to all creation).[129] Consequently, God infuses his *gbɔgbɔ* (breath/spirit) into us, and since the breath comes direct from God, it makes human unique among all creatures and said to be in the image of God. Then God appointed humans who are in his image "*be miakpɔ xexemenuwo katã dzi*" (to be stewards of all creation), but both humans and the rest of creation are under God's care. He believes procreation is part of humanity's role and a means of showing God's love

---

127. Alhassan Ibrahim, telephone interview, 7 April 2017.
128. Imam Alhaji Ali, telephone interview, 7 April 2017.
129. Rev. M. K. Adikpe, telephone interview, 7 April 2017.

as co-creator. Humans are to live out God's loving nature by obeying all his laws and worshipping him. Answering the same question Mercy Akafo of Sokpoe holds similar views: humanity is created in God's image to show his loving nature in our relationships with him and others. Humans, in her view, are thus to "*kpɔ efe asinudɔwɔwɔwo dzi*" (be stewards of all his handiworks) and continue his creativity in procreation.[130] For these Christians, then, God created humankind to image him in their conduct of life daily, be stewards of creation and be co-creators through procreation.

Now, as earlier indicated, analyzing these religious worldviews has one aim: to find commonalities that may influence cooperation in the practice of religious eco-ethics in a context of religious pluralism.

Common Ground in Sokpoe-Eʋe Religious Worldviews for Concerted Eco-Praxis

Although there are some differences, to a large extent there are similarities or common ground amongst the primal religionists, Christians and Muslims in conceiving of *xexeme* as our environment in the cosmos. In all three religious traditions the exact concept is not easy to articulate from the responses of the interviewees in the Sokpoe-Eʋe ecological community. However, all three religious traditions undoubtedly use the term in daily life experience with a dual sense: on one hand, *xexeme* is bad ecological ethos (that is, human behaviors and not something intrinsically cosmic); on the other, it is our cosmic living habitat or "gecosphere."

For the primal religionists, the *xexeme* way of living may incur ecological sin by offending *trɔ̃wo* (Earth deities), with possible resultant untold retribution upon the entire eco-community. For instance, disobediently picking an oyster from someone's staked oyster preservation enclave in the river, or greedily picking more than one from a "mountain" of oysters in the deep river, grieves the oyster deity. It may lead to the drowning of the culprit. Harvesting wood from a forbidden or sacred forest may incur untimely deaths and great sorrow to bereaved families. In addition, misconduct such as conjugal sex in the forest or on bare ground in the farm may result in drought and poor harvest of crops for the farming community. Consequently, pacification rites such as *kpokpɔkplɔ* (land purification) may be required to cleanse the ecosystem and enable the deities to bring rain and good harvests. In a similar vein *xexemegbenɔnɔ* (worldly living) among the Christians and Muslims includes ungodly/unethical eco-relational behaviors (such as pilfering, disregard of the poor, sexual immorality and

130. Mercy Akafo, telephone interview, 7 April 2017.

improper disposal of fecal matter), which need to be recognized as ecological sins. They are punishable by God in the end.[131] Theoretically, then, this could be an impulsion, a motivational warning, to shun not *xexeme* as "gecosphere" but *xexeme* as "eco-misconduct." This could mean living in obedience (Christians) or submission (Muslims)[132] to the will of God in the ecosphere.

On the other hand, all three religious traditions in this study conceive *xexeme* as *anyigba kple edzinuwo* or "gecosphere," which is our earthly living space in the cosmosphere. I argue that the concept of "gecosphere" has theocological significance in that it may ground the Sokpoe-Eʋe as earthlings more than "cosmosphere" or even "ecosphere" or "biosphere." Evolutionary cosmology teaches that the physical "world" or cosmos, and hence cosmosphere, is a vast "universe with numerous galaxies, stars and planets," which is the "Earth's home."[133] In other words, the Earth, the only planet where life and its interrelationships exist, is itself a microcosm in a macro-universe system. Michael Dowd says:

> We have no existence outside the ecological cycles of the Earth, which in turn has no existence outside the solar system. The solar system has no existence outside the Milky Way Galaxy. The Milky Way has no existence outside the Universe. And the Universe has no existence outside the Ultimate Reality, [God for the Christian]. Everything is interrelated and interdependent. The entire process oozes divinity.[134]

Since "our home" is where we can exert moral energy for pragmatic creation care, which of the two—the macrocosmic universe or the microcosmic—ecologically translates *xexeme* for the Sokpoe-Eʋe as "our home"? While "cosmos" or "cosmosphere" leaves the individual with a sense of "loss" in an incomprehensible extragalactic space, the term "biosphere" tends to limit earthlings to biologically known living things; yet for the Sokpoe-Eʋe *xexeme* is holistic. "Ecosphere" is the term ecologists employ when we speak of the cosmic spatial regions that constitute home for all life (creation), hence the limited place of the cosmos for environmental actions. However, "ecosphere" as a word does not specifically mention or unequivocally point to the Earth as that cosmic home space the way *xexeme* emphasizes "earthly home" in the Sokpoe-Eʋe religious cosmology. Earth as our home is only implied in "ecosphere." "Gecosphere," contrarily, is straight forward

---

131. Wright, "World in the Bible," 207.
132. Foltz, "Introduction" to Foltz et al., eds., *Islam and Ecology*, xxxix
133. Swimme and Tucker, *Journey of the Universe*, 1.
134. Dowd, *Thank God for Evolution*, 229.

The Religious Mind-Views of Creation and Humanity 141

in describing the Earth (*ge*) as our home. Thus the best theocologically inclusive and earthly implied English word to communicate the concept of *xexeme* as in the Sokpoe-Eʋe religious cosmology may be "gecosphere," at least literally. "Gecosphere" may interpret David Bookless's use of the word "creation" from an ecological point of view as "the Earth and all that it contains: [including] the atmosphere and the oceans, the mineral resources and the wildlife",[135] rather than "ecosphere." "Gecosphere" for me describes emphatically and specifically the Earth's surface, and its atmospheric regions up to the sky observable with unaided eyes and no scientific calculations, as the home where *we* (human and other-than-human creation) live and act in holistic interrelationships.[136]

For all three traditions, *aʋlime* or *tsīefe* is the subterrenean place for corpses and the world of the living dead. It is not part of *xexeme*, but rather inferrably the gateway, after transiting the gecosphere at death, into the other side, the spiritual side, of existence. The spiritual state of existence can be in either *anyigbaxexeme* (gecosphere) for ŋɔlĩ/luvɔ vɔ̃ɖiwo (non-godly ghosts/souls) or *dzifoxexeme* (celesphere) for ŋɔlĩ/luvɔ kɔkɔewo (godly ghosts/souls).[137] Some of the primal religionists are not sure whether *aʋlime* is a permanent abode of their living dead, nor do they conceive *dzifoxexeme* as a possible abode after physical death. But they believe that some living dead, favored by God to correct their past evil lives, do return from *aʋlime* to the Earth as *amedzɔdzɔ* (a reincarnate) or *ametefe* (a replacer) in the *anyigba xexeme/kodzogbe*. The rest of the souls, both the incorrigible and ancestral spirits, remain in the spirit state, shuttling and roaming between *aʋlime* and *kodzogbe* (the Earth's surface).

Although a few of the Christian respondents also believe in reincarnation, generally the "souls or ghosts" (of Christians) and "departed spirits" (of Muslims) do not remain permanently in *aʋlime*. Christians picture *aʋlime* as a rendezvous appointed by God where their ghosts await judgement day. Muslim departed spirits move out of *aʋlime* and keep roaming the Earth till judgement day. For both Christians and Muslims the souls of the departed

135. Bookless, *Planetwise*, 29.

136. Etymologically "ge" connotes Earth, "cos" from *oikos* as home, and "sphere" as the regions around the Earth, atmosphere and stratosphere (sky). These are the three major ideas conceptualised in *xexeme* in the Sokpoe-Eʋe mind-picture of the world.

137. I see this word *aʋlime/tsīefe* as a mind-picture carried from traditionalists or primal imagination, where it is known to be the abode of corpses, but also for ŋɔlĩwo/luvɔwo (ghosts/souls), which according to Grey Kwame seem ubiquitous, easily moving from subterrestrial to terrestrial systems. In terrestrial systems they can remain in either spirit form or wear physical bodies temporarily; when in temporal physical bodies they appear to living eyes as *nukpekpe* (strange encounter), since they are not expected in physical state again in *kodzogbe*.

reunite with their earthy bodies in *aʋlime* for resurrection on judgement day. All three religious traditions then conceive *aʋlime* (the underworld below the Earth or subterresphere) serving as the cosmic interface for the transition between the physical and the spiritual states of life, the temporal and the eternal, the Earth and the heavens, the human world and the ancestral world.

Thus, I suggest that the English words that may best provide a closer and literal translation of the three dimensions of existential space in the Sokpoe-Eʋe religious worldviews may be "celesphere" for *dzifoxexeme* (in the case of Christians and Muslims only), "gecosphere" for *anyigba xexeme* and "subterresphere" for *aʋlime*, the transitional rendezvous between gecosphere and celesphere.

Since my penultimate concern is how the religious cosmologies thus analyzed and outlined influence moral ecological relations of the Sokpoe-Eʋe for ultimately informing the African Theocology curriculum design, it is necessary to investigate their religious eco-values and ethical praxis also.

CHAPTER 6

Religious Eco-Valuing and Ethical Praxis

Introduction

A SIGNIFICANT EMPHASIS IN the proposed African theocology curriculum for PUCG and other African Christian higher educational institutions is that it has potential to stimulate practical African religious and moral eco-sustainability. This is because meaningful responsibility for creation goes beyond academic belief and touches our personal lives, our lifestyles and how we personally affect the environment. It engenders commitment to concrete or practical ecological actions,[1] a commitment believed to be more effective when rooted in our eco-cultural contexts.[2]

Pragmatically this requires ecological ethics, the moral (right and wrong) relationships between humans and the world around us.[3] But eco ethics is based on our cosmologies and it directs how we ought to live and act to sustain our ecological community.[4] For an African example, in designing the proposed African theocology I investigated the religious eco-ethical praxis of the Sokpoe-Eʋe, based on their religious cosmologies analyzed in the previous chapter. But I began with a fundamental feature of practical ecological ethics: ecological values.

Two hypothetical questions drawn from living scenarios in the ecological area were used to assess the religious ecological valuing systems of the Sokpoe-Eʋe who participated in this study. The first was from the Eʋe name *amewuga*, literally "the human being is more than money." The second was

1. Nebel and Wright, *Environmental Science*, 13.
2. Agbanu, interview at Legon, 15 November 2015; Curry, *Ecological Ethics*, 156.
3. Cunningham and Saigo, *Environmental Science*, 37.
4. Curry, *Ecological Ethics*, 3.

from a historical flooding event in the area in 1963 due to the construction of the Akosombo dam. It asked for participants' preferred order of rescuing some drowning representatives of creation—human, goat, gold nugget/money and tree—within a limited time, with reasons.

To the question, "As a Traditionalist how will you explain the Eʋe name *Amewuga*?," all twelve out of twenty-five primal religious interviewees gave similar responses from separate interviews. They did not only espouse the message or philosophy behind the name but would so name their children for the same purpose. Enyi Avenɔgbo, for instance, considers it *ahamaŋkɔ* (insinuating name), but will name his child accordingly to remind himself and others that "when I die my money will not carry me to my grave by itself."[5] He explained the name with many more instances, all to indicate that money cannot take initiative, reason on life issues or affect emotionally and so cannot fellowship like humans do. Hence "humans are of more value than money," he concluded. Klayi Avi argues that "money cannot serve by itself; it requires human to use it."[6] He means that without servicing human beings, a gold nugget or its minted coin as money, for instance, does not have any worth by itself. On his part Efoe Avinyo Atiglo said:

> Gold or money does not talk; only human can talk with me. What can counsel or share thoughts with me is more valuable than all things around me.[7]

Avinyo's logic may be assembled as follows: rational beings who communicate are more of value than anything else; only humans are rational and communicate; humans then are most valuable of all things around him in the ecosystem. It is not difficult to infer that the primal religionists' comparative valuing of human and abiotic (the other-than-human creation that is non-living) is anthropocentric. Generally, from their responses, the criteria for valuing include qualities of volition or initiative taking, reasoning ability or rationality, having affection or emotions and sharing or possessing communication skills. For them, in contrast to aspects of other-than-human creation such as gold minerals, only humans manifest these qualities and, therefore, are of value in themselves. The abiotic creation such as gold mineral has only instrumental value in that they are to service humankind to be of value. What about human relations with other-than-human but living creation?

---

5. Enyi Avenɔgbo, interview at Sokpoe-Elavanyo, 2 February 2016.

6. Klayi Avi, interview at Sokpoe, 2 February 2016.

7. Kofi Atiglo, interview at Sokpoe-Elavanyo, 15 February 2016. See appendix, A7, for transcript.

The second question derived from the 1963 deluge scenario also received varied answers, but with reasons that led to same conclusions (table 6.1).

Table 6.1: Eco-Valuing of Primal Religionists Indicated by Order for Rescuing Drowning Creatures

Descending Order of Rescuing Creatures	Number of Respondents	Some Major Reasons
Human-Gold-Goat-Tree	19	"The human can work for me, gold can purchase human needs; goat and tree may die."
		"Gold cannot purchase human life. Human is thus more important. Gold can buy another goat for me."
		"Human is my fellow being. He can help me if alive. Gold will help purchase my needs."
		"Human is fellow living being. Gold purchases needs of the man. Goat also is living; tree does not breathe like man and goat."
		"Human is fellow living being. Gold purchases food for the man. Income from goat is faster and more than from trees."
Human-Goat-Tree-Gold	3	"Human is fellow living being. Goat for food; tree for housing. Gold has no life."
Human-Goat-Gold-Tree	3	"Human is fellow living being. Goat for food; gold is money or power to purchasing; tree for housing and fire."

For instance, Amega Enyi Avenɔgbo explains that "The human can work for me, gold can purchase human needs. As for the goat and tree, they may die."[8] Here valuing ecological components is based on the magnitude of how each item benefits human, and thus is highly anthropocentric. Both George Grey and Klayi Avi gave similar anthropocentric reasons, but introduced also the idea of life, and hence biocentrism. "Gold cannot purchase

8. Enyi Avenɔgbo, interview at Sokpoe-Elavanyo, 2 February 2016.

human life," says George Grey. "Human is thus more important than the other things. Gold can buy another goat for me."[9] His main criterion is "life," but particularly human life; even gold's instrumental value is because it can provide animal life to benefit human life eventually. Klayi Avi adds, "Human is my fellow being. He can help me if alive. Gold will help purchase my life needs."[10] While the responses of Agboklu and Avinyo also suggest biocentrism, they prioritize human and animal life against tree life, and thus appear zoocentric in the biosphere. As Avinyo said, "Human is fellow living being . . . Goat also is living, but human is my fellow being; a tree does not breathe like man and goat."[11] Similarly, for Agboklu, "Human is fellow living being" and "Goat can kid quicker for sales than fruiting of a tree."[12] Their criteria then seem to be primarily "life," but in the order of human, animal then tree. This is biocentrism, but particularly zoocentrism. And gold's value as a non-living thing is based on its benefitting human life—anthropocentrism. Generally, then, valuing of creation by participating primal religionists in Sokpoe ecological area is a mixture of biocentrism, zoocentrism and anthropocentrism. Only humans have intrinsic value; all that is other-than-human—both biotic and abiotic—has instrumental value.

Thus, for the primal Sokpoe-Eʋe, like other African primal religionists, ecological values and ethics are ultimately anthropocentric. Agbanu's study on the indigenous environmental ethics of the Mafi-Eʋe of North Tɔŋu in Ghana makes almost similar observations. He concludes that their ecological ethics is anthropocentric but mixed with biocentrism and ecocentrism.[13] Ogbu Kalu expresses surprise at this, wondering that, "In spite of the remarkable awareness of spiritual forces, the African places man [sic] at the center of the universe."[14] Kwame Bediako makes a similar observation for most African cultures.[15]

Christian and Muslim participants in the study answering the same questions indicated similar ecological valuing of creation. For instance, the Christian participants espoused both the literal meaning and axiological implication of the name *Amewuga*, humans are more valuable than money. Their reasons included humans possessing qualities of emotionality, rationality, lingual skills, initiative taking and relatively higher versatility, which,

---

9. George Kwame Grey, interview at Sokpoe, 2 February 2016.
10. Klayi Avi, interview at Sokpoe, 2 February 2016.
11. Kofi Atiglo, interview at Sokpoe-Elavanyo, 15 February 2016.
12. Agboklu, interview at Sokpoe, 2 March 2016.
13. Agbanu, "Environmental Ethics in Mafi-Eʋe Indigenous Culture," iii.
14. Kalu, "Precarious Vision," 41.
15. K. Bediako, *Jesus in Africa*, 92.

in their view, non-living aspects of other-than-human creation lack. Further evidence was from the question of the flood victims' rescuing scenario. Margaret Asuma, a deaconess of the Church of Pentecost (COP), was among 61 percent (14 out of 23 interviewees) who followed the descending order of man, gold, and goat before the tree.[16] She gave her reasons as follows:

> Although God created all things before humanity, yet human beings are more important among all the things. Gold/money follows because as money it enables humans to be complete; the goat will be for food, and so will be the third. As for the tree it may drown. No problem. Even today the order of rescue will not change.[17]

For Mary Adzabeng, like Deaconess Margaret Asuma, and those with similar views, the human has life and is created in God's image; both the rescued human and the rescuer are fellows, *Homo sapiens*.[18] Analysis of all the other explanations by these respondents indicated, however, that their criteria for valuing creation generally included life, breath and economic worth. Both human and goat breathe *tsixetsixe* (visibly inhale and exhale) and so are of more sympathetic value than trees; but a human is more important than a goat since biblically only the human is created in God's image and must attract compassion when in trouble.[19] Thus this first group appear more zoocentric than just biocentric, and eventually anthropocentric. The remaining 9 of 23 (39 percent) were even more succinct with this axiological stance. They would rescue in descending order of man, goat and tree before gold, an indication of anthropocentrism, zoocentrism and biocentrism. Explaining in separate interviews, Dickson Degbe Blasu and Maxwell Agbewɔvi, both of the Apostolic Revelation Society (ARS), minced no words: "*Nusiwo me agbe le la xɔ asi wu nuwo katã; eyata maɖe ame, egbɔ̃ kple ati hafi aɖe ga*" (Living things are worthier than all things; hence I shall rescue the man, goat, tree before gold).[20] Clearly, for this second group of Christian respondents, life is of more value than non-life, animal life is more valuable than plant life, and human life is of most value among all animals.

16. Actually 5 of 23 (22 percent) had the goat instead of the tree to be last in the rescue order, but the reasons advanced were almost like those (9 of 23—39 percent) who would rescue the tree last. In both groups the emphasis seems to be anthropocentric and biocentric.

17. Margaret Asuma, interview at Sokpoe-Elavanyo, 25 February 2016. See appendix, A8, for transcript,

18. Mary Adzabeng, interview at Sokpoe, 21 June 2016.

19. James Cudjoe, interview at Sokpoe, 26 June 2016.

20. Dickson Degbe Blasu, interview at Sokpoe, 3 February 2016; Maxwell Agbewɔvi, interview at Sokpoe, 26 February 2016.

Like the primal religionists, the Christian participants' eco-valuing of creation in this study mixed biocentrism with zoocentrism but is practically more anthropocentric.

Neither were the results different from the participating Muslims. Their Islamic eco-valuing was guided by considering factors of biological life, sentience, breath, economic worth, livelihood or preoccupation, Islamic devotedness to pleasing God and the geographical location. Like both the primal and Christian respondents, the Muslims' ecological values are anthropocentric but mixed with biocentrism and zoocentrism.

It is significant, however, to note that, like the Christians, two sets of responses were analyzed from the participating Muslims. Apparently, geographical location appears to influence both some Christians and Muslims in their biocentric eco-valuing. In this work, all the respondents appear to generally mix biocentrism and anthropocentrism, but practice anthropocentrism. All the same, rural dwellers seemed to value floral components of the ecosystem relatively more than large town residents. For instance, we saw earlier how respondents like Deaconess Margaret Asuma, who lives in Bodzoḍife, a suburb of Sokpoe Township, concluded her response by saying, "As for the tree it may drown. No problem."[21] Meanwhile she is a bread baker who depends heavily on wood fuel. A similar observation was even more noticeable among the Muslims. Sixty-three percent (10 out of 16) of the interviewees who dwell in the capital town, Sogakɔfe, seemed to value trees less compared with the 37 percent (6 of 16) living in the savanna grasslands of Dabala. The rescue plan of the town dwellers was from man to gold, goat then tree. For instance, Hajia Fatti Sanni of the Sogakɔfe Zongo eco-community explained her flood victims rescue plan as follows:

> First will be the man because he is my fellow human being; if rescued he will help me work to get the goat and money. However, if time allows, I shall go for the goat since it also is living. Then the third item will be the gold/money, which will help care for my children. As for the tree it may drown, I can plant another.[22]

In the same way the chief Imam Abu Bakar at Sogakɔfe Zongo ended his response with, "as for tree it is not of any importance."[23] Idrisu Ibrahim, son of the Zamarama *sarachi* (chief) of Sogakɔfe Zongo, thinks "the

---

21. Margaret Asuma, interview at Sokpoe-Elavanyo, 25 February 2016. See appendix, A8, for transcript.

22. Hajia Fatti Sanni, interview at Sogakɔfe, 20 April 2016. See appendix, A11, for transcript.

23. Imam Abu Bakar, interview at Sogakɔfe Zongo, 5 May 2016.

tree may go; if it is lost we can look for another to plant."[24] For this group floral components of the ecosystem seem worthless, having no immediate thought of benefits to human beings and so do not matter if lost. But I pointed out to Idrisu that he had responded to an earlier question, "When the weather is hot where do you expect some cooling effect?," that "Trees provide shade and coolness in the environment." Then he remembered that "both Qur'an and a hadith of the prophet Mohammed promise Allah's blessings on anyone who encourages planting or caring for trees to provide shade for human beings."[25] He could not remember, nor was it possible to locate, the particular *"surakatu jaria"* he alluded to from the Qur'an. However, some *hadiths* (words and deeds) of Prophet Mohamed indicate his concern for the protection of natural resources as a desert dweller.[26]

The second set of Muslim interviewees, the savannah dwellers, on the contrary, gave their rescue plan as man, goat, tree and gold/money. By putting the tree in third position, lining up the biotic before the abiotic elements, suggests stronger biocentrism (though with anthropocentric reasons) and more concern for flora than the first group, who placed the tree last.[27] Their Sahalian background and current geographical location in the research area, where they reside in huts with grass roofs in the dry open grassland outside Dabala town,[28] would mean that they tend to value trees more than the other Muslims living in the towns of Dabala and Sogakɔfe. Unlike the town dwellers, these open savannah dwellers exposed to vagaries of the weather saw the instrumental worth of a tree in providing shelter, rafters for their huts, rainfall and browsing material for their ruminants. Mohammed Abdullah explained from home experience as a Sahelian from Niger that "trees are of great concern for savannah life, because the absence of adequate trees in Burkina Faso, Mali, Niger and even Mecca account for their low rainfall."[29]

As I indicated in the introduction of this chapter, axiology is fundamental to ethical praxis. Having analyzed the religious eco-valuing systems of the Sokpoe-Eʋe, I move next to learn how this religious eco-valuing influences their moral ecological actions to sustain creation.

24. Idrisu Ibrahim, interview at Sogakɔfe, 23 April 2016.

25. Idrisu Ibrahim, interview at sogakɔfe, 23 April 2016.

26. Foltz, "Introduction" to Foltz et al., eds., *Islam and Ecology*, xxxviii.

27. Those in this second category included Alhaji Hammah (a Fullani), Musah Mohammed (Malian), Musah Salleh (Nigerien), Idrisu Shaibu (Nigerien), Mohammed Abdullah (Nigerien) and Mahazui Awudu (Hausa).

28. See map 2 on page vii.

29. Mohammed Abdullah (trainee imam) and Musa Salleh, interview at Dabala, 25 May 2016.

Impulsion for and Praxis of Eco-Ethics by Primal, Christian and Islamic Traditions

To gain an insight of the Sokpoe-Eʋe's motivation for and praxis of religious eco-ethics, I posed questions about their knowledge of and reasons for ecological regulations and rules. From the responses of the primal religionists there are varied situations that influence or motivate the eco-ethical praxis of the Sokpoe-Eʋe. These include desire for good harvest, altruistic social concerns, avoidance of legal actions and fear of punishment by deity. Sometimes the motivating factor is at the same time an ecological action or ethical praxis in disguise. The eco-ethical principles and norms that sustained both ecosystem harmony and good yields in pre–Akosombo dam days were mainly taboos or prohibitive and inhibitive rules to determine who, how and when to access ecological services for the best and sustainable results from the ecosystems—water, land and forest.

Sokpoe is predominantly a riverine ecological area on the Volta River.[30] Yet, significantly primal religionists in Sokpoe do not sacralize the great *Amutɔsisi* (Volta River) itself as per the responses from the entire interviewees in this study. I know it for a fact myself, too. There is neither veneration nor fear of *Amutɔsisi* as a deity. There are, for example, no religious restrictions, as in some African cultures, pertaining to accessing its water resources by menstruating women, and no religious prohibition or inhibition of anyone directly fetching water from, washing laundry in, wading through, and crossing with canoe, bathing in the waters or subsistent fishing in *Amutɔsisi*.[31] Even though some regard a few of the tributaries as sacred,[32] there are no special or regular religious rites and rituals associated with the water bodies *per se*.[33] Instead, in all cases the water eco-ethical regulations in the Sokpoe ecological area are concerned about the contents of the water bodies, the fish, oyster/clam and alluvial soil: how they are exploited, by

30. See maps 1 and 2 on pages vi and vii.

31. George Kwame Grey, interview at Sokpoe, 2 February 2016.

32. It appears the creeks on the Xevie clan farming lands are considered sacred as per the submission of Efoe Kofi Avinyo Atiglo in an interview at Sokpoe-Elavanyo, on 15 February 2016. He says this in respect of the Agasigbe taboo, which he thinks is "the day of a spirit in the creek." However, other narratives place the Agasigbe taboo as a regulation of a chief of the Agave traditional area called Aga. He set that day apart for settling issues brought to his court. Hence, most people would not go to farm or fishing in order to attend the court. In the process, the day became adopted as a traditional taboo. Geoffrey Siame, in a personal phone communication on 25 October 2016, espoused this view and added, "This is why some elders of Sokpoe do not obey Agasigbe so as not to appear subservient to the Agave traditional council."

33. Anthony Kɔwu Yɔhokpɔ, interview at Sogakɔfe, 17 February 2016.

whom, at what time and for what purposes. Apart from clam-picking laws, the eco-ethical regulations and practices relating to water bodies in Sokpoe ecological area are not necessarily motivated by fear of any deities or spirits of the water *per se*. They are rather anthropocentrically based on concerns for social and economic benefits.

For instance, fishing is eco-regulated mostly with inhibitive taboos that ecologically "buy" time for a good yield at harvest. In separate interviews with Enyi Avenɔgbo and Klayi Avi, they each recalled that before 1963, when the Volta flooded and filled the *tɔvuwo* (creeks, rivulets), *tavewo* (ponds) and *tagbawo* (lakes) by July-August, creek fishing would be temporarily banned (inhibited)[34] until the high water levels of the *Amutɔsisi* (Volta) started dropping by the second week in October or early November.[35] The Alɔlɔ (Zoyi) clan of Sokpoe, for example, were often motivated by social altruism to regulate fishing in their creeks. That is to say they would not sell the produce from their creeks and lagoons to any other person(s) to harvest; rather fishing in the creeks would be delayed until March, when the *hlɔ̃tatɔ* (clan head) would lift the ban for the entire clan to go and harvest themselves. In this way they believed the fish developed well, the water volume ebbed very low to enhance their selective fishing methods that aimed at ensuring even children and women had a catch by simply scooping the fish with baskets.[36] Suggestively, for the Alɔlɔ, the moral motivation for complying with the creek-fishing ban after flood season is altruism, a selfless concern for the majority interest; all the clan members must benefit, and do so from the best of yields possible in the season. Compliance may also prevent possible loss of lives during high water levels.

In other situations, fear and avoidance of the troubles associated with legal enforcement of ecological taboos and regulations is both an influence of and action for sustaining eco-justice related to fishing. The high anthropocentric and economic valuing of creeks meant that "ownership of the creeks was jealously prized"[37] and associated with tribal and inter-clan conflicts regarding who could and when to fish in them. Avinyo Atiglo bemoaned how that sometimes the litigation compelled title holders, against their grain, to presell a season's expected catch in a creek or lagoon to fund

---

34. Enyi Avenɔgbo, interview at Sokpoe-Elavanyo, 2 February 2016; Klayi Avi, interview at Sokpoe, 2 February 2016.

35. Sitɔ Loli, interview at Sokpoe, 4 March 2016.

36. Enyi Avenɔgbo, interview at Sokpoe-Elavanyo, 2 February 2016; George Kwame Grey, interview at Sokpoe, 2 February 2016. Usually, since the water volume is already low, they build semicircular mud dams that trap both water and fish between the bank and the wall of the dam; the water is scooped out and the fish fetched with baskets.

37. Moxon, *Volta*, 190.

legal defense of the land and the creek on it, even before harvesting time.[38] Enyi Avenɔgbo was very specific: "As for *Balatsui* lagoon, fishing in it was always sold ahead of time."[39] The sales were arbitrarily estimated from the previous season's catch, with a high risk factor for both seller and buyer, though the latter was often more advantaged.[40] Legal interventions to determine ownership were then ecological actions motivated by the need for eco-justice administered by either traditional authorities or constitutionally established courts. Cunningham and Saigo state that legal actions are "important ways of protecting our environment."[41] In the process peace and harmony in the ecological community concerning the ownership, use of and good economic yields from the water bodies and their alluvial lands could be sustained.

Oyster or clam is the next economic produce of the Volta River in Sokpoe eco-area with ecological importance. It is the only water produce eco-regulated with religious taboos, because it is considered by most primal religionists in the ecological area as a *trɔ̃* (female deity). That oyster could be a deity stems from its peculiar and awesome characteristics. It lives in shallow sandy beds where fishers pick them with toes through torso (body) wriggling and levering them up from the sand with toes.[42] But clams can occupy sandy clay river beds in deep waters where they become relatively big with dark tough shells and meaty bodies. Pickers dive from canoes into one or two fathoms (6–12 feet or 1.8–3.6 meters) of water to pick them.[43] According to Avinyo, some clam pickers claim from experience that in the deep waters oysters can pile themselves up into a mound or pillar and be guarded by a crocodile. The unusual or wondrous scene is *nukpekpe* (fearful encounter), which in the primal belief system can induce death. Therefore, the eco-rule is to pick either none or only one clam, and not more, at a time in such an encounter, or else there is a fear of drowning. Clams are said also to float on the water surface despite their heavy finless shells and they can "swim" rapidly with a frightening sound due to spewing water from their proboscis, particularly when migrating.[44] In addition, I am personally aware, even as reported by Moxon also, that some oyster pickers would lay out clam farms in the shallower waters by staking them "early in the

---

38. Efoe Avinyo Atiglo, interview at Sokpoe-Elavanyo, 15 February 2016.
39. Enyi Avenɔgbo, interview at Sokpoe-Elavanyo, 2 February 2016.
40. Efoe Avinyo Atiglo, interview at Sokpoe-Elavanyo, 15 February 2016.
41. Cunningham and Saigo, *Environmental Science*, 216.
42. Moxon, *Volta*, 191.
43. Moxon, *Volta*, 191.
44. Foe Avinyo Atiglo, interview at Sokpoe-Elavanyo, 15 February 2016.

Religious Eco-Valuing and Ethical Praxis   153

season and left them to fatten by as much as 60 percent" before reharvesting later.[45] The wonder here is that the clams may leave to feed elsewhere but will always return and never depart from the farm until reharvested by the farmer. Neither could other people have courage to pilfer them from the farm, because of fear that "clam is a deity"[46] and may punish them.

The commonest eco-regulation in the clam industry is its annual picking taboo. This is a trimester inhibitive suspension put in place usually by the traditional administrative authority, from November until February. For instance, the Agave traditional area is only about five kilometers south of the Sokpoe traditional area and falls within the ecological boundary of this study. Clam pickers freely operate within and across the eco-area irrespective of belonging to different traditional administrative authorities. Thus, to ensure social harmony between Agave and the other people commonly sharing resources of the river, and to allow time for full clam development in their part of the eco-area before harvest, the Agave Traditional Council would preinform all stakeholders about the ban as well as when it is lifted. More often than not, the majority of the people who believe do comply. I chanced on one such communication of the ban during this research in the area. It was a circulated letter about the 2015–2016 ban addressed to the sister traditional areas—Sokpoe and Ada—and the district law enforcing agencies. The ban began on November 24, 2015 and ended on February 17, 2016. The last two paragraphs read:

> The aim of the ban, to recall, is to help the clam breed to replenish its stock to continue to generate employment for the youth of Agave traditional area and beyond.
> For peace and tranquility during the period of the ban, we are by this letter informing and seeking the cooperation of the security agencies and alerting our neighbor traditional areas to bring the ban to the notice of their subjects for compliance.[47]

The direct ecological import for the clam picking suspension then is to ensure the clam population is sustained by allowing time—the taboo period—for self-replenishment through breeding. It happens that such inhibited times coincide with the reproductive periods of the fish and clams, perhaps because the elders have learnt this from their long close association

---

45. Moxon, *Volta*, 191.
46. Kofi Avinyo Atiglo, interview at Sokpoe-Elavanyo, 15 February 2016.
47. I stumbled on this letter from Andrews Ahado, interview at Sokpoe, 5 February 2016. Andrews is the son of the late *dufia* (paramount chief) of Sokpoe traditional area, Togbe Zogah I. Hence, he has access to such documents coming to the traditional authority.

with aquatic life.[48] Indirectly, the suspension expects possible economic gains in terms of youth employment in the eco-community. In addition, circulating the letter announcing the suspension may be an ecological action in so much as it seeks peace and cooperation as a socioecological requirement to secure the direct ecological expectations of the ban. Here it is respect for traditional authority and expected economic gain rather than fear of the clam as a deity that underlies commitment to the taboo suspending clam picking.

Conversely, the story is different with the terrestrial ecosystem relations. Here the responses of primal religious interviewees about human-land-forest relationships contained two frequently occurring expressions: "*Ekpoa ƒe kɔe*" (It is a dislike of the land deity) and "*Trɔ̃ku awu wo*" (The deity will kill you). They are expressions that at once, from the tone and body language of interviewees, suggest so much sacralization of land and forests that, in their belief, to disobey *kpoa ƒe kɔ* (the forbidden of the land) is to necessarily suffer *trɔ̃ku* (death by the gods). Asked what happens if someone disobeys land and forest taboos, Enyi Avenɔgbo had this to say: "*Eku wu nawo godoo*" (They surely die).[49] And Anthony Yɔhokpɔ was more succinct: "*Etrɔ̃kui wu na wo, menye tɔgbe ŋolĩwo o*" (It is the deity that kills them not ancestral spirits).[50] Herein is an indication that ancestors do not form a strong component like deities in the primal religious worldview and eco-ethical concerns of the Sokpoe-Eʋe. According to Andrews Walls, the difference in emphases of dominating components underscores the difference in cosmologies among Africans.[51]

That the forests and land are considered more sacred than water systems is perhaps consequential to the migration and settlement history of the Sokpoe-Eʋe. Like many African primal communities observed by B. A. Ogot, Sokpoe has migration histories indicating that they were led by hunters.[52] The hunters invariably were also spiritual leaders in as much as they had in custody the *trɔ̃wo* (deities/spiritual powers) believed to have aided in their migratory encounters. They would house such deities/powers in special places on the newfound land, usually in a forest. Then that forest, and hence the land carrying it, becomes designated *trɔ̃ve* (the deity's sacred forest), where rituals are performed by the *trɔ̃nua* (priest of the deity).[53] Yet

---

48. Harry Agbanu, interview at Legon, Accra, 23 November 2015.
49. Enyi Avenɔgbo, interview at Sokpoe-Elavanyo, 2 February 2016.
50. Anthony Kɔwu Yɔhokpɔ, interview at Sogakɔƒe, 17 February 2016.
51. Walls, *Cross-Cultural Process in Christian History*, 124.
52. Ogot, ed., *General History of Africa*, 25.
53. Togbe Dagadu, interview at Sokpoe, 4 March 2016.

the physical image of the deity/power itself, "being a precious and envious religious property at the time,"⁵⁴ may not be "dwelling" there, but kept home. As Geoffrey Siame explained,

> Trɔ̃ve (sacred or deity's forest) is a ritual performing ground, a place to commemorate the deity's deeds and petition it. But the deity itself remains home. Only during purification ritual is it brought out, clad in white, carried into the forest for the purpose. It returns home thereafter.⁵⁵

He implies that a sacred forest is a ground for petition prayer, ritual sacrifices of appreciation, renewal of faith and allegiance to the clan deity and commemoration of its past providence. Though the physical image of the clan deity does not dwell in the forest, and hence the land, it is believed its spirit does, for which reason it is fearful. Agbanu notes a similar belief among the Mafi-Eʋe.⁵⁶ Perhaps in the people's mind, the thicker and larger the forest the more sacred it is, the more powerful the deity and so fearful are its taboos. Geoffrey Siame did not think that our forebears necessarily set forest taboos as means of sustainable care, at least not consciously or directly. They only knew that a forest, like a mountain, tends to be "*nuvɔvɔ̃ le eɖokui si*" (fearful by itself or naturally numinous) and attracts religious attention. In their view, "the thicker the forest the more numinous and religiously respectable or fearful the deity in it and its taboos are perceived."⁵⁷

All the same, the taboos "demanded by the deities"⁵⁸ and enforced or supervised by owners of the forests—the clan cult leaders—do maintain harmonious relations between the deities, the forests and the people. This perhaps explains why *Balave*, the only non-sacralized forest in the area, suffered complete destruction, especially with the disregard of its taboos, led by Amega Gbadago, a Christian, according to Edward Kattah.⁵⁹ As Avinyo Atiglo explained, "the major difference between forests designated sacred and those not, is the sustained actively functional taboos associated with the former."⁶⁰ Some of the religious taboos of sacred forests are listed in table 6.2.

---

54. Geoffrey Siame, interview at Sogakɔfe, 17 February 2016.
55. Geoffrey Siame, interview at Sogakɔfe, 17 February 2016.
56. Harry Agbanu, interview at Legon, Accra, 23 November 2015.
57. Geoffrey Siame, interview at Sogakɔfe, 17 February 2016.
58. Togbe Dagadu, interview at Sokpoe, 4 March 2016.
59. Edward Kattah, interview at Sokpoe, 11 March 2016.
60. Kofi Avinyo Atiglo, interview at Sokpoe-Elavanyo, 15 February 2016.

Like the primal religionists, the Sokpoe-Eʋe Christians and Muslims also answered the same questions to show their translation of eco-values into eco-ethical actions to care for the cherished riverine ecosystem. It was obvious from their responses that there are no eco-ethics or norms (practical regulations) and rituals to guide ecological actions toward creation care that could be described distinctively as Christian or Islamic. They all knew and could speak of only the primal religious eco-ethics and praxis that have been in the ecological area to date discussed above. The study, therefore, sought further to understand how Christians and Muslims perceive and engage with such primal religious ecological ethics and praxis.

Among the responses typical of most of the Christian participants was that of Isaac Avi of the Church of Pentecost (COP). For him the ecological taboos are not evil for the Christian; they are institutions that reveal the mind of God about how we should relate with and maximize our use of the water and land resources sustainably. Pertaining to water taboos, for instance, he says:

> As a Christian I see nothing wrong with the water taboos. However, it is improper to have the taboos ascribed to *trɔ̃wo* (local deities). The Christian must understand that naturally fish must be well developed before being harvested. The regulations are of God. All humans, both *trɔ̃subɔlawo* (traditionalists) and *Kristotɔwo* (Christians) need to recognize the taboos as God's provision implanted in our minds; they are not rules made by humans who worship deities.[61]

---

61. Isaac Avi, interview at Sokpoe, 2 February 2016. See appendix, A9, for transcript.

Table 6.2: Sacred Forests and Associated Taboos in Sokpoe

Name of Forest	Location	Religious Taboo	Primal Religious Reason
Alɔlɔdzove and Dzixeve[62]	Sokpoe-Bodzodjfe and Sokpoe-Votenu, respectively	No entering on *Agasigbe*.	The resting day of the land and forest deities—"Ebo" and "Alɔlɔdzo." It is the day for *nuxexe* (ritualistic sacrifices).
		No entry for women, especially if in menses.	It is impurity before the deities and desecrates the forest.
		May harvest food/fruits only. No harvesting of wood—dry or fresh—for fuel or building.	Vegetation removal is nudity of the deities. They do not permit forest wood for fueling domestic fire.
		No clearing nor weeding of forest	Vegetation removal is nudity of the deities.
Kɔtive	Sokpoe dume	Inside the forest don't respond vocally when called. Just walk to the caller.	It is unnecessary noise; it disturbs the tranquility for relaxation of the deity.
		Leave a third of harvested sweet berries under baobab tree (*Adansonia digitata*).	Failure incurs dwarfs' fury to mysteriously make you lose the way out of the forest.
		No defecation in forest.[63]	It messes room of dwarfs/gods
		No entering on *Agasigbe*.	The resting day of the land and forest deities. It is the day for *nuxexe* (ritualistic sacrifices).

---

62. Enyi Avenɔgbo, interview at Sokpoe-Elavanyo, 2 February 2016.
63. George Kwame Grey, interview at Sokpoe, 2 February 2016.

Name of Forest	Location	Religious Taboo	Primal Religious Reason
Nyaɖeŋgɔve[64]	Sokpoe-Kutudɔkɔfe	No entering on *Agasigbe*.	The resting day of the land and forest deities. It is the day for *nuxexe* (ritualistic sacrifices).
		No entering if indulge in sexual intercourse within twenty-four hours.	
		No harvesting of firewood or building rafters.	It makes forest deity naked or unclothed.
		May cut wood for building but only after special ritualistic prayer by and supervision of the priest.[65]	
Mɔkɔdzɛve	Sokpoe-Mɔkɔdzɛ	Shirt, shoes and hats must not enter forest (enter with bare chest and feet).	Not to obey is a disgusting show of haughtiness to the forest deity.
		No entering on *Agasigbe*.	The resting day of the land and forest deities. It is the day for *nuxexe* (ritualistic sacrifices).

Isaac Avi, like others, understands that the water taboos in the Sokpoe ecological area are theistic religious instruments to help discipline ourselves against interfering with God's natural law or time line for fish to develop before being made available for human consumption. In his expectation, Christians should already know that God is the creator and provider of all human needs, including the water and fish. As such they cannot excuse themselves by being ignorant of this natural order of God, which should intuitively prompt us to keep the water bodies undisturbed from time to time for their maximum output to benefit us. He sounds like Saadia Khawar Khan Chishti, who argues from an Islamic worldview that humankind has *fitra*, an instinctive predisposition for creation care that need not be instilled

---

64. Kofi Avinyo Atiglo, interview at Sokpoe-Elavanyo, 15 February 2016; Togbe Dagadu, interview at Sokpoe, 4 March 2016; Samuel Agboklu, interview at Sokpoe, 2 March 2016.

65. Kofi Avinyo Atiglo, interview at Sokpoe-Elavanyo, 15 February 2016.

but only awakened by Islamic ecology from the *Sharī'a*.⁶⁶ Isaac Avi similarly is disgusted by ascribing to Earth deities of primal religion what God originated and planted instinctively in us.

The main argument of Christians like Isaac Avi is that the setting and obeying of the taboos should be in honor of the creator and provider, God. They seem to advocate for a Christian theocentric eco-valuing and praxis rather than shrouding them in primal religious myth. With this understanding and expectation most of them tend to practically devalue the taboos, yet they do not actively or always disobey them. A nonagenarian and former presbyter of Presbyterian Church of Ghana (PCG), Mary Awusi Blasu, is not happy with the primal religious fears associated with the taboos, but cannot challenge an old ancestral institution that was before her birth. As she put it:

> *Medze ŋunye ya o gake eya wɔm wo nɔ hafi va dzim. Nye mateŋu agbe nu le egbɔ o, togbɔ be mènye Kristotɔ hâ.* (I do not like it [the taboo], but it has been long there in practice before I was born. I cannot refuse to recognize it, though I am a Christian).⁶⁷

In other words, she does not value nor fear the taboos yet will not intentionally, on grounds of being a Christian, flout them either.⁶⁸

But there were other Christian responses, like that of Winner Eworyi, who will not enter nor harvest firewood from a *trɔ̃ve* (sacred) forest for fear of the deity that resides there. She acknowledges that

> God is powerful, but *abosam* (Satan) also has its power. *Trɔ̃subɔlawo* (traditionalists) perform religious rites in the *trɔ̃ve* (sacred forest), because the deity's power is there. I so believe even as a Christian. I shall never contend them and enter the sacred forest, for fear of the *trɔ̃* (deity).⁶⁹

Miss Eworyi shall inferably obey the primal religious taboo that forbids women from entering let alone harvesting firewood from sacred forests primarily, because of fear of some possible punishment by the forest deity; at least, not due to any implicit ecological importance of the taboo or for the sake of honoring God. On his part, Daniel Agbota represents yet a third category of Christian responses. He does not think the indigenous religious taboos entail any ecological significance or fearful respect for forest/land

---

66. Chishti, "*Fitra*," 67.
67. Mary Awusi Blasu, interview at Sokpoe-Elavanyo, 1 February 2016.
68. Mary Awusi Blasu, interview at Sokpoe-Elavanyo, 1 February 2016.
69. Winner Eworyi, interview at Sokpoe, 3 February 2016. See appendix, A10, for transcript.

deities, because Christian teachings have demystified the fears associated with the forests. As he expressed it,

> Now Christian faith *ɖe vɔvɔ̃ ɖa* (has removed the fear) around sacred forests rendering the rites performed in them useless. In fact, some of us Christian youngsters wish that all the sacred forests are cleared for building projects. I have already started; I bought part of *Kɔtive* for my building project.[70]

Daniel Agbota does not only advocate for all primal religious forest/land taboos to be proscribed to free the forested lands for physical developmental purposes, he has himself initiated the move and bought part of *Kɔtive*. My personal inspection after listening to him revealed how this forest (*Kɔtive*) has indeed reduced drastically in size from what I knew of it from my basic school days in the early 1960s, suggesting a high rate of encroachment. Ben-Willie Kweku Golo, at a Christian-Muslim interfaith lecture, argued from research that by disenchanting the natural world, and especially when an expected eco-deity's retribution against violation fails, Christians and Muslims disregard and defy the eco-taboos.[71]

Indeed, a similar attitude was observed among the Muslim participants. In separate interviews some of them remembered, for instance, that before the Akosombo dam-caused deluge of 1963, *Avadzakɛ* and *Aɖɔdzi* were the main and sacralized creeks or tributaries at the Eastern bank of the Amu (Volta) River. They recollected also forests around these water bodies as well as eco-regulatory systems enforced by the indigenous Eʋe amongst whom they lived. But their responses indicated that they disregarded such eco-regulations as satanic concepts and practices of *dutɔwo* (indigenes). Zongo *sarachi* Abdullah Muhammad, for instance, knew that at Sogakɔfe before the 1963 deluge, "*Wome klɔa agbelimakusi le Amu tɔsisi me o*" (It was forbidden to wash a cassava dough carrier basket in the river Volta).[72] Yet when asked: "What is your comment on the primal religious water regulations and rituals as a Muslim?," he answered:

> Taboos and rituals are for *dutɔwo* (the indigenous Eʋe) landlords. They are not good for Muslims. Muslims observe no such *dekɔnuwo* (cultural rituals, rules), in order not to stray. We obey only that which is of and from God's word. If *dekɔnutɔwo* (cultural or primal religious persons) tell me not to wash cassava

70. Daniel Agbota, interview at Sokpoe, 5 February 2016. See appendix, A16, for transcript.

71. Golo, "Environment and Spirituality."

72. Abdullah Muhammad (zongo *sarachi*), interview at Sogakɔfe, 5 April 2016. See appendix, A12, for transcript.

dough basket in the river I shall not obey. As an example, because only Qur'an forbids pork, we do not eat it.⁷³

Answering the same question in another interview, an Eʋe, Memuna Kudi, who converted to Islam, believes, with her primal background, the reality of the religious ecological taboos and rites. But now as a Muslim she does not observe rules that Islam forbids. She claimed that

> Muslimtɔwo ya la kɔ aɖeke mele mía ŋu o. Eyata nye ya mateŋu atsɔ ze yibɔ ayi kutsi eye naneke mawɔm o. (Muslims have no taboos or rituals to observe. So, I can fetch water with soot-tainted pot from the river without suffering any danger).⁷⁴

She implies that as a Muslim her faith expunges the existence of water spiritual forces or deities, let alone being afraid of their punishment for flouting their taboos. Similarly, Ademu Ibrahim, the Zamarama (Nigerian) *sarachi* of Sogakɔfe zongo, born to an Aŋlɔ-Eʋe woman, remembered forests around *Avadzakɛ* and *Aɖɔdzi* creeks.⁷⁵ But he did not know any primal religious eco-ethical regulations associated with them, nor did he think any such taboos, if there were, could negatively affect him as a Muslim if and when flouted. His reason was that as long as he did not believe in the deities, flouting taboos associated with them would not affect him.

Apart from disenchanting nature, the Muslim participants in the study seemed not to be aware of Islamic ecology and held a strong anti-primal religious disposition that did not motivate them for Earth-keeping. Ademu Ibrahim, like Hajia Fatti Sanni, was highly convinced that the Qur'an says nothing about such forest laws; rather God as creator has gifted forests for our use without any restrictions. For him and Hajia Sanni, to prohibit forest use with primal religious taboos is to deprive people of God's gift; it is "not what God told us," and hence it is sinful. "No Muslim," Ademu asserted, "will observe such taboos unless it can be found in Qur'an."⁷⁶ Obviously he and Hajia Sanni had no idea of keeping sacred forests, called *harim* zones or green belts, in *sharī'a* as a legal Islamic means of environmental conservation praxis. Llewellyn states that according to Islamic law every settlement (*'amir*) should have a surrounding *harim* resembling a green belt with the right to acquire or develop it restricted.⁷⁷ The high anti-primal

73. Abdullah Muhammad (zongo *sarachi*), interview at Sogakɔfe, 5 April 2016.
74. Memuna Kudi, inerview at Sogakɔfe, 13 April 2016.
75. Ademu Ibrahim (Zamarama *sarachi*), interview at Sogakɔfe, 5 April 2016.
76. Ademu Ibrahim (Zamarama *sarachi*), interview at Sogakɔfe, 5 April 2016; Hajia Fatti Sanni, intrview at Sogakɔfe, 14 April 2016.
77. Llewellyn, "Basis for a Discipline of Islamic Environmental Law," 210.

religious feeling of these participants was exemplified more particularly in the unequivocal submissions of Alhaji Hama. He feared that the *agasigbe* taboo, which sets one day in a five-day week aside, like a Christian Sabbath, for not farming was and still is a religious practice that may stray a Muslim from submitting to only Allah as required by the Qur'an. He contended that *agasigbe* is essentially a primal religious taboo, and hence satanic. To him it contradicts Islam as it deprives the Muslim from using the free or unrestricted hours given by Allah at will to work and glorify him. Therefore, he suggested, "if there is any good in this taboo, and for which even Muslims must obey, then it should be put forward purely as an administrative instrument or measure of the chief, and not by the *trɔ̃nuɔ* (priest of the deity)." He insisted that if the chief also passes any environmental law through the supervision of primal religionists or Christian religious leaders or vice versa, Muslims will not obey.[78]

Practical Re-Evaluation of the Primal, Christian and Islamic Religious Eco-Ethics

Rationally, the retrieved primal religious taboos and undergirding reasons suggest that the taboos can be both eco-regulation principles and creation care actions at the same time. Although in most cases shrouded in religious myths, yet they have plausible and possible eco-care implications. Some of the taboos tend to undergird ethics of eco-conservation and eco-restoration while the others promote eco-preservation, eco-moral transformation and eco-justice. For instance, *Agasigbe* is a sacred day taboo believed to be demanded by the deities. It falls on every fifth market day on the local calendar where a week has five market days. Ecologically, *Agasigbe* perhaps is an unplanned primal religious practice of conservation ecology[79] that ensures health replenishment or self-renewal of the ecosystem. It involves "stopping the abuse" by continuous extraction from the ecosystem, at least once a week, and allows for land's self-replenishment to support vegetation regrowth.[80]

Another ecological rule that also enables nondisturbance or "resting" for the ecosystem is *tɔsisisewo* (fishing regulations), such as *tɔve kple*

---

78. Alhaji Hama, interview at Dabala, 25 May 2016.

79. Cunningham and Saigo, *Environmental Science*, 116, explain that "Although there are many similarities between restoration and conservation, stewardship or management the former often entails more direct intervention to achieve a predetermined end than do these other fields."

80. Nebel and Wright, *Environmental Science*, 46.

tame sewo (creek and lagoon rules) as well as *afɔlĩ ɖeɖesewo* (clam-picking taboos). As noted earlier, they are more of inhibition (delay/suspension) than prohibition (stopping) regulations. For instance, fishing in creeks and lagoons are annual and last for a brief period of about three months, when flood water fills the creeks. Hence *tɔvesisise* is not to stop a once-a-year opportunity; it simply delays in order to maximize output/benefit. For the suspension of activity leaves an undisturbed condition in the creeks, which encourages fish growth, maturity and multiplication to some expected individual size and population level before harvest.[81] The same understanding, aim and effect go with *afɔlĩ ɖeɖese*, though the water system in this case is perennial.

The regulations for creek-fishing during the short periods of annual flood and clam-picking in the river then may be traditional versions of "re-creation" as a specific form of restoration ecology.[82] For in effect these regulations help to virtually recreate temporal fish and clam "ponds" in the creeks and the river, respectively, after the previous year's good harvest to ensure "maximum sustainable yield."[83]

Conversely, taboos connected with sacralized forests are prohibitive and tend to promote preservation rather than either conservation or restoration. It can be deduced that they have an objective to ensure continuity regardless of potential for utility of the species and the entire forest ecosystem.[84] They generally insist, as an example, that wood from a sacred forest must not provide domestic fuel or building and constructional material.

The third category of primal eco-ethical praxis discovered in the study is the use of rituals to correct or offset the effects of flouting ecological taboos excessively. It appears there is an indirect effect by which the rituals may prime the community for moral transformation with eco-character education and development. This is the case for taboos considered as *busu* (unpardonable ecological crimes), such as having sexual intercourse in the bush. These offenses are generally believed to result in drought and famine as manifestations of divine wrath (of deities/God) against not only offenders, but the entire ecological community. Yet it appears that besides averting or offsetting the drought and famine, the experiences of costs involved, suffering of the sacrificial animals, the bashfulness of unclothed intercessors and public education for self-controlled attitudes by the traditional

---

81. Enyi Avenɔgbo, interview at Sokpoe-Elavanyo, 2 February 2016; Kwame Grey, interview at Sokpoe, 2 February 2016; Klayi Avi, interview at Sokpoe, 2 February 2016.

82. Cunningham and Saigo, *Environmental Science*, 116.

83. Nebel and Wright, *Environmental Science*, 497.

84. Nebel and Wright, *Environmental Science*, 496.

authority during the rituals may impact offenders or/and the entire community with moral remorse. Such religiously influenced remorse may help offenders and the community at large to develop ecological virtues of self-discipline, especially in sexuality and ecological repentance from wanton destruction of ecosystem life. Finally, legal interventions are also ecological actions of enforcing eco-justice regarding ownership, timing and method of fishing in creeks instead of the otherwise annual disputes and litigations. Environmental justice combines civil rights with environmental protection to demand a safe, healthy, life-giving environment for everyone.[85]

In the case of Christians, there seem to be three analyzable categories of responses to ecological relationships. The first group of respondents I call the "indigenized or acculturated Christians." They rightly maintain and are influenced by their primal religious cosmology as an African reality. For them, both God and Satan are powerful spiritual entities that influence the ecosystem in different ways and for different and opposite purposes. However, Satan, associated with primal religion, is more proactive directly, quickly and intensively in dealing with violations of eco-ethical rules than the Christian God. They, therefore, tend to fear Satan and his instructions such as the primal religious taboos and rituals. So, despite their Christian faith in God as Almighty and Creator of all things, they also seriously fear forest and Earth deities as powerful agents of Satan. They strictly respect the associated primal religious (or what they see as satanic) forest taboos for fear of and to avoid punishment by the deities. This attitude results from Western missionary evangelization.[86]

The second group are the "passive or suspended Christians," who appear undecided for or against primal religious eco-ethics and praxis, as it were, holding back active faith. They appreciate ecological goodness in the "old ancestrally instituted" ecological taboos except for their ascription to "Satan's" agencies, the land and forest deities. To them this denies God his due glory as not only the creator and owner, but more so the one who initiates and instinctively inspires us to naturally appreciate the need for creation care. In their view it is theologically sinful to deny God this glory; yet they will not challenge primal religious taboos. Rather, they avoid any relations with such primal religionists' sacralized ecosystem places, and hence any temptations to obey the taboos. But their choice of passivity is in effect a positive ecological action indirectly, for their noninterference with taboos eventually leaves the ecosystem anthropologically undisturbed. Thus, as it

---

85. Cunningham and Saigo, *Environmental Science*, 44.

86. Meyer, *Translating the Devil*, xvii, concludes among the Peki-Eʋe that demonisation of Eʋe primal religion did not take away converts' fear of the local deities and spirits in their practical Christian lives.

seems from their attitudes and behaviors, both the "acculturated" and "passive" Christian respondents maintain some level of enchantment of nature indirectly, which may result in eco-preservation and eco-conservation implicit in the primal religious taboos.

The third group, the "deculturated or Western-influenced Christians," however, may pose danger to the forests/land, considering their Christian disenchantment of nature. For them Christianity has demystified the fears of forest deities and taboos—a system that only unnecessarily hinders physical and agricultural development in their mind—and spells freedom for all forested lands to be cleared for developmental needs of humans. As one of them asked, "What is a taboo when humans are hungry?" and a second declared, "Left to us, the Christian youth, all sacred forests must be cleared for our building projects." Both their Christian understanding and subsequent exploitative ecological attitude reflect a Western Christian "dominion" theology and creation doctrine. This was theology backed with an Enlightenment view of all things as lifeless (and spiritless) commodities to be understood scientifically and to be used mainly for human ends.[87] Emmanuel Adow Obeng observes that though this teaching of the church "was wrong, narrow-minded and destructive," it influenced uncontrolled subjection of the Earth to manipulations to serve human needs.[88] Worst of all, it was void of primal spirituality—a situation Gillian Bediako describes as "erroneous and ignorant theology."[89] That the negative ecological effect of this Christian doctrine descended to Africa through missionary influence may be implied from missionary Craig Sorely's experiences.[90] Harvey Sindima argues that it is the mechanistic or Enlightenment worldview (and theology) imported to Africa by the West that has been largely responsible for many eco-crises faced by Africa[91] as part of the tropical regions where most of the deforestation has been taking place since the twentieth century.[92]

It is not difficult, then, to infer that the "deculturated Christians" in this study still maintain the Western Christian missionaries' teaching void of primal spirituality. They tend to disenchant nature and anthropocentrically value the land and forests as to meet only agricultural and infrastructural development needs of humanity. The serious ecological implication of their

---

87. Sindima, "Community of Life," 137–47.

88. Obeng, "Healing the Groaning Creation in Africa," in Getui and Obeng, eds., *Theology of Reconstruction*, 10.

89. G. Bediako, "Primal Religion and Christian Faith," 14.

90. Craig, "Christ, Creation, Stewardship and Missions," 137.

91. Sindima, "Community of Life," 137–47.

92. Houghton, *Global Warming*, cited by Osafo, "Reducing Emissions from Tropical Forest Deforestation," 64.

position is that by eroding the fears associated with sacred ecosystem places, their type of Christianity may negatively impact any implicit eco-caring effects of the traditional taboos. Ernestina Afriyie opined that traditionally Africans are likely to treat the environment with little or no respect when their belief in the relationship of the deities and ancestors with nature is undermined.[93]

In summary, the African perception of nature is generally theistic, which, when properly interpreted by the gospel and converted to a theocentric view, may be a sufficiently fundamental motivation for African Christians to naturally reduce deforestation just from a religious awe of God.[94] In other words, I presume that a new group, the "culture-converted Christians," who, using Kwame Bediako's words, allow "Scripture as hermeneutic" for ecological issues, are likely to approach ecology with Christian theocentric worldviews, eco-ethics and praxis. They are more likely to appreciate and respect not only the positive aspects of primal religious taboos when "refracted through the prism of the Gospel," but also to attribute them ultimately to the sovereign God of creation. Admittedly, it will, not be an easy project as reasoned from most of the responses, because with ecological issues the Christian God is not as "fearful as local deities."[95]

Like the Christians, it is difficult to determine any distinctively Islamic motivation for and praxis of eco-ethics from the responses of Muslims. The seemingly lack of practical Islamic ecological values, ethics and norms may be due partly to the observation that though the Sokpoe-Muslim's life and living is highly determined by the teachings of Qur'an, they, like "the majority of Muslims in the Islamic world," are unaware of the "powerful and persuasive spiritual teachings of Islam about the natural world and the relations of human beings to it."[96] Idrisu Ibrahim, son of the Zamarama *sarachi* of Sogakɔfe zongo, laments how that imams do not teach "these things; they have only one message instead of addressing pertinent issues in our lives."[97] Idrisu was virtually echoing the same feelings of Seyyed Hossein Nasr, who, writing on "Islam and the Environmental Crisis," decried that even the *ulamă* (traditional guardians of Islamic knowledge in its various dimensions) do not teach or preach the Islamic views on the environment.[98] And

---

93. Ernestina Afriyie, personal comment based on field experience as research fellow, cited in Blasu, "Compensated Reduction," 24.

94. Blasu, "Compensated Reduction," 24.

95. Martin Doade, interview at Sokpoe, 3 February 2016; Edward Kattah, interview at Sokpoe, 11 March 2016; Stella Xɔmeku, interview at Sokpoe, 29 February 2016.

96. Nasr, "Islam, the Contemporary Islamic World," 85.

97. Idrisu Ibrahim, interview at Sogakɔfe, 23 April 2016.

98. Nasr, "Islam, the Contemporary Islamic World," 87.

maybe the imams do not address environmental issues because generally the exceedingly rich contributions that Islamic law and ethics have to offer in addressing environmental concerns in the Islamic world as a whole remain largely unarticulated (not promoted) and unrealized.[99] Chief Imam Mahmud Abu Bakr of Sogakɔfe zongo admitted that it is not everything that "I know because of the level of my education."[100]

Yet Islamic dogmatism seems a great challenge in their religious motivation (or rather demotivation) for and praxis of ecological ethics. Anything not attributable to Qur'an, and for that matter Allah, is devilish and an anathema for their religiocultural self-understanding as Muslims in the Sokpoe ecological area. Alhaji Hama insisted that as long as an ecological regulation is imposed with a primal or Christian religious fervor, the Muslim will simply not regard it.[101] Consequently, as it seems, their strong anti-primal-religious attitude made it hard for them to perceive any affinities between the primal ecological ethics and praxis and those possibly in Islam. In addition, perhaps the meaning of the word "zongo" as a place for non-domiciled but "awaiting and passer-by strangers"[102] has a significant psychological effect of not being motivated to be morally responsible for the land that they consider not theirs but for *dutɔwo* (indigenes). This "zongo mentality" may not make Muslims in zongo "rooted"[103] enough in the ecological community in which they sojourn to exhibit *fitra* (natural impulse) in caring for creation.[104]

A hopeful deduction, however, is that theoretically all the Muslim participants in the study will obey eco-ethical rules and regulations if only they are void of non-Islamic religious tones—primal or Christian—in order not to compromise their Islamic faith. Once an ecological regulation can be proven to be sourced from the Qur'an there is high probability they will comply. Similarly, if even not from Qur'an, but known emphatically not to be from primal religion, but shown to be of general sociological value and importance to the eco-community, the probability is still high that the Sokpoe-Mulsim will comply with ecological regulations. Such regulations may only follow an Islamic ethical principle of "universal and individual

---

99. Llewellyn, "Basis for a Discipline of Islamic Environmental Law," 186.
100. Imam Mahmud Abu Bakar, interview at Sogakɔfe, 5 April 2016.
101. Alhaji Hama, interview at Dabala, 25 May 2016.
102. Abdullah Muhammad (zongo *sarachi*), interview at Sogakɔfe, 5 April 2016.
103. Bookless, *Planetwise*, 50.
104. Chishti, "*Fitra*," 67.

welfare."[105] The chief Imam Mahmud Abu Bakar,[106] Zamarama *sarachi* Ademu Ibrahim[107] and Madame Memuna Kudi[108] are of this opinion. In separate interviews, they realized in the end the possible and plausible ecological implications of the river and forest taboos, especially their valuable involvement in rain formation and hence agricultural importance. This was when in ascertaining the consistency of their ecological views I reminded them of their answers to earlier questions. For instance, to the question, "What will happen if a forest is not regulated as *dutɔwo* [the indigenous Eʋe] do, and everyone freely cuts trees from that forest?," Imam Mahmud Abu Bakr responded, "*Aveɛ gbɔna tsɔtsrɔ̃ ge, eye tsidzadza nu atsi. Evɔ míawoe le tɔ kple ave ŋuti hele wo zam na agbledede kple lã ɖeɖe. Medze be míawɔe be woava tsrɔ̃ o*" (The forest will die down and there will be no rains. Since we live near the forests and rivers and use them for farming and fishing, we must not destroy them). Then I reminded him: "But you told me earlier that forest taboos have no good for Muslims, because they are unnecessary and evil prohibitions of *dutɔwo*." He responded with a smile: "*Azɔ meva kpɔ be numa wɔm wo le la eleme; Azɔ mese egɔme nusi ta wode se mawo ɖo*" (Now I see that what they are doing is right; now I know why the forest taboos are put in place).

They then suggested that a way to get Sokpoe-Muslims to appreciate ecological regulations, even if not from Qur'an, is to plainly explain their nature and good rather than enshroud them mystically as primal religious taboos. Perhaps a significant aspect of such an Islamic ecology curriculum needs to emphasize the sacralization of creation as a religious view not limited to only primal religion. Seyyed Hossein Nasr suggests "the solution to the [environmental] crisis requires the most urgent action, the turning to a sacralized vision of nature, as well as performing concrete actions on the earthly plane."[109] Perhaps the story may also be different if they have a little more education on what the Qur'an says about creation and the Muslim's relationship with it, since only the Qur'an determines their ethics, attitudes and behaviors. Moreover, as Saadia Khawar Khan Chishti argues, Muslims have *fitra*, the natural instinct for creation care that need only be awakened by Islamic ecology from the *Sharī'a*.[110]

---

105. Llewellyn, "Basis for a Discipline of Islamic Environmental Law," 195.
106. Imam Abu Bakar, interview at Sogakɔfe, 5 May 2016.
107. Adamu Ibrahim, interview at Sogakɔfe, 5 April 2016.
108. Memuna Kudi, interview at Sogakɔfe, 13 April 2016.
109. Nasr, "Islam, the Contemporary Islamic World," 99.
110. Chishti, "*Fitra*," 67.

It is noteworthy that the story of eco-praxis in Sokpoe does not end with only eco-ethics; there is also ritualistic priming for eco-care, particularly in birthing and funerary rites.

CHAPTER 7

Religious Birthing Rites and Ecological Relations

The Religious Birthing Rites of the Sokpoe-Eʋe

IN ADDITION TO THE religious eco-ethical actions or practices of the Sokpoe-Eʋe toward creation care that I investigated and reported in the previous chapter, I observed also and was intrigued with their performance of birthing and funerary rites. In my opinion, and for the study of African theocology, these birthing and funerary rites are religious eco-anthropological rites; that is, anthropological observances with significant ecological implications. In this chapter, I discuss the potential of religious birthing rites to influence a sense of connection to the land and people, and thus prime babies (initiates) to develop morally sustainable ecological relationships with and in the "gecosphere."

I sourced the evidence for this discussion by investigating the primal, Christian and Islamic religious symbols for inducing creation care as enacted in the birthing rites, and how emotionally powerful they are in promoting particular ecological moral codes. To this end the respondents' practical knowledge undergirding rational and hence ecological import of the birthing rites were interrogated.

The varied responses analyzed suggest that attitudes toward the rites, procedural details and emphases on types and number of rituals involved in each rite differ slightly throughout the ecological area and among the various religious traditions. For instance, both the primal religionists and Christians consider birthing rites as *dekɔnu* (cultural), something characteristic of and hence uniquely identifiable with the eco-cultural community of the Sokpoe. As a Church of Pentecost (COP) elder, James Cudjoe strongly argues:

> Performing a cultural rite has nothing to do with being *Kristotɔ* (a Christian) or *trɔ̃subɔla* (worshipper of deities). Things that have been laid down by ancestors to identify us as the Sokpoe-Eʋe remain same to date and bind us all irrespective of religious persuasion.[1]

In other words, Cudjoe, like other Christian participants, suggests that "Christian" birthing rites need to follow the same pattern of those for the primal religion; they are only enacted with different forms of liturgical symbols to convey the same meanings. Hence, the birthing rites of Christians are basically adaptations of the primal religious practices with no distinctive Christian outdooring rites observed in the study. Muslims, on the contrary, regard the rites performed in the primal and Christian traditions as devilish.[2] Yet they virtually do similar things with different symbolisms to suggest that the basic undergirding principles, beliefs, fears and expectations are similar, to a large extent, in all the religious traditions. Essentially the religious birthing rites are derived from their religious cosmologies (mental pictures of *xexeme* or gecosphere) and subsequent ecological cultures (practical daily relational experiences with and in the ecosystem). Knowledge of the ecological implications of these rites can contribute to our attitudinal change both in respecting their eco-significance and performing them with hope of impacting ritualistic priming for sustainable ecological relations.

Generally, the eco-oriented religious birthing rites identified are *fukatsotso* (pregnancy liberation), *amenɔɖiɖi* (placenta burial), *viɖeɖeɖego* (baby outdooring) and *vewɔwɔ* (winning accordance rite). However, in this chapter I will present only the data on *viɖeɖeɖego* (baby outdooring) to illustrate how the birthing rites may prime for harmonious eco-relations. Moreover, *viɖeɖeɖego* seems to be both a summary and culmination of the ecological import—the enactments of priming for eco-relations—beginning from *fukatsotso* and *amenɔɖiɖi*.

---

1. James Cudjoe, interview at Sokpoe, 26 June 2016. See appendix, A12, for transcript.

2. Abdullah Muhammad (zongo *sarachi*), interview at Sogakɔfe, 5 April 2016.

Vidededego as Primal, Christian and Islamic Religious Priming for Creation Care

For analytic purposes I built a general and logical outline of the liturgy or procedure for primal religious outdooring rite from the various responses collated.

1. Mother and child remain indoors from day one up to day seven postpartum, when the umbilical cord falls off.[3]

2. The fallen umbilical cord is buried by the child's parents, usually behind the local bath place and a tree seedling, such as coconut, nursed or planted on it by its father.[4]

3. On average the ceremony begins very early morning on day seven after birth, by 6:00 a.m. or with the early rising rays of the sun.[5]

4. The officiator, necessarily an elderly man from the child's paternal family, opens program with prayer.[6]

5. The elderly officiator brings out the child from the room, and in soliciting all best omen *in xexeme* (geocosphere) lifts it up towards the rising sun in the East, saying, "Welcome into light; ours is the East." Then to the West, saying, "The sun sets here, the place for our enemies."[7]

6. He turns the baby to the witnessing congregation and formally introduces it for all creation to see aright, saying, "We begat this child in peace. Now that the sun shines its bright rays on it all eyes can behold and know that a new person has joined us." Then he curses whoever sees the child with evil eyes "to go before [the child] goes."[8]

---

3. Francis Hordo, interview at Sokpoe, 11 February 2016.

4. Geoffrey Siame, interview at Sogakɔfe, 17 February 2016.

5. Hordo, interview at Sokpoe, 11 February 2016.

6. Yɔhokpɔ, interview at Sogakɔfe, 17 February 2016.

7. Klayi Avi, interview at Sokpoe, 2 February 2016; Gladys Ahado, interview at Sokpoe, 26 June 2016. She is a Christian but talking with a primal worldview. Her church (COP) does not follow this procedure in outdooring, though. Contrarily, while Klayi Avi and Gladys Ahado consider East as the rising light for life of the baby and West as the setting sun of death for baby's enemy, Kɔwu Yɔhokpɔ and Avinyo Atiglo interpret East as rising rays of heat for the enemy and setting rays with coolness for the baby. Avinyo Atiglo, for instance, gives the alternative opening prayer of the Xevie clan as follows: "To the evil one, to the evil one, to the evil one; ours is the cool evening, not just one but all evenings. Some people cannot stand seeing new babies, but mine shall be seen because anyone who sees with evil eyes shall go ahead of my child."

8. Atiglo, interview at Sokpoe-Elavanyo, 15 February 2016; Francis Hordo, interview at Sokpoe, 11 February 2016.

7. The child lays unclothed on bare ground and urinates onto the ground, or cool water in calabash is sprinkled from the rooftop down the eaves onto the child and it cries out for help.⁹

8. A female from the maternal family picks up and presents the crying child to its mother as a baby lost but found, comforted and wrapped up before being laid on a reed mat on the ground.¹⁰

9. The officiator pours libation with gin (hard liquor) to the deities and ancestors and solicits their care and protection for the child. Evil forces are cursed so as to ward them off. The child is blessed by pronouncing all good required for success and admonished to live a good life.¹¹

10. The officiator presents *dzatsi* (unroasted cornmeal mixed with fresh water) to the ancestors in prayer, saying, "You cared and sent this child to join the family; continue to care for and bless it and the entire family."¹²

11. The officiator drops with a finger the remaining *dzatsi* in the calabash onto the tongue of the child and besmears its toes also with it, saying, "Today, you also begin to take in *li* (literally, millet, but stands for grains) that we eat here. Work up the soil so it can yield *li* for you; avoid laziness so as not to bring disgrace to our family."¹³ At this juncture some clans will formally welcome the child, saying, "You came with one hand we receive you with two."¹⁴

12. Sometimes saline solution and hard liquor are dropped onto the child's tongue, one after the other, with instructions to distinguish between the two liquids and avoid the burning one in life.¹⁵

13. The officiator then asks the baby's father for its name since everyone is called by a name and not "heh," and the name is provided by the father with *nyikɔtsɔha* (naming drink), "because we inherit paternally."¹⁶

9. Siame, interview at Sogakɔfe, 17 February 2016; Francis Hordo, interview at Sokpoe, 11 February 2016.

10. Kɔwu Yɔhokpɔ, interview at Sogakɔfe, 17 February 2016; Francis Hordo, interview at Sokpoe, 11 February 2016.

11. Atiglo, interview at Sokpoe-Elavanyo, 15 February 2016.

12. Hordo, interview at Sokpoe, 11 February 2016.

13. Yɔhokpɔ, interview at Sogakɔfe, 17 February 2016; Efoe Avinyo Atiglo, interview at Sokpoe-Elavanyo, 15 February 2016.

14. Martin Doade, interview at Sokpoe, 3 February 2016.

15. James Cudjo, interview at Sokpoe, 26 June 2016; Francis Hordo, interview at Sokpoe, 11 February 2016.

16. Atiglo, interview at Sokpoe-Elavanyo, 15 February 2016.

14. The officiator pronounces the name thrice and says, "So shall you be known and called henceforth here at *kodzogbe* (the living world) and among your ancestors in *avlime* (the living-dead world)." Then he sips a little of the *nyikɔtsɔha* to end the ritual.[17]

All those present are then given tots to do similarly; even non-alcoholics symbolically put an empty glass to their lips accordingly or pour out any little liquor in it on the ground as they repeat the child's name. This is explained to symbolically emboss the name in their memory.[18]

Upon analysis of the outline I perceive three interrelating potentially practical ways by which the religious birthing rites impact harmonious eco-relational priming. They are what I term (1) gecospheric fortification and acclimatization, (2) grounding into land of birth and (3) sociocultural integration.

"Gecospheric" Orientation by Fortification and Acclimatization as Eco-Priming

In the religious worldview of the Sokpoe, acclimatization and fortification begin during pregnancy with *fukatsotso* (pregnancy liberation) and continue through the first week postpartum. Particularly on the first day postpartum the process prevents the baby's possible development of an unwanted personal health condition called *dzigbeɖi* (broinhidrosis or repellent odor) with a ritualistic *vudzitslele* (parturition bath). An elderly woman or the midwife first besmears the neonate with *blimumuwɔ* (unroasted cornmeal).[19] Next she uses a soft sponge and three buckets of warm water and *amedzalẽ* (local soap made from oil palm and ash from plantain peels) to bath the baby. The social ecological import of this ritualistic neonatal bath is that *dzigbeɖi* (broinhidrosis) may be a challenge for the child in mingling with people in the eco-community.[20]

From the day of birth both mother and child are kept indoors for the next six days in a room called *ɖiɖexɔme* (maternity room). It is to ensure the baby *trɔ ɖe xexeme ŋu* (turns to the atmosphere, i.e., acclimatizes) gradually in preparation for the formal exposure to the vagaries of the weather and

---

17. Atiglo, interview at Sokpoe-Elavanyo, 15 February 2016.
18. Castro Abotsi (Fodze), interview at Sokpoe, 5 February 2016.
19. Matthew Agbatɔ (DHCC), interview at Sokpoe-Vogɔme, 24 February 2016.
20. Matthew Agbatɔ (DHCC), interview at Sokpoe-Vogɔme, 24 February 2016; John Bosoka (CEM), interview at Sokpoe-Vogɔme, 24 February 2016.

climatic phenomena in the earthly environment, on the seventh day.[21] It is essential then that the mother is kept close as much as possible to the baby for constant maternal body heat exchange while the child adjusts to the new environment.[22] Therefore, the mother and child are often kept in a special room or the mother's old room is refurbished to look cleaner and warmer. The mother may go out when necessary, but not very frequently within the first three days, and even after that she must not go far off nor delay in returning to her ɖiɖexɔme. Moreover, in going out the primal religious mother must be without a top covering, perhaps to let any vagaries of the weather she encounters outside remind her of the lonely baby's situation inside and be moved empathetically to hurry back to it.

All these arrangements may be to ensure the baby's accessing enough maternal body heat simulating the uterine environment as well as colostrum lactation for immunoglobulin fortification, according to midwife Evelyn Ama Blasu.[23] Consequently, a fresh mother depends on the support of relatives to care for her, particularly in providing her with ɖiɖɛkple (maternity meals) usually made of roasted corn flour, red palm oil and salted fish, to ensure her good health and lactating freshness.[24] In some cases where the belief in and fear of malevolent spirits' possible attack on the baby is strong, there is also spiritual fortification with tidodo, a procedure of inserting ti (black herbal powder) through an incision on the child's body, before outdooring.[25] In addition, among the Aŋlɔ-Eʋe, for instance, a special xɔnudzɔgoe (spirit-exorcising object, often made of food stuffs packed into

21. Winner Eworyi, interview at Sokpoe, 3 February 2016

22. W. Eworyi, interview at Sokpoe, 3 February 2016

23. Evelyn Blasu, personal communication, 27 August 2016. Speaking from over thirty years' of nursing experience; currently a Principal Midwifery Officer (PMO) and head of the Neonetal Intensive Care Unit (NICU) at Atibie Government Hospital, Ghana, Mrs. Evelyn Blasu observes that a few minutes after birth the midwife places the baby skin-to-skin on the mother's chest for maternal heat exchange and filial bonding. The filial bonding is believed to work as symbiosis via baby suckle-stimulation that secretes oxytocin from maternal posterior pituitary for milk let down and evacuation of uterine congesta. The umbilical cord is clamped and severed about three minutes after birth; and about twenty-two minutes thereafter (that is within twenty-five minutes after cord severance) a healthy baby begins to suckle fingers and anything close to its mouth. Mothers are encouraged to give breast milk from this time on, particularly within the first twenty-four hours and up to seventy-two hours postpartum. This ensures baby's access to colostrum for immunoglobulin fortification or natural immunization before the colostrum ceases to flow.

24. As members of the family or relations offer free helping hands to the fresh mother, social caring and friendly relationship in the family and eco-community is promoted and sustained. This is a socioecological effect.

25. Rev. H. Aveteh, interview at ACI, Akropong-Akuapem, 22 May 2015.

a small gourd) is hanged with tender oil-palm leaf on the door post of the *ɖiɖɛxɔme*. People believe that any evil forces and spirits of homophagy such as *adzetɔwo* (witches and wizards) intending to eat the flesh of the child may be attracted to the food particles and spare the human victim.[26]

Gecospheric acclimatization and fortification is observable in the birthing rites of both Christians and Muslims also. They also fortify the child against possible development of the unwanted health condition of *dzigbeɖi* (broinhidrosis or repellent odor) with *vudzitsilele* (parturition bath) in their own ways. The testimonies of Matthew Agbatɔ[27] and Hajia Amina Awudu[28] for Christians and Muslims, respectively, refer in this case, with the same socioecological implications. According to Pastor Matthew Agbatɔ, Christians use the same materials in the *vudzitsilele* (neonatal bath) as do the primal people.[29] Then also follow similar indoor acclimatization and fortification practices of keeping the baby indoors, for eight days in the case of Christians, but for Muslims either eight (Tijaniyya) or seven (Sunni) days postpartum.[30] As in the primal religious understanding, they believe the baby gradually adapts its irritability to the exo-uterine environment, changing from internal maternal warmth to external atmospheric weather vagaries. It is noteworthy that Christians and Muslims are careful to consciously direct the baby to God/Allah for its ultimate spiritual fortification, using other symbols than the traditionalists' *xɔnudzɔgoe*. Though in this study only the Apostolic Revelation Society reported offering prayers "for safe delivery and continuous safety of mother and child,"[31] I personally know it is a common Christian practice in the eco-area from birth to outdooring. For the Muslims, pointing God to the child textually on the day of birth may perhaps be a seeking of ultimate reliance on God for protection from start to finish. Zongo *sarachi* Abdullah Muhammad narrates that on the second day postpartum, "*Malam ava xlẽ Mawunya kpuikpui alo kartu aɖewo ɖe ɖusi kple mia tome na ɖevi la*" (Malam comes to recite some Qur'an texts,

---

26. Aveteh, interview at ACI, Akropong-Akuapem, 22 May 2015.

27. Matthew Agbatɔ (DHCC), interview at Sokpoe-Vogɔme, 24 February 2016; John Bosoka (CEM), interview at Sokpoe-Vogɔme, 24 February 2016.

28. Hajia Amina Awudu, interview at Dabala, 25 May 2016. See appendix, A30, for transcript.

29. Matthew Agbatɔ (DHCC), interview at Sokpoe-Vogɔme, 24 February 2016; John Bosoka (CEM), interview at Sokpoe-Vogɔme, 24 February 2016.

30. Abdullah Muhammad (zongo *sarachi*), interview at Sogakɔfe, 5 April 2016. He explains that the Tijaniyya start counting the week from the day of birth, and the Sunni start a day after, but both end up naming the child on its first day of birth in the first week postpartum.

31. Maxwell Agbewɔvi (ARS), interview at Sokpoe, 26 February 2016; John Bosoka (CEM), interview at Sokpoe-Vogɔme, 24 February 2016.

"*kartu*," into the right and left ears of the baby), as instructed by the Prophet Mohammed.[32] John Azumah identifies the actual word "whispered into the ears of a newborn and into the ears of a dying Muslim" is the *Kalima*: "*La ila ha illa Allah: Muhammad Rasul Allah*" (There is no God but Allah, Muhammad is the Messenger of Allah), which actually is the *Shahadah* (confession of faith).[33] Azumah explains that "of all the pillars of faith" in Islam, "this alone is absolutely essential . . . It should be the first thing one hears upon entering the world and the last thing one hears before leaving the world to meet one's creator."[34]

Thus, due to the vulnerability of the freshly born baby to the vagaries of biophysical energies and malevolent forces in the ecosystem, the baby is kept in *ɖiɖexɔme* for six or seven days' acclimatization and fortification. It affords and ensures that the baby continues the process, started prenatally with *fukatsotso*, to gradually get oriented to the realities of gecospheric biophysical energies and spiritual forces as well as preparedness to mitigating their vagaries. This sets the tone for and thus anticipates the other two movements: further grounding or rooting the baby in its land of birth and sociocultural integration into the ecological community.

Religious Grounding or Rooting in Land of Birth as Eco-Priming

Practically, primal religious outdooring as an initiation rite involves two distinct but inseparable liturgical orders: *vitsɔtsɔfiawo* (showing baby to the sun) followed by *nyikɔtsɔtsɔ* (naming). The first part, *vitsɔtsɔfiawo*, seems to formally introduce the baby mainly to the other-than-human (physical and spiritual) elements in the gecosphere and enroots it in the particular geographical part of the Earth that it can regard as its land of birth. It is thus a completion on day seven of the ecological grounding process started on day one with *hɔka kple amenɔɖiɖi* (umbilical cord and placenta burying). For all the religious traditions, the fall of the short piece of umbilical cord left on the baby after severance of the placenta on parturition day determines the day for the outdooring rite. Usually this happens on day seven, which then, as the day for the ritual, must not coincide with the day of birth, in the case of primal religionists. This is unlike the Aŋlɔ-Eʋe, particularly the Nigokpo ecological community, where the rite is on day eight or day

---

32. Abdullah Muhammad (zongo *sarachi*), interview at Sogakɔfe, 5 April 2016.
33. Azumah, *My Neighbor's Faith*, 34.
34. Azumah, *My Neighbor's Faith*, 34.

sixteen, as it must necessarily fall on the day of birth.[35] Similarly, as we noted earlier, Christians and Muslims in Sokpoe eco-area, like the Aŋlɔ-Eʋe, tend to outdoor on the eighth day.[36] The fallen umbilical cord is buried just like the placenta, sometimes in the same hole or another behind the bath place to begin *vitsɔtsɔfiawo*.

Unlike the placenta, the short umbilical cord burial more often than not tends to be by parents themselves and not relatives. Usually it is the father, who plants a seedling such as coconut, oil palm or any food tree on it. According to Rev. P. H. Aveteh, while the seedling is being planted the names of both the tree and the child are pronounced to link them up so that the baby will grow to love caring for the tree and benefit from its produce. As he puts it, talking with the background of sea beach ecosystem, "from the one coconut tree planted on the umbilical cord the child may get a large coconut plantation if it cares for it well."[37] In an interview Mrs. Rebecca Ahoto from Dzodze did not know why her father planted a coconut tree on her umbilical cord, nor was she urged to and so did not personally care for it. Yet she knew the tree was for her and she benefits nutritionally and money-wise from the fruits borne by the tree. Moreover, it connects her to her hometown as she visits the tree when in need of the fruits or when responding to any other duty back home.[38]

It may not be an overstatement to say that burial of the umbilical cord on the outdooring day grounds or connects a baby to and "reminds it of its land of birth"[39] as potentiating for creation care. Yet it is not a common practice among Christians and Muslims in the eco-area; at least it is not done as often or as consciously as in the case of the primal religion. But the grounding, rooting and connection as potentiating for creation care is further observable from the other symbols and rituals, such as showing the baby to the sun and laying it bare on the ground.

As earlier stated, among the Sokpoe-Eʋe the primal religious rite of outdooring a baby is sometimes simply described as "*vitsɔtsɔ fia wò*" (showing baby to the sun). An elderly man officiating opens the program with prayer saying, "Agoo, agoo, agoo; the sun rises from the East, runs up on top of us and sets to the West. Let everything around us remain quiet and calm as we perform this rite to outdoor our child, the human baby born for

---

35. Rev. H. Aveteh, interview at ACI, Akropong-Akuapem, 22 May 2015.

36. For ARS only boys are outdoored on the eighth; but for girls' outdooring is on the sixteenth day. Maxwell Agbewɔvi, interview at Sokpoe, 26 February 2016.

37. Rev. P. H. Aveteh, interview at ACI, Akropong-Akuapem, 22 May 2015.

38. Mrs. Rebecca Ahoto, interview at Sokpoe, 18 June 2016.

39. Dickson Degbe Blasu, interview at Sokpoe, 3 February 2016.

Religious Birthing Rites and Ecological Relations 179

us."[40] Cosmologically the Sokpoe-Eʋe represents or symbolizes *xexeme* (the gecosphere) with the sun. James Cudjoe of COP avers, "When day breaks, we get out into *xexeme*."[41] He implies that unlike an enclosed dark space, an open bright space gives one the sensation of being in *xexeme*. Thus for the Sokpoe-Eʋe *xexeme* translates the spatially open vast arena where we experience alternation of day/sun light and night/darkness[42] lying between *dzifo* (the sky), where we can see and point to above us, and *anyigbadzi* (Earth's surface), where humans live and put their feet.[43] To show the baby to the sun is then to formally present and integrate it into and as part of *xexeme*, which is seen also as "the Earth and all that is in it,"[44] including all phenomena pertaining to life on Earth. The rising and setting of the sun, for instance, signifies cycling of time and affirms life and death as a characteristic earthly phenomenon. While the light of solar rays from the East in the morning guarantees general safety for life in the gecosphere, its setting in the West in the evening reminds us of death or termination of earthly life.[45] This explains performing the outdooring rite usually early in the morning when the sun rises from the East to wish and immerse the baby into good life in the world it has entered. The West, on the other hand, is undesired for the baby, but rather for its enemies for whom death is wished.[46]

Thus, the ritual of turning the child to the East and then to the West potentiates it for the sense of time or temporality as a significant phenomenon in the ecosystem. In other words, the child's consciousness of temporality, and hence the need to respect time, is necessary for survival and success in the ecological community. Time consciousness affects the baby's survival decisions and actions, such as discerning the right seasons/periods to farm and fish in the ecosystem for sustainable yields. So, the baby is ritually admonished during the program to work hard with the seasons so that

---

40. Yɔhokpɔ, interview at Sogakɔfe, 17 February 2016. Instead of saying "agoo, agoo, agoo" the officiant may gently hit his heel against the entrance wall thrice as asking permission from *Mawu* (God), who cared and brought the child into being. Hordo Francis, interview at Sokpoe, 11 February 2016.

41. James Cudjoe, interview at Sokpoe, 26 June 2016. He is a Christian but like many others responded to the questions mainly with his primal worldview.

42. Atiglo, interview at Elavanyo, 15 February 2016.

43. Enyi Avenɔgbo, interview at Elavanyo, 2 February 2016.

44. Efoe Avinyo Atiglo, interview at Sokpoe-Elavanyo, 15 February 2016.

45. Yɔhokpɔ, interview at Sogakɔfe, 17 February 2016. He is a ninety-five-year old Christian of the Roman Catholic Church but responded to questions with a primal worldview.

46. Klayi Avi, interview at Sokpoe, 2 February 2016.

the Earth (land and river) can yield the baby's required basics of life: food, clothing and shelter.[47]

Apparently, the Earth's nurturing with good yield in rewarding the child's hard work depends on the ecological link—filial and moral (respectful) relationship—between baby and the Earth. This is ritually enacted by laying the baby, without body covering, on the bare ground with the expectation that it urinates. Some informants indicate that where the baby fails to urinate, cold fresh water is either sprinkled between its thighs[48] or thrown from calabash onto a thatched roof top to drip down at the eaves onto the baby.[49] The latter practice, however, appears unknown to a few other respondents.[50] For the majority, such as Dickson Blasu, who reported its practice, it may be done irrespective of whether the baby urinates on the ground or not.[51] The ecological significance of laying an uncovered baby on the ground, the baby urinating on the ground and/or making water drip from roof eaves onto baby on the ground have been explained by the respondents. All the explanations point to grounding or rooting the baby in its land of birth as potentiating for respecting and caring for creation.

For instance, the laying of the baby to have direct or bare contact with the Earth is to remind it of having been materially made of it and so shall return its materiality to the Earth.[52] In addition, it compares rationally with the skin-to-skin laying of a newly born baby on its mother's chest "for maternal heat exchange and filial bonding."[53] This practice is observed among other ethnic groups as noted by Robert Clobus.[54] Asare Opoku suggests that perhaps it signifies that the child is made essentially of clay from the Earth and so is "expected to revere and cooperate with it."[55] Similarly, the micturition symbol also reminds the child that out of the soil it came and its material substance, represented by the urine, like the placenta and umbilical cord, will return to the soil.

All these rituals, in my view, suggest and are emphatic about inducing the baby's filial respect for the Earth with which it must relate

47. Atiglo, interview at Sokpoe-Elavanyo, 15 February 2016.

48. Abotsi, interview at Sokpoe, 5 February 2016; Geoffrey Siame, interview at Sogakɔfe, 17 February 2016.

49. Dickson Degbe Blasu, interview at Sokpoe, 3 February 2016.

50. Enyi Avenɔgbo, interview at Sokpoe-Elavanyo, 2 February 2016; Efoe Avinyo Atiglo, interview at Sokpoe-Elavanyo, 15 February 2016.

51. Dickson Degbe Blasu, interview at Sokpoe, 3 February 2016.

52. Siame, interview at Sogakɔfe, 17 February 2016.

53. Evelyn Blasu, personal communication, 27 August 2016.

54. Clobus, "Ecofarming and Land Ownership," 70.

55. K. Opoku, "Cooking on Two Stones of the Hearth?," 5.

anthropomorphically as a kind of "mother." It is commonly the case among the Eʋe that on a mother's lap her child urinates innocently, yet the mother does not reject nor destroy the innocent child for soiling her lap.[56] Rather the baby's innocent soiling strengthens the filial bond between mother and child by stirring up the maternal care instincts of the mother. Hence, the baby's urination on the bare ground may signify its symbolic invoking of the maternal love and care of "mother" Earth. Amega Kɔwu Yɔhokpɔ explains that "Urinating on the ground shows the child is kɔkɔe (pure) for the land that welcomes it unto her lap as a mother."[57]

Asked what he means by "kɔkɔe" and what happens if the baby does not urinate, *Amega Yɔhokpɔ* clarified that when a baby hesitates to urinate the Earth regards it as *efe dzimemekɔ o* (it is not pure in heart, i.e., not innocent). Rationally it may imply that spontaneous micturition establishes the baby's innocence, having no awareness of good or evil before entering *xexeme*, and so can ritually stir the maternal instinct of and acceptance by "mother" Earth. Perhaps this suggests the primal religious way of explaining that human beings are primordially innocent just as in Judaeo-Christian religion the nakedness of Adam and Eve before God indicated their innocence; "they had nothing to hide from each other or God."[58] Hesitation and failure to urinate may suggest the child is not innocent enough and for whatever reason is reluctant to soil its "mother" (the Earth's) lap contrary to her loving expectation for acceptance. For an unaccepted child may be denied access to "mother" Earth's nurturing roles and hence uncertainty of the baby's survival in *xexeme*. Consequently, where this is strongly believed, Castro Abotsi and Geoffrey Siame observe that the officiating elder may sprinkle water in the laps to symbolically represent the urine for a baby that fails to urinate naturally.[59] Mother Earth is by this ritual informed, so to speak, to accept and caringly provide basic needs of life for the vulnerable and innocent baby.

The cosmological enactment here establishes the worthiness or inviolability of human identity with the Earth due to the Earth's nurturing values and function in relation to human life. Logically the baby is in turn set to respect and care for the Earth as its ecological "mother" so it can continue to nourish it. Native Americans hold a similar perception, who

---

56. An Eʋe proverb endorses this understanding when it says, "A mother does not cut off the fecal mess of her baby on her lap with a knife."

57. Yɔhokpɔ, interview at Sogakɔfe, 17 February 2016. See appendix, A13, for transcript.

58. Bookless, *Planetwise*, 36.

59. Abotsi, interview at Sokpoe, 5 February 2016; Geoffrey Siame, interview at Sogakɔfe, 17 February 2016.

when encountering environmental threats in their holistically perceived ecosystems look into themselves and ask, "Are we nourishing our Mother Earth as she has nourished us, so that she will continue to nourish future generations?"[60]

Apart from substituting for urine where a baby fails micturition, the dripping of water from roof eaves onto the baby as explained by interviewees implies a further orienting the baby to the reality of weather vagaries. I explained above that the ritual of showing the baby to the sun informs the baby about heat, light and darkness. The dripping water ritual, on the other hand, focuses on the weather elements of cold temperature and rainfall in the ecosystem. Explaining what these rituals signify, Doade Martin's response suggests that both the dripping water ritual and that of showing baby to the sun together are meant to teach the baby the weather and climatic elements as well as seasonality and temporality in the gecosphere. He observes, speaking from a primal religious perspective, that

> Bringing out the child from the room they show it to the East and West. It implies teaching the child to take note of time and timeliness for life activities in the world. In addition, it is to make the child appreciate the seasons for heat and cold in the world. Then they pour water on rooftop to drip unto the child. This also reminds the child about rainy season and reality of being beaten by rain on Earth.[61]

It stands to reason that the primal religious outdooring orientates and integrates (or grounds) the baby by awaking its consciousness of the geobiophysical phenomena in the gecosphere and the temporality of ecosystem life. But it also fortifies the baby spiritually because the ecosystem life is not only temporal; it is also precarious due to the presence of malevolent forces that threaten its sustenance. The child should be made aware not only of their presence and endangering manoeuvres, but more importantly how to relate with them for the integrity, success and sustenance of life. To help the innocent and vulnerable child secure its life in the precarious world, the fortification started earlier from conception through the first six days postpartum and is brought to climax during outdooring. Special libation prayers are offered that ward off the evil spirits before blessings are pronounced on the baby, just as happens among the Ga primal religious system. Citing the case of Ga culture to emphasize belief in the power of cursing, B. Y. Quarshie sees African outdooring rites as occasion not only to invoke

---

60. Gonzales and Nelson, "Contemporary Native American Responses," 497.
61. Martin Doade, interview at Sokpoe, 3 February 2016.

material blessings to the baby, but also to deal with malevolent forces that may overturn the blessings by cursing them.⁶²

Evidentially "*vi tsɔtsɔ fia ɣe*" (showing the child to the sun), as the first stage of *viɖeɖeɖego*, is often either overlooked or not very elaborately performed by Christians; and Muslims do not do it at all. In an explanation Catechist Robert Avenɔgbo remarks:

> Parents tell the pastor to come and show their child to the sun, which in their mind is in accordance with *dekɔnunu* (primal religious rite). But we church agents take it that they only want the child named just as it was biblically done to Jesus.⁶³

He shows that, contrary to Christian parents' understanding, church elders who officiate outdooring ceremonies think that showing baby to the sun is *dekɔnu*, something non-Christian, and so "ignore this part and concentrate on only naming."⁶⁴ This, for them, is because the Bible records only christening in the outdooring ceremony of baby Jesus, and that was in the temple. In the same vein, church elders also prefer the chapel more than the home as the venue for the outdooring ceremony.⁶⁵ Perhaps the interpretation given by the church elders seriously influenced some of the church members to think similarly that showing baby to the sun is "unchristian." Atsuƒe Xɔmeku, a mother of twin girls, testifies that the outdooring of her children by catechist Avenɔgbo and Presbyter Andrews Ahado took place in the chapel instead of home. Performing the rite in chapel alone is enough to make it Christian for her, and she is glad that "the ceremony was more of Christian naming than the unchristian *dekɔnuwɔwɔ* (primal religious rituals)."⁶⁶ Although during the ceremony in question the girls were taken out and lifted briefly to the sun outside the chapel, she did not complain at that time only due to ignorance; with her level of Christian understanding today, she "will not tolerate such unchristian *dekɔnu* during the ceremony."⁶⁷

These Christians in the Sokpoe ecological area may not be unique. Professor Joshua Kudadjie, a Christian ethicist of the Methodist Church of Ghana, conducted research among the Ada, whose outdooring rites are similar to those of the Sokpoe-Eʋe in many respects. Perhaps bereft of theological background or being more focused on ethics than theocology, he

---

62. Quarshie, "Paul and the Primal Substructure of Christianity," 12.
63. Robert Avenɔgbo, interview at Sokpoe, 13 March 2016. See appendix, A15, for transcript.
64. Robert Avenɔgbo, interview at Sokpoe, 13 March 2016.
65. Robert Avenɔgbo, interview at Sokpoe, 13 March 2016.
66. Atsuƒe Xɔmeku, interview at Sokpoe, 29 Feb 2016,
67. Atsuƒe Xɔmeku, interview at Sokpoe, 29 Feb 2016.

downplayed and discarded some aspects of the ritual that he regarded as unchristian from his reconstructed outdooring liturgy.[68] For instance, he construes the ritual of "abandoning child and calling on a woman to pick it" as an "act of [human] redemption," which perhaps, to him, is contrary to promoting Christ's divine redemption. He then "expunged this act" on grounds that "the child is a gift of God and its arrival thus calls for thanksgiving to God, not redemption."[69] Similarly the Church of Pentecost (COP) leaders at Sokpoe ecological area delete the ritual of "pouring and dripping water from roof eaves onto baby" because it is *egodotɔwo tɔ* (for non-Christians).[70] Generally the ritualistic actions expunged by Christians from primal religious *viɖeɖeɖego* liturgy include:

- Ritualistic burying of the piece of umbilical cord that falls off on the seventh day postpartum: Not much attention is given to it. Yet it may be grounding or linking child with land of birth and death.

- Planting a tree on the buried umbilical cord: This is not done at all. Yet it could be orienting or priming baby to be concerned for other-than-human creation care, particularly for floral care and agricultural income earning.

- Ritually "taking baby out" or lifting the baby to the sun and turning it toward the East for early sun rays, signifying rising life, and turning it to the West to signify sundown or ending of life: Even where and when done, it is without ecological undertone, at least not consciously.[71] Yet this believably primes baby to be consciousness of time, temporality of earthly life, as well as weather (temperature) and season changes as realities in the ecosystem.

- Placing and abandoning the baby uncovered on bare ground; having it found and picked up by a woman and dropping *dzatsi* (corn meal solution) on the tongue of the baby, with instruction to fend itself with produce of the land: No Christian does it. Yet this could prime the baby to see itself as an earthling and so respect the nurturing function of the Earth as "mother." It also introduces the baby to the eco-value of hard work and to appreciate locally or eco-culturally produced staple food. Implicit also is the sense of belonging to a loving family, having been found by a caring woman and not lost in vast cosmos. However,

68. Kudadjie, "Researching Morals and Rituals," 35.
69. Kudadjie, "Researching Morals and Rituals," 35.
70. James Cudjoe, Church of Pentecost, interview at Sokpoe, 26 June 2016.
71. Only Church of Pentecost indicates they do this part. See Gladys Ahado, interview at Sokpoe, 26 June 2016.

this priming will only occur if someone explains this to the child when he/she is able to understand. Otherwise, the child will not know it has been done.

- Sprinkling cold water from roof eaves onto the baby on the bare ground: This is again not done by Christians. Yet it may prime the baby for rainfall and cold weather conditions in the ecosystem.

- Dropping water, honey or liquor in turns on the tongue of the baby with instruction to distinguish contrasts: This is occasionally done by some Christians. It may, using alternative symbols, prime the baby for moral training in contrasting good and bad, truth from lie, sweet and bitter and sin from holiness.

- Presenting *ŋkɔtsɔha* (naming drink) to all those who hear the child's name for the first time: This believably is a kind of mnemonic or a symbolic reminder for witnesses to remember the names and is also proof of true paternal heritage for the child. He who presents *ŋkɔtsɔha* is the recognized responsible father. This may ensure paternal responsibility.

Apparently, some other Christian parents are not satisfied with the "Christian" version of *viḍeḍeḍego*, which lacks the aspects for showing the child to the sun. They miss the "*dekɔnu* feeling"—the African cosmological and cultural meanings and purposes—that give the sense of completeness and effectiveness of the rite. Castro Abotsi is a Presbyterian. In an interview he observes from experience that usually, for some parents, the rite in the chapel is "topped up" back home because "*mede o*" (it is not complete).[72] Asked if this is true and why, Andrews Ahado, a presbyter who often assists or represents the minister in outdooring ceremonies, replied in affirmation and said: "We rebuked them several times yet some believe in it so much that they see it as a continuation of committing the child into God's hands."[73]

Muslims in this study did not present any rituals to suggest *vitsɔtsɔfiawo* also takes place during their baby outdooring ceremonies. A noteworthy point in the case of the primal people is that in dealing with evil forces in the ecosystem the child needs the assistance of both benevolent deities and their human devotees who can manipulate the deities in favor of the child in accordance with sociocultural understandings. This moves the outdooring liturgy into the next stage for sociocultural integration of the baby.

---

72. Castro Abotsi, interview at Sokpoe, 5 February 2016.
73. Andrews Ahado, interview at Sokpoe, 5 February 2016.

Sociocultural Orientation and Integration as Ecological Priming

I see that this section of the liturgical practice in primal religious outdooring ceremony, called *nyikɔtsɔtsɔ* (naming), moves the focus from the other-than-human to fellow human beings, and to integrate the child in their social relationships and cultural ethos in the ecological community. From a social ecology viewpoint, the Sokpoe-Eʋe practice paternal heritage[74] and desirously respect old age. This may underscore the insistence that an elderly male officiates the outdooring rite. Kɔwu Yɔhokpɔ speaks of the officiator as necessarily being *ŋutsu nutefewɔla* (a worthy or faithful man).[75] People believe that this impacts the child morally to respect old age as well as be inspired to adopt the good character and relationships that promote long life in the ecological community.[76] Citing an example from his hometown Nigokpo, Rev. P. H. Aveteh explains the reason primal religionists in the Aŋlɔ-Eʋe insist on only an aged and well respected man to officiate outdooring ceremony. They believe and expect that the baby will take after the man in terms of age and character.[77] Ogbu Kalu believes that the cultivation and practice of a "green" or an ecologically virtuous character is the best way for establishing harmonious ecological relationships, and hence abundant life in the ecosystem.[78] A person's character or eco-character is formed as a human quality through inherited traits and influences of interactions with fellow humans in the social and cultural environment. Such sociocultural interactions may provide primordial understanding of the environment and how it functions in the historical and traditional context, which, according to Agbanu, the child needs to know first before science can later help to improve on it.[79]

Therefore the outdooring rite integrates the baby into the society as implied by the statement "*Wodee amehawo dome*" (It is literally put into the people)[80] when the officiator ceremonially presents the baby by lifting it towards the witnessing participants at the ceremony, saying, "Let you who know not know this child from today."[81] In other words, the child must be welcomed as a member of, and so ritualistically exciting its sense of belonging

---

74. Isaac Avi, interview at Sokpoe, 2 February 2016.
75. Yɔhokpɔ, interview at Sogakɔfe, 17 February 2016.
76. Klayi Avi, interview at Sokpoe, 2 February 2016.
77. Aveteh, Interview at ACI, Akropong-Akuapem, 22 May 2015.
78. Kalu, "Precarious Vision," 44.
79. Agbanu, interview in his office at Legon, Monday 23rd November 2015.
80. Atiglo, interview at Sokpoe-Elavanyo, 15 February 2016.
81. Klayi Avi, interview at Sokpoe, 2 February 2016.

to, an ecological community on the Earth. It becomes a citizen of Earth, and hence an earthling. But the Earth is part of an extra-galactic universe; even by itself it is vast with many communities located geographically at different cardinal points. As a new entrant, the child is considered lost and vulnerable to ill fates in the vast, extra-galactic and precarious universe. It needs to be identified, loved and guided by and in a particular community or family, taking its place specifically as an earthling in *xexeme* (gecosphere).

These worldviews are enacted to impress them upon the infant during the outdooring rite by leaving the child alone on the ground to cry until a close relative picks him/her up, saying, "I found a lost child, whose innocent child is lost this way?" Then the mother, on behalf of society, receives and lovingly comforts to quieten the child. It may signify a parental caring quality that the child is to experience and learn to emulate in the bewildering community, particularly to estranged persons. Next the child is identified by naming it, the names having meanings and purposes based on the day of birth (day name), a significant event (insinuating name) and paternal heritage (surname).[82] However, more often only the day name and surname are pronounced at the ceremony; the other names come later as parents consider life events that may be memorabilia.[83] To legally establish and affirm the particular paternal family or line of heritage of the child, only males officially release the name to the event officiator for publicizing, with a *nyikɔtsɔha* (naming drink). "Certainly, among the Eʋe, in general, it is traditionally accepted that only males do name children; and the legal evidence of paternity is the answer to the question "who submitted *nyikɔtsɔha* during outdooring?"[84] The naming ritual is followed with introduction to *tɔgbeŋɔliwo* (ancestors).

The Sokpoe-Eʋe, like many other African primal cultures, hold a holistic view of the world, where community consists of visible and invisible, human and other-than-human members in diverse but clearly known and ethically valued structural relationships.[85] An important group of invisible community members are the *tɔgbeŋɔliwo kple mamaŋɔliwo* (male and female ancestors) in *aʋlime* (world of the living dead), from whom the child is believed to have come and who also must bless its life at *kodzogbe* (the world of the living living). The child is introduced to them with hope that he/she will respect them who sent and shall watch over him/her. So the ancestors are invoked to dine with the child. For it is said among the Eʋe that

82. Klayi Avi, interview at Sokpoe, 2 February 2016.
83. Aveteh, interview at ACI, Akropong-Akuapem, 22 May 2015.
84. Aveteh, interview at ACI, Akropong-Akuapem, 22 May 2015.
85. Kalu, "Precarious Vision," 42.

only a child who washes his/her hands well—that is, respects—eats with elders. The communal food is *fomedzatsi* (family meal made of a mixture of fresh corn flour in fresh water), representing the culturally most staple food (grain and water) in the typical riverine ecosystem of Sokpoe. The ancestors eat theirs from the ground, but that of the child is dropped onto its tongue. The officiator makes it clear to the ancestors that "You sent this child to us. Here receive our family *dzatsi* and bless your child so it can fend for itself with its own produce from the river and soil."[86] Similarly, the child is also admonished to work hard to earn a good living from the river and land, and not to disgrace the family with laziness.[87]

With this communal dinning ritual, the child is culturally potentiated for moral values of respecting human elders and the deities who bless it, caring for the river and land that yields his/her food, grateful for and satiated with the staple, locally produced food stuffs and also see hard work as real necessity for sustaining good life in the ecological community. The teaching on moral responsibility in the eco-community seems to be completed with the ritual of dropping saline solution and alcohol on the child's tongue. They are symbolically to help the child appreciate the reality of contrasts in the ecosystem. The child is instructed to distinguish between water and alcohol, good and bad, right and wrong, truth and lie even where the situation seems very much alike, but must keep to the good.[88] The moral impartation ritual is concluded with prayer for the child to develop good character as it grows up.[89] Thus it appears the entire birthing rituals from conception to outdooring unconsciously point to and prime the child to ultimately develop and practice eco-character or virtue toward creation care. Curry describes a child with eco-character, from his Western understanding, as a "green citizen of the Earth Community," the kind reported about in primal cultures not entirely colonized by modernity.[90]

As noted earlier, *nyikɔtsɔtsɔ* (naming ceremony), the second stage of the outdooring rite, is the part that both Christians and Muslims tend to emphasize. Despite some denominational differences, I collated a logical generalized liturgical order for the outdooring ceremony from responses of the Christian participants in this study.[91]

86. Klayi Avi, interview at Sokpoe, 2 February 2016.
87. Yɔhokpɔ, Interview at Sogakɔfe, 17 February 2016.
88. Aveteh, Interview at ACI, Akropong-Akuapem, 22 May 2015.
89. Atiglo, interview at Sokpoe-Elavanyo, 15 February 2016.
90. Curry, *Ecological Ethics*, 49 and 159.
91. Actually, the liturgy for Church of Pentecost is far shorter, mainly concerned with praying in the room, bringing out the baby, lifting up child to the sun, exhortative homily, naming, gifting and blessing of child. See James Cudjoe, interview at Sokpoe,

Religious Birthing Rites and Ecological Relations 189

a. Both baby and mother remain indoors for seven days postpartum. This prevents *diɛlélé* (perinatal fever or jaundice).[92]

b. On the eighth day[93] after the day of birth, the family members, well-wishers, officiating minister and catechist/elder gather at 6:00 a.m. for the outdooring ceremony. It may be at home or in the chapel.[94] If the program is at home, the child's father or mother[95] or paternal aunt[96] or minister[97] brings the child out from the *diɖexɔme* (maternity room) and keeps the child in her arms as the program proceeds. In the chapel either the parents step forward with the child in their hands,[98] or a female presbyter receives the child from the parents and carries it.[99]

c. Either the father of the child[100] or the officiating minister[101] announces the purpose of the gathering, saying, "Unto us a child is born, and we gather *be woatsɔe afia wò*" (to show it to the sun).[102]

d. The ceremony begins with a hymn and the minister prays thanking God for the safe delivery and asking God to grant success all through the ceremony.[103] For both COP[104] and DHCCC,[105] the opening prayer is offered in the *diɖexɔme* before the minister carries the child out to signify "outdooring."[106] Similarly in CEM an elder carries the baby out of the chapel as "outdooring," where the minister lifts it up to the sun,

---

26 June 2016.

92. Evelyn Blasu, interview at Abetifi, 16 January 2016.

93. For ARS only boys are outdoored on the eighth; but for girls' outdooring is on the sixteenth day. See Maxwell Agbewɔvi, interview at Sokpoe, 26 February 2016.

94. Francis Hordo, interview at Sokpoe, 11 February 2016.

95. Andrews Ahado, interview at Sokpoe, 5 February 2016.

96. Maxwell Adikpe, interview at Mepe, 2 June 2016.

97. For Church of Pentecost a female church elder takes the child from mother and give to the minister in the room. See James Cudjoe, interview at Sokpoe, 26 June 2016

98. Winner Eworyi, interview at Sokpoe, 3 February 2016.

99. Francis Hordo, interview at Sokpoe, 11 February 2016.

100. Robert Avenɔgbo, interview at Sokpoe, 13 March 2016

101. Winner Eworyi, interview at Sokpoe, 3 February 2016; Rev. M. K. Adikpe, interview at Mepe, 2 June 2016.

102. Robert Avenɔgbo, interview at Sokpoe, 13 March 2016; Gladys Ahado, COP, interview at Sokpoe, 26 June 2016.

103. Francis Hordo, interview at Sokpoe, 11 February 2016.

104. James Cudjoe, interview at Sokpoe, 26 June 2016.

105. Matthew Agbatɔ, interview at Sokpoe- Vogɔme, 24 February 2016.

106. James Cudjoe, interview at Sokpoe, 26 June 2016.

pronouncing its name given by the father thrice. He prayerfully seeks the baby's protection by cursing and casting off endangering evil spirits and blessing the child to prosper in life before returning to chapel.[107]

e. The minister then gives a short scriptural homily exhorting both the new and other parents concerning nurturing children in the way of the Lord, reminding them of the roles of both parents and children.[108]

f. The minister receives the child in his/her arms[109] and requests for the child's name.[110] The father writes the set of names out just as Zechariah did when his son John the Baptist was born.[111] The meaning is briefly discussed for parents to know what the names imply and give their approval[112] before the minister prays on the names as social identifying symbols.[113] Usually the set of names include biblical, day-of-birth and surnames in that order.[114]

g. Either the child's father[115] or the minister[116] pronounces the name three times[117] and the congregation repeats after him, thrice, in the name of the Trinity. After the third time the minister says to the child: "I commit you into God's hands as his child, but not for Satan. You shall be known and called by this name among the saints on Earth."[118]

h. Like Simeon did for Jesus, the minister or a presbyter now receives the child into his/her arms and blesses it by pronouncing blessings.[119] Also prophetic words from Psalms 23 or 91 are pronounced by the minister, addressing the child by calling the new names at various stages, as God

---

107. John Bosoka, interview at Sokpoe-Vogɔme, 24 February 2016.

108. Francis Hordo, interview at Sokpoe, 11 February 2016.

109. For COP it is the father who hands over the baby to the minister. See James Cudjoe, interview at Sokpoe, 26 June 2016.

110. Winner Eworyi, interview at Sokpoe, 3 February 2016.

111. Robert Avenɔgbo, interview at Sokpoe, 13 March 2016.

112. Robert Avenɔgbo, interview at Sokpoe, 13 March 2016.

113. Winner Eworyi, interview at Sokpoe, 3 February 2016.

114. Francis Hordo, interview at Sokpoe, 11 February 2016.

115. Robert Avenɔgbo, interview at Sokpoe, 13 March 2016.

116. Winner Eworyi, interview at Sokpoe, 3 February 2016.

117. For COP the minister pronounces the names only once. See James Cudjoe, interview at Sokpoe, 26 June 2016.

118. Castro Abotsi, interview at Sokpoe, 5 February 2016. In CEM the minister gives the name earlier outside the chapel when he lifts up the baby to the sun saying, "I outdoor you in the name of the Father, I outdoor you in the name of the Son, I outdoor you in the name of the Spirit, amen."

119. Andrews Ahado, interview at Sokpoe, 5 February 2016.

is petitioned for fulfilling his divine purposes and destiny for the child: long life, health, prosperity and a God-fearing spirit.[120]

i. The minister or presbyter returns the baby to its father, who then may give it to its mother to signify paternal inheritance, as Eʋe hymn 407 v. 5 is sung.[121] The minister reminds the child of the lyrics of this hymn, which affirms that wise parents are gifted the child and, hence, instructs it to obey its parents and live longer and prosper.[122]

j. The congregation sings hymns interspersed with optional exhortations from one or two church members. The exhortations re-emphasize the need for Christian nurturing of children so they can develop holistically in both the physical and spiritual dimensions.[123]

k. At the same time congregants as witnesses to the rite donate in Christian love for the upkeep of the child items including, money, powder, body cream, toilet soap etc.[124]

l. The minister ends the rite with a closing prayer, blessing the child, parents and congregation to be useful instruments for the Lord, church, society and family.[125]

m. If they can afford, the parents provide some refreshment like a hot beverage or soft drink in the midst of singing and merry making.[126]

Ecologically, since this part of the outdooring is for sociocultural orientation and integration, the symbolic rituals signify naming, establishing paternal heritage, admonishing for Christian moral conduct, spiritual (prayer) and material (gifts) support for the newly introduced member of the community and welcoming the baby into the community joyously. The practice is not very different from that of Muslims except that Muslims actually begin naming on the very day of birth. According to Hajia Amina Awudu,

---

120. Robert Avenɔgbo, interview at Sokpoe, 13 March 2016.

121. Eʋe Hymn 407, verse 5, says: "*Ena dzila kple nufiala anukwaretɔwom. Wofe nufiafia tso gbɔwò, Wò, si nye keli gã*" (You gave me parents who are true teachers. Their teachings come from you, who is the Great Light).

122. Robert Avenɔgbo, interview at Sokpoe, 13 March 2016.

123. Winner Eworyi, interview at Sokpoe, 3 February 2016.

124. Castro Abotsi, interview at Sokpoe, 5 February 2016.

125. Winner Eworyi, interview at Sokpoe, 3 February 2016; Robert Avenɔgbo, interview at Sokpoe, 13 March 2016.

126. Winner Eworyi, interview at Sokpoe, 3 February 2016.

On the day of birth women around sound yur . . . yur . . . yur thrice, as done when a bride is outdoored into a public space. With every "yur" they whisper the birth-day name, such as Kɔku, if born on Wednesday, into its ears. This is to enable babe to internalize and ever recognize that name as belonging to it.[127]

Like the Christians, the naming program on day eight postpartum, sometimes called *suna*, takes place either at home or in *masalachi* (mosque). Depending on the ability of parents the program may end with or without *sadaqa* or freewill offering. If it is without *sadaqa*, the program may start at dawn, during the 5:00 a.m. *salat-az-subbh* prayers; otherwise it starts formally at 9:00 a.m., as instructed by the Prophet Mohammed.[128] The entire program, according to participants, may be summed up as follows:

1. More often than not the umbilical cord falls off on the seventh/eighth day and is buried in the same way as the placenta: it is wrapped in *Calotropis procera* ("wagashi" herbal) leaves, and sometimes covered with a piece of calico, put in *kutu* (a small clay pot) and buried one and half feet deep in the soil, "depicting burial of a complete human, dead."[129]

2. Family and well-wishers gather in the house for the outdooring program at 6:00 a.m. Some may have been there since the day of birth helping with various chores in preparation for the ceremony.[130]

3. The father of the child presents a "naming ram," which is served as *sadaqa* either as fresh mutton or cooked meal.[131] Although this is not mandatory,[132] yet by God's grace, every father is able to afford at least one ram for the occasion.[133]

4. Joyful welcome of babe, with feasting and social recreational interactions, continues until the imam or malam arrives into the house at about 9:00 a.m.[134] If for any reason, such as the father of the child travelling, the naming ritual, that is, the official pronouncement of the

---

127. Hajia Amina Awudu, interview at Dabala, 25 May 2016. See appendix, A14, for transcript.
128. Abdullah Muhammad (zongo *sarachi*), interview at Sogakɔfe, 5 April 2016.
129. Hajia Fatti Sanni, personal telephone communication, 12 December 2016.
130. Hajia Amina Awudu, interview at Dabala, 25 May 2016.
131. Abdullah Muhammad (zongo *sarachi*), interview at Sogakɔfe, 5 April 2016.
132. Hajia Hawusatu Eleas, interview at Sogakɔfe, 12 April 2016.
133. Hajia Fatti Sanni, personal telephone communication, 12 December 2016.
134. Hajia Hawusatu Eleas, interview at Sogakɔfe, 12 April 2016.

names by the imam, would have taken place earlier in the mosque during dawn prayer time.[135]

5. The imam or malam prays to bless the child, before the formal or ritualistic pronouncing of its names, to be successful in life.

6. The imam then officially or ritually pronounces the names (including the day-of-birth name, Islamic and surnames) given by the child's father. For a girl to be called "Hawusatu," as example, he says *"Ariraya Hawusatu"* four times, and an old lady then responds with a *"gunda"* (yurrra, yurrra, yurrra) after each pronouncement. For a boy the pronouncement and subsequent response is only thrice. This is because in life a woman receives a special bath four times: at birth, marriage, maternity and death. With the boy that of maternity is out. One of the names may be after a chosen elderly relative.[136]

7. In his final blessings the imam admonishes the babe to emulate the good character of the person it is named after, often its grandmother or grandfather.[137]

8. Freewill offering (*sadaqa*) and refreshing the congregants continues for long time.[138] In their joy congregants also invoke goodwill and blessings on the child as they call its names, saying: "Welcome, having joined us do stay well and be of help to us and to yourself. We wish you happy living."[139]

To summarize this chapter, it is evidently clear that the primal religious birthing rites of the Sokpoe-Eʋe are highly potent with implications of priming babies for harmonious ecological relations or creation care. When appropriately re-evaluated and reconstructed with the gospel as hermeneutic these rites may provide vital and pragmatic knowledge for an African Christian theocology curriculum. Yet both the Christians and Muslims in the ecological area appear not to be taking advantage of this opportunity, perhaps due to influence of their Western Christian and Islamic-inherited missionary theologies, respectively. How a baby eventually knows or may come to know of and actualize the ecological implications of its religious birthing rites as it grows through physical life to its end in the ecosystem

---

135. Hajia Hawusatu Eleas, interview at Sogakɔfe, 12 April 2016.
136. Hajia Hawusatu Eleas, interview at Sogakɔfe, 12 April 2016.
137. Hajia Hawusatu Eleas, interview at Sogakɔfe, 12 April 2016.
138. Abdullah Muhammad (zongo *sarachi*), interview at Sogakɔfe, 5 April 2016.
139. Hajia Amina Awudu, interview at Dabala, 25 May 2016.

is beyond this research. However, it is significant to notice that even their funerary rites may also have ecological implications.

CHAPTER 8

Eco-Sustainability Associated With Funerary Rites

Introduction: Funerals as Antithesis of Birthing Rites of the Sokpoe-Eʋe

SINCE THE SOKPOE RELIGIOUS worldview is holistic, where life is experienced on a cyclic pattern, ecological relations do not end up only at *kodzogbe* (physical/human world), but continue into *aʋlime* or *etsīe* (the underworld) and *dzifo* (heaven)—all describing the spiritual world of the living dead. The religious funerary rites, like the birthing rites, are enactments of their holistic worldviews and the anthropocentric valuing of humanity in all three religious traditions—Primal, Islamic and Christian. Socio-ecologically, just as only human entrance into the ecological community at birth is celebrated with birthing rites to initiate it, so only humans' departure from the earthly community of the living is commemorated with the burial and funerary rites to bid them farewell. Therefore, funerary rites, as the antithesis of birthing rites, celebrate departure from as against initiation into the ecological community on Earth. But they also have significant socioecological implications based on the conception of death as a transition and translocation from the gecosphere to terresphere and celesphere rather than a termination of life. The specific location of the departed soul of a deceased person in the cosmos and the state of its continuity of being is contingent, at least in a sense, on ecological relationships on Earth prior to death. What then is death to the religious in Sokpoe ecological area and how can this influence religious ecological actions?

The Sokpoe-Eʋe Religious Concept of Death and Its Influence on Eco-Praxis

The primal Sokpoe-Eʋe religionist looks on death as both the opposite of *kodzogbe nɔnɔ* (living as material being on Earth) and a transition to *aʋlime* (living as immaterial being in the world beneath). Death occurs when, according to their religious anthropology, the enlivening of the *ʋu-kple-gbɔgbɔ* (blood and breath/spirit) coupling ceases to function. At this point the *ŋutilā* (flesh or body) is dead or enters a new state of no *agbe* (enlivening). The dead *ŋutilā* is then referred to as *amee* (the being or thing).[1] At death, therefore, there is a separation between the blood, breath/spirit and the flesh. Then the blood either sleeps[2] or turns back into water in the body and both eventually turn into soil in *yɔdome* (grave).[3] Samuel Agboklu does not know where the spirit/breath departs to at death. However, it may either return to *Mawu* (God), from whence it came,[4] or becomes *ŋɔlĩ* (ghost).[5] Being the same as *luʋɔ* (soul),[6] *ŋɔlĩ* may continue to roam in *yame le anyigbadzi* (the Earth's atmosphere), and/or may become *amedzɔdzɔ* (a reincarnate),[7] although the permanent abode of *ŋɔlĩ* is not known.[8] It seems from the responses that the fate of the *luʋɔ* (soul) depends on the type of death, particularly *trɔ̃ku* (deity-induced death). From a theocological point of view, it is *trɔ̃ku* that potentially can induce thoughts of and decisions of the living to develop and practice eco-ethical relationships in the gecosphere. For *trɔ̃ku* often results believably from unethical attitudes and behavioral relationships and practices in the holistic but precarious ecological community.[9] I

---

1. Geoffrey Siame, interview at Sokpoe on 17 February 2016.
2. Geoffrey Siame, interview at Sokpoe on 17 February 2016.
3. Samuel Agboklu, interview at Sokpoe, 2 March 2016. Avinyo Atiglo, interview, 15 February 2016, explains this conclusion that blood turns into water at death is based on the observation that when there is breath/spirit a cut on the living being oozes blood; but at death a similar cut brings out water instead.
4. Geoffrey Siame, interview at Sogakɔfe on 17 February 2016.
5. Enyi Avenɔgbo, interview at Sokpoe-Elavanyo, 2 February 2016.
6. Geoffrey Siame, interview at Sogakɔfe on 17 February 2016.
7. Klayi Avi, interview at Sokpoe, 2 February 2016.
8. George Kwame Grey, interview at Sokpoe, 2 February 2016.
9. Avinyo Atiglo, interview at Sokpoe-Elavanyo, 15 February 2016. He explains with an example from oyster picking that: staked oysters are a cluster of oysters intentionally kept in the open river with fence poles planted around them, but they are not necessarily enclosed. Despite the openness, staked oysters never move away from the staked arena; even after going out for food they would return to the arena. The purpose is to conserve them till the next conducive market season. Oyster is generally considered a deity, particularly when in a cluster, whether self-organized or by someone.

shall elaborate more on *trɔ̃ku* and its influencing eco-sustainable relations later in this chapter.

On their part the Muslim participants believe that death is the condition we enter when all the predetermined quantity of days and the basic needs of life—water, food and air—provided by God at birth for an individual finish.[10] An Islamic theologian, Muhammad Taqi-ud-Din Al-Hilali, explaining this belief argues from Qur'an 72:28 that "God keeps count of or knows the exact number of everything he has provided to his people whom he protects," especially the messengers he has chosen from humankind.[11] In addition, God decrees the fate of all things according to the Islamic belief in predestination.[12] Muhammad Abu Bakar is the chief imam of the Zongo community in Sokpoe-Sogakɔfe ecological area. In his understanding, *eku* (death) occurs when *Mawu* (Allah/God) takes back life from humans.[13] For Idrisu Ibrahim, "*Ne ame ku la gbɔgbɔ ɖe ɖa eye ŋutilã alo lãkusi tsi anyigba.*" He means that at death *gbɔgbɔ* (breath/spirit) separates off from the *ŋutilã* (body), leaving *lãkusi* (flesh) on the *anyigba* (ground).[14] Thus, in the Islamic thought of the participants in this research, death is separation of the *gbɔgbɔ* (life-giving spirit) from its encasement, *ŋutilã* (the body). The separation can and is effectuated only by God, otherwise death cannot occur. Thus for the participants it is God who kills or at least allows occurrence of death, perhaps based on Qur'an 45:26. In an internet article, "Muslim Views of Death," Prof. Omid Safi and Anna Bigellow explain that Muslim views about death, as in Christianity, begin with the premise that the eternal human soul is God-given.[15] In other words, only God decides to take what he had given back or not. "But at death," I asked, "what happens to the constituents of the being of human?"

The view of most of the participants answering this question is that on leaving the body at death *gbɔgbɔ* (the spirit/breath) is taken back by God but may be kept either with or somewhere else away from God. Idrisu Ibrahim believes that at death God receives the spirit unto himself in the seventh heaven.[16] For Memuna Kudi, an Eʋe proselyte to Islam, human spirits go

---

Stealing from the staked cluster or picking more than one from self-organized cluster in the deep river bottom may result in the culprit drowning as the deity's punishment for being unethical.

10. Alhassan Ibrahim, interview at Sogakɔfe, 14 April 2016.
11. Al-Hilali et al., *Noble Qur'an*, www.noblequran.com.
12. Azumah, *My Neighbour's Faith*, 33.
13. Imam Muhamad Abu Bakar, interview 5 April 2016.
14. Idrisu Ibrahim, interview at Sogakɔfe, 23 April 2016.
15. Safi and Bigelow, "Muslim Views of Death."
16. Most of the Muslim participants in the study mention seven heavens; only one

to heaven only for persons with *dzimekɔkɔe* (clean heart or righteous). She is not certain where a "non-righteous" person's spirit goes, though it may be roaming on the Earth awaiting Judgment Day.[17] On his part Imam Muhammad Abu Bakar thinks God keeps the spirits of all dead people safe at an unknown place awaiting Judgment Day.

The Islamic views of Muslims in the study about the whereabouts of a person's *gbɔgbɔ* (spirit/soul) postmortem are thus inconclusive. However, the respondents are clear in their minds that the fate of a deceased's *gbɔgbɔ* is ultimately determined by God and this will be during judgment at the eschatological end. Judgment will take place by the weighing of deeds, "for in Islam salvation has to be earned."[18] If one's good deeds, including ecological relationships, outweigh the bad then one qualifies admission into the seventh paradise or *janna*. But if the bad deeds outweigh the good, one will be condemned to hell or *jahanna*.[19] Until then and even thereafter, participants were not very certain where a deceased person's *gbɔgbɔ* specifically abides after departing *ŋutilã*, because only God knows where we shall be after judgment.[20] This notwithstanding, Abu Bakar Ademu, a dealer in metal scraps at Dabala Junction, strongly believes if he as Muslim cheats on Earth his spirit goes straight into *dzomavɔ* (hell fire) after death.[21] From a theocological point of view, he means that sinfulness *per se* and, hence, possibly ecological sin in the gecosphere is surely the way for one's spirit to go into hell in the celesphere. It is in this sense that the concept of death can influence a Muslim to pursue righteous and harmonious socioecological relations on Earth. These ideas correspond in some respects with similar ones in Christianity.

The concept of death among the Christian participants in this study relates directly to their anthropological understandings of the human constitution, which is either of three or two components. Castro Abotsi, a Presbyterian, and Mathew Agbatɔ of Divine Healing Church of Christ in Christ

---

(Abdul Aziz Muhammad) thinks there are eight heavens with God in the eighth one called paradise or *fidaus*; and two participants, Memuna Kudi and Hawusatu Eleas, who are proselytes, do not know the heavens are more than one. Yet Azumah, in his *My Neighbour's Faith*, 33, indicates that the Qur'an describes eight paradises (*janna*).

17. Memuna Kudi, interview at Sogakɔfe, 13 April 2016. She is an Eʋe who became a Muslim. Since many Ghanaians associate Islam more with northern ethnic extractions than southerners, the latter who adhere to Islam are described as tuba', meaning proselytes.

18. Azumah, *My Neighbour's Faith*, 33.

19. Abdallah Mohamed, interview at Sogakɔfe, 5 April 2016.

20. Imam Muhamad Abu Bakar, interview at Sogakɔfe, 5 April 2016.

21. Abu Bakar Ademu, interview at Dabala Junction, 19 May 2016.

(DHCCC), for instance, share their understandings based on the three components view: ŋutilā, luvɔ and gbɔgbɔ. Although interviewed separately, each approached explaining his understanding of the constitution of human being antithetically from the phenomenon of death, illustrating it with our dream-state experiences. In a dream *luvɔ* parts with *ŋutilā* temporarily, but no death occurs because *gbɔgbɔ* remains present,[22] connecting *ŋutilā* and *luvɔ* as if in a state of ḍimeyiyi (coma).[23] At the point of death, *luvɔ* is first to exit *ŋutilā* yet remains connected in a sense to *gbɔgbɔ*. Subsequently, as *gbɔgbɔ* follows to exit gradually the person enters a state of *kudɔfofo* (gasping for breath).[24] This happens when the *kadodo* (cord) between *ŋutilā* and *gbɔgbɔ* disconnects and frees the latter to follow *luvɔ* out of the body. The body is then left in a state of lifelessness as had been at its creation; this is death.[25]

All the same, some other respondents, including Jacob Azuma of Church of Pentecost (COP), pastors Agbewavi of Apostolic Revelation Society (ARS) and M. K. Adikpe, a Presbyterian, explain death with a two-component view of the human constitution—*ŋutilā* and *gbɔgbɔ*. For them death is the exit of *gbɔgbɔ* from the *ŋutilā*,[26] then *ŋutilā*, made up of muscle and blood, returns to soil from which it is created, after internment.[27] Similarly, Andrews Ahado, a Presbyterian, bases his view on the scriptural assertion in Ezekiel 18:4 (RSV). By quoting this text that "the soul that sins shall die" he argues that dying occurs when a human being loses out the enlivened, rational and sentient constituent, leaving the lifeless and nonsentient body. In the mind-world of the Sokpoe-Eʋe Christian, death on Earth then is separation of the human living soul (being a conjoined created soul and enlivening breath of God) from the lifeless body (made up of flesh and blood). In short, death to the Sokpoe-Eʋe Christian is essentially a disjoining of the psychosomatic confluence of the spiritual and the physical aspects of a human being.

Like the primal religionists and Muslims, the fate of the living soul of a Sokpoe Christian after departing the body at death depends on the quality of life lived in the eco-community on Earth prior to dying. As Pastor Agbewɔvi and Martin Doade view it, the departed soul roams the Earth's

---

22. Castro Abotsi, interview at Sokpoe, 5 February 2016.
23. Mathew Agbatɔ, interview at Sokpoe-Vogɔme, 24 February 2016.
24. Mathew Agbatɔ, interview at Sokpoe-Vogɔme, 24 February 2016.
25. Castro Abotsi, interview at Sokpoe, 5 February 2016.
26. Maxwell Agbewɔvi, interview at Sokpoe, 26 February 2016 and Maxwell K. Adikpe, interview at Mepe 2 June 2016.
27. Maxwell K. Adikpe, interview at Mepe 2 June 2016.

surface for at least forty days, after which only *kɔkɔetɔwo* (righteous souls) ascend to God in heaven, leaving the unrighteous ones on Earth.[28] Mercy Akafo espoused this view, but did not specify the duration of soul roaming before ascending.[29] On their part, M. K. Adikpe, Mathew Agbatɔ and Edward Kattah think all departed souls keep roaming on the Earth awaiting God's Judgement Day before their permanent abode in either heaven or hell can be determined.[30]

Generally, in the view of most of the Christian participants, roaming souls of dead persons, including the righteous ones prior to ascension, may "wear" human bodies temporarily and reappear as *ŋolīwo* (ghosts) to living people on the Earth.[31] Citing personal instances, pastors Agbewɔvi and Adikpe as well as Edward Kattah strongly believe ghosts do exist, being departed souls reappearing in human body form. More so, "the word *ŋolī* exists and only exists because something exists to be called *ŋolī*."[32] Agbewɔvi's daughter Vivian died and was buried at Tadzeʋu. Yet within two weeks postmortem Vivian was believed to have visited and called her father twice at Sokpoe in the night.[33] In addition, during the funeral rites at Sokpoe, Vivian's first cousin Dzɔka Atsuƒe saw and recognized her, but she (Dzɔka Atsuƒe) had tightened lips and so was unable to communicate with her.[34] M. K. Adikpe did not see, but clearly heard both his late mother and a nephew, Edo, speak to him during their respective funeral rites.[35] Edward Kattah knew his friend Adenyo had died, and so was surprised when at a bank in Ho he saw Adenyo, who, however, vanished before he could get closer to exchange greetings.[36] Shortly after his father's death, Daniel Agbota believes the deceased came as or in a whirlwind. For Daniel, that he saw the whirlwind lifting a bottle of liquor on his dwarf wall, and the fact that the previous night he had heard a knock, though he found no one upon

28. Maxwell Agbewɔvi, interview at Sokpoe, 26 February 2016. Martin Doade, interview at Sokpoe, 3 February 2016.

29. Mercy Awo Akafo, interview at Sokpoe-Elavanyo, 28 December 2015.

30. M. K. Adikpe, interview at Mepe 2 June 2016 and Matthew Agbatɔ, interview at Sokpoe-Vogɔme, 24 February 2016, Edward Kattah, interview at Sokpoe, 11 March 2016.

31. Martin Doade, interview at Sokpoe, 5 February 2016; Castro Abotsi, interview at Sokpoe, 5 February 2016; Andrews Ahado, interview at Sokpoe, 5 February 2016. See also Maxwell K. Adikpe, interview at Meƒe 2 June 2016.

32. M. K. Adikpe, interview at Mepe 2 June 2016.

33. Sokpoe is about one hundred kilometers from Tadzeʋu.

34. Maxwell Agbewɔvi, interview at Sokpoe, 26 February 2016.

35. M. K. Adikpe, interview at Mepe 2 June 2016.

36. Edward Kattah, interview at Sokpoe, 11 March 2016.

opening the door, were enough evidence for his conclusion.³⁷ More often than not the visual or audible encounter between living humans and ghosts is rather transient and considered *nukpekpe* (an astonishing encounter).³⁸ The theocological implication of the concept of ghosts is the belief that the spirits of the ancestors can influence the living in the eco-community, either for good or evil.

Ghosts as Ancestral Spirits and Their Influence on Religious Eco-Ethical Praxis

The Aŋlɔ-Eʋe describe ancestors as *tɔgbeŋɔlĩwo* (male ghosts) *kple mamaŋɔlĩwo* (female ghosts), and that they are invisible community members.³⁹ Describing the components of the Akan spirit world, Kwame Bediako calls ancestors *Nsamanfo* or "spirit fathers"⁴⁰ who dwell in the "realm of ancestor spirits."⁴¹ In African primal cultures that have ancestral dominance in their worldviews, like the Akan, the ancestors or ghosts of respected living dead serve as custodians of traditional moral laws, including ecological ethics. They have power to punish or reward breakers or upholders of the laws, respectively,⁴² because death has changed and translocated them from the human to the "realm of spirits and the 'gods.'" Bediako argues that in the African primal worldview, the spirit world, which provides the pattern for the human world, is the place of both power and resources for living as well as terrors and misfortunes that threaten and destroy life.⁴³ Thus in the primal culture and spirituality of Africans the effectiveness of taboos as eco-ethical tools in sustaining the ecosystem arises as a matter of strong faith in and from either the fear of divinities or respect for ancestors (the living dead).⁴⁴ However, both Christians and Muslims in the Sokpoe eco-area tend to generally abhor ancestral veneration and repudiate ancestral influence on eco-ethical praxis.

The suggestion that a deceased's *gbɔgbɔ* (spirit) may reappear on the Earth as *ŋɔlĩ* (ghost) or *amedzɔdzɔ* (reincarnate) is completely inconceivable to the Islamic mind of the Muslim participants. Hajia Hawusatu is a

37. Daniel Agbota, interview at Sokpoe, 11 February 2016.
38. M. K. Adikpe, interview at Mepe 2 June 2016.
39. Aveteh, interview at ACI, Akropong-Akuapem, 22 May 2015.
40. K. Bediako, *Jesus in Africa*, 23.
41. K. Bediako, *Jesus in Africa*, 26.
42. Gyekye, *African Cultural Values*, 166.
43. K. Bediako, *Jesus in Africa*, 27.
44. Blasu, "Compensated Reduction," 24.

southerner who lives in Sogakofe but hails from Ada in the Greater Accra region of Ghana. Through association with northern Ghana Muslims sojourning in Ada she became a proselyte to Islam. Asked to describe and distinguish *ŋɔlĩ* (ghost) and *luvɔ* (soul) from an Islamic point of view, she responded assertively: "*Awusatɔwo menya ŋɔlĩ o*" (Muslims do not know of *ŋɔlĩ*); and *luvɔ* is the shadow we cast on the ground and to which we are connected.[45] Hajia Hawusatu shows she has no ideas about, let alone believing in, concepts of "ghosts" and "souls" in connection with the making and dying of humans. Similarly, Imam Muhammad Abu Bakar does not believe in the existence of *ŋɔlĩ* because death terminates a person's *xexeme* (state of a being). In other words, once a person loses its *gbɔgbɔ* (breath/spirit) to God at death, every earthly involvement of that person as a being is completely ended; it can no longer influence anything in the ecological community.[46] Both the Zongo *sarachi* of Sogakɔfe, Abdullah Mohamed, and Hajia Amina Awudu of Dabala do not believe in the existence of ghosts, and hence ancestors as living dead. However, they know of the Tujania Islamic sect, who tend to believe this.[47] Hajia Amina recalls a case in which a Tujania friend claimed to have encountered the *fetoluwa* (Hausa word for ghost) of her (Hajia Amina's) late sister.[48] Madam Adizza Garba is a Muslim, being the daughter of a transhumant pastoralist from northern Ghana, but sojourned in Tɔŋu.[49] She also tends to affirm the concept of ghosts, perhaps because of influence from her long years of close interactions with the Tɔŋu Eʋe—both primal religionists and Christians—in the many villages where her father had lived as a cattle business dealer. She explains:

> I have only heard about but never seen a ghost. Yet the testimonies of our Eʋe neighbors about ghost activities make me believe it exists. The concept of ghost is from the indigenous religious Eʋe and not from Muslims. The indigenous Eʋe speak of *ŋɔlĩ* (ghost) as the *luvɔ* (soul) of a deceased which manifests itself as if a living human enters another person and influences the host person to be mischievous. Thus, I believe in ghosts though I am also aware Muslims generally do not.

45. Hajia Hawusatu Elias, interview at Sogakɔfe, 12 April 2016.
46. Imam Muhamad Abu Bakar, interview 5 April 2016.
47. Abdullah Muhammad (zongo *sarachi*), interview at Sogakɔfe, 5 April 2016.
48. Hajia Amina Awudu, interview at Dabala, 25 May 2016.
49. Transhumance pastoral practice involves both migration of livestock (shifting camp) in the dry season and returning to (settling on) the same fertile place in the wet season for some level of sedentary crop cultivation. They settle at a place for one to three years before shifting.

Inferably Madam Adizza Garba, though a Muslim, tends to believe that ŋɔlĩ is the same as luvɔ and hence the departed gbɔgbɔ (spirit) of a deceased. In her view, when encountered in the eco-community, ŋɔlĩ is a "spirit-in-body" person: a living human who hosts and is influenced by the departed gbɔgbɔ (spirit) of a deceased person. She does not see the phenomenon as reincarnation, though. In addition, she considers that a characteristic by which a person who has actually died may be identified as a ghost is a notable mischief of the ghost.

For Idrisu Ibrahim, although the ghost concept is absent in an Islamic religious worldview, there are things that may be similar to ghosts in that they are spirits that can appear in bodily form.[50] They are called *jinns*; some are good and others bad. According to Islamic theologians *sura* 72:11 of the Qur'an speaks of creatures called *jinns* who eavesdropped the recital of the Qur'an to Prophet Mohamed. However, only some believed and became Muslims in submitting to Allah; the others became *al-qâsitûn* (disbelievers).[51] John Azumah describes *jinns* as supernatural beings that Muslims believe have been created of smokeless fire (Qur'an 15:27). They can behave like humans, procreate with humans and can appear and disappear from people at will in the form of animals and humans. Idrisu Ibrahim, in an interview, thinks the difference between ghosts and *jinns* is in the ease and frequency of encountering them. The latter unlike the former are no longer encountered in our human world since the times of Isa (Jesus), Suleiman (Solomon) and Musa (Moses).[52]

It is not difficult to conclude that the Muslims in this study generally do not know the whereabouts of the departed spirit of a deceased person between the time of death and the expected divine judgment in the eschatological end. Unlike in primal religion, the Muslim counterparts conceive no ancestral spirits as living dead anywhere, nor do they believe ancestors can influence any eco-ethical matters of the living in the ecosystems of the Earth. Nonetheless, the southern Ghana Muslim participants, perhaps with influence from their original pre-Islamic Eʋe cultural background, tend to believe that ghosts may be roaming on the Earth or at least have ability to interact with the living in the ecological community while waiting Judgment Day.

Like the Muslims, most of the Christians in Sokpoe ecological area are disgusted with the thought of ancestors having interests in and being able to influence compliance with eco-ethical regulations. Gladys Ahado of the

---

50. Idrisu Ibrahim, interview at Sogakɔfe, 23 April 2016.
51. Al-Hilali et al., *Noble Qur'an*.
52. Idrisu Ibrahim, interview at Sogakɔfe, 23 April 2016.

Church of Pentecost (COP) believes in ghost existence, but not in ancestors influencing the living, because the dead cannot be sensitive to nor are they able to affect issues in the world of the living. Unlike Gladys Ahado, the majority of the Christians in the study are either not certain about or do not believe in the existence of ghosts at all, let alone their influencing the living. Dickson Blasu of ARS reasons that the dead cannot appear in life form again on Earth until resurrection day. He denies the existence of ghosts of ancestors although ghosts are reportedly seen among the living living (*kodzogbe*). He contends that any such reportedly seen ghost of an ancestor is only the working of an evil spirit. To him the evil spirit camouflages itself by "wearing" or interpenetrating the roaming *luvɔ* (soul) and assuming the bodily face of the deceased.[53] In my opinion, since it is still the soul and face of the deceased that the supposedly evil spirit "wears" and manifests, Dickson Blasu's argument does not actually deny the existence of ghosts, but rather means their manifestations are more of the manipulation of evil spirits than natural occurrences.

In the view of Mary Azuma, since in Christianity it is not conclusive that ancestral spirits exist in the eco-community after death, it is abhorrent that some Christians tend to venerate ancestral spirits for various reasons. She knows of a man who attends the same church with her. Yet during traditional festival celebration this man performs a ritual dancing with a wartime flag believed to be inhabited with the war spirit that helped our founding ancestors.[54] For fear of incurring the wrath of the ancestors who captured the flag in a war, if the dance is not properly performed he pours a libation soliciting their help. In another instance, Mary Azuma recalls disagreeably a middle-aged Christian lady who wondered why her dead father did not cause her only child who died as an infant to be reincarnated.[55] In other words, the bereaved Christian woman believed the living dead in *avlime* could influence issues of the living living in *kodzogbe* (earthly life) even to the extent of sending back to life a dead beloved relative.

From the foregoing discourse I see that in the real socioecological life of the Sokpoe-Eʋe, the existence of an ancestral spirit or ghost is not inconceivable in the religious mind of the eco-community. Even some Muslims, particularly proselytes to Islam from the indigenous Eʋe and their Ada close neighbors who have similar primal worldviews, tend to uphold such

53. Dickson Blasu, interview at Sokpoe, 3 February 2016.

54. This flag is a traditional insignia of military bravery during the migratory and settlement battles of the Sokpoe people. People believe it contains some spiritual power that possesses the flag-bearer. Pouring libation to invoke ancestors for help in bearing the flag is considered non-Christian among the Sokpoe-Eʋe.

55. Mary Ame Azuma, interview at Sokpoe, 1 March 2016.

a conception. This observation is evidentially affirmed by the belief of all three religious traditions in life after death. Harold Turner theorizes that the sense of or belief in life after death is one characteristic of primal religious consciousness.[56] In the case of the Christians there is a further evidence of confessing belief in "communion with the saints" in their creed. It suggests that some interaction exists, at least conceptually in the mind of the three traditions of the religious community, between the living dead in *avlime* (the teresphere) and the living living here in *kodzogbe* (the gecosphere). The critical question, however, is, in the words of Kwame Bediako, "whether such an understanding faithfully reflects biblical revelation and is rooted in true Christian experience." In other words, does this conceptual interaction mean that the living dead (or cult of ancestors) in real terms do function as real persons—custodians and supervisory enforcers of eco-ethical regulations on the living-living?

Kwame Bediako's insightful explanations come to mind in answering this question. Bediako suggests that ancestors are more of mythical than real entities, and that they do not originate from transcendent realms.[57] He argues from an intellectual point of view that ancestors are the products of the myth-making imagination of the living community they left behind on Earth.[58] As he puts it, "the potency of the cult of ancestors is not the potency of the ancestors themselves; . . . [it] is the potency of myth."[59] However, for ancestor-dominant cultures "the cult of ancestors as myth points to the role of the cult in ensuring social [and ecological] harmony"[60] by enforcing environmental relational taboos and regulations. In performing this role, the ancestors exercise the sacralized authority conferred on them by the community through traditional leadership that is itself sacralized by the same myth making. Indisputably, in ancestor-dominant cultures the eco-harmony-promoting potency of the ancestral myth is commonly observable in the commitment of primal religionists to comply with environmental taboos. It is a different situation in the Sokpoe ecological area, where the dominant component in the worldview is different.

Among the Sokpoe-Eυe, although the ancestral concept exists, ancestors are not a dominant component of their religious worldviews; neither does the eco-community (primal religionists, Muslims and Christians) generally fathom ancestral veneration as a religious motivation for creation

56. Turner, "The Primal Religions of the World and their Study," 31.
57. K. Bediako, *Jesus in Africa*, 30.
58. K. Bediako, *Jesus in Africa*, 30.
59. K. Bediako, *Jesus in Africa*, 30.
60. K. Bediako, *Jesus in Africa*, 30.

care. Mercy Akafo, a presbyter, like many other Christian participants, rightly asserts,: "the souls of departed ancestors in *aʋlime* (terresphere) cannot influence life situations in the ecosystem of the living in *kodzogbe* (gecosphere)."[61] From an Islamic perspective, Muhammad Abu Bakar shares similar views: "once a person loses its *gbɔgbɔ* (breath/spirit) to God at death every earthly involvement of that person as a being is completely ended; it can no longer influence anything in the ecological community."[62] For the primal religionists there are ancestors, but it is not necessarily the ancestors, rather the deities, which they believe are responsible for enforcing eco-regulations, because "*ŋɔlĩ mewua ame o, trɔ̃e wua ame*" (ghost or ancestral spirit does not kill; it is deity that kills).[63] Thus the primal religionists and the group of Christians that I have earlier described in chapter 6 as the "indigenized or acculturated" comply with ecological taboos for fear of and to avoid *trɔ̃ku* (deity-induced death).

Fear of *Trɔ̃ku* (Deity-Induced Death) as Impulsion for Eco-Ethical Praxis

To the Sokpoe-Eʋe primal religionist the cause of every death necessarily must be investigated before funerary rites are performed. There are at least two socioecological reasons. On one hand, it enables performing the appropriate funerary rituals befitting the deceased by virtue of their socioethical status prior to dying. On the other hand, more importantly, it helps to prevent recurrence of avoidable deaths in the eco-community. As Samuel Agboklu and Tɔgbe Dagadu insist in separate interviews, it is necessary to inquire and understand the death of a person so as to know how to organize the funerary rites[64] and so the survivors may not die similarly.[65]

The socioecological significance of the latter reason stems from their precarious vision of the gecosphere. Amega Enyi Avenɔgbo strongly believes that the gecosphere is full of many lethal malevolent spirit entities to which human beings are vulnerable. "We live in a dangerous world, filled with unpredictable challenges and unseen perils."[66] This perspective is similar to Harold Turner's third feature of the worldviews of primal eco-communities:

61. Mercy Awo Akafo, interview at Sokpoe-Elavanyo, 28 December 2015.
62. Imam Muhamad Abu Bakar, interview 5 April 2016.
63. Yɔhokpɔ, Interview at Sogakɔfe, 17 February 2016.
64. Samuel Agboklu, interview at Sokpoe, 2 March 2016. This is the position of Enyi Avenɔgbo and Avinyo Atiglo, among others also in separate interviews.
65. Tɔgbe Dagadu, interview at Sokpoe-Ahogaƒeme, 4 March 2016.
66. Enyi Avenɔgbo, interview at Sokpoe-Elavanyo, 2 February 2016.

humans are not alone in the cosmos. There are myriad spiritual entities, both benevolent and malevolent, more powerful than humans, unpredictable and yet the causers of many events in human experience.[67] Hence, there is the need to desist from ecological *ethoi* or relational behaviors in the ecosystem that may be provocative, perhaps, to even the unseen spirits, particularly the malevolent ones. Otherwise the consequence will be *trɔku*, that is, a punitive death recurring in a family, believed to have been caused by a deity whose wrath is incurred by some ecologically unethical behavior of the victim. As explained earlier in chapter 6, among the Sokpoe-Eʋe, unlike other African cultures like the Akan in Ghana, it is deities rather than ancestors that are custodians of environmental regulations and taboos. It is deities then that reward or punish responses to eco-ethical taboos. Enyi Avenɔgbo did not mince words; his vocal, facial and body language was firm: "*Amesiame le trɔku vɔm*" (Everyone fears deity-induced death), especially when indicted before the court (shrine) of the deity for some misconduct in the social or physical environment.

A person avoids incurring *trɔku* by prudently complying with ecological taboos. It is a serious demand from a primal religious point of view, because to curtail the otherwise resultant recurring punitive death in the family is usually expensive. It may involve sending a young lady to serve sacrificially in the shrine of the offended deity on behalf of the affected family as *trɔkosi* (slave maid of deity). If the affected family has no such person, they may have to "borrow" her from another family at a bargained fee. In the shrine, the young *trɔkosi* becomes a maid slave and wife of the deity, and hence the *trɔnuɔ* (the shrine priest), for a given period or even for life.[68] Apparently the expensiveness of *trɔku* lies in the possibility of changing the destiny of an innocent girl or woman, against her wishes, to become *trɔkosi*; and the many lives to be lost in toll of recurring death if no person is found to become *trɔkosi*.

Trɔku is thus the first suspect and inquired for elimination when investigating cause of death. The inquiry involves *ŋɔlīyɔyɔ* (divination), by which the deceased's *ŋɔlī* (ghost) is made to describe the type of death, who is involved and/or how he/she must be buried. Often, necromancy takes place while the corpse is put on *donu* (a dugout) to drain out all visceral and renal fluid into the soil. Emptying the internal contents of the corpse helps to preserve the body. Sometimes inquiry of the cause of death may involve public display by the *ŋɔlī* (ghost) of the deceased under the instruction of a *nukala* or *ŋɔlīyɔla* (diviner). The corpse races its wooden bier and

---

67. Turner, "The Primal Religions of the World & Their Study," 31.
68. Enyi Avenɔgbo, interview at Sokpoe-Elavanyo, 2 February 2016.

bearers to a secret spot where some personal effects of the deceased, such as underpants, towel and sponge, are hidden. The spot is known only to the diviner or a chosen member of the family who alone had earlier hidden the items secretly there. The diviner instructs the corpse, borne on a wooden bier by two carriers on their heads, to go and locate its hidden clothing. If it is *trɔku*, people believe the ghost forcefully and speedily moves the carriers but halts suddenly and surprisingly at the hidden spot. Then the corpse is further instructed to move to an identified object such as a tree ahead. The speedy rush forward towards the object, as against sluggish and reluctant or even reverse movement, confirms *trɔku*.[69]

As mentioned above, *trɔku* often results from unethical attitudes and behavioral relationships and practices in the holistic but precarious ecological community. Some of such unethical ecological behaviors include pilfering staked oysters in the river. Another is entering and/or harvesting wood and fish from sacred or regulated forests and water bodies, respectively.[70] Sometimes ecological pollutions such as illicit sexual intercourse in the bush and improper disposal of human waste may incur the displeasure of deities. George Kwame Grey reports that in 2015 the daughter of a woman called Woonyɔ suffered a disturbing gastrointestinal condition on her way from farm back home. She was compelled to ease herself in a nearby sacred forest. Suddenly a man in white apparel approached and accused her of messing his "room" with fecal matter. She rushed home to narrate her fearful encounter but died soon thereafter.[71] In a separate interview, Amega Klayi Avi espoused the same story and recollects that the cause of the death was inquired and confirmed by the diviner as *trɔku* while the corpse was on *donu*.

Unlike the primal religionists, Muslims and Christians do not normally investigate cause of death before burial,[72] except on medical or legal grounds, and even that is done by a pathologist in a hospital and not by a diviner. The primal religionists argue fervently that not inquiring to know the cause of death, particularly with religious approaches, denies Christians the opportunity of knowing whether they fall victims to *trɔku* (death from the wrath of a deity). The primal religionists say this in connection with Christians' wantonness in disobeying traditional ecological regulations and

---

69. Enyi Avenɔgbo, interview at Sokpoe-Elavanyo, 2 February 2016.

70. Enyi Avenɔgbo, interview at Sokpoe-Elavanyo, 2 February 2016; and Geoffrey Siame, interview at Sogakɔfe, 17 February 2016. Both believe that Amega Asamevi Langla died at the hands of *Nyaɖengɔ trɔ̃* (deity) when he felled some trees in *Nyaɖengɔve me* (forest).

71. George Kwame Grey, interview at Sokpoe, 2 February 2016.

72. Enyi Avenɔgbo, interview at Sokpoe-Elavanyo, 2 February 2016.

taboos, which for them invariably incurs *trɔku*.⁷³ This allegation is of significant theocological interest for two reasons. First, there appears to be some evidential affirmation of the allegation, particularly that Christians tend to disregard *trɔku* and so wantonly disobey traditional ecological regulations and taboos. As I have earlier pointed in chapter 6, Edward Kattah speaks of his grandfather, Gbadago, a Christian, who cleared part of *Balatsui* forest to provide more food than please earthly deities. He believes Gbadago's fearlessness of the deities and wanton ecological actions encouraged many other Christians and even non-Christians to follow suit denuding the entire forest.⁷⁴ In another instance, Daniel Agbota, a presbyter, abhors the designating and declaring of some forests in Sokpoe as *trɔve* (sacred forest for a deity). He supports any moves to clear the entire *Kɔtive* (the forest of *Kɔtitrɔ*) for development purposes rather than pleasing deities. He has even already purchased and cleared part of this sacred forest for his building project.⁷⁵

This leads to the second reason of the theocological importance of the allegation. The allegation underscores the need for an appropriate African Christian theology of the environment that can accommodate and motivate Christians to be part of a concerted effort of all the religious traditions to address their common ecological concerns. As noted in the Introduction, Patrick Curry argues that because we live in a world of diverse views on same issues,⁷⁶ values and ethical praxis sometimes conflict, with no generally accepted absolute or painless resolution in the pluralistic context. Therefore, pragmatic religious ecologies need to accommodate as many virtuous ideals as possible, especially "where there is real potential common ground on a particular issue,"⁷⁷ although they may possibly not accommodate all.

Even though Muslims and Christians do not involve themselves in divination, they also observe the ritual of placing a corpse on *donu* in *yɔxɔme* (the funeral parlor).⁷⁸ This signifies a beginning of the fulfillment and a reminder to the living of God's judgmental fiat in Genesis 3:19 that the materiality of the deceased shall return to its material origin, the Earth. The ritual ensures discharging all visceral and renal contents back into the soil

---

73. Enyi Avenɔgbo, interview at Sokpoe-Elavanyo, 2 February 2016; and Efoe Kofi Avinyo Atiglo, interview at Sokpoe-Elavanyo, 15 February 2016.

74. Edward Kattah, interview at Sokpoe, 11 March 2016.

75. Daniel Agbota, interview at Sokpoe, 11 February 2016.

76. Curry, *Ecological Ethics*, 156.

77. Curry, *Ecological Ethics*, 156.

78. Klay Avi, interview at Sokpoe, 2 February 2016.

and, as noted earlier, enhances local preservation of the corpse for burial and funerary rites.[79]

Funerary Rites as Socioecological Deintegration and Translocation in the Cosmos

Among the Sokpoe-Eʋe all three religious traditions maintain a socioecological perception that undergirds funerary rites. Death does not terminate but simply translocates the deceased, and their relational duties and roles in the eco-community from *kodzogbe* to *avlime*. In addition, the same anthropocentric valuing that singles out humans among other creatures for ritualistic initiation into the cosmos at birth remains the same reason for burial of a corpse at death. Andrews Ahado, a Presbyterian, does not see any vast difference between indigenous religious and Christian practices of burial and its undergirding beliefs in the Sokpoe ecological area. In both religious traditions, the corpse of a human being, among creatures in the ecosystem, must be specially and formally disposed of with required rituals in funerary rites.[80] For Muslims, the corpse must be disposed off without undue delay, ideally within the next twenty-four hours, because it has no value any longer except to be discarded.[81] Yet it is still a human,[82] and, like traditionalists and Christians, the disposal must be done with accorded respect to dignify the corpse. Idrisu Ibrahim states with great concern and emphasis about a corpse:

> *Amegbetɔ wònye! Agbe nɔ eme! Eyata menyo be woatsɔe afugbe ko abe lã aɖe ene o. Ke boŋ woa ɖii ɖe tome.* (It is human! There had been life in it! So, it cannot be discarded just like an animal; it must be buried into the soil.)[83]

These cultural self-understandings require the living community to necessarily perform socioecological rites, which symbolically free the corpse from human roles in *kodzogbe*. I call it eco-social "deintegration" to suggest a reversal of the sociocultural "integration" into *kodzogbe* at birth as discussed in chapter 7. To deintegrate means to sign out and free the deceased's soul and its known credentials among the living living of *kodzogbe*

---

79. Samuel Agboklu, interview at Sokpoe, 2 March 2016.

80. Andrews Ahado, interview at Sokpoe, 5 February 2016.

81. Imam Mahamud Abu Bakar, telephone communication from Sogakoɔfe to Abetifi, 14 September 2016.

82. Idrisu Ibrahim, interview at Sogakɔfe, 23 April 2016.

83. Idrisu Ibrahim, interview at Sogakɔfe, 23 April 2016.

(gecosphere) so as to be integrated or signed into the community of the living dead in *avlime* (terresphere) and *dzifo* (celesphere). Like the sociocultural integrating rituals at birth, the eco-social deintegrating rituals at death are based on a holistic worldview—the understanding that the human and ancestral worlds open seamlessly into each other. The deintegrating rituals include *hlɔ̃tsilele* (clan ritual bath), *ameḍoḍo agba* (laying corpse in state) and *ameḍiḍi* (interment).

Hlɔ̃tsilele (Clan Ritual Bath) as Priming for Integration into *Avlime* (Ancestral World)

Before laying in state and burial the corpse is given *hlɔ̃tsilele*. This is a clan ritual bath, which rationally fulfills a dual purpose. As it deintegrates from *kodzogbe* it also primes or prepares the deceased for integration in *avlime*. The Sokpoe-Eʋe believe that *hlɔ̃tsilele* ensures eco-social identity and moral qualification for acceptance in *avlime*.[84] The primal religious belief is that to enjoy warm welcome and integration in the company of the ancestors and loved ones gone ahead in *avlime*, the deceased must bear a testimony of having proved, while in life, to be a true member of the family, without any questionable character. It may be recalled from chapter 7 that during outdooring at birth the sociocultural integration into an eco-community in *kodzogbe* instructs the baby to "prove whose child you are." Perhaps *hlɔ̃tsilele* in *yɔxɔme* (funeral parlor), as the last bath at the terminus of and departure into life below the Earth, corresponds to *dzigbeḍi tsilele* (bath to remove broinhidrosis or repellent odor) in *ḍiḍɛxɔme* (maternity room) as the first bath at the entrance into earthly life. The one deals with repulsive body odor (chemical pollution) in the eco-community, while the other answers questions on whether some attitudinal and behavioral shortcomings (ethical pollutions) unbecoming of the family are being transited from *kodzogbe* into *avlime*, also known as *etsīewode* (world of the living dead).

Some Christians also practice *hlɔ̃tsilele*, not as a moral correction and priming ritual, but for clan identification in the other world.[85] It suggests the persistence of the primal religious consciousness in their Christianity, "the application of the material of Christian tradition to already existing African maps of the universe."[86] Andrew Walls argues that "What happens in African Christianity is intelligible only in the light of what has gone before

---

84. Agnes Abla Blasu, interview at Sokpoe-Bodzoḍife, 21 June 2016.
85. Agnes Abla Blasu, interview at Sokpoe-Bodzoḍife, 21 June 2016.
86. Walls, *Cross-Cultural Process in Christian History*, 122.

in the African religious story."[87] In Zoyi (Ablɔ) clan for instance, the officiators of *hlɔ̃tsilele* are themselves Presbyterians and the same types of materials, procedures and textual prayers are used for both primal religionists and Christian corpses. For both primal religionists and Christians who practice *hlɔ̃tsilele*, women representatives of the two parental families of the deceased join hands to perform this ritualistic bathing. The process requires *ayisawukutsa* (local sponge made from beating a soft tree stem), *amedzaleˇ* (local soap from palm oil and plantain peel ashes), *tsilenu* (towel), *tsidzodzoe gago ɖeka* (one bucket of hot water), *tsifafɛ gago ɖeka* (one bucket of cold water) and *etre* (calabash). Agnes Abla Blasu is a regular performer of *hlɔ̃tsilele* for the Zoyi (Ablɔ) clan of Sokpoe. She narrates the liturgical process as follows:

> We first pray for effectiveness of the ritual. Then we turn to the corpse and speak to it: "We have come as your parents to bath you with *hlɔ̃tsi* [clan bath] just as you were given *dzigbeɖitsi* (broinhidrosis bath) into the clan at your birth. Be pure enough to be welcomed by your male and female ancestors." Then as one of the two women cleanses the corpse with soapy sponge from head to toes, the other pours warm water from calabash on it. The women then change over hands; the second now does the cleansing while the first pours cold water on the corpse. On emptying both buckets of water one woman would dab the corpse with the towel and the other besmears it with fragrant herbal preparations.[88]

According to her, where one family representative is unavailable at the ritual bath prior to laying the corpse in state, she will necessarily perform a symbolic one with a shorter liturgy when the body is laid in state. There she uses soapy sponge to dry-clean the soles and palms of the corpse, saying, "I have bathed you this *hlɔ̃tsi*; show it to the ancestors so they can welcome you into their midst." The bathing ritual ends when elders of the clan express gratitude to the two women who bathed the corpse. They present them with one bottle of schnapps, saying, "Well done. You have purified your kin person for the ancestors in *tsĩɛ* (living dead world). Wash your hands with this drink." Then just before the coffin is closed for internment, one of the women who performed the ritual bath puts all the items used—sponge, towel and the soap—at the foot of the corpse inside the coffin. It is believed the deceased person needs them for life in *etsĩewode*. Moreover, the living in *kodzogbe* would not need to use them, perhaps to avoid contracting any

---

87. Walls, *Cross-Cultural Process in Christian History*, 120.
88. Agnes Abla Blasu, interview at Sokpoe-Bodzodɟife, 21 June 2016.

health problems of the deceased; nor should they be left accessible to a diabolical person who may use them for spiritual attacks against the family.

To primal religionists the ritual bathing serves two purposes: as a cultural cleansing of socioecological sins, and hence priming (qualifying the deceased) for identification and acceptance by and integration into the community in *avlime*. For Muslims it is neither. A ritual bath is simply the last respect accorded a deceased, and so a close relation does it.[89] On the contrary, some Christians follow the same procedures as the primal religionists; they, however, do not hold unto the first, but the second purpose for this ritual—that it guarantees clan identity and integration in the other world. From my personal observation, experience and interaction with the Christians in the Zoyi clan of Sokpoe, enacting this aspect of their pre-Christian map of the universe with the practice of ritual bath does not make them feel less Christian. This is contrary to Western observation that the continuance of pre-Christian universe makes African Christianity less Christian, an observation Andrews Walls rightly objects to and describes as what "has been the most fruitful single source of misunderstanding."[90]

In my opinion, the Christian ritual bath is a *praeparatio evangelica*; it is indicative of a sense from the religious primal worldview that humans, rightly, need to have some moral quality for acceptance in the spirit world of the living dead. It is then an eco-cultural preparation that enables the Sokpoe-Eʋe to appreciate the gospel teaching on and need for Christ's washing away of sin, consequently qualifying the believer for heavenly citizenship and identity on Earth before death. Thus it "is not intended as an act of apostasy from Christianity."[91] Nevertheless, from a Christian perspective I am convinced that, apart from being a *praeparatio evangelica*, the ritual bath is neither necessary nor a true means of attaining its objectives when engaged with the gospel. It does not in reality prime by cleansing socio-ecological sins nor guarantee clan lineage identity in the spirit world. The Bible interprets the cleansing of eco-social sin very clearly in the Epistle of Hebrews 9:22–28 and 10:1–18 through the blood of Jesus Christ, which washes away sin (Matt 26:28) and reconciles all creation (human and other-than-human) to himself (Col 1:19–20). This is why water baptism does not cleanse sin; it only symbolically announces the outward cleansing of what has already happened inwardly and graciously by faith in the blood of Jesus. Consequently, the identity we should seek in the celestial community is not necessarily earthly clan lineage, but that of God himself, and this identity or

---

89. Safi and Bigelow, "Muslim Views of Death."
90. Walls, *Cross-Cultural Process in Christian History*, 122.
91. Walls, *Cross-Cultural Process in Christian History*, 123.

mark of belonging to God's family is guaranteed when we receive the Holy Spirit (Eph 4:30).

Nevertheless, this does not mean that our earthly ethnic and clan identities will be lost; they shall only be superseded in Christ by a new spiritual bond. In other words, I am not denying that Christians have no further linkage with their family when they die. For the Christian, we have a dual identity. Although our spiritual identity is in Christ, our human identity is still there, even in heaven, in my understanding of Revelation 7:9. As Clement of Alexandria sings in *Protreptikos*, the miracle of heaven is that our clan identities will be gloriously harmonized with all other clan identities in some incomprehensible way. So, the Sokpoe-Eʋe language will be represented in heaven, singing in harmony with other languages like Kasem etc. That means there is a possibility of clan identity, and for the Sokpoe-Eʋe an eco-moral quality or status needs to be attained during gecospheric life to qualify for both entering and reuniting with one's clan members who make it into the heavenly celesphere.

Therefore, I reiterate the African Christian theocological significance of *hlɔtsilele*. I propose that *hlɔtsilele* as a ritual bath of the dead can remind Christians of some biblical socioecological realities in earthly life that have eternal consequences, and therefore the need to manage them appropriately on Earth before death. For instance, it reminds that we need to belong to an eco-social community both on Earth and in heaven. But the guarantee of being identified with and integrated into the community in heaven is contingent on how we manage righteous socioecological and ethical relationships on Earth, based on faith in Christ, love for God the Father and empowerment of the Holy Spirit.

Laying in State and Interment as Eco-Social Deintegration from *Kodzogbe*

After the ritual bath, the corpse is clad in one of his/her traditional dresses or in such attire that depicts his/her status in life. For both Christians (sometimes) and Muslims (all times) the corpse is clad in a white *aklala* (calico) burial *awuʋlaya* (shroud) or cloak. Particularly in the case of Muslims, the burial cloak consists of a pair of loose or airy *aklala* trousers stretching from the toes to the waist, where it is tied with a belt made from the same white fabric. On top of the trousers is a white sleeveless tunic being *awugɔmewui* (underwear) from neck to knees. Finally, on the tunic is worn a white *awuʋlaya* (burial shroud) that virtually wraps up the corpse from the head (except the face) down and covering the toes. It has a hood that can be pulled to cover the face of the corpse, though.

In all cases the dressed corpse is then laid in state in the specially provided room in the clan house called *yɔxɔme* (funeral parlor) for all mourners to take a final look and give last homage and bid farewell amidst *avigbexexlē* (mournful oratory) and wailing. In other words, the bereaved families and sympathetic friends, usually women, painfully recount personal experiences with the deceased and question the loss or vacuum created in the relationship due to the death. In this way the living living commemorate the deceased's credentials, on one hand, and on the other, sorrowfully express affirmation of discontinuity of same credentials at *kodzogbe*. Others cry because the current death reminds them of previously lost relatives. As part of the mournful wailing, primal religionists send verbal messages of felicitation and petitioning for providence through the current corpse to their departed loved ones in *avlime*. These rituals then provide a special means for eco-social communication between the ecological communities of the living dead in *avlime* (subterresphere) and the living living in *kodzogbe* (gecosphere). The rituals, commencing in the morning, continue amidst drumming, dancing and gifting of things, especially pieces of coins, believed to be needed for the journey to *avlime*. At early sundown the corpse is finally sent to *yɔme* (graveyard) for interment.

Muslims also lay the dressed body in state for final public viewing and paying of last homage through mournful wailing, drumming and dancing. After sometime of public viewing the face of the corpse is covered with the headgear, the white-shroud wrapped body put in a simple wooden coffin and taken to the graveyard for burial.[92] For Christians the corpse may be laid in state in either the *yɔxɔme* (funeral parlor) or the chapel, depending on either the choice of the family or standing of the deceased in the church before death. *Avigbexexlē* (mournful oratorical crying) goes on, especially by the women. Christians, however, do not always practice gifting items for the *tsiēfe* journey; where and when they do, it is mainly handkerchiefs. In addition, no alcohol is officially permitted at the funeral ground, and since 1980s the usual night vigils or wake-keeping on the eve of interment has been abolished.[93] The main difference between Christian and primal religious funerals lies in the use of Christian lyrics in the drum music, absence of alcoholic drinks and libation as well as preaching consolatory sermons.[94] A preburial church service is held where the corpse has been laid in state;

---

92. Abdullah Muhammad, interview at Sogakɔfe, 5 April 2016.
93. Andrews Ahado, interview at Sokpoe, 5 February 2016.
94. Andrews Ahado, interview at Sokpoe, 5 February 2016.

however, if it is laid in the clan funeral parlor, the coffin may either be taken to chapel or remain in the clan house for preburial church service.

Interment marks the climax of the symbolic deintegration ritual. It may take the form of either *ame ḍiḍi ḍe yɔdo me* (burial in a grave), dug six feet down in the ground, or by *ame meme* (cremation). Jacob Azuma believes that a wicked person such as a witch or wizard must be cremated or else it never experiences freedom at *etsīe* (world of the dead).[95] However, the decision on the type of interment depends on the findings of the cause of death from the *nukala/ ŋɔlīyɔla* (diviner) consulted at the time of death. In some cases, the people believe that a wicked dead person inflicts the family with unusual sicknesses or recurring deaths as a means of announcing its desire to be cremated.[96] Agbanu observes similar beliefs and practices among the Mafi-Eʋe of North Tɔŋu.[97] Cremation may be either in a bonfire outside the grave or application of special herbs inside the grave.[98] However, only primal religionists practice cremation; Muslims and Christians do not. Perhaps it is because the Tɔŋu in general associate cremation with being guilty of evil and wickedness in life,[99] an eco-cultural stigma and abomination with which no Christian wants to be disgracefully associated. Consequently, according to Castro Abotsi, wicked people sometimes may maliciously leave certain herbs in the grave of a Christian, which may influence the deceased's ghost to request cremation. This may occur when the wicked person decides to ridicule and disgrace a deceased Christian and its family for a purpose.[100]

Where the corpse is not cremated but to be buried at the graveyard, the coffin is placed on two strong ropes, one toward the head region and the other at the foot side. Four men, two on each side holding the ends of the ropes, let the coffin down the *yɔdome* (grave) with the head Westwards, because "that signifies sunset or ending for life in *kodzogbe* and transition into *aʋlime*."[101] In primal religion, any male clan elder from the deceased's family can officiate the burial ritual. He pours a libation with hard liquor in praying for revenge of the death and safe journeying into *aʋlime*, saying:

> Let your journey be peaceful. Remember your killer and revenge your death. Let the nipples of your killer's mother never

---

95. Jacob Azuma, interview at Sokpoe, 5 February 2016.
96. Jacob Azuma, interview at Sokpoe, 5 February 2016.
97. Agbanu, "Environmental Ethics in Mafi-Eʋe Indigenous Culture," 118.
98. Jacob Azuma, interview at Sokpoe, 5 February 2016.
99. Agbanu, "Environmental Ethics in Mafi-Eʋe Indigenous Culture," 118.
100. Castro Abotsi, interview at Sokpoe, 5 February 2016.
101. Gladys Ahado, interview at Sokpoe, 26 June 2016.

be suckled by children on her laps; may her tears fill the buckets in *yɔxɔme* (funeral parlor) for bathing her children laid in state. But safeguard your children and the entire family. *Mɔme ne kɔ* (Safe journey)![102]

This type of prayer underscores the belief in primal religion that someone (not necessarily something) is responsible for death in the universe. Commenting on Harold Turner's third feature of primal religious eco-communities, the conviction that humans are not alone but there are beings more powerful and ultimate than us, Kwame Bediako observes that the primal religious universe is so *personalized* that "the appropriate question is not 'what caused this or that?' but '*who* did it?'"[103] The belief that the dead person is actually not dead but only transiting into life on the other side, *etsīewode* or *avlime*,[104] explains the insertion of other human needs into the *yɔdo* (grave), apart from the clothing put in the coffin. Usually foodstuffs, pieces of utensils, dinning plates and cups are some of the human needs provided the deceased. Some people may even add coins to pay for the ferry at the riverside.[105] The young men around then heap the dug-out soil back onto the coffin until the grave is overfull into a mound.

From the responses, Muslims bury and do so as a sign of respect for the deceased. But it is obviously also to prevent possible scavenging and air pollution with noxious odor from putrefaction of the body if not buried.[106] This explains why Hajia Hawusatu Eleas and zongo *sarachi* Abdullah Mohamed are particular about the dimensions of the final resting place of a corpse, the grave. It must be about "six feet deep below this first of the seven Earths"[107] or simply "up to the waste of an average man."[108] In some cases, especially where the main grave is shallow, a horizontal cut is made like a shelf into the sidewall. The corpse is removed from the coffin and laid wrapped in the shroud either on the floor of the grave or the side shelf. In the latter case broad leaves serve as curtain between the body and the soil heaped into a mound on the grave.[109] Abdullah believes that a dead person can still hear prior to putrefaction,[110] and may explain why the imam ends

102. Castro Abotsi, interview at Sokpoe, 5 February 2016.
103. K. Bediako, *Jesus in Africa*, 87 (italics original).
104. Geoffrey Siame, interview at Sogakɔfe, 17 February 2016.
105. Castro Abotsi, interview at Sokpoe, 5 February 2016.
106. Abdullah Mohamed, interview at Sogakɔfe, 5 April 2016.
107. Hawusatu Eleas, interview at Sogakɔfe, 12 April 2016.
108. Abdullah Muhammad, interview at Sogakɔfe, 5 April 2016.
109. Abdullah Muhammad, interview at Sogakɔfe, 5 April 2016.
110. Abdullah Muhammad, interview at Sogakɔfe, 5 April 2016.

the burial ritual with the funeral prayer (*salat al janaza*)[111] and by reciting the *Kalima* into its ears. John Azumah observes that the *Kalima* is the last thing a deceased must hear before leaving this world just as it was the first thing whispered into its ears on entering the world.[112] According to the participants, the grave then is the last home of the deceased's body, where it is expected to putrefy and wait resurrection and Judgment Day. But before putrefaction the corpse is prepared to face the creator's judgment. Two angels come immediately after burial and assist it recollect its own deeds in the eco-community and write them on the shroud. The good deeds are on the right half while the bad are on the left. In this way the dead person may have foreknowledge of its fate and "keep reflecting on it"[113] even before Judgment Day. This is like participatory verification of a person's deeds prior to God's declaration of sentence. It explains why and how, to the Muslim, God is a righteous judge. For a person becomes fully aware of and confirms his/her deeds and thereby becomes a self-witness and self-judge. He/she thus reflects on and concedes the eventual concluding sentence before God's pronouncement of it on Judgment Day. As Abdullah Muhammad puts it, "*Ame ŋutɔe drɔ̃a vɔnu edokui, ke menye Mawu yo o*," meaning one judges oneself and not God.

Unlike the indigenous situation, a deceased Christian is buried at most by midday or just a little beyond. At the graveside the coffin is let down the grave with insistence that the head-to-toe axis aligns with a West-East direction, just as in the indigenous system. For Gladys Ahado of COP this way of placing the corpse in the grave is necessary and significant. It informs both living and dead that the end of physical life on Earth has truly come for the person being buried.[114] The officiating minister ends the brief graveside rituals of singing and an exhortative homily with symbolically throwing three shovels full of soil onto the coffin as committal, saying:

> Dust thou art and unto dust hast thou returned. We bury your *ŋutilā* (body) into this grave, but your *gbɔgbɔ* (soul) we hand over into the hands of the God from whom it came. Fare thee well till we meet again.

According to Ahado this text of the commital prayer indicates that "*amekuku la fe ŋɔli le agbe*" (the soul/ghost of the deceased lives on). Thus,

---

111. Safi and Bigelow, "Muslim Views of Death."

112. Azumah, *My Neighbour's Faith*, 34. The Kalima is the Muslim creed, *Ashahadah la ilaha ila Allah; Muhammad Rasul Allah* (I bear witness that there is no God but Allah, and that Muhammad is the messenger of Allah).

113. Safi and Bigelow, "Muslim Views of Death."

114. Gladys Ahado, interview at Sokpoe, 26 June 2016.

the soul, and not the rotten body, is what shall arise on the resurrection day promised by Jesus Christ.¹¹⁵ As in the case of the traditionalists, the young men around then heap the dug-out soil back onto the coffin until the grave is over full into a mound.

Primal religionists continue the yɔfewɔwɔ (funeral) after burial with social gathering and celebration of the life of the departed through mixture of mournful crying and wailing, drumming and dancing, dining and wining alongside freewill donations in cash and kind to help defray the funeral costs. This may continue for a couple of days and end with *agbamekaka* (rendering of the funeral accounts) on an appointed day and time, within three weeks postinterment. In the case of Muslims, three days after burial family and friends of the deceased gather for another special prayer. Generally, in Islamic practice, a forty-day mourning period is usually observed, after which normal family activities such as weddings or other celebrations may resume.¹¹⁶

Regarding Christians, the rest of the yɔfewɔwɔ (funeral) continues with a thanksgiving church service on the immediate Sunday after interment. The bereaved family expresses gratitude, usually with some amount of money, for a peaceful funeral. Often they request a Bible text or/and hymn of gratitude to accompany the symbol of gratitude. The minister and congregation would pray for them to enjoy God's condolence and providential care, particularly if the deceased had been a breadwinner or great support for them. Individual donations to help them defray funeral expenses continue until the second and third Sundays following burial. On the third Sunday after burial the funeral ends with a brief memorial service at church. The minister exhorts the bereaved family from Scripture, calls the deceased by full name thrice and commits it again finally into the bosom of the Lord, in faith and hope of resurrection when Christ comes again. The congregation goes to mourn with consolatory singing and final opportunity for later funeral donations. The bereaved family head then closes the funeral with *agbamekaka* (rendering of the funeral accounts).¹¹⁷

Some theoecological relevance can be deduced from the religious interment practices of the religious traditions in the Sokpoe ecological area. The general disgust of interment by cremation due to its association with

---

115. Andrews Ahado, interview at Sokpoe, 5 February 2016. When considered as immaterial and immortal entities gbɔgbɔ (spirit), luvɔ (soul) and ŋɔli (ghost) become interchangeable in the mind and daily usage of the Sokpoe-Eʋe Christian.

116. Safi and Bigelow, "Muslim Views of Death."

117. These days the memorial and thanksgiving service takes place the Sunday after burial; but *agbamekaka* by the bereaved family waits till the third Sunday without involving the church.

evil socioecological behaviors in the eco-community could be an impulsion for all the religious traditions to desire, develop and practice positive ecological character and harmonious relationships. Whoever wants to avoid his or her corpse being cremated needs to avoid being guilty of any crime or sin against and in the ecological and social community. With Muslims in particular, I perceive that the Islamic anthropology derived in this study can provide strong basis for developing kinship with nature and hence motivation for creation care through respect for the Earth. This follows from the reasons noted in the submissions for burying dead humans, which suggest ecological grounding and nurturing even in death. The body must not be scavenged, but rot and become soil, hence the need to bury well.[118] Yet the body must wait (be preserved) for Judgment Day, when it will resurrect, upon the return of the spirit into it, to face judgment.[119] However, as it appears ironically, to be well preserved the corpse must putrefy and return its material components into the soil (Earth) from which it was created at birth. In this way the body remains grounded in and identified with the same ecological community it had belonged to in life.

Apparently, according to Idris Ibrahim, the Earth's readiness to preserve a corpse "peaceably" by nurturing it depends on the *kadodo* (understanding or unwritten ecological agreement) between the Earth and humans. This is how he puts it:

> *Ne ènye amegbetɔ la kadodo le miakple anyigba dome. Elabe Koran gblɔ be anyigbadzi zɔm nèle. Eyata de bubu anyigba ŋuti. Eyata ne èfɔ ŋdi la awɔ "sudaja" gbedoɖa si enye be natsɔ ŋgonu atɔ anyigba. Esia ana anyigba nakpɔe be amenyui nènye hafi nava ku. Mawu be esi wònye anyi wotsɔ me wòe ta la anyigba aheto nawò ne woɖi wò ɖe anyigba tome. Anyigba agblɔ be le wò be malemale ta mède bubu ye ŋu o.*[120]

> As humans there is *kadodo* (a cord of understanding) between us and the Earth. The Qur'an reminds that because we walk on the Earth, we need to respect it. Hence, in the morning we perform the "sudaja" or praying with genuflection till our forehead touches the ground. The Earth imputes it as our good relations with it before dying. God states it that since we are made of clay the Earth has right to punish us when our bodies are buried in it, with explanation that we did not take care of it while in life.

---

118. Imam Mahmud Abu Bakar, interview at Sogakɔfe, 5 April 2016.
119. Abdullah Muhammad, interview at Sogakɔfe, 5 April 2016.
120. Idrisu Ibrahim, interview at Sogakɔfe, 23 April 2016.

Inferably, there is a natural and non-negotiable demand on us humans to respect the Earth, because we are made from it and in response to its supportive functions as we dwell on it. Consequently, the Earth has divine permission to punish our buried corpses if we failed in life to keep the *kadodo* (agreed ecological relations), such as not bowing in humility and respect at prayers. In response to such disrespect, the Earth will make the grave constricted, uncomfortable and difficult as they wait between burial and resurrection. But for the respectful and faithful persons the grave is expansive, comfortable and easy.[121]

Other Aspects of Funeral Rites Depicting Socioecological Grounding

It is noteworthy, however, that socioecologically the deintegration of roles and translocation of being from *kodzogbe* does not deny the deceased a continued belonging to and grounding in the land of birth. In the cultural understanding of the Sokpoe-Eʋe the land of birth needs to be the land of death. Therefore, despite the Eʋe adage "*Afia ɖeke nyigba megbe ame ɖiɖi o*" (Everywhere may be a burial ground), both Sokpoe-Eʋe primal religionists and Christians believe that it is important to bury a deceased citizen necessarily in *tefe si wòdzɔ tso* (home soil from where it hails).[122] Generally, the first option in choosing burial ground should be the land of birth. Consequently, corpses deposited in morgues or of deaths occurring outside Sokpoe are transported home with appropriate rituals for burial. Castro Abotsi observes that at the place of the death the family representative responsible for carrying the corpse home ritualistically clears the road for the journey with pouring libation. On arrival the family head and elders back home inspect to affirm that *ameε* (the corpse) is their child before it is taken out of the hearse. It may be a motor hearse or hired commercial passenger truck. Then the deceased's *luvɔ* (soul) is also ritualistically "removed" from the vehicle to avoid incurring its wrath and subsequent interference with the operations of the carrier vehicle, particularly if it is a commercial passenger truck. Some drivers will themselves insist on the soul-removal ritual to avoid unnecessary accidents caused by the infuriated *ŋɔli* (ghost) of the deceased. The family head breaks a fertilized egg from a local hen—not a commercially produced poultry egg—against the bumper. Then he pours a libation with hard liquor, saying, "We brought you safely home with this vehicle; we have also ritually taken you out of it into our funeral parlor; now

121. Safi and Bigelow, "Muslim Views of Death."
122. Geoffrey Siame, interview at Sogakɔfe, 17 February 2016.

therefore permit this vehicle and its driver to continue operations normally and even more successfully."[123]

Sokpoe-Eυe Christians maintain the same belief as the primal religionists that it is important to bury a deceased citizen necessarily in *tefe si wòdzɔ tso* (home soil from where it hails).[124] Impliedly, Christians uphold the indigenous religious belief that a person necessarily belongs to a land of birth and a culture even in death. So, they would ideally have the corpse of relatives dying abroad brought home for interment in the very land that had engulfed their umbilical cords at birth. They welcome corpses of deaths occurring or deposited in morgues outside Sokpoe and transported home with appropriate rituals on the day of burial in Sokpoe soil. However, instead of libation, Christian prayers are said for safe carrying of the corpse home by the family representative assigned this responsibility. On arrival the family head and elders back home inspect to affirm *ameε* (the corpse) is their child before it is taken out of the carrier vehicle. Like the primal religionists the deceased's *luvɔ* (soul) is also ritualistically removed from the vehicle to avoid incurring its wrath and subsequent interference with the operations of the carrier vehicle, particularly if it is a commercial passenger truck.[125] In other words, some Christians also believe that without the ritualistic removal, the deceased's infuriated *ŋɔli* (ghost) may cause accidents involving the vehicle and its passengers. To this end the family head prays, but without using any egg, simply to assure the driver that all will be well thereafter. In my own experience and strictly for the same reason of reassuring the driver who insisted on the ritual, I offered such prayer in 2010 when a dead relative (Cephas Akafo) was brought home for interment. I prayed:

> Thank you God for bringing our deceased family member safely home with this vehicle; by this prayer we take its body and soul out of it into our funeral parlor; now therefore may no evil spirit act in its name against this vehicle and driver; May God continue to let the services of this driver and his vehicle be even more successful, in the name of Jesus. Amen.

The second aspect of the socioecological returning of the materiality of a deceased to and grounding it in its soil of origin is called *luvɔ tsɔtsɔ va afee* (bringing the soul home). In this case circumstances beyond control must have compelled burial outside Sokpoe eco-area. The *luvɔ* (soul) needs be taken home and buried in the land of birth. *Luvɔ* in this case is represented with some body parts of the deceased: pieces of hair cut from the

---

123. Castro Abotsi, interview at Sokpoe, 5 February 2016.
124. Geoffrey Siame, interview at Sogakɔfe, 17 February 2016.
125. Andrews Ahado, interview at Sokpoe, 5 February 2016.

front and back of the head as well as from the pubis, together with pieces of nails trimmed from the phalanges (fingers and toes). These are put in a matches-box and wrapped in a cloth of the deceased. It is transported home on appointed day when family members home gather to welcome the *luvɔ* and perform its funeral. The entire funeral as described above may be performed as if the real corpse were available, except on a reduced scale. Patronage is less, being limited usually to only relatives and close friends, and the funeral duration lasts for only one or two days. Geoffrey Siame explains that in this way the *luvɔ* is assisted to come and dwell on homeland peacefully even if, for any insurmountable reason, the *ŋutilā* (corpse) itself could not return to its original soil.[126]

Christians in Sokpoe ecological area do not enact the home-grounding cultural view by bringing the *luvɔ* (soul) of a person who died and was buried abroad. They organize a befitting memorial service instead. In August 2015 the Langhorst Congregation of the Presbyterian Church of Ghana at Sokpoe held one such memorial service for the late Mrs. Emma Apeti-Hoggar. She died and was buried in London. Her *luvɔ* was not brought home; rather there was a brief ritual of remembering her. The congregation stood in silence for a moment, then the minister pronounced her name thrice and prayed for her soul to rest in perfect peace. After singing a hymn of hopeful reunion with the faithful departed, the minister petitioned God's providential care for the bereaved family. In turn the bereaved family offered some cash gift in gratis to God, and after the service provided some refreshment to relatives and congregants.

There is yet a third case of *ametsivumewo* (the dead from fatal accidents). These include deaths from lorry accidents, maternal mortality at parturition, fallen from a height, drowned in water bodies or shot with a gun and the like.[127] Even if the accident occurs at Sokpoe they are also considered as having died away from home, except that the death is rather sad and painful to the deceased—a situation that can make them wild, furious and vindictive in the eco-community.[128] All items used in preparing them for burial are later burnt. The corpse is laid in state, not in the normal funeral parlor of the clan, but at *kpɔgɔme* (outskirts of town) and buried in *vubɔme* (bloody cemetery). Most often the burial takes place at *tɔgodo* (over the riverbank) or far off from the township,[129] because *woa va nye nukpekpe*

---

126. Geoffrey Siame, interview at Sogakɔfe, 17 February 2016.
127. Geoffrey Siame, interview at Sogakɔfe, 17 February 2016.
128. Geoffrey Siame, interview at Sogakɔfe, 17 February 2016.
129. Mercy Awo Akafo, interview at Sokpoe-Elavanyo, 28 December 2015.

(they may be encountered frightfully) in the eco-community of the living living.[130]

That the souls of such dead may keep roaming and frightening the living people in the ecological community is due to the belief that they are disgusted with their type of death and act accordingly with fury.[131] Burying them outside the town reduces them to having died abroad, materially disconnected from home, and hence may not meet anyone to vent their anger on. Yet at the same time, being citizens, they must have their ŋɔlĩwo guided to come home soberly with a peculiar consoling ritual, which believably pacifies their anger. According to Geoffrey Siame, the ghost-consoling-and-homecoming ritual begins at the riverbank at midnight or at early dawn when all other people are asleep. No one else must see it or else a bad omen awaits any such an inquisitive person. Yet it is perhaps because the performers are elderly men and women, usually widows and widowers, dressed almost in nudity. The men cover theirgenitals with *kamegoe*, a slender piece of cloth wrapped around the waist and through the thighs as if an underpant. The women *tsra ama he tsɔ avɔvu xe nyɔnu mee* (wear only a set of waist stringed beads with which they also hold a slender piece of cloth through the thighs to cover their genitals). They march around the village with music from knocking empty oyster shells against each other to produce a *ko-ko-ko* beat that accompanies *atrikpe* drum songs (a type of war song). Calling out the name of the deceased, they express condolence, saying, "*Babaa! mlɔetɔ nye esia. Mega dzɔ azɔ gbedegbede o*" (Have our condolence. This is the last. May it not so happen again). Before daybreak they prepare and serve a ritual meal at the riverbank and say, "*Wo de amevɔ̃wo tɔ le eme*" (literally, that of the evil one is taken care off). Thus, this ritual is believed to have cleared any evil associated with the accidental death and the ghost consoled enough

---

130. Geoffrey Siame, interview at Sogakɔfe, 17 February 2016.

131. Geoffrey Siame, interview at Sogakɔfe, 17 February 2016. It is worthy to note that while I was working on this chapter on 29 July 2018, at about 8:30 p.m. TV3 in Ghana telecast an African (Akan) movie entitled *Empere Me* (may it not happen to me). The movie depicts the Akan worldview of a ghost of an accident victim, the identical twin brother of one Amoako who died in an accident in a village. His ghost went to marry in the city. But the wife, ignorant of her husband being a ghost, compelled him to return to the village for interacting with his family, her in-laws. There circumstances made the lady to unknowingly have the living twin brother of her ghost husband as her actual suitor. But she suffered continued torments in dreams of someone that resembles her husband preventing her from sleeping with the "new" husband. Eventually the truth was revealed in a scenario that made her see both brothers physically in her room one day; the "new" husband also frightfully screamed out her dead brother's name, and upon beholding both her ghost and "new" husbands the lady collapsed and died. Such an occurrence will be interpreted at Sokpoe as the ghost not being properly buried with the necessary rituals.

to return peacefully to its homeland. It will no longer frighten anyone who might meet it in the eco-community. With the rising sun of the new day they ceremonially *kplɔ luvɔ* (walk the soul) back home amidst singing and *akaya* (maracas) music. The rest of the funeral is as happens normally after burial—wailing, drumming, dancing and voluntary donations to defray the funeral cost.[132] Similarly, Christians in Sokpoe ecological area know of *ametsivumewo* (the dead from fatal accidents), which are same as for the primal religionist. Yet there is no special liturgical practice for their interment. They are buried and funeral conducted just as for ordinary deceased.

In conclusion, as I have earlier indicated at the close of chapter 6, the story of eco-praxis in Sokpoe ecological area does not end with only their knowledge of religious eco-ethics. The discussions in chapters 7 and 8 suggest that their religious anthropology also generates religious rites that underpin and can promote socioecological relationships to sustain ecological integrity. Particularly, there is possible ritualistic priming and motivation for sustainable eco-relations implicit in their religious birthing and funerary rites. These ideas prompted and formed the basis for developing the proposed African theocology curriculum.

---

132. Geoffrey Siame, interview at Sogakɔfe, 17 February 2016.

Part 3

African Theocology

CHAPTER 9

A Proposed African Alternative to Enviromental Science Curriculum

Introductory Remarks

I BEGAN THIS PROJECT when motivated by some challenges in teaching undergraduate environmental science as a missional and morally transformative subject in Presbyterian University College, Ghana. Since the experience was contrary to my personal expectation of Christian higher education, I embarked on this investigation to understand better what was amiss, with a hope in the end, if necessary, to propose an alternative curriculum for the environmental science course. The processes involved both literary study and two different types of field research. In particular, the field research among the Sokpoe-Eʋe was to learn from the daily life experiences of their religious ecologies—primal, Christian and Islamic—to inform the design of the African theocology curriculum. It was not strictly a comparative phenomenological study of the ecologies of these religious traditions. However, it sought to and identified three minimum common grounds on which to base constructive understanding, motivating discussion and concerted action. As I conclude, I propose to reiterate the three common grounds that were retrieved and re-evaluated from the studies among the Sokpoe-Eʋe in as much as they contribute to the design of the African theocology curriculum. These were their religious worldviews, religious impulsion for and praxis of creation care, and religious priming for harmonious ecological relationships.

Religious Worldviews of Creation, Its Purpose and Humanity's Role in It

The research shows in chapter 5 that although the details have significant differences, generally, all three religious traditions in the Sokpoe ecological area in Ghana hold theistic, but not theocentric worldviews. The three religions in the eco-area conceive *xexeme* (the world as a cosmic environment) with a dual meaning: it is, first, *agbenɔnɔ baḑa* (detestable cultural ethos, i.e., unacceptable human ways of life and situations). As a way of life *xexeme* is detestable to all three religions, but for both Christians and Muslims *xexeme* in this sense must be decidedly avoided to qualify for eternal life in heaven as taught by their scriptures. On the other hand, *xexeme* is *amenɔfe/agbenɔfe* (the geographical space where we live, the gecosphere). For the three religions, the gecosphere is structurally the open vast geographical arena consisting of the Earth's surface (lithosphere) and air mass (atmosphere) up to the sky (stratosphere). It is created by the supreme being (*Mawu*/God/Allah). It is holistic, containing human and other-than-human creations existing in interwoven relationships. It is precarious due to numerous malevolent spiritual forces that oppose both the benevolent forces and humans. Beneath but opening into *xexeme* is *avlime* (terresphere, the spirit world), which is either home for the spiritual existence of dead humans or a transitory gate for the dead to return as *amedzɔdzɔ* (reincarnates) or roam as *ŋolĩwo* (ghosts) in *xexeme*. Among the three religious traditions, only the Muslims do not believe in ghosts or reincarnates, and only the Christians and Muslims believe that the spirits of deceased devotees of their religions pass on from *avlime* to either *dzifovii* (heaven of heavens) if the person is of good spiritual standing or *dzomavɔme* (hell) if bad, both places being differently located somewhere in the celesphere. The purpose of *xexeme* is to be home for and nurturing of living humanity, the most valuable of all creations as seen by all three religions.

Humanity for these religions is created by God out of clay, though some of the primal religionists do not know the origin of humanity. Constitutionally, God first created *ŋutilā* (body), and breathed *agbegbɔgbɔ* (life-giving spirit/breath) into the *ameɛ* (thing) to become *amegbetɔ* (human being). Humans are thus composed of created *ŋutilā* (body, being flesh/muscle) and *evu* (blood), and so are material and mortal, and *gbɔgbɔ*, which is the uncreated immaterial spirit/breath of God conjoined to *luvɔ* (soul), which is created but immaterial. The role of humankind is to image God as caregivers/ stewards/*khalifas* of creation so it can in turn nurture humans, and to be co-creators with God through procreation. The Muslims add, however, that the primary role, before others, is for humanity to "worship" or "submit" to God as a Muslim.

Religious Impulsion for Eco-Valuing and Praxis of Eco-Ethics

A second area of findings that emerged related to the axiological conception of creation by all three religions, as in chapter 6. The conception is a mixture of biocentrism, zoocentrism and anthropocentrism, but is generally more of anthropocentrism. The primal religionists argue that only humans have intrinsic value because they alone have qualities of initiative taking, rationality, having emotions and possessing communication skills. To these qualities the Christians and Muslims add that humans' intrinsic value is derived from the fact that only humans are made in the image of God, with a responsibility of being his vicegerents/*khalifas* (representatives). The other-than-human creation, such as rocks, flora and fauna, has only instrumental value in that it is to service humankind to be of value.

Among all three religious traditions only the primal religionists sacralize land, forests and some water bodies, especially creeks and lagoons. While they all recognize the prevalence of malevolent spirits and hence the precariousness of the ecosystems, only the primal have elaborated inhibitive and prohibitive taboos that ultimately promote eco-harmony through praxis of ethics of eco-conservation, eco-restoration, eco-preservation, eco-character formation and eco-justice. Disobeying sacred land/forest taboos is an eco-crime and results in *nukpekpe* (astonishing encounter), ill health, death and drought. Thus, fear of punishment by deities, avoidance of land/water body litigations and respect for traditional authority constitute the impulsion or basis for keeping the eco-taboos. Ecological actions to restore and/or sustain eco-harmony, eco-health and eco-justice include eco-rituals like *ekpokpɔkplɔ* (land purification rite) and legal enforcements at traditional or law courts.

There are no distinctly identifiable Christian or Islamic eco-ethics or norms (practical regulations) in the Sokpoe eco-area. Yet in order not to compromise their faith the Muslims vehemently oppose primal eco-ethical praxis and demonstrate neither religious impulsion for nor praxis of creation care. They claim that the Qur'an does not regulate use of nature for human needs, unaware that it does. The Christians, on the contrary, as I argued, relate to primal religious eco-ethical praxis in three ways or groups: first is the "acculturated" Christians, who, being influenced by their primal religious cosmology more than their Christology, strictly comply with primal religious eco-taboos for fear of the deities. The second group is the "passive Christians," who neither object nor comply so as not to practice "syncretism." The third group is the "deculturated Christians," who have demystified the fears of ecological deities and taboos and freely clear forested lands for developmental needs of humans. I suggested in chapter 6 that a better approach is perhaps to be "culture-converting Christians" who engage Scripture as hermeneutic for ecological issues, aimed at life-long transformational development of eco-virtues. In that case, African Christian eco-ethical impulsion for and praxis of creation care may rest on the self-understanding as being made in the image of God, being vicegerents of creation, having kinship with creation and being disciples of the doctrine of "love God, love neighbor."

Birthing and Funerary Rites as Religious Promoters of Sustainable Ecological Relations

Summarizing chapters 7 and 8, this research analyzed the liturgies and symbols for birthing and funerary rites of the three religions in the Sokpoe ecological area. Though I noted four main birthing rites—*fukatsotso* (pregnancy liberation), *amenɔdidi* (placenta burial), *vidededego* (baby outdooring) and *vewɔwɔ* (twin accordance rite)—I reported on only *vidededego* as in chapter 7. I argued in the findings that the birthing rites suggest significant ecological implications as a means of priming for sustaining harmonious ecological relations in their common holistic view of the world. Concerning *vidededego* there are differences in the details and emphases within and between religious traditions. In the primal tradition these rites have the potential of preparing a child for sustainable eco-relations through (1) "gecospheric" acclimatization and fortification, (2) grounding into the land of birth and (3) socio-cultural orientation and integration.

Christians attach the same meaning but use different symbols for the birthing rites—*fukatsotso, amenɔdidi* and *vidededego*—as in primal religion. They recognize these birthing rites as *dekɔnu* (cultural), that is, something characteristic of and hence uniquely identifiable with the eco-cultural community of which they are part. However, not all the Christian churches perform all these rites or with the same liturgical emphasis and elaboration. For gecospheric acclimatization and fortification, some reported some liturgical practices of *fukatsotso* and *didɛxɔmenɔnɔ*. As grounding into one's land of birth only some of the Christians practice *amenɔdidi* (placenta burial), *hɔkadidi* (umbilical cord burial) and *vitsɔtsɔfiawo* (showing baby to sun, as first part of *vidededego* or baby outdooring). However, none of the

Christians, including those who practice parts of these rites, do so with the mind of performing religious rituals or with any ecological implications. Consequently, they expunge from their reconstructed liturgies some of the primal religious rituals that together give meaning and eco-grounding implications to the birthing rites. The most common form of Christian birthing rite is limited to only the sociocultural orientation and integration performed as a *nyikɔtsɔtsɔ* (naming) ceremony.

The research analyzed the birthing rites that Muslims perform. These practices are not necessarily understood or approached with the mind that they are *dekɔnu* (cultural rites), which to them are satanic primal religious practices of the indigenous Sokpoe-Eʋe. Yet their birthing ceremonies portray some of the primal religious birthing rituals, and hence have implicit ecological priming potencies. For instance, they have no rituals for *fukatsotso* (pregnancy liberation) but keep mother and neonate indoors in *ɖiɖexɔme* for seven days, for gecospheric acclimatization and fortification. They practice *amenɔɖiɖi* (placenta burial) in their own way, which implies grounding in the land of birth, and they perform the *nyikɔtsɔtsɔ* (naming) aspect of *viɖeɖeɖego* (baby outdooring), which ecologically is a sociocultural orientation and integration ritual.

It is intriguing that funerary rites of the Sokpoe-Eʋe also have implicit impulsions for religious care of creation by informing the need to develop eco-ethical relationships with all creation in the ecological community. The two most significant rituals with this potential to impact appropriate moral and sustainable eco-relationships are associated with *trɔ̃ku* and *hlɔ̃tsilele*. The dominant component in their primal religious consciousness responsible for ecological taboos is their belief in deities. Committing ecological sin by violating ecological taboos, in the views of primal religionists and some Christians, results in *trɔ̃ku*. The fear of *trɔ̃ku* thus becomes an impulsion for maintaining positive ecological relations, and hence socioecological harmony. Similarly, the desire to be morally acceptable in and by one's community in the afterlife world, as depicted by *hlɔ̃tsilele*, can inform the living to pursue eco-ethics and justice. *Hlɔ̃tsilele* then is a *praeparatio evangelica*, which can remind the living Christians of the need to deal rightly with sin through faith in the finished work of Christ and washing in his blood in the gecosphere before transitioning out of it by death. Thus, these common religious ecological understandings and praxis from the primal, Christian and Islamic traditions in the Sokpoe ecological area suggest they can be plausible and possible grounds or philosophies for reconstructing African Christian paradigms or responses—the paradigm I propose is African theocology. An African theocology curriculum designed on these common African religious worldviews and praxis of eco-ethics can enable constructive discussions and motivate concerted actions in a religiously plural educational context.

Description or Philosophy of the African Theocology Curriculum

The African theocology course is designed as a mandatory subject to provide moral ecological orientation to undergraduate students in all academic disciplines of study in Christian higher educational institutions, particularly in Ghana. It introduces the newly emerging field of religion and ecology, or theocology for short, as a hopeful missional alternative that may pragmatically encourage moral responsibility for creation, rather than "environmental science" as a secular subject. It explores human relations to the natural world as understood in African Christianity, but incorporates phenomenological parallels from primal and Islamic traditions, since "pluralism has important implications for any project to bring about a more ecological society."[1] The course draws on both African religious worldviews and modern scientific concepts of the field of ecology for an understanding of the orientation of humanity to the creator and creation as well as the dynamic processes of Earth's ecosystems and their function.

As John Grim and Mary Evelyn Tucker observe, "for many years, science, engineering, policy, law, and economics were considered indispensable for understanding and resolving environmental problems," based on Western Enlightenment and secular views of the world. They argue that

> We now have abundant knowledge from these disciplines about environmental issues, but still not sufficient *moral will* to engage in long-term change for the flourishing of the Earth community. Thus, there is a growing realization that religion, spirituality, ethics, and values can make important contributions, in collaboration with science and policy, to address complex ecological issues.[2]

The course proposes to examine those contributions, particularly from African perspectives, acknowledging both the problems and promises of religions, especially Christianity. David Mutasa observes that teaching about the environment in Africa has usually been teacher centered, thus the teacher is the transmitter of knowledge.[3] He suggests that today environ-

---

1. Curry, *Ecological Ethics*, 25.
2. Grim and Tucker, "Online Course."
3. Mutasa et al., "Ngano," 35.

mental education requires taking the learners outdoors to the biophysical environment. He believes that "by teaching in the environment, an emotional bond will be established between the learner and the environment,"[4] as has been the experience in our indigenous African eco-cultures. African theocology is designed with a mindset of being not only a holistic missional curriculum for moral transformation toward creation care, but also to be delivered with a pragmatic and balanced pedagogy including integration of faith and dependence on the Holy Spirit's enlightenment. Students need to be exposed to real environmental situations as much as possible, participate in an ecological culture of the institution and use Scripture as hermeneutic of the ecological issues encountered, whether from an ecological science (fact-based) or religious ecology (faith-based) perspective.

This twelve-week contact (non-online or non-distance) and field course is offered as a non-major course in ecological studies to engage students in Ghanaian Christian universities and colleges, but particularly the Presbyterian University College, Ghana (PUCG), in the first year.[5] However, it may be a prerequisite for the major program on Environmental and Natural Resources Management at PUCG. Three credits will be offered for the course.

Course Objectives

1. To help students appreciate the importance of the Earth and all that is in it as God's creation (natural and built environment), particularly humans and their place in it.

2. To raise students' awareness of current ecological issues, particularly anthropogenic eco-crisis, and hence the need for education for sustainability by all humanity.

3. To assist students to know and understand how the world works and can be sustained with methods undergirded by both African religious worldviews and scientific understandings.

4. To induce impulsion for moral ecological responsibility in students, using critical thinking, problem-solving skills, and Scripture (backed with prayer and Holy Spirit guidance) as ecological hermeneutics.

---

4. Mutasa et al., "Ngano," 35.

5. According to Stewart, "Transforming Higher Education," 5, it is important that students should have a foundational knowledge of sustainability by the end of their first year.

Course Content/Format

African theocology as an interdisciplinary subject embraces a wide variety of topics from different areas of study, particularly ecological science and theology. There are several major unifying constructs, or themes, that cut across the many disciplines included in the study of theocology, and the choice of themes for this curriculum takes into consideration the Christian missional and African contextual needs. For instance, in order to properly understand the nature of the environmental crisis in Africa, we need to understand the ways in which both primal and modern social structures and technoscience have led to environmental degradation.[6] Moreover, as Agbanu avers, missional teaching of "environmental science cannot be in a vacuum," but must be with students' prior understanding of the environment and how it functions from their cultural setting. Then science can help them to improve on it.[7] In addition, Fainos Mangena suggests acknowledging the moral status of other-than-human creation is a starting point for any discourse on environmental ethics in Africa.[8] The following themes provide a foundation for the structure of the African theocology course.

Ecological Problems and Relevance of Mandatory Theocological Studies

a. *A planet in peril*: the Earth as our gifted home (environment); historical awareness of ecological problems in the world, Africa and Ghana; major eco-problems, e.g., waste, degradation, pollution, ozone layer depletion, global warming, biodiversity loss, eco-injustice, eco-feminism, poverty, moral decadence etc.

b. *Natural and anthropogenic eco-crisis—causes and remedies*: disasters, population, lifestyle (human need and greed), organization (politics), technoscience and secularization; debates against anthropogenic eco-crisis; scientism as remedy for eco-crisis in the secularized world.

c. *The missing link*: limitations of secularized approaches, especially modern technoscience, in mitigating eco-crisis; religious ecology (or theocology) as emerging alternative (complementary and supplementary) means for resolving eco-crisis; African theocology explained/defined and role of moral impulsion for creation care; shared phenomenological ideas from primal, Christian and Islamic religions.

---

6. Ogungbemi, "African Perspective on the Environmental Crisis."
7. Agbanu, interview at Legon, 23 November 2015.
8. Mangena, "Discerning Moral Status in the African Environment," 25.

d. *Sailing or sinking together*: pluralism and concerted effort required for ecological projects; justification/need for mandatory creation care education for all academic disciplines in higher educational institutes; practical examples from various disciplines of study and profession are required, especially at local levels.

Toward Resolving Eco-Crisis: Understanding Our World with Faith (Religion) and Facts (Science)

a. *African holistic worldviews*: the Earth as one interconnected system and home (environment) for the life of other-than-human creation (animate and inanimate, natural and artificial); relationships of creation, creator and humanity; discuss similar theistic but non-theocentric and precarious views from primal, Christian and Islamic traditions.

b. *Scientific view of how the world works*: ecological science defined/explained; scientific concepts of "gecosphere," its origin and ecosystems; ecosystem structural components and function; eco-communities and species interactions; ecosystem life as interplay of matter, energy and their operational laws of nature.

c. *Nature's life-nurturing function*: Earth's endowed resourcefulness; natural resources—definition, importance and measurement; natural resources of Ghana—their locations, level of development and exploitation, measurement and economic value/uses.

d. *Human impact on environment*: anthropogenic damage to the ecosystem and secular approaches of remedy; challenges of Western scientism in resolving eco-crisis.

Integrated Approaches to Earth-Keeping in the Twenty-First Century

a. *God's natural self-conservation laws in ecological science*: cosmic balance/equilibrium and self sustenance; biogeochemical systems as Earth's divinely endowed abilities to recover from perturbations/disturbances; moral implications of cosmic balance for creation care; discuss ideas from primal, Christian and Islamic traditions.

b. *Practical scientific conservation principles and methods*: restoration ecology; creating artificial ecosystems; international conventions and their historical limitations.

c. *African Christian eco-care praxis*: promises and problems; God's creation as good, valuable and purposeful; eco-ethical principles of *imago Dei*, vicegerency, kinship with nature and loving God and loving neighbor as impulsion for eco-care; biblical examples of eco-praxis; ecological crime or sin; discuss similar ideas from primal and Islamic traditions, especially ecological rituals as priming for creation care.

d. *Revision and end-of-semester examinations*: quick review of major topics, examination regulations and prayer for success.

The study leading to the discussions and postulations in this book has provided evidence of a few factors from both the literary and field work for the future of Christian higher education in general and specifically for studying theocology in Ghana and Africa. For instance, it affirms that the moral motivation required for Christian environmentalism may be retrievable and reconstructive from both primal religious ecological knowledge systems and other world religions,[9] because such shared pluro-religious eco-experiences have important implications for any project to bring a more ecological society, as argued in chapters 2 and 6 of this book.[10] No longer will ecological science and technology alone, but rather their synthesis with religious ecology, be the valid or true way for resolving eco-crisis.

Furthermore, it is imperative for African Christian higher educational institutions to consider retrieving, adopting and adapting appropriate cultural thoughts and categories if the teaching and learning process for environmental moral transformation is to be effective and innovative. For, to be effective, studying ecological science in Africa needs the foundation of African religious worldviews to provide eco-cultural context and self-understanding of students. African theocology, unlike Enlightenment-influenced Western theology and ecotheology, acknowledges the importance of kinship with nature in its primal worldviews. This makes it plausible to influence, among others, "human responsibility for the continuity of life, and restoration of both humans and ecosystems for the flourishing of life."[11]

Finally, the ideas generated from the research that has fed this book provide a significant amount of primary data and basis for more work to be done among the Sokpoe-Eʋe in particular, but the Tɔŋu-Eʋe in general, in the areas of religion, ecology and ethics in our search for appropriate cultural contributions to resolving global eco-crisis. In addition, the retrieved primary data may assist in reconstructing practical Christian theologies

---

9. Grim and Tucker, *Ecology and Religion*, 8.
10. Curry, *Ecological Ethics*, 25.
11. Grim and Tucker, *Ecology and Religion*, 8.

and pastoral liturgies for eco-related ceremonies like birthing and funerary rites that prime for creation care, at least for Tɔŋu-Eʋe Christians. Thus, the study has implications not only for holistic Christian education at church and institutional levels, but also for practical Christian and pastoral involvement in ecological praxis or creation care.

Appendix
Transcripts of Interview Responses

A1   Samuel Agboklu, Sokpoe: On Mawu as Creator
Trɔ̃subɔlawo nyae be Mawu dzifovĩtɔe wɔ ame kple nusiwo katã le anyigbadzi. Eyata woyɔe be Sogbolisa, Okitikata. Adaɲuwɔtɔ, Dɔnyuiwɔtɔ. Ewɔ asi kple afɔ, anyigba kple edzinuwo keŋ. Eyae me ame kple anyi hegbɔ gbɔgbɔ de eme.¹

A2   Geoffrey Siame, Sokpoe: On purpose of human and other-than-human creation
Le tsitsiawo fe gɔmesese nu la Mawu wɔ amegbetɔ be ame nanɔ yetefe alo de edokui tefe. Eyata wòwɔ mí de efe nɔnɔme nu. Eye esi miekpɔnɛ o ta la míe wɔa legba abe ame alo nuwɔwɔ bubu ade de etefe. Legba siawoe tsɔa míafe nyawo yina na Mawu. Ne dɔ ade gakpe de eŋu la eya koe nye dzidzi. Abe wɔla ene la ena mí mɔnukpɔkpɔ be míadzi, eye wòwɔ nusiwo akpe de míaŋu na efe dɔwɔwɔawo la foxlã mí be mía zã.²

A3   Alhaji Ali of Dabala Junction: Zongo ethnography as ecological challenge
Le zongo me la amewo tso tefe vovovowo va: wotsɔ susu vovovowo tso wofe de vae. Wo katã wova fofu le zongo deka. Eyata wofe gɔmesese mesɔ o. Eye wome doato wonɔewo o. Amesiame dia be yeawɔ nu alesi ye nyae tso yewo de nuwɔnawo me la ko. Hekpe de eŋu la esi wònye gbegbɔgblɔ vovovowo abe Hausa, Fafra, Dagati kple zamarama yae fofu ta la, wome sea nugɔme na

---

1. Samuel Agboklu, interview at Sokpoe, 2 March 2016. The same understanding and names of God were expressed by Geoffrey Siame, interview at Sokpoe on 17 February 2016.

2. Geoffrey Siame, telephone interview, 6th April, 2017.

wonɔewo o. Amesiame bube nusi yenya tso yeƒe de la nyo wu ame bubu sitso du bubume la tɔ.³

A4   Alhassan Ibrahim, Sogakoƒe: Islamic view on creation of humanity
Gbãla, le Koran me la, Mawu dɔ dɔla ɖeka wò va ku anyi eye Mawu me ame he siae ƒe bla ene. Le ƒe bla ene sia megbe la ede agbe gbɔgbɔ eme; eyae nye Adamu. Emegbe Mawu tsɔ Adamu ƒe axa ƒu ɖeka he me Hawa. Etsɔ wo da ɖe paradisobɔ me.⁴

A5   Zongo sarachi Abdullah Muhammad, Sogakoƒe: Islamic view of human creation
Ame ɖesiaɖe la nyɔnu kple ŋutsu ye dzie. Ne nyɔnu fɔfu la etsi si ŋutsua trɔ ɖe eƒe vidzi kotoku me la trɔa zu ʋu le ŋkeke bla ene megbe. Le ŋkeke bla ene bubu vɔ me la eʋu la trɔ zua lãkusi. Ke le ŋkeke bla ene si ga kplɔe ɖo megbe la, si fia be dzinu enelia megbe la, Mawu dea gbɔgbɔ lãkusi la me be wòazu ame agbetɔ si woavadzi.⁵

A6   Andrews Ahado, Sokpoe: On constitution of humanity
Ame enye ŋitilã kple gbɔgbɔ si Mawu gbɔ de eme. Mawu yɔe be luʋɔ gbagbe. Eyata ne amegbetɔ ku la wo mega yɔa eƒe ŋkɔ o; wogblɔ na be 'amee' ko evɔ. Gbɔgbɔ mee susu, dzimedidi, kple sese le lãme le. Eyata Biblia be luʋɔ si wɔ nuvɔ̃ la luʋɔma aku. Amegbetɔ si sea nu alo hea susu la yɔm Biblia le be 'luʋɔ gbagbe'.⁶

A7   Kofi Avinyo Atiglo, Sokpoe: Primalist eco-valuing of creation
Ga alo sika meƒoanu o; gbetɔ koe aƒo nu kplim. Nusi aɖo aɖaŋu alo ahe susu kplim la xɔ asi wu bubuawo keŋ le xanye.⁷

A8   Margaret Asuma, Sokpoe-Bodzodiƒe: Christian view on eco-valuing
Togbɔ be Mawu wɔ xexeme nuwo katã hafi wɔ amegbetɔ hã la amee hiã gbâ le nuawo katã dome. Nusi akplɔe ɖo enye sika alo ega; gae kpeɛ ɖe gbetɔ ŋu hafi wòa de blibo. Gbɔ̃ nye nuɖuɖu ta eya ava etɔ̃lia. Ne ati la tsrɔ̃ hã la mewɔ naneke o. Ate ŋu ayi faa. Egbegbe hã ɖoɖoma nu ko mawɔe.⁸

---

3. Imam Alhaji Ali, interview at Dabala Junction, 17th May 2016
4. Alhassan Ibrahim, interview at Sogakɔƒe, 14 April 2016.
5. Abdullah Mohamed (zongo sarechi), interview at Sogakɔƒe, 5 April 2016.
6. Andrews Ahado, interview at Sokpoe, 5 February 2016.
7. Efoe Avinyo Atiglo, interview at Sokpoe-Elavanyo, 15 February 2016.
8. Margaret Asuma, interview at Sokpoe-Elavanyo, 25 February 2016.

Appendix 243

A9 Isaac Avi, Sokpoe: Christian view of primal eco-taboos

Abe Krsitotɔ ene la nye me kpɔ vɔ̃ le seawo ŋu o. Gakē menyo be wòanye trɔ̃subɔlawoe dee o. Edze be Kristotɔ nase egɔme be ehĩa be woana mɔ lâwo be woatsi hafi alewo. Eyata seawo la Mawu ƒe se wonye. Edze be amesiame (trɔ̃subɔla kple Kistotɔwo sia) nade dzesii be Mawu gbɔ seawo tso hafi va míaƒe susuwo me; menye amegbetɔ siwo nye trɔ̃subɔlawo ƒe se wonye o.[9]

A10 Winner Eworyi, Sokpoe: Christian view of primal eco-taboos

Mawu ƒe ŋusē li gake abosam hã tɔ li. Trɔ̃subɔlawo wɔa kɔnunu le trɔ̃vewo me eyata trɔ̃ ƒe ŋuse le avea me. Mexɔe se, togbɔ be Kristotɔ mènye hã. Nye me le atsindzie ɖige ayi ɖe trɔ̃veme akpɔ o, ɖe vɔvɔ̃ na trɔ̃ la ta.[10]

A11 Hajia Fatti Sanni, Sogakɔƒe: Islamic valuing of creation

Amegbetɔ gbâ, elabena nɔvinye ame yo. Ne etsi agbe la akpe ɖe ŋunye awɔ dɔ be makpɔ gbɔ kple sika. Gake ne ɣeyiɣi li la male gbɔ, elabe eya hã agbe le eme. Azɔ etɔ̃lia anye ga; ga menye ƒeƒenu o, eyae kpeɖe ŋunye mekpɔ vinyewo dzi. Ati ya ne ebu hã madi bubu ado.[11]

A12 Zongo sarechi Abdullah Muhammad: Islamic view of primal eco-taboo

Dutɔwo ƒe kɔnuwoe nye ma. Womenyo na Muslim o. Muslim la dekɔnu aɖeke meli wowɔ na o. Ava na míatra mɔ. Nusi nye Mawu tɔ alo ƒe nya koe hĩa. Ne dekɔnutɔwo gblɔ be maga klɔ agbelimakusi le tɔme o la nyemele se sia dzi wɔge o. Le kpɔɖeŋu me, esi Koran meɖe mɔ be míaɖu ha lâ o ta la míɖuɛ o.[12]

A13 Kɔwu Yɔhokpɔ, Sogakɔƒe: Primal view on urinating during birthing rite

Aɖuɖɔ ɖoɖo ɖe anyigbadzi fia be eŋu le kɔkɔe na anyigba si xɔe ɖe eƒe ata dzi abe vinɔ ene.'[13]

---

9. Isaac Avi, interview at Sokpoe, 2 February 2016.
10. Winner Eworyi, interview at Sokpoe 3 February 2016
11. Hajia Fatti Sanni, interview at Sogakɔfe, 20 April 2016.
12. Abdullah Muhammad, (zongo sarechi), interview at Sogakɔƒe, 5 April 2016
13. Yɔhokpɔ, interview at Sogakofe, 17 February 2016.

A14   Hajia Amina Awudu, Dabala: Islamic birthing rite outlined
Gbesigbe wodzi vi la wo lea tsi nɛ nyuie be dzigbeɖi maga tsi eŋu o. Nyɔnuwo awɔ yurr . . . yurr . . . yurr zi etɔ̃, abe alesi wowɔna na amariya be egbe edogo ɖe amewo dome. Yurr ɖesiaɖe megbe la woyɔa ɖevia ƒe aɖagbe ŋkɔ, nenye egbe Kuɖagbe wodzii la woa yɔe be Kɔku, ɖe eƒe towo me. Esia gɔmee nye be ɖevia na lé ŋkɔ ɖe tame eye wòava de dzesi be yee woyɔ na nenema.[14]

A15   Robert Avenorgbo, Sokpoe: Christian view of birthing rites
Dzilawo gblɔa na nunɔla be ne va tsɔ ɖevia ƒia wò le woƒe dekɔnu gɔmesese nu. Gake mí nunɔlawo ya sea egɔme be ŋkɔ koe wo di be woava tsɔ na ɖevia. Eyata ŋkɔ tsɔtsɔ ta ko míe yi na ɖo le Biblia ƒe ɖase ɖiɖi tso Aƒetɔ Yesu ɖeɖeɖego ŋu ƒe gɔmesese nu.[15]

A16   Daniel Agbota, Sokpoe: Christian view of primal eco-taboos
Fifia la Kristo dzixɔse wɔe be vɔvɔ̃ na trɔ̃awo me li o eye viɖe mele kɔnuawo wɔwɔ le aveawo me ŋu o. Le nyateƒe me la enye mí Kristotɔ ɖekakpui aɖewo ƒe didi be woagba trɔ̃aveawo ne míakpɔ xɔ tu ƒe. Nye ya me dze egɔme xoxo; me ƒle kɔtive ƒe akpaɖe be matu xɔ ɖe gama.[16]

A17   James Cudjoe, Sokpoe: Culture of Sokpoe not limited by religion
Kɔnu wɔwɔ la menye trɔ̃subɔla alo Kristotɔnyenye hãa hafi woawɔe o. Nanewo li la alesi tɔgbewo wɔe alo gblɔe ɖaɖi si ƒia be Sokpoetɔwo mienye la nenema ko woga le na míkata. Alesi woɖoe ko la nenema ko wòle. Eƒe trɔ̃subɔla nyenye kple Kristotɔnyenye me li o.[17]

---

14. Hajia Amina Awudu, interview at Dabala, 25 May 2016.
15. Robert Avenɔgbo, interview at Sokpoe, 13 March 2016
16. Daniel Agbota, interview at Sokpoe, 5 February 2016.
17. James Cudjoe, interview at Sokpoe, 26 June 2016.

Glossary

THE EʋE USED IN this study predominantly reflects the Eʋe spoken by the Tɔŋu districts of Southern Volta Region of Ghana. Many of the words are, however, similar to those used by the Aŋlɔ and the Peki or Ʋedomeawo. My translations into English are almost literal, which means the English expression and grammar is somewhat distorted. In addition, there are some new English words that I have coined for lack of close equivalents that preserve the conceptions or thought forms and understandings in the Eʋe expressions about the religious worldviews of the Sokpoe-Eʋe.

Eʋe Expression	English Equivalent
Abosam	Satan, Devil
Agasigbe	Chief Aga's instructed market day, one day of rest out of a five-day week. It is also the day for performing sacrificial rituals in primal religion
Ame	Created thing, human as a creature. The word is used as neutral noun only for humans.
Ameɛ	Lifeless or dead human body, corpse.
Amegbetɔ	Enlivened created body, human being, humanity.
Amewuga	Human is more than money; humanity is the most valuable of all things.

Eʋe Expression	English Equivalent
Aʋlime	The world of the living dead beneath the Earth's surface, what I call "terresphere." For the primal religionists *aʋlime* opens contiguously back to the world of the living living on Earth (*kodzogbe*), which I call "geosphere." This explains why *ŋɔliwo* (ghosts) can freely move between *aʋlime* and *kodzogbe*. Christians and Muslims use this term to imply the gateway from the human world on Earth (geosphere) through which *luʋɔ* (soul/spirit) of the dead pass into either *dzifoʋī* (highest heaven) or *dzomavɔme* (hell) in the spiritual world above the Earth, which I call "celesphere."
Awusatɔ	A person belonging to Hausa ethnic extraction, but often implies a Muslim.
Aziza	Dwarf, short human-like creature with feet turned backwards, believed to possess spiritual powers.
Dzifoʋī	Highest heaven or Paradise. This is the place of blissful and glorious eternal living for godly souls, as believed by both Christians and Muslims in Sokpoe eco-area. It is the blissful side of the celesphere.
Dzifoxexeme/Dzifo	The eternal or perpetual world or place of abode of the living dead, located above *dziŋɔli/alilikpo* (sky) in the mind-view of Christians and Muslims. It is the cosmic space for life post-mortem, the spatial arena within which is located both *dzifoʋī* (highest heaven) and *dzomavɔme* (hell). This is the space I call "celesphere."
Dzigbeɖi	Dirt of parturition, broinhidrosis, persistent repulsive body odor that results from poor post-parturition skin care of the baby.
Dziŋɔli/alilikpo	Sky, clouds, firmament, stratosphere.
Dzomavɔme	Hell, or place of eternal fire. It is the place of punishment for ungodly souls/spirits as believed by both Christians and Muslims in Sokpoe eco-area. It is the painful side of the celesphere.
Ɖidɛxɔme	Maternity room, the special place for a new baby and mother at home.
Kodzogbe	The place of physical existence on the Earth; physical state of human being. This is what I call the "geosphere."
Legba	Molded image, statue, idol.
Luʋɔ	Soul, the real being of a human, which is a created but immortal mirror of the created but mortal *ŋutilā* (body); shadow of a living person under partial light.
Lī	Millet, sorghum, grain.

Glossary

Eʋe Expression	English Equivalent
Ŋɔlĩ	Ghost, spiritual form of human existence, or spirit of a deceased inhabiting and seen in human body. Primal religionists sometimes equate it with luʋo, but Muslims do not have the concept of ŋɔli.
Ŋutilã/Lãkusi	Body, flesh. It is the part of being created with or from clay, into which *Mawu* (God) breathed *gbɔgbɔ* (breath/spirit). Thus, it is the created, physical and mortal aspect of humans and animals.
Tɔgbeŋɔlĩ	Ancestor (male). *Mamaŋɔlĩ* is female ancestor but used mainly by the Aŋlɔ-Eʋe. The Tɔŋu-Eʋe refer to ancestors more often simply as *tɔgbetɔgbewo*, and this often is generic for both male and female ancestors, though *mamawo* may also be used specifically for female ancestors.
Trɔ̃	Local god, deity.
Trɔ̃nua	Person in charge of a deity, priest of a deity.
Trɔ̃subɔla	Worshipper or devotee of *trɔ̃*, primal religionist.
Tsixetsixe	An adjective qualifying breathing, visible inhaling and exhaling.
Viɖeɖeɖego	Taking a baby out, outdooring rite.
Xexeme	(1) (*agbe gbegblẽ nɔnɔ*) detestable human behaviours, e.g., *Ametsitsimabumabu le gbɔ sɔm elabe xexeme le gbegblẽm* (Increasing disrespect of the elderly amounts to deteriorating *xexeme*.) Thus the expression *xexeme le gbegblẽm* actually refers to living conditions, socially, religiously and ecologically, not in tandem with how the creator purposes it to be, at least according to the Sokpoe-Eʋe worldview.

(2) (*lãme gbegblẽ atraɖii*) chronic or persisting ill-health conditions, e.g., *Nye gbɔgbɔtsixe xexeme ga ʋlu* (My chronic asthmatic *xexeme* (condition) is back.

(3) (*Agbenɔƒe/anyigbadzi/kodzogbe*) Gecosphere or cosmic environment for physical life; the Earth's surface and its atmospheric regions up to the sky observable with unaided eyes and no scientific calculations, as the home where we (human and other-than-human creation) live physically and act ecologically in holistic interrelationships. The spatial arena consisting of lithosphere, atmosphere and stratoshere. |
| Xexemetɔ/Egodotɔ | Worldly person, person outside Christianity, non-believer. |
| Xɔnudzɔgoe | Guarding gourd, a gourd packed with foodstuff to lure evil spirits off. |

Bibliography

Agbanu, Harry L. K. "Environmental Ethics in Mafi-Eʋe Indigenous Culture." PhD diss., University of Ghana, Legon, 2011.

Agrawal, Arun, and C. C. Gibson. "Enchantment and Disenchantment: The Role of Community in Natural Resource Conservation." *World Development* 27/4 (1999) 629–49.

Al-Hilali, Muhammad Taqi-ud-Din, and Muhammad Mushin, translators. *The Noble Qur'an*. http://www.noblequran.com.

Anderson, Fulton H. *The New Organon and Related Writings*. New York: Macmillan, 1960.

Asante, Frank. "Environmental Education Integrated in School Syllabi." Government of Ghana Official Portal, April 10, 2014. http://ghana.gov.gh/index.php/media-center/news/469-environmental-education-integrated-.

Avenɔgbo, Stephen Kofi. "Aesthetic Impact of Ghanaian Socio-Cultural Practices on the Environment and Its Protection in Ghana." PhD diss., Kwame Nkrumah University of Science and Technology, 2008.

Azumah, John. *My Neighbour's Faith: Islam Explained for Christians*. Nairobi: Hippo 2008.

Bauckham, Richard. "The New Testament Teaching on the Environment: A Response to Ernest Lucas." *Transformation* 16/3 (July 1999) 99–101.

Bediako, Gillian Mary. Editorial to "Primal Religion as the Substructure of Christianity—Theological and Phenomenological Perspectives." *Journal of African Christian Thought* 11/2 (December 2008) 1–4.

———. "Primal Religion and Christian Faith: Antagonists or Soul-Mates?" *Journal of African Christian Thought* 3/1 (June 2000) 12–16.

———. "Reflections on the Scholarship of Kwame Bediako and Its Importance for African Theology." *Journal of African Christian Thought* 12/2 (December 2009) 19–22.

Bediako, Kwame. "Christian Faith and African Culture: An Exposition of the Epistle to the Hebrews." *Journal of African Christian thought* 13/1 (June 2010) 47–57.

———. "Gospel and Culture: Some Insights for Our Time from the Experience of the Earliest Church." *Journal of African Christian Thought* 2/2 (December 1999) 8–17.

———. *Jesus in Africa: The Christian Gospel in African History and Experience*. Oxford: Editions Clé and Regnum Africa, 2004.

———. "Scripture as the Hermeneutic of Culture and Tradition." *Journal of African Christian Thought* 4/1 (June 2001) 2–11.

———. *Theology and Identity: The Impact of Culture upon Christian Thought in the Second Century and in the Modern Africa.* Oxford: Regnum, 1999.

Bergant, Dianne. *The Earth Is the Lord's: The Bible, Ecology and Worship.* Collegeville, MN: Liturgical, 1998.

Berry, Sam. "A Christian Approach to the Environment." *Transformation* 16/3 (July 1999) 73–74.

Berry, Wendell. *What Are people for? Essays by Wendell Berry.* New York: North Point, 1990.

Birch, Charles, William Eaken, and Jay B. McDaniel, editors. *Liberating Life: Contemporary Approaches in Ecological Theology.* Maryknoll: Orbis, 1990.

Blasu, Ebenezer Yaw. "'Compensated Reduction' as Motivation for Reducing Deforestation: An African Christian Theological Response." *Journal of African Christian Thought* 18/1 (June 2015) 18–24.

———. "Our Earth, Our Responsibility." *Evangelical Review of Theology* 41/3 (July 2017) 254–68.

Boff, Leonardo. *Sacraments of Life—Life of Sacraments.* Washington, DC: Pastoral, 1996.

Bonk, Jonathan J. "Mission and the Groaning of Creation." *International Bulletin of Missionary Research* 32/4 (October 2008) 169–70.

Bookless, David. *Planetwise: Dare to Care for God's World.* Nottingham: InterVarsity, 2008.

Carson, Rachael L. *Silent Spring.* New York: Mariner, 1962.

Carter, Howard Kris. "Looking Up . . . the Majesty of God and Our Place in Creation Psalm 8 . . . Theo-Cology: The Breath Print of God and Renewal of Creation Care in the Nature Psalms (Part 1)." *How in the World!!* (blog), October 6, 2013. https://howard-carter.blogspot.com/2013/10/looking-up-majesty-of-god-and-our-place.html.

Chishti, Saadia Khawar Khan. "*Fitra*: An Islamic Model for Humans and the Environment." In *Islam and Ecology: A Bestowed Trust*, edited by Richard C. Foltz, Frederick M. Denny, and Azizan Baharuddin, 67–81. Cambridge, MA: Harvard University Press, 2003.

Chryssavgis, John. "The World of the Icon and Creation: An Orthodox Perspective on Ecology and Pneumatology." In *Christianity and Ecology*, edited by Dieter T. Hessel and Rosemary Radford Reuther, 83–96. Cambridge, MA: Harvard University Press, 2000.

Clarke, Mathew. *Development and Religion: Theology and Practice.* Cheltenham, UK: Edward Elgar, 2011.

Clobus, Robert. "Ecofarming and Land Ownership in Ghana." In *Missionary Earthkeeping*, edited by Calvin B. DeWitt and J. Mark Thomas, 63–89. Macon, GA: Mercer University Press, 1992.

Cunningham, William P., and Barbara Woodworth Saigo. *Environmental Science: A Global Concern.* 6th ed. New York: McGraw-Hill, 2001.

Curry, Patrick, *Ecological Ethics: An Introduction.* 2nd ed. Cambridge: Polity, 2011.

Daneel, M. L. *African Earthkeepers: A Holistic Interfaith Mission.* Maryknoll, NY: Orbis, 2001.

Deane-Drummond, Celia. *Eco-Theology.* London: Darton, Longman and Todd, 2008.

Dowd, Michael. *Thank God for Evolution.* San Francisco: Council Oak, 2007.

Dutton, Yasin. "The Environmental Crisis of Our Time: A Muslim Response." In *Islam and Ecology: A Bestowed Trust*, edited by Richard C. Foltz, Frederick M. Denny, and Azizan Baharuddin, 323-40. Cambridge, MA: Harvard University Press, 2003.

Edwards, Denis. *The God of Evolution: A Trinitarian Theology*. New York: Paulist, 1999.

Eliade, Mircea. *The Sacred and the Profane: The Nature of Religion*. Translated by Willard R. Trask. New York: Harcourt, Brace, 1959.

Environmental Protection Agency of Ghana. *Ghana State of Environment Report 2004*. ACCRA: EPA, Ghana, April 2005.

———. *National Programme on Sustainable Consumption and Production (SCP) for Ghana (2011-2016), Volume 2, Final Report*. EPA and UNEP, December 12, 2019 https://europa.eu/capacity4dev/file/12626/download?token=NnfczEUo

Ester, and B. Seuren. "Religious Beliefs and Environmental Attitudes: An Empirical Test of the Lynn White Hypothesis in Fourteen Nations." *Sociale Wetenschappen* 35/1 (1992) 20-39.

Foley, M. W. "Who Cut Down the Sacred Tree? Replying to Lynn White Jr's Popular Thesis that Christianity Is the Root of All Environmental Evil." *CoEvolution Quarterly* 15 (1997) 60-67.

Foltz, Richard C., Frederick M. Denny, and Azizan Baharuddin, editors. *Islam and Ecology: A Bestowed Trust*. Cambridge, MA: Harvard University Press, 2003.

"Forum on Religion and Ecology at Yale." http://fore.yale.edu/files/Forum_Overview.pdf.

Fueter, P. D. "Theological Education in Africa." *International Review of Missions* 27 (1956).

Gathogo, Julius. "Environmental Management and African Indigenous Resources: Echoes from Mutira Mission, Kenya (1912-2012)." University of South Africa Institutional Repository. http://uir.unisa.ac.za/bitstream/handle/10500/13127/Gathogo.pdf?sequence=1.

Geisler, Norman L. *Christian Ethics: Contemporary Issues and Options*. 2nd ed. Grand Rapids, Michigan: Baker, 2010.

Getui, Mary N., and Emmanuel Obeng, editors. *Theology of Reconstruction: Exploratory Essays*. Nairobi: Acton, 1999.

"Ghana Goes for Green Growth: Discussion Document – Summary." Accra: Ministry of Environment, Science and Technology, November 2010. http://cdkn.org/wp-content/uploads/2011/04/NCCPF-Summary-FINAL.pdf.

Glatthorn, Allan, *Writing the Winning Dissertation: A Step-by-Step Guide*. London: Corwin, 1998.

Godfrey, Robert W. *God's Pattern for Creation: A Conventional Reading of Genesis 1*. New Jersey: P&R, 2003.

Golo, Ben-Willie Kwaku. "Environment and Spirituality: The Climate Crisis as a Spiritual and Moral Challenge." Paper presented at the Presbyterian Inter-Faith Research Resource Centre (PIRRC), Seventh Annual Interfaith Symposium, Ebenezer Presbyterian Church Hall, Osu Accra, October 14, 2015.

———. "Redeemed from the Earth? Environmental Change and Salvation Theology in African Christianity." *Scriptura* 111/3 (2012) 348-61.

Gonzales, Tirso A., and Melissa K. Nelson. "Contemporary Native American Responses to Environmental Threat." In *Indigenous Traditions and Ecology*, edited by John A. Grim, 495-538. Cambridge, MA: Harvard University Press, 2001.

Grim, John A., editor. *Indigenous Traditions and Ecology.* Cambridge, MA: Harvard University Press, 2001.

Grim, John A., and Mary E. Tucker. *Ecology and Religion.* Washington, DC: Island, 2014.

———. "Online Course: Introduction to Religion and Ecology." F&ES 783E, REL 903H course syllabus, Spring 2015. Yale School of Forestry and Environmental Studies. http://fore.yale.edu/files/Introduction_to_Religion_and_Ecology.pdf.

Gyekye, Kwame. *African Cultural Values: An Introduction.* Accra: Sankofa, 1998.

Losslky, Nochoas, Jose Miguez Bonino, John Pobee et al., editors. *Dictionary of the Ecumenical Movement.* Geneva: WCC, 2002.

Hallman, David G., editor. *Ecotheology: Voices from the South and North.* Eugene, OR: WCC, 1994.

Haq, Nomanul S. "Islam and Ecology: Toward Retrieval and Reconstruction." In *Islam and Ecology*, edited by Richard C. Foltz, Frederick M. Denny, and Azizan Baharuddin, 121–54, eds. Cambridge, MA: Harvard University Press, 2003.

Hayes, Victor C., editor. *Australian Essays in World Religions.* Bedford Park, South Australia: AASR, 1977.

Henry, John. *The Scientific Revolution and the Origins of Modern Science.* 2nd ed. Basingstoke: Palgrave, 2002.

Hessel, Dieter T., and Rosemary Radford Ruether, editors. *Christianity and Ecology.* Cambridge, MA: Harvard University Press, 2000.

Hitzhusen, Gregory E. "Judeo-Christian Theology and the Environment: Moving beyond Skepticism to New Sources for Environmental Education in the United States." *Environmental Education Research* 13/1 (February 2007) 55–74.

Holmes, Arthur F. *Building the Christian Academy.* Cambridge: Eerdmans, 2001.

Houghton, L. T. *Global Warming: The Complete Briefing.* Cambridge: Cambridge University Press, 2004.

House, Paul R. "Creation in Old Testament Theology." The NTS Library. http://www.ntslibrary.com/PDF%20Books/Creation%20in%20OT%20Theology.pdf.

Howell, Allison M. "African Spirituality and Christian Ministry: 'Discerning the Signs of the times' in Our Environment and Community." *Journal of African Christian Thought* 20/1 (June 2017) 12–23.

Ilori, Joseph Abiodun. "Networking and Partnership as Tools for Improving Christian Higher Education in Africa." *West African Journal of Higher Education* 3 (2014) 4–9.

Kalu, Ogbu U. "Precarious Vision: The African's Perception of His World." In *Readings in African Humanities: African Cultural Development*, edited by Ogbu U. Kalu, 37–44. Nigeria: Fourth Dimension, 1980.

———, editor. *Readings in African Humanities: African Cultural Development.* Nigeria: Fourth Dimension, 1980.

———. "The Sacred Egg: Worldview, Ecology, and Development in West Africa." In *Indigenous Traditions and Ecology*, edited by John A. Grim, 225–48. Cambridge, MA: Harvard University Press, 2001.

Keitzar, Renthy. "Creation and Restoration: Three Bible reflections." In *Ecotheology: Voices from the South and North*, edited by David G. Hallman, 52–61. Eugene, OR: WCC, 1994.

Kudadjie, Joshua. "Researching Morals and Rituals." *Journal of African Christian Thought* 2/2 (December 1999) 35–43.

Kwamena-Po, Michael A. *Vision and Achievement: A Hundred and Fifty Years of Presbyterian Church of Ghana.* Accra: Waterville, 2011.
Lee, Hannah, et al. "Human Disturbance and Natural Habitat: A Biome Level Analysis of a Global Data Set." *Biodiversity and Conservation* 4/2 (1995) 128-55.
Llewellyn, Othman Abd-Ar-Rahman. "The Basis for a Discipline of Islamic Environmental Law." In *Islam and Ecology*, edited by Richard C. Foltz, Frederick M. Denny, and Azizan Baharuddin, 185-247. Cambridge, MA: Harvard University Press, 2003.
Lucas, Ernest. "The New Testament Teaching on the Environment." *Transformation* 16/3 (July 1999) 93-99.
MacArthur, John. "The Theology of Creation." *Grace to You*, August 24, 2008. https://www.gty.org/library/sermons-library/90-359/the-theology-of-creation.
MacDonald, Mary N. "Changing Habits, Changing Habitats: Melanasian Environmental Knowledge." In *Indigenous Traditions and Ecology: The Interbeing of Cosmology and Community*, edited by John A. Grim, 591-617. Cambridge, MA: Harvard University Press, 2001.
Mangena, Fainos. "Discerning Moral Status in the African Environment." *Phronimon* 14/2 (2013) 25-44.
Mante, J. O. Y. *Africa: Theological and Philosophical Roots of Our Ecological Crisis.* Accra: SonLife, 2004.
Marans, Daniel. "Obama EPA Head Savages Donald Trump's Environmental Policies." *Huffington Post*, March 4, 2017. http://www.huffingtonpost.com/entry/gina-mccarthy-savages-donald-trump_us_58bb08cee4b0d2821b4e977e.
Mbiti, John S. *African Religions and Philosophy.* 2nd ed. Oxford: Heinemann, 1990.
———. *Introduction to African Religion.* 2nd ed. Long Grove, IL: Waveland, 1975.
Meiners, Roger, Pierre Desrochers, and Andrew Morris, editors. *Silent Spring at 50: The False Crisis of Rachael Carson.* Washington, DC: Cato Institute, 2012.
Meyer, Birgit. *Translating the Devil: Religion and Modernity Among the Ewe in Ghana.* Edinburgh: Edinburgh University Press, 1999.
Moe, Thang David. "A Trinitarian Theology of Religions: Themes and Issues in Evangelical Approaches." *Evangelical Review of Theology* 41/3 (July 2017) 234-53.
Moltmann, Jürgen. *God in Creation: An Ecological Doctrine of Creation.* London: SCM, 1985.
Moncrief, L. "The Cultural Basis for Our Environmental Crisis: Judeo-Christian Tradition Is Only One of Many Cultural Factors Contributing to the Environmental Crisis." *Science* 170/3957 (1970) 508-12.
Moran, Gabriel. *Design for Religion: Toward Ecumenical Education.* New York: Herder, 1970.
Moutinho, Paulo, and Stephen Schwartzman, editors. *Tropical Deforestation and Climate Change.* Washington, DC: Amazon Institute for Environmental Research, Environmental Defense, 2005. https://www.edf.org/sites/default/files/4930_TropicalDeforestation_and_ClimateChange.pdf.
Moxon, James. *Volta: Man's Greatest Lake.* London: Andre Deutch, 1969.
Mutasa, Davie E., Shumirai Nyota, and Jacob Mpara. "Ngano: Teaching Environmental Education Using the Shona Folktale." *Journal of Pan African Studies* 2/3 (March 2008) 33-54.
Muzorewa, Gwinyai. *The Origins and Development of African Theology.* Maryknoll, NY: Orbis, 1985.

Myers, Bryant L. *Walking with the Poor: Principles and Practices of Transformational Development*. Rev. ed. Maryknoll, NY: Orbis, 2011.

Narh, Cephas Richard. *Moral Linkage: A Practical Approach to Integration in Learning*. Accra: Combert Impressions, 2012.

Nasr, Seeyed Hossein. "Islam, the Contemporary Islamic World, and the Environmental Crisis." In *Islam and Ecology*, edited by Richard C.Foltz, Frederick M. Denny, and Azizan Baharuddin, 85–105. Cambridge, MA: Harvard University Press, 2003.

Nebel, Bernard J., and Richard T. Wright. *Environmental Science: The Way the World Works*. 5th ed. Upper Saddle, NJ: Prentice Hall, 1996.

Nehring, Andreas, editor. *Ecology: A Theological Response*. Madras: Gurukul Lutheran Theological College and Research Institute (Summer Institute), 1993.

Northcott, Michael. "Christians, Environment and Society." *Transformation* 16/3 (1999) 102–9.

———. *A Moral Climate: The Ethics of Global Warming*. London: Darton, Longman and Todd, 2007.

Ogot, Bethwell Allan, editor. *General History of Africa*, vol. 5: *Africa from the Sixteenth to the Eighteenth Century*. Paris: UNESCO, 1999.

Ogungbemi, S. "An African Perspective on the Environmental Crisis." In *Environmental Ethics: Readings in Theory and Application*, edited by L. J. Pojman, 330–37. Belmont, CA: Wadsworth, 1997.

Ojomo, Philomena A. "An African Understanding of Environmental Ethics." *Thought and Practice*, n.s., 2/2 (December 2010) 49–63. https://www.ajol.info/index.php/tp/article/view/64100.

Opoku, John Kwaku. "African Traditional Ethics: An Appraisal of Its Impact on Human Development in the Kumasi Metropolis." *Journal of Applied Thought* 4/2 (May 2015) 286–304.

Opoku, Kofi Asare. "Cooking on Two Stones of the Hearth? African Spirituality and the Socio-Cultural Transformation of Africa." *Journal of African Christian Thought* 13/1 (June 2010) 3–9.

———. *West African Traditional Religion*. Accra: FEP International, 1978.

Oxford Advanced Learner's Dictionary. 8th ed. Oxford: Oxford University Press, 2010.

Pachuau, Lalsangkima. "Primal Spirituality as the Substructure of Christian Spirituality: The Case of Mizo Christianity in India." *Journal of African Christian thought* 11/2 (December 2008) 9–14.

Presbyterian Church of Ghana, Department of Education. *Policy Document on General Education*. Accra: Presbyterian Press, 2015.

Quarshie, B. Y. "Paul and the Primal Substructure of Christianity: Missiological Reflections on the Epistle to the Galatians." *Journal of African Christian Thought* 12/1 (June 2009) 8–14.

Rahman, Fazlur. *Major Themes of the Qur'an*. Minneapolis: Bibliotheca Islamica, 1980.

Ruether, Rosemary Radford, editor. *Women Healing Earth: Third World Women on Ecology, Feminism and Religion*. Maryknoll, NY: Orbis, 1996.

Safi, Omid, and Anna Bigelow. "Muslim Views of Death." Islamic Research Foundation International. https://www.irfi.org/articles3/articles_4301_4400/muslim%20views%20of%20deathhtml.htm.

Sapir, Edward. *Selected Writings of Edward Sapir in Language, Culture and Personality*. Edited by D. G. Mandelbaum. Berkeley: University of California Press, 1958.

Schloss, Jeffrey. "Wisdom Traditions as Mechanisms for Organisational Integration." In *Understanding Wisdom*, edited by W. S. Brown, 153–91. Philadelphia: Templeton Foundation, 2000.

Schwarz, Hans. *Creation*. Cambridge: Eerdmans, 2002.

Silverman, David. *Doing Qualitative Research: A Practical Handbook*. London: SAGE 2000.

Sindima, Harvey. "Community of Life: Ecological Theology in African Perspective." In *Liberating Life: Contemporary Approaches in Ecological Theology*, edited by Charles Birch, William Eaken, and Jay B. McDaniel, 137–47. Maryknoll, NY: Orbis, 1990.

Sorely, Craig. "Christ, Creation, Stewardship and Missions: How Discipleship into a Biblical Worldview on Environmental Stewardship Can Transform People and Their Land." *International Bulletin of Missionary Research* 35/3 (July 2011) 137–43.

Stewart, Mark. "Transforming Higher Education: A Practical Plan for Integrating Sustainability Education into the Student Experience." *Journal of Sustainability Education* 1 (May 2010) 1–13. http://www.jsedimensions.org/wordpress/wp-content/uploads/2010/05/Stewart2010.pdf.

Stokols, Eli. "Trump to Pull U.S. Out of Paris Climate Accord." *Wall Street Journal, What's News* (podcast), June 1, 2017. http://www.wsj.com/podcasts/trump-to-pull-us-out-of-paris-climate-accord/0FBC2FBC-2A0B-40B3-B14C-AF72587043DF.html.

Swimme, Brian Thomas, and Mary Evelyn Tucker. *Journey of the Universe*. New Haven, CT: Yale University Press, 2011.

Sylvan, Richard, and David Bennett. *The Greening of Ethics: From Human Chauvinism to Deep-Green Theory*. Cambridge: White Horse, 1994.

Tuan, Y. F. "Our Treatment of the Environment in Ideal and Actuality." *American Scientist* 58/3 (1970) 247–49.

Tucker, Catherine M., editor. *Nature, Science and Religion*. Santa Fe: SAR, 2012.

Tucker, Mary Evelyn, and John A. Grim. "The Emerging Alliance of World Religions and Ecology." *Daedalus* 130/4 (2001) 1–22. http://www.jstor.org/stable/20027715.

———, editors. *Worldviews and Ecology*. Lewisburg, PA: Bucknell University Press, 1993.

Victus, Solomon. *Eco-Theology and the Scriptures: Revisit of Christian Responses*. New Delhi: Christian World Imprints, 2014.

Vriezen, T. C. *An Outline of Old Testament Theology*. Oxford: Basil Blackwell, 1958.

Walls, Andrews F. *The Cross-Cultural Process in Christian History*. Maryknoll, NY: Orbis, 2002.

Wenham, Gordon. "The Old Testament and the Environment: A Response to Chris Wright," *Transformation* 16/3 (July 1999) 86–92.

Westermann, Claus. *Genesis*. London: T. & T. Clark, 1987.

Westermann, Dietrich. *Gbefiala or Eve-English Dictionary*. Berlin: Dietrich Voshen, 1930.

"What Is ECOTHEOLOGY What Does ECOTHEOLOGY Mean? ECOTHEOLOGY Meaning, Definition & Explanation." Audiopedia (YouTube channel), October 5, 2016. https://www.youtube.com/watch?v=o4-KyAN03Kg.

White, Lynn, Jr. "Historical Roots of Our Ecological Crisis." *Science* 155 (March 10, 1967) 1203–7.

Williams, R. J. *Renewal Theology: God, the World and Redemption*. Grand Rapids: Zondervan, 1996.

Wilson, Suzan M., and Penelope L. Peterson. *Theories of Learning and Teaching: What Do They Mean for Educators?* Washington, DC: National Education Association Research Department, July 2006.

Wright, Chris J. H. "Theology and Ethics of the Land." *Transformation* 16/3 (1999) 81–86.

———. "The World in the Bible." *Evangelical Review of Theology* 34/3 (July 2010) 207–19.

Young, Richard A. *Healing the Earth: A Theocentric Perspective on Environmental Problems and Their Solutions.* Nashville: Broadman & Holman, 1994.

Zizioulas, John. "A Comment on Pope Francis' Encyclical *Laudato Si'* by Elder Metropolitan John (Zizioulas) of Pergamon." June 18, 2015. https://www.patriarchate.org/-/a-comment-on-pope-francis-encyclical-laudato-si-.

Index

Italicised words are Eʋe expressions (a Ghanaian language); words in parenthesized (*italics*) are Islamic terms, and <u>Underlined names</u> are some of the interviewees mentioned in the book.

A

Abbreviations, xi
(*Ābd-Allah*) servant of God, 57
<u>Abdullah Muhammad</u>, 120, 132–33, 160–61, 167, 171, 176–77, 192–93, 202, 215, 217–18, 220, 242, 243
Abosam (Satan), 126, 159
<u>Abotsi, Castro</u>, 174, 181, 185, 190–91, 198–200, 216–17, 221–22
Abiotic factors, 28
Acceptance, 181, 211, 213
Accidents, 64, 221–24
Acclimatization, 174, 177
 gecospheric, 176, 232–33
Acculturated or indigenized Christians (see Christians), 164, 231
ACI (Akrofi-Christaller Institute of Theology, Culture and Mission) xi, xiv-xv, 7, 175–76, 178, 186–88, 201
Acknowledgements, xv
Ada, 2
Adam, 68, 92, 95, 98, 131–32, 138, 181
Adamah, (the equivalent of Hebrew "erets," or Greek "ge," or "cosmos"), 62, 93

<u>Adikpe, Maxwell Kwasi (Rev.)</u>, 121, 133, 136, 138, 189, 199–201
<u>Adzabeng, Mary</u>, 147
Adze, (witchcraft), 126
Affirmation, 34, 80–81, 83, 185, 215
Africa, 3, 10–13, 37–39, 41–45, 47, 50–52, 58–59, 92–94, 135–37, 165, 201, 205, 236, 238, 251–54
African child, 78, 84–85
African Christian, 11, 58, 94, 143, 214, 232, 238, 249, 252, 254
 ethics, 97, 99, 101, 112–14
 response to global ecocrisis, 1
 theology, 7, 58, 209
 thought, 249–50, 252, 254
African Christianity, 4–5, 11–12, 211, 213, 234
African
 conception of space, 45, 124
 cultural development, 252
 culture, 41, 42, 45, 62, 73, 119, 146, 150, 207, 249
 earthkeepers, 6–7, 95, 98, 250
 environment, 38, 41, 236, 253
 Indigenous Christianity (AIC), 5, 7
 precarious vision, 104
 primal cultures, 10, 72, 74, 187, 201
 primal worldviews, 44, 72, 76, 78, 201
African Religions, 7, 19

257

and Philosophy, 48, 253
African religiosity, 7, 48
African religious worldviews, 7, 13, 234–35, 238
African theocology, i, iii-iv, ix, xiv, 5–9, 15, 19, 109, 119, 142–43, 170, 227, 233–36, 238
  curriculum, 5–6, 13, 115, 119, 225, 229, 233–34
African worldviews, 38–39, 42–44, 46–50, 72–73
Afriyie, Ernestina (Believes Africans' fear of deity is impulsion for ecocare), 166
Afɔlĩ (see clam, oyster)
Agasigbe (the fifth market day on the local, 5-day week of the Sokpoe-Eʋe), 150, 157–58, 162
  taboo, 150, 162
Agbanu, Harry L. K., 12–14, 45–47, 72–73, 75, 79, 105, 107, 120, 143, 146, 155, 186, 216, 236, 249
Agbatɔ, Matthew, 121, 133, 174, 176, 198–200
Agbenɔfe, *xexeme*, (world as a living space, biosphere), 123, 230
Agbewɔvi, Maxwell, 130, 133, 147, 176, 178, 189, 200
Agboklu, Christiana, 128
Agboklu, Samuel, 49, 71, 125, 127–28, 130–31, 137, 146, 158, 196, 206, 210, 241
Agbota, Daniel, 136, 159–60, 200–201, 209, 244
Agrawal, Arun and C. C. Gibson, 103, 105, 249
Ahado, Andrews, 123, 128, 133–36, 153, 185, 189–90, 199–200, 210, 215, 219, 222, 242
Ahado, Gladys, 64, 121, 124, 172, 184, 189, 203–4, 216, 218
Ahamaŋkɔ, (insinuation name), 144
AIC (African Indigenous Christianity), 5, 7
Aiōn, 62
Air, 20, 22, 50, 60, 66–67, 89, 92, 126, 128, 131, 197
Akafo, Mercy, 129–30, 139, 200, 206

Akrofi-Christaller Institute *see* ACI
Akropong-Akuapem, 175–76, 178, 186–88, 201
Alhaji Hama, 162, 167
Allah, 71, 80, 82–83, 88, 90, 122, 130–31, 162, 177, 203, 218
All creation (cosmosphere), 63
Alɔlɔ, or *Zoyi* (a clan in Sokpoe), 151, 212
Amanuke (A Nigerian community with significant primal conservation philosophy), 106
Amedzɔdzɔ (reincarnate), 201, 230
Ameɖiɖi, (burial), 211, 216, 221
Amegbetɔ (human, humanity), 50, 130, 132, 134, 136, 230, 242
Ame meme (cremation), 216
Amenɔɖiɖi, (burial of placenta), 171, 177, 232–33
Ametsivume (the dead from accident occurrence), 213, 225
Amewuga, (human is worthier than money), 143–44
Amutɔsisi (Volta River), 150–51
Ancestors, 42, 47–48, 73, 75, 77, 106, 123, 154, 166, 171, 173–74, 187–88, 201–7, 211–12, 247
  cult of, 205
  female, 187, 212, 247
Ancestral world, 50, 142, 211
Anderson, Fulton A. (explains why Francis Bacon insists on God's book of nature), 66
Androgene (17*a*-methyl-testosteron), hormone to unisex fryers, 115
Angels, 126–28, 131, 218
Anthropocentric, 2, 11, 52, 71–72, 75–76, 89, 95, 138, 144–48, 195, 210
Anthropocentrism, 72, 91, 146–48, 231
Anthropogenic, 1
Anyigbadzi (surface of Earth), 123–24, 179, 196, 241
Anyigba kple edzinuwo, (gecosphere), 64
Apostolic Revelation Society *see* ARS

Index

Appendix, 49, 51, 108, 130–32, 137, 144, 147–48, 156, 159–60, 171, 176, 181, 183, 192, 241
ARS (Apostolic Revelation Society), 130, 133, 147, 176, 178, 189, 199
Asiedu-Amoako, Samuel, xv
Asuma, Margaret, 147–48, 242
Atiglo, Avinyo Kofi, 50–51, 123, 130–31, 151, 153, 155, 158, 172–74, 179–80, 186, 188, 196, 242
Atmosphere, 29, 54, 64, 67, 92, 123–27, 141, 174, 230, 247
Australian Essays in World Religions, 13, 43, 252
Authority, traditional, 152–54, 231
Autotrophic green plants, 28
Avenɔgbo, Robert, 183, 189–91, 244
Avenɔgbo, Enyi, 120, 123, 127, 130, 137, 144
Aveteh, Patrick Hans, 175–76, 178, 186–88, 201
Avi, Isaac, 156, 158–59, 186, 243
Avi, Klayi, 186–88, 196, 209
Avlime (subterranean abode), 124–25, 128, 141–42, 174, 187, 195–96, 204–6, 210–11, 213, 215–17, 230, 246
(*Ăwamir*) natural laws (singular, *amr*), 55, 86
Awuvlaya, (shroud), 215
(*Ăyat or* singular *aya*) pointer to God, 55, 71, 89, 129
Aziza, (dwarf), 126
Azuma, Jacob, 126, 133, 216
Azuma, Mary Amɛ (mama), 204
Azumah, John, 53, 80, 121, 126, 133, 177, 197–98, 218, 249

B

Babylonian myths of origin, 65
Baby outdooring, 171, 232–33
Bacon, Francis (Scholastic Christian, father of modern science), 66
Balatsui (Bala-pond), 152
Balave, (Bala-forest), 155
Balcomb, Anthony, xv

Bartholomew, Ecumenical Patriarch, of Eastern Orthodox Church, 98
Basel Missionaries (BM), 12, 94
Bawku, 1–2
Bediako, Gillian Mary, 92
Bediako, Kwame, 26, 40–42, 45, 47–48, 51–52, 59, 62–63, 73, 79, 92, 122, 125, 201, 205, 249
Behaviors, ecological, 41, 43–44, 52, 64, 85, 108, 120–21, 165, 168
  human, 9, 139
Belief, 25–26, 38, 41, 48, 53, 73, 80–82, 93, 126, 154, 166, 171, 175, 205, 217
  religious, 10, 83, 92, 102, 105, 211, 222
Benefits, 3, 31, 34, 88–89, 145–46, 149, 151, 158, 178
Bereaved families, 139, 215, 219, 223
Bergant, Dianne, 34–36, 250
Bible, 20, 59, 62–63, 66, 92, 101, 110, 112, 134, 183, 213, 250, 252, 256
  world in the, 62–64, 124, 127, 140
Biblical creation stories, 67, 96
Bigelow (see Safi, Amid and Anna Bigelow), 197, 213, 218–19, 221
Biocentric, 72, 147–48
Biocentrism, 72, 91, 145–49, 231
Biodiversity (loss), 28, 31, 33, 236
Biogeochemical processes, 28, 86
Biogeophysical cycles, 56
Biome, 27
Biosphere, 140
Birds, 2, 66–67, 92, 126
Birgit (See Meyer, Birgit)
Birth, 28, 49, 76–79, 108, 159, 172, 174–77, 180, 184, 191, 193, 195, 210–12, 220–22, 232–33
  day of, 174, 176–78, 187, 189, 192
Birthing, 77, 115, 138, 169–70, 232, 239
Birthing rites, 92, 101, 170–71, 176, 195, 232–33, 243
  religious, 94, 170–71, 193
Blasu, Agnes Abla, 211–12
Blasu, Ebenezer Yaw iii–iv
Blasu, Evelyn Ama xvi, 123, 128–29, 133, 175, 180, 189

Blasu, Mary Awusi, 129, 159
Blasu, Dickson Degbe, 126, 133, 136, 147–48, 178, 180, 204
Bless, 173, 187–88, 190, 193
Blessings, 78, 182–83, 188, 190–91, 193
Blood, 50, 95, 131–34, 136, 196, 199, 213, 230, 233
BM (Basel Missionaries), 12, 94
Body, 28, 68, 76, 86, 130–32, 133–37, 152, 180, 196–97, 199, 207, 217–18, 220, 230, 245–47
Bodzodife, (a town in Sokpoe), 148, 157
Bonk, Jonathan J., 9
Book of nature, God's, 66
Bookless, David, 54, 61, 108, 110–11, 141, 167, 181, 250
Bosoka, John, 174, 176, 190
Breath/spirit, 50, 67, 130–31, 134, 136, 138, 147–48, 196–97, 199, 202, 206, 211, 246
Broinhidrosis (*dzigbedi*), 174, 176, 211, 246
Buckets, 174, 212, 217
Burial, 79, 178, 192, 195, 208, 210–11, 215–16, 218–19, 221–23, 225
  placenta, 171, 232–33
  ground, 221
  ritual, 216, 218
Bury, 218, 220–22

C

Calabash, 77, 173, 180, 212
Calotropis procera ("wagashi" herb for wrapping placenta by Muslims), 192
Caring activities, 51, 137
Carson, Rachael, (*Silent Spring*), 22
Carter, Howard Kris (concurrently and independently also used the word 'theocology' when I coined it), 8
Celesphere (see meaning in glossary, 246), 125, 127, 141–42, 195, 198, 211, 214, 230, 246

CEM (Christ Evangelical Mission), 174, 176, 189–90
Ceremony, 76–77, 92, 172, 183, 186–87, 189, 192, 233
Chapel, 126, 183, 185, 189–90, 215–16
Chief, 77, 120, 126–28, 132, 148, 150, 153, 162
Child, 77–78, 84, 92, 144, 172–76, 178–93, 204, 221–22, 232
Children, 1, 144, 148, 151, 183, 190–91, 217
Christ, 14, 92–93, 95, 98–99, 110–12, 165, 214, 219, 233, 255
Christian,
  creation care praxis, 113
  birthing rites, 171
  environmentalism, 8, 238
  participants, 121–23, 128–30, 146, 148, 156, 171, 188, 198, 200, 206
  religions, 10, 109
  respondents, 141, 147–48
  responses, 110, 125, 159, 255
  salvation theology, 93–94
  theocentric worldview, 91, 100, 113
  theology, 8, 58–59, 91
  thought, 249–50
  worldviews of creation, 62
Christianity, 3, 11–14, 39, 52, 56–57, 85, 94–96, 101, 109–11, 121, 165–66, 197–98, 204, 211, 250–52
  ecological heritage, 95, 110
Christians, 11–15, 59–60, 90–91, 93–95, 111–12, 121–25, 139–42, 148, 156, 158–59, 170–71, 176, 183–85, 204–6, 208–16, 222, 231–33
  acculturated or indigenized, 164, 231
  and Muslims, 124, 139, 141–42, 148, 156, 160, 176, 178, 188, 193, 201, 230–31, 246
  culture-converted, 166, 232,
  deculturated or western-influenced, 164, 232,
  in Sokpoe ecological area, 203, 223, 225

passive or suspended, 164, 232
Chronos and Kairos, 45
Chryssavgis, John (human is a paradoxical duality), 96
Church of Pentecost *see* COP
City (*zongos*) community of West African Muslims among non-Muslims in Ghana, 107–8
Clams (oyster, *afɔlĩ*), 152–54, 163
Clan identity, 213–14
  ritual bath (see *hlɔ̃tsilele*), 211
Clarke, Matthew, 10
Clay, 77, 130–32, 135, 180, 220, 230, 247
Climate, change, 1–2, 5, 24, 253
  skeptic, (Scott Pruitt),, 23
Clobus, Robert, 77, 180, 250
Co-creators, humans as, 96–97, 139, 230
Coffin, 212, 216–19
Common Ground in Sokpoe-Eʋe Religious Worldviews, 139
  for concerted eco-praxis, 139
Community, 11, 40–41, 46, 68, 76–78, 90, 105, 163–64, 187, 191, 205, 211, 213–14, 233, 252–53
  creative, 29, 86
  of life, 11, 44, 72–73, 165, 255
Comply, 153, 167, 205, 231–32
Components, 13, 27, 41–42, 125, 127, 130, 132–33, 154, 198–99, 201
Concept, 5, 10–11, 19, 21, 28, 30, 35, 45, 49, 56, 82 84, 119–20, 140–41, 198, 201–2
Congregation, 190–91, 219, 223
Conservation, 10, 26, 29, 31, 38, 106, 162–63, 253
Constituents, 50, 133–34, 136, 197
Constitution, human, 130–31, 198–99
Contemporary Islamic World, 12, 55, 57, 87, 90, 104, 107, 109, 166, 168, 254
Contemporary Native American Responses, 75, 77, 106, 182
Contents, ix
Control, 36, 56–57, 104, 222
Converts, 4

COP (Church of Pentecost), 94, 121, 124, 133, 147, 156, 171–72, 184, 188–90, 199, 204, 218
Corpse, 79, 141, 207–12, 214–18, 220–23, 245
Cosmic, 56, 85–86, 93, 139
  exclusivity and ethical impotence, 35–36
Cosmologies, 13, 37, 42–43, 63, 65, 105, 125, 143, 154, 253
  pre-evolutionary, 63
Cosmos, 26, 37, 39–40, 45, 53–56, 61–64, 76, 80, 82, 84, 86, 91–93, 127, 139–40, 210
  biblical concepts of, 64
Cosmosphere, 63, 140
Country, 1–2, 24, 83
Course, African Theocology
  objectives, 235
  contents, 236
  relevance, 236
Courts, 88, 150, 152, 207
Creation, ix, xiii, 7–9, 43–45, 49–68, 71–72, 80–81, 83–85, 90–101, 109–13, 119–20, 133–35, 137–41, 146–48, 165–68, 230–35, 250–53
  activity, 137–38
  all, 63, 127
  doctrine of, 62, 165
  good, 63, 112
  in Old Testament Theology, 59–60, 63, 252
  integrity of, 34, 63, 83
  love, 58, 80
  manifests God's wisdom (Isa., 40:25–26), 65, 67
  role of humanity in, 96, 111
  stories of, 8, 67, 76, 92
  sustain, 25, 149
  theology of, 60
Craig (see Sorley)
Creation and restoration, 62, 65, 67–68, 98, 129, 252
Creation care, 5–6, 11, 19, 30, 35, 37–38, 70, 72, 76, 79, 84, 90, 92, 178, 235–39
  in Religious Traditions of Africa, 70

praxis of, 6, 79, 90, 92, 100–101, 108, 115, 229, 231–32
Creative activity, 50, 60, 92, 137
Creativity, 20, 45, 60, 138–39
Creator, 6–7, 34, 43, 51–52, 54–55, 57–58, 61–63, 68, 73, 80, 91–92, 97–98, 113, 158–59, 164
  good, 63, 71
  real, 53, 80
  in Primal religion, 120
  in African Primal Worldviews, 43
  in Islamic Worldviews, 52
  God as, 54, 62, 67
  of Our Home, 53, 59
  purposes for creation, 122, 247
Creatures, 20, 34, 51, 56–57, 66–67, 71, 73, 80–82, 89, 91, 96–97, 131, 137–38, 203, 210
  human, 50, 131
  short human-like (i.e. dwarfs), 246
Creeks, 150–52, 163–64, 231
Cremation, 79, 216, 219
Crop failure, 1
Cross-Cultural Process, 12–13, 40–42, 44, 48, 154, 211–13, 255
Cudjoe, James, 94, 147, 171, 179, 184, 188–90, 244
Cultures, 40–42, 48–50, 59, 63, 73, 78, 103, 105, 107–8, 222, 249–50, 254
  ancestor-dominant, 205
Cunningham, William P. and Barbara Woodworth Saigo, 6, 9, 20–22, 24–27, 29–33, 35, 70, 86, 111, 143, 152, 162–64
Curriculum(a), 5, 23, 25, 229, 236
Curry, Patrick, 1, 13, 30, 35, 39, 56–58, 70–71, 74, 76, 81, 84–86, 89, 99, 110, 143, 188, 209

D

Dabala, 121, 148–49, 162, 167, 176, 192–93, 202, 244
Dabala Junction, 108, 138, 198, 241–42

Dagadu, Tɔgbe (from Agave, but lives with Loli Sitɔ in Sokpoe), 154–55, 206
Daneel, M. L., 5–7, 95, 98, 250
Deane-Drummond, Celia, 21, 28, 31, 33–34, 36–38, 110, 250
Death, 49, 64, 76, 78–79, 94, 121, 125, 132, 136, 139, 179, 195–99, 201–8, 210–11, 213–24
  deity-induced, 196, 197, 206–7
Deculturation, 58, 232
Deities, 46, 48, 50–51, 72–73, 75, 104–5, 122, 137, 150–51, 154–55, 157, 159–62, 206–9, 231–33, 247
  clan, 155
  earthly, 209
Dekɔnu,, 170, 183, 233
  mede o, 185
Deluge (1963, flood), 145
Denny, Frederick M., 12, 250–54
Deoxyribonucleic acid (DNA), 61
Desertification, 2
Design, 2, 4, 9, 142, 229, 253
Destiny, 51, 121, 132, 191, 207
Devastation of harvested crops, 1
Development, 5, 7, 9–10, 12, 24, 36, 58, 65–66, 74, 84, 102, 106, 163, 237, 253–54
Devil, 11–12, 15, 38, 93–94, 126, 164, 245, 253
DHCCC (Divine Healing Church of Christ in Christ), 133, 174, 176, 189, 198–99
Diagrammatic, worldview, 43
Dimensions, of space in African worldview, 24, 37, 47, 53, 57, 81, 87, 124, 142, 166, 217
(*Din al-fitra*) Islamic instinctual knowledge, 84
Discerning moral status, 38, 236, 253
Discipline of Islamic Environmental Law, 53, 70–71, 80–84, 87–89, 99, 161, 167–68
Diviner (*nukala*), 207–8, 216
Divinities, 42, 46–47, 55, 72, 74, 201
Doade, Martin, 182, 199, 200
Dominion, 56, 96–97, 99
  to God be (1 Pet., 5:11)

Dowd, Michael, 63–64, 140, 250
Doxological contemplation, 85
Dripping water ritual, 182
Drowning creatures, rescuing, 145
(*Dunia*) Hausa word for creation, See *xexeme*, 122, 124–25
Dutɔwo (indigenous landlords), 108, 160, 167–68, 243
Dwarfs, 126, 157
Dyson, Freeman (Physicist and cosmologist), 36
Dzatsi, (special beverage from unroasted corn), 173
Dzi (heaven), 64, 121, 123–25, 127–28, 141–42, 179, 195, 211, 230, 246
Dzigbeɖi (Broinhidrosis), 174, 176
Dzifovi (highest heaven), 124–25, 127–28, 230
Dzifoxexeme (celesphere), 64, 125, 141–42

Ɖ

Ɖiɖexɔme (maternity room), 174–76, 189, 211, 232–33
Ɖiɖekple (special meal for lactating mother),, 175
Ɖiɖelélé, (post parturition unwellness), 189

E

Ears, whisper Islamic scripture into, 177, 192, 218
Earth, 40, 54, 56, 65, 67, 82–83, 124, 127, 135, 217
  first, 55, 124, 127
  community, 76, 188, 234
  deities, 47, 126, 139, 159, 164
Earth-keeping, 83, 161
  Integrated approach, 237
Earthlings, 57, 92, 140, 184, 187
Earthly,
  involvement, 202, 206
  life, 77, 79, 179, 184, 204, 211, 214
Earth's,
  ecosystems, 234
  surface, 54, 123–27, 141, 179, 230, 246–47
East, as symbol of life beginning, 172, 178–79, 182, 184
Eaves, roof, 77, 180, 182, 184–85
Eco-area, 153, 176, 178, 230
Eco-character, 74–76, 78, 186, 188
Eco-community, 3, 70, 73–74, 76, 89, 91, 101, 120, 122–23, 128, 139, 174–75, 203–6, 210–11, 223–25
Ecocrisis, 2, 5, 10, 24, 90–91, 95, 100–101, 112–13, 165, 236
  resolving of, 103, 236–38
Eco-cultures, 14, 74, 78
Eco-ethical regulations, 122, 150–51, 203, 205
Eco-ethics, 70, 73, 99–100, 106, 143, 150, 156, 166, 169, 231, 233
Eco-farming and Land Ownership, 77, 180
Eco-Sustainability ix
Eco-Theology, 6, 8–9, 11, 21, 28, 31, 33–34, 36–37, 58–60, 64–65, 67–68, 91, 96–97, 99–100, 109–11, 250, 255
Eco-transformation, 6
Ecological,
  actions, 22, 26, 34, 38, 57, 64, 71, 74, 81, 91, 104, 119, 150, 152, 154
  balance, 21, 28, 85
  biblical, 100–101
  community, 26, 39, 41, 44, 71, 76, 78, 143, 152, 163, 167, 177, 186–88, 195, 202–3
  crimes, 74, 76, 238
  crisis, 11, 35, 58, 84, 95, 99, 110–11, 253, 255
  deities, 74, 232
  doctrine of creation, 253
  ethics, 1, 11, 13, 25–26, 35, 56–58, 70–71, 74, 84–86, 89, 96–97, 99–100, 103, 110–14, 143, 156, 209
  grounding, 76, 220
  implications, 11, 64, 91, 165, 171, 193–94, 233
  import, 81, 170–71

issues, 166, 232, 235
practical Islamic values, 87, 166
reframers, rejoice in decay of Earth, 112
regulations, 88, 150, 167–68
relations ix, 72–73, 91, 170, 195, 221
rituals, 75–76, 238
science, 8, 21, 86, 235–38
sin, 74, 97–98, 100, 139–40, 198
taboos, 151, 156, 206–7, 233
Theology in African Perspective, 11, 255
traditional, 208–9
values, 70, 143, 146, 148
wisdom, 34
Ecologists, 30, 97
Ecology, xv, 6–10, 12–14, 26, 35, 37–38, 40, 52, 58–59, 84, 96–97, 105, 110–11, 113–14, 234, 250–55
Ecology and Religion, 6, 9, 11, 26, 37–38, 76, 98, 110–11, 238, 252
Ecosphere, 20, 26, 47, 49, 73–74, 95, 97, 104, 123, 140–41
Ecosystem(s),, 6–8, 10, 30, 39, 41, 48–49, 59, 65–66, 77–79, 84–86, 148–50, 162, 184–86, 238
function, natural, 26, 27–28, 32–33
life, 26, 75, 100, 164, 182, 237
management, 26, 30–31, 38
creating artificial, 237
human-dominated, 31
Ecotheology, 58, 93, 238, 252, 255
Education, 2, 5, 24, 42, 88, 112–13, 167–68, 235, 254
missional ecological, 14
Edwards, Denis, 60–61, 251
Egodotɔwo, (see *xexeme*) worldly, 64, 94, 184
Ekpokpɔkplɔ (land purification rite), 231
Elavanyo (a town in Sokpoe), 50–51, 120, 122–23, 125, 127, 130–31, 137, 179
Eleade, Mircea, 49
Emerging Alliance of World Religions and Ecology, 105, 255
Energy, 27, 29, 54, 61, 100, 113, 237

Entities, spiritual, 38, 47–48, 72–73, 126, 164, 207
Environmental, 231, 233, 235, 237, 239
change and salvation theology in African Christianity, 11, 251
crisis, 8, 12, 31, 52, 66, 87, 110, 166, 236, 251, 253–54
issues, 23, 26, 28, 36, 87, 167, 234
laws, 70, 99, 162, 253
responsibility, 4, 11, 81
science, 4–7, 9–10, 19–37, 70, 86, 107, 111, 113–14, 119, 143, 152, 162–64, 229, 234, 236
taboos, 48, 74, 205
Environment, 1–3, 6–7, 9–10, 19–22, 25–28, 34–37, 48, 84–85, 98–99, 103–5, 107–8, 110–11, 114–15, 160, 234–37, 249–55
earthly, 175
Environmental Ethics, 12, 14, 52–56, 58, 71, 80–81, 83, 85–88, 90, 105, 122, 146, 236
global, 5, 7
in Mafi-Eʋe Indigenous Culture, 12–13, 45–47, 72–73, 75, 79, 105, 120, 146, 216, 249
Environmental Management and African Indigenous Resources, 48, 251
Environmental Protection Agency *see* EPA
Enyi Avenɔgbo, 50, 120, 123, 127, 130, 144–45, 151–52, 154, 157, 163, 180, 196, 206–9
EPA (Environmental Protection Agency), 1–2, 5, 10, 23–24, 33, 251
Ethical,
praxis, 13, 142–43, 149–50, 209
impotence, 35–36
Ethics, 6, 37, 70–71, 74, 87–88, 91, 99–100, 104–5, 111, 146, 166–68, 183, 231, 234, 254–55
Ethos, 41–42, 73–74
Evil spirits, 47, 75, 182, 190, 204
Evolution, 34, 37, 60–61, 63–64, 71, 140, 250–51

Eve (an ethnic and lingual group in West Africa), 11, 77, 122, 124, 126, 161, 171, 181, 187, 198, 245
Eve-English Dictionary, 121–22, 124, 255
Eve Expression English Equivalent, 245–47
Evu (blood), 131–33, 136, 230, 242
Eworyi, Winner, 123–24, 133, 159, 175, 189–91, 243
Excrement, cover (Deut., 23:13), 101
Exemplar of eco-praxis, God, 100
Existence, 34, 38, 40, 47, 53, 57, 60, 67, 70, 76, 81, 91, 105, 123, 140–41
Exit, 78–79, 199

F

Faith, 13–14, 19, 26, 34–35, 38, 60–61, 66, 91–92, 112–14, 126, 155, 177, 213–14, 219, 231
  Christian, 34, 62, 92, 160, 164–65, 249
Family, 50–51, 77–78, 89, 137–38, 173, 175, 187–88, 191–92, 207–8, 211–17, 221–22, 224
  head, 77, 221–22
Father, 95, 172–73, 178, 189–92, 200, 202, 214
  child's, 189–90, 193
Fear, 15, 24, 33, 38, 72–73, 75, 105, 107, 150–54, 159–60, 164–66, 171, 175, 206–7, 232–33
Fellow, 145–48, 186
(*Fi ahsānī taqwim*) best of forms, 57
(*Fiqh*) Islamic science of jurisprudence, 88
First Adam, 95, 97–98
Fish, 2, 67, 126, 150–51, 153, 156, 158, 179, 208
Fishing, 150–52, 163–64, 168
(*Fitra*) Islamic belief in instinct, 52, 84–85, 109, 158–59, 167–68, 250
Flesh, 50, 68, 92, 98, 131–34, 136, 176, 196–97, 199, 230, 247
Flood, 1

Foltz, Richard C., 8, 12, 52, 81, 84, 110, 123, 140, 149, 250–53
Forest deities, 157–59, 164–65
  Alɔbdzove, 157
  Nyaɖeŋgɔve, 64, 158
Forest taboos, 154, 164, 168
Forests, 46, 90, 93, 106, 111, 126, 139, 150, 154–55, 157–60, 165, 168, 208–9, 231
Foreword, xiii
Fortification, 174, 176–77, 182, 232–33
Forum on Religion and Ecology, 7–8, 251
Fukatsotso (liberating pregnant woman), 171, 174, 177, 232–33
Funeral, 219, 223, 225
  parlor, 209, 211, 215, 217, 221–22
Funerary rites, 79, 115, 138, 169–70, 194–95, 206, 210, 225, 232–33, 239

G

Gaia theory, 56
"*Galamsey*" (illegal small-scale mining in Ghana), 114
Galaxy, Milky way, 140,
Gathogo, Julius, 48
Gbefiala (dictionary), 121–22, 124, 255
gbɔgbɔ (spirit/breath), 50, 130–36, 138, 197, 199, 202, 206, 218, 230
Gecosphere, 40, 64, 76, 94, 125, 127–28, 138–42, 170–72, 177, 179, 182, 195–96, 205–6, 230, 246–47
Geisler, Norman L., 97–99, 100–101, 112–14, 251
Genesis, 14, 59–60, 65, 67–68, 92, 94–98, 110, 209, 255
Ghana, 1–3, 5–6, 8–11, 14, 24–25, 33, 37–39, 45, 68, 71, 93, 107, 236–38, 249, 251
Ghana State of Environment Report, 2, 10, 24, 33, 251

Ghosts, 126–27, 133, 141, 196, 200–204, 206–8, 219, 221–22, 224, 230, 246–47
  existence of, 202, 204
Gibson (see Agrawal, Arun and C. C. Gibson), 103, 105, 249
Glithorn, Allan A., 4
Global concern, environmental, 10, 20, 22, 250
Glory, 55, 62, 65, 71, 85, 164
GNSP (General Science Program), 4–5, 19–20, 25, 37, 119
Goat, 144–49
God, v, xvi, 6–9, 46–51, 53–58, 60–68, 71, 80–86, 88–89, 91–101, 121–23, 127–41, 147–48, 158–61, 196–200, 218–19, 230–32
  children of, 47, 94
  -creation-human relations, 110
  humanity images, 51, 137
  of Evolution, 60–61, 251
Godfrey, Robert W. (God never tire of creative work), 100
Gold, 144–48
Golo, Ben-Willie Kwaku, 5, 11–12, 58–60, 63, 93–94, 160, 251
Gonzale, Tirso and Melissa Nelson, 75, 106
Gospel, 14, 38, 112, 166, 193, 213, 249
  and culture, 40–42, 47, 79, 249
Gratitude, 80, 212, 219
Grave, 144, 196, 216–19, 221
Graveyard, 215–16
Greek Gnostic understanding of cosmos, 65
Grey, George Kwame, 125–26, 149–50, 208
Grim, John A., 12, 103, 105, 251–53, 255
Grim, John A. and Mary Evelyn, Tucker, 6, 9, 11, 26, 37–38, 76, 98, 110–11, 234, 238
Groaning of Creation, 110–11, 250
Ground, 67, 77, 92–93, 135, 140, 155, 173–74, 178, 180–81, 187–88, 197, 202, 216, 220
  bare, 75, 77, 139, 173, 180–81, 184–85

Grounding, 6, 9, 76–77, 174, 177–78, 180, 184, 221–22, 232–33

H

(*Hadith*), 88–89, 149
Hajia Amina Awudu, 176, 191–93, 202, 244
Hajia Fati Sanni, 123, 126–28, 148, 161, 192, 243
Hajia Hawusatu Eleas, 107–8, 123, 126–27, 192–93, 217
Hallman, David, 58
Haq, Nomanul S., 39, 53, 55–57, 81–82, 86, 88–90, 129, 252
(*Harām*) sacred territory, 90, 161
Harvest, 67, 139, 151, 153, 163
Healing, 91, 110, 112, 165
Hearth, 77–78, 85, 180, 254
Heavens, 54–56, 60, 62–64, 71, 85, 121, 124–25, 127–28, 133, 135, 142, 197–98, 200, 214, 230
  first, 55, 124
  highest, 124–28, 246
  second, 125, 128
Hebrews, 60, 62, 96, 249
Hell, 121, 125–26, 128, 198, 200, 230, 246
Heterotrophs, 28
(*Himā*) (reserved forest/land in Islam), 89–90
History, Christian, 12–13, 40–42, 44, 48, 154, 211–13, 255
Hitzhusen, Gregory E., 110, 252
Hlɔ̃tsilele (clan bath), 211–12, 214, 233
Holistic,
  education, 4–5, 9
  mission, 3, 5
Holy Spirit, 14, 93, 95, 128, 214, 235
Home, 36, 53, 59, 66, 81, 93, 108, 140–41, 155, 178, 183, 189, 221–25, 230, 246–47
  earthly, 114, 140
  transported, 221–23
  soil, 221–22
Hordo, Francis, 123, 125, 134–35, 172–73, 189–90

Index

House, Paul, 59-60, 63, 77, 154, 192, 252
Howell, Allison Mary. xiv, 52, 103
Human(s),, 1-2, 1-2, 35, 50-51, 58, 63, 70-73, 81-84, 97-98, 130, 133-39, 143-44, 230-32
  activities, 64, 98
  beings, 4, 38, 42, 53, 56-57, 62, 67, 79, 82-83, 86-87, 96, 113, 131, 134, 149
  body, 50, 200, 247
  -built world, 20
  creation, 242
  dead, 220, 230,
  disturbance and natural habitat, 31-32, 253
  -Earth relations, 4
  existence, 51, 68, 247
  habitation, 124, 129
  hands, 70, 99, 101
  life, 3, 49-50, 56, 72, 74, 79, 89, 122, 126, 129, 145-47, 181
  -natural environment relations, 52
  perpetuate, 50, 137
  relations, 56, 123, 144, 234
  role of, 5, 14
  spirits, 47, 197
  world, 47, 50, 78-79, 123, 125, 142, 201, 203, 246
Humanity, 37, 43, 49-52, 55-58, 64-65, 67-68, 74, 80-86, 91-92, 94-97, 99-100, 111-12, 128-32, 136 39, 230-31
  creation of, 68, 135
  creator of, 49, 130
  estate of, 21, 66
  fallen, 95, 98, 112
  origin of, 130, 133, 230
  role of, 7, 50-51, 137
  theomorphic status of, 80, 90
  in Islamic Worldview, 57
Humankind, 9, 56, 68, 82, 92, 129, 139, 158, 197, 230
Hymn, 189, 191, 223

I

Ibrahim, Alhassan, 130-32, 138, 197, 242
Ibrahim, Idrisu, 87, 120-21, 123, 126-28, 130, 132, 148-49, 166, 197, 203, 210, 220
Identity, 40, 44, 59, 65, 76, 213, 250
  human, 181, 214
Iheanacho, Maureen, xv
Image, 12, 14, 51, 96-98, 137-39, 147
  of God, 4, 14, 68, 95, 97-98, 138, 231-32
Imago Dei, 4, 68, 90, 95-96, 98, 112, 238
  demut (likeness), 96
  tzelm (image), 96
Imam Alhaji Ali, 108, 138, 242
Imam Abu Bakr, chief, 167
Imams, 87, 123, 126, 129, 166-67, 192-93, 217
Impulsion, 3, 5, 10-11, 15, 71-72, 79-80, 82, 90-91, 96, 101, 140, 150, 220, 231, 233
  religious, 6, 229, 231
Incongruous ecosystem life, 79
Indigenized or acculturated Christians (see Christians), 164
Indigenous,
  Eve, 160, 168, 202, 204
  Sokpoe-Eve, 126, 233
  Traditions and Ecology, 12, 103, 105, 251-53
Inhibition, regulations, 163
Integration, 9, 186, 191, 210-11, 213, 232-33, 254
Interment, 79, 211, 214-16, 219, 222, 225
Interview, 1, 25, 49-51, 87-88, 107-8, 115, 120-37, 143-63, 166-68, 171-81, 183-93, 196-204, 206-12, 215-25, 241-44
  responses, 135, 241
  separate, 107, 120, 123, 127-29, 131, 133-34, 144, 147, 151, 160, 168, 206, 208
Interviewees, 129, 137, 139, 147-48, 150, 154, 182
  religious, 137, 144, 154

268 Index

Intrinsic and instrumental values, 71
Introduction, 8, 52, 70, 84, 99, 113, 123, 140, 143, 149, 187, 195, 209, 250, 252
  to African Religion, 48, 253
Isaac Newton and Nicolaus Copernicus, 60
Islam, 8, 12–14, 39, 52–55, 57–58, 71, 79–84, 87–90, 107, 109–10, 126, 161–62, 166–68, 198, 250–54
  persuasive spiritual teachings of, 87, 166
  and Ecology, 8, 12, 39, 52–53, 55–57, 81–82, 84, 86, 88–90, 110, 123, 129, 140, 149, 250–54
  explained for Christians, 12, 249
Islamic, 5–6, 10, 52, 56, 83, 87, 90, 109, 120, 128–31, 148, 156, 166, 197–98, 242–43
  earth-keeping, 82
  eco-ethics, 87–88, 231
  ecology, 99, 159, 161, 168
  traditions, 12, 38, 150, 233–34, 237–38
  view of human creation, 242
  world, 87, 166–67
  worldviews, 53, 56–57, 79–80, 86, 109, 125, 133, 158
Italics, 22, 34, 53, 71, 81, 86, 88–89, 110, 114, 217

J

(*Janna*) heaven, 121, 198
(*Jahanna*) hell, 121, 198
Jesus, 45, 47, 51–52, 62, 73, 94–95, 98, 122, 125, 127, 146, 183, 190, 201, 205
(*Jinns*) Islamic concept of "ghost-like" creatures, 126, 138, 203
Job, 38–39, (God quizzes Job's ecological knowledge), 65
John (Epistle of), 2, 68, 91, 94, 98, 249–50, 252–53, 256
Journal, 249–50, 252, 254
Journey, 20, 27, 29, 36–37, 50, 54, 61, 78, 86, 129, 140, 215–16, 221, 255

Jubilee, law of, (Lev., 25:23–28), 101
Judeo-Christian Theology, 58, 110, 252
Judgement Day, 121, 141–42, 198, 200, 218, 220, 203,

K

Kadodo (relation/relationship), 199, 220–21
(*Kalima*), 177, 218
Kalu, U. Ogbu, 12–13, 40–50, 72, 74–75, 77–79, 104–6, 122, 124, 146, 186–87, 252
  diagram of, 44–45, 47
Kattah, Edward, 123, 128, 133, 155, 166, 200, 209
Keitzar, Renthy, 62, 65, 67–68, 98, 129, 252
Keta, 2
(*Khalifa Allah*) vicegerent of God, 57, 80
(*Khalīfacy*) vicegerency, 82–84
(*Khalīfat*) vicegerent, 80–82, 138, 230
Kinship, 13, 92, 232, 238
  humanity's, 90, 93
Klayi Avi, 128, 144–46, 151, 163, 172, 179, 186–88, 196
Knowledge xiii, 13, 20–21, 26, 29, 34–35, 54, 97, 150, 171, 225, 234, 253
Kodzogbe (physical world), 124–25, 141, 174, 187, 195, 204–6, 210–12, 214–16, 221, 246
Kofi Atiglo (See Atiglo, Avinyo Kofi)
Kpɔgɔme (outskirts or outside clan house), 223
Kudadjie, Joshua, 77–78, 184, 252
Kudi, Memuna, 161, 168
Kudɔfofo (gasping for breath), 199
Kunz, Sandra, xv
Kɔtive (a forest at Sokpoe), 157, 160, 209, 244
Kwame Bediako, 40, 45, 47, 51, 59, 62, 122, 125, 146, 201, 205, 217
Kwamena-Po, Michael A., 3

Index

L

Lagoons, 151, 163, 231
Lākusi (flesh/body), 131–32
Land, 45–46, 52, 67, 75, 77–79, 89, 95, 97–98, 100–101, 154–55, 157–58, 164–65, 180–81, 188, 255–56
   of birth, 108, 174, 177, 180, 184, 221–22, 232–33
   degradation, 1
Laws, 29, 40–41, 52, 59, 70, 85, 87–88, 100–101, 121, 123, 139, 201, 234
Learning, 4, 6, 9, 36, 74, 76, 85, 106, 114, 254, 256
   scientific, limitations, 21
Leonardo, Boff (human and all things are sacraments, signs of the transcendent), 96
Leopold, Aldo, (Sandy County farm), 30
Libation, 215–16, 221–22
Light green ecology, 56
Living, 27, 34, 49, 67, 72, 77, 84, 87, 121, 123, 139–40, 145–49, 195–96, 200–201, 203–4
   creatures, 60, 67, 92
   humanity, 128, 230
   soul, 134–36, 199
Llewellyn, Othman Abd-Ar-Rahman, 53, 70–71, 80–84, 87–89, 99, 161, 167–68, 253
Locations, geographical, 148–49
Loli, Sitɔ, 151
Lord, 34–36, 53, 65, 80, 82, 84–85, 112, 190–91, 219, 250
Love creation, 57, 58, 65, 68, 91, 138, 214
Loving nature, 138–39
Lucas, Earnest, 95
   Luvɔ, gbagbe (soul, living), 133–36, 196, 199, 202–3, 219, 221–23, 230, 242, 246–47

M

(*Mādari*) traditional training ground for Islamic leaders, 109
Mafi-Eʋe, 45–47, 73, 75, 79, 155
(*Malayikum*) angels, in Hausa, 127
Management, environmental, 48
Mante, J. O. Y., 11, 58–59, 135–37, 253
Maps vi-vii
Market days, 162
Martey, Emmanuel, Rev. Prof. (a moderator, PCG), 4
(*Māslih* and *māfasid*) law of benefits and detriments, 88–89
Mass, 27–29, 41, 54, 61, 107
Matter, 27, 35, 45, 54, 57, 61, 65, 67, 84, 86, 88, 97, 112, 149, 201
Mawu (God), 49, 73, 121–22, 127, 130–32, 179, 196–97, 220, 241, 243, 247
Mbiti, John (Africa notoriously religious), 48
McDonald, Mary N. (primal cosmology informs tackling present ecocrisis), 105–6
Megbe (behind), 124, 242, 244
Memuna Kudi, 120–23, 161, 168, 197–98
Mepe/Mefe (a town in North Tɔŋu, Ghana), 133, 138, 189, 199–201
MEST (Ministry of Environment, Science and Technology), 1, 33, 251
Metaphysical, 53
Meyer, Birgit, 11–12, 38, 93–94, 164, 253
Mind, 35, 40, 42, 63–64, 76, 80, 120, 127–28, 136, 156, 165, 183, 198, 205, 233
Minister, 185, 189–91, 219, 223
Ministry of Environment, Science and Technology (see MEST)
Mission, 4, 8–9, 35–36, 59, 110–11, 165, 250–51, 255
(*Mīzān*) cosmic balance, 56, 84
Mmusu/busu, (deadly evil), 74, 163
Modernity, 10–11, 76, 102–5, 107, 188, 253
Moe, Thang David (Christians share with other faiths in ecocare), 13
Moltmann, Jürgen, 99–100, 253
Money, 93, 143–48, 191, 219, 245
Moral environmentalism, 2–3, 15, 17

Mother, 172–76, 181, 183–84, 187, 189, 191, 233, 246
  Earth, 75, 181–82
Motivators, 79, 81, 90, 92
Mound, 152, 217, 219
Moxon, James, 151–53, 253
Muslim(s), 54–56, 80–81, 85–90, 108–9, 122–24, 126–29, 138, 148–49, 160–62, 166–68, 197–99, 202–5, 213–16, 218–20, 230–31
  interviewees, 149
  participants, 54, 126–27, 133, 146, 160–61, 167, 197, 201
  writers, 83
  in Sokpoe riverine ecological area in South Tɔŋu, 87
Mutasa, David et al., (teaching environmental science in Africa has been teacher-centered), 234
Myers, Bryant L., 4, 65–66, 92, 254
Myths, 37, 43, 205

N

Names, 3, 6, 8, 35, 53, 134, 144, 157–58, 173–74, 178, 185, 187, 190, 192–93, 222
  child's, 174, 185, 190
Naming, 6, 176–77, 183, 186–88, 191, 233
Narh, Cephas, 113–14
Nasr, Seeyed Hossein, 12, 55, 57, 87, 90, 104, 107, 109, 166, 168, 254
Native Americans, 75, 181
Natural,
  Ecosystem Conservation and Motivation for Creation Care, 30
  environment, 12, 26, 52–53, 89
  habitat, 32–33, 253
  laws, 28, 34, 55–56, 76, 86, 158
  world, 10, 19–21, 25, 30–32, 37, 53, 56–58, 66, 81, 84, 87, 160, 166, 234
Nature, 10–11, 29–30, 34, 36–37, 52–56, 65–66, 71–72, 75–76, 80, 84–86, 92–93, 96–98, 105–6, 165–66, 236–38

Nature Psalms, 8, 250
Nebel, Bernard J. and Richard T. Wright, 22–23, 25–29, 31–34, 70, 143, 162–63
Nelson, Arthur, 75, 77, 106, 182
Nephesh haya (living being, Gen., 1:24;, 2:7b), 67
Neurobiological possibilities, humans have, 96
New creation, 62, 98
Nicolaus Copernicus and Isaac Newtown, 60
NMG (Norddeutsche Missionsgesellschaft), 11–12, 93
Non-Christians, 94, 183–84, 204, 209
Non-polluting and non-depletable, 28
Northcott, Michael S., 11, 101
Nunyuiwɔla, Mawu (Good Creator), 71
Nurturing, 99, 129, 220, 230
Nuxexe (sacrifice), 157–58
Nwosu, H. N. and Kalu, U. Ogbu, 41–42, 74
Nyaɖeŋgɔve (a forest at Sokpoe), 158
Nyajeka, Tumai, 49
Nyikɔtsɔtsɔ (naming), 186, 188, 233

Ɖ

Ɖɔlĩ, (ghost), 125–26, 196, 200–202, 207, 218
Ɖɔlĩyɔla/nukala (diviner/necromancer), 216
Ɖutilã, (body), 130, 132–36, 196–97, 199
Ɖkɔtsɔha, or *nyikɔtsɔha* (naming drink), 173–74, 185, 187
Ɖkɔtsɔtsɔ or nyikɔtsɔtsɔ (naming), 177, 186, 188, 233
Ɖutsu nutefe wɔla (a faithful or worthy man to officiate outdooring), 186

O

Objectives, African Theocology course (see course objectives), 235

Observations, similar, 120–21, 146, 148
Officiator, 172–74, 186, 188, 212
Ogbu U. Kalu, 40, 42, 49–50, 75, 104, 106, 146, 186
Oikos, 65
Opoku, Kofi Asare, 73–75, 77–78, 85, 180, 254
Orienting, 76–77, 182, 184
Origin, 36–37, 39, 43, 52, 65–66, 86, 108, 113, 119–20, 130, 132, 222, 237
Osafo, B. Y. (on global warming), 165
OT (Old Testament), 62–63, 65, 68, 96, 99, 127
Other-than-human, 7, 50, 54, 58, 64, 66, 70–71, 76, 80, 89, 112, 144, 146, 177, 186
    creation, 49, 51, 53, 55–57, 62, 64, 72, 86, 90, 97, 128–29, 137, 144, 230–31, 236–37
    creation care, 184
    creation lack, 147
    creatures, 45–46, 51, 55, 60, 67, 72, 92, 125, 138
    moral extensionism, 89
Otherworldly, 63
Outdoor, 178, 190
Outdooring, 172, 175–76, 178, 182–83, 187–89, 191, 211
    ceremonies, 78, 183, 185, 188–89
    rite, 77–78, 177, 179, 183, 186–88, 247
Overgrazing, 28, 33
Oxford, 249–50, 253–55
Oysters (clam), 139, 152, 153, 196, 163
Özdemir, Ibrahim, 12, 52–56, 58, 71, 80–81, 83, 85–88, 90, 122

P

Pathological factors, 1
Paradise, 127, 131, 198, 246
Parents, 178, 183, 185, 187, 189–92, 212
Participants, 26, 51, 120, 123, 128–29, 144, 162, 192, 197–98, 218

PCG (Presbyterian Church of Ghana), 2–5, 9, 121–22, 124–25, 128, 133, 159, 223, 253–54
Perichoretic, 137
Person, 40–41, 72, 79, 130, 132–35, 151, 193, 198–99, 202–3, 206–7, 218, 222–23, 230, 246–47
    dead, 200, 217–18
    human, 41, 96, 135
Perspective, 8–9, 11, 27, 34, 36, 38, 40, 52, 74, 96, 206, 235
Pests and diseases, 2
Philosophies, educational, 2–4
Photosynthetic products, 28–29
Physical/human world, 49, 195
Placenta, 92, 177–78, 180, 192
Planet Earth, 10, 119
Planets, 8, 23, 26, 60, 125, 128, 140, 236
Planetwise (by David Bookless), 54, 61, 108, 110–11, 141, 167, 181, 250
Pluralism, religious, 13, 39
Policy, 2–4, 104, 106, 234
    Document on General Education, 2–4
Potency, 96, 132, 205
Potentiating, 178, 180
Praeparatio evangelica, 213, 233
Praxis, 3–4, 6, 10, 12–14, 24, 66, 69, 72, 88, 99–100, 106, 115, 150, 156, 166–67
    of religious creation cares, 115
    of Creation Care in Christianity, 90
    of Creation Care in Islam, 79
Prayer, 172–73, 176, 178, 188–89, 191, 217, 221–22, 235, 238
Precarious Vision, 13, 40, 43, 45, 72, 74–75, 104, 124, 146, 186–87, 206, 252
Presbyterian, 3, 133, 185, 198–99, 210, 212
Presbyterian Church of Ghana see PCG
Presbyterian University College, Ghana, 4–5, 7, 9, 19, 24, 35, 113, 119, 229, 235

Priestly or P (Gen., 1:1—2:4a) and Yahwist or J (Gen., 2:4b-24), 59
Primal, 5-7, 13-14, 38-39, 51, 71, 73-74, 93-94, 103-6, 128-31, 159-68, 170-72, 175-78, 181-84, 231-34, 236-38
  communities, 105
  cosmologies, 105, 122
  cultures, 188, 201
  eco-taboos, 243-44
  ecological ethics, 15, 167
  religion, 13, 42-43, 48-49, 71-72, 92, 105, 123, 159, 164-65, 167-68, 171, 178, 203, 216-17, 249
  religionists, 49, 101, 120, 124-25, 127-30, 139, 141, 146-47, 150, 205-6, 208, 212-13, 206, 222, 230-31, 247
  Sokpoe-Eʋe, 50, 125, 146
  Sokpoe-Eʋe religionist, 196
  spirituality, 123, 165, 254
  substructure of Christianity, 78, 183, 254
  worldview, religious, 123, 125, 172, 179, 238
  worldviews in Africa, 45
Principles, 3, 10, 28-29, 31, 33, 41, 52, 56, 81, 89, 99-100, 106, 254
Problems, 4, 11, 24-25, 32, 37, 44-45, 59, 81, 111, 113, 147-48, 234, 238, 256
Procreate, 50-51, 137, 203
Procreating, 50, 138
Procreation, 50-51, 128, 130, 132-33, 137-39, 230
Program, 4, 24-25, 172, 178-79, 189, 192
Prohibition regulations, 163
Protreptikos, of Clement of Alexandria, 214
PUCG (see Presbyterian University College, Ghana)
Purpose of Creation and Humanity in Primal Religious Worldview, 50
Putrefaction, 217-18

Q

(*Qadar*) measure, 56, 86
Qualities, 29, 40, 134-35, 144, 146, 199, 231
Quarshie B. Y., 78, 182-83, 254
Qur'an, 15, 52-53, 55-58, 80-85, 87-88, 90, 109, 123-24, 127, 129, 149, 161-62, 166-68, 197-98, 203
Qur'anic,
  cosmology, 80-81
  worldview, 53, 86

R

Raised temperatures, 1
Re-creation, 63, 163
Readings in African Humanities, 41-42, 252
Reconstructing,
  Christian theology, 96, 111
  creation care theology, 5
Redemption, 92-95, 112, 184, 255
Regulations, 71, 99-100, 150-51, 156, 163, 167, 205
Reincarnation, 49-50, 78-79, 141, 203
Relatives, 175, 178, 222-23
Religions, 6-14, 26, 37-38, 76, 84, 88, 98, 102-3, 105, 109-13, 125, 230-32, 234, 237-38, 250-55
Religious,
  approaches, 6, 8, 208
  beliefs and environmental attitudes, 110, 251
  cosmologies, 7, 72, 119, 129, 140-43, 164, 171, 231
  ecologies, 5-8, 10-12, 15, 39, 81, 84, 101, 103, 115, 119, 229, 235-36, 238
  practices, 8, 162, 171, 233
  priming for creation care, 172
  rituals, 183, 233
  taboos, 152, 155, 159, 161-62, 164-66, 168
  traditions, 6, 8, 11, 13, 39, 43, 52, 70-71, 76, 127-30, 139-40, 170-71, 209-10, 219-20, 229-32

Index 273

worldviews, 6, 38–39, 43, 51, 115, 122, 139, 142, 154, 174, 195, 205, 229, 230, 245
Resolving ecocrisis, 237
Resources, 25–26, 97, 101, 104, 112–13, 201
  natural, 2, 75, 149, 237
Respondents, 120, 122, 128–29, 133, 145, 147–48, 164, 170, 180, 198–99
Responsibility, 3, 25, 36, 57–58, 61, 82, 98–99, 114, 138, 143, 222, 231, 250
  human, 91, 238
Resting day, 157–58
Return, 57, 67, 78–79, 103, 141, 153, 180, 196, 209, 220, 223–25, 230
Righteous, 198, 200, 218
Rites, 74, 76–78, 138, 160–61, 170–71, 177–78, 183, 185, 191, 193, 232–33
Ritual(s), 7, 40, 73–79, 87, 101, 104, 154–56, 160–61, 163–64, 177–82, 184–85, 209, 211–13, 215, 221–24
  bath, 212–14
  bathing, 212–13
Ritualistic sacrifices, 157–58
River, 33, 90, 114, 139, 153, 160–61, 163, 168, 180, 188, 208
Riverbank, 223–24
Role, 26–27, 29, 38, 51, 61–62, 97–98, 105, 112, 129, 132, 137, 190, 205, 210, 221
  humanity's, 137–38, 230

S

Sabbath rest, law of (Exod., 23:12), 99–100
Sacred Egg, 12, 40–50, 75, 77–79, 104–6, 122, 252
Sacred forests, 139, 154–55, 159–60, 163, 165, 208–9
Sacred Forests and Associated Taboos in Sokpoe, 157
(*Sadaqa*), 192–93

Safi, Omid and Anna Bigelow, 197, 213, 218–19, 221, 254
Sahelians from Niger, 149
Salvation, 61–63, 92–94
Sanitation, law of (Lev., 13:9–14), 101
Sapir, Edward,, 40
Satan, 138, 159, 164, 190
Schwarz, Hans, 11, 58–65, 67–68, 92, 96–97, 100, 255
Science, 7–10, 19–21, 30–31, 33–34, 36, 54, 59, 61, 66, 104, 107, 113–15, 234, 236–37, 255
  conservation, 31, 33
Scientific learning, 21, 36
Scientism, 114
Scripture,, 2, 6, 11, 13, 20, 26, 58–60, 63–65, 67–68, 91, 93, 96–97, 99–100, 109–12, 235
  as hermeneutic for ecological issues, 166
Sea,
  level, 2
  erosion, 2
Season, 106, 151–53, 179, 182
Seasonal, 2
Secondary literature, 9
Self-conservation or self-sustainability, 29
Separation, 196–97, 199
Series Foreword, 8, 103, 105, 110
Sexual intercourse in the bush, 75, 138
(*Shari'a*), 52, 161, 168
Shift, 21, 66, 100
Shrines, 46, 126, 207
Siame, Geoffrey, 50–51, 122, 125–28, 130–31, 137–38, 150, 155, 172, 180–81, 196, 217, 221–25, 241
Signs, 14, 41, 55, 71, 94–96, 112, 129, 210, 217, 252
Silent Spring, 22, 110, 253
  at-50, 22
Sin, 22, 64, 93, 95, 98, 134, 138, 185, 213, 220, 233, 238
Sindima, Harvey, 11, 44, 72–73, 165, 255
Sky, 45, 47, 54, 77, 122–25, 127–28, 141, 179, 230, 246–47

Society, 66, 101, 105, 114, 122, 186–87, 191, 254
  human, 84, 123
Sogakɔfe, 107–8, 120–21, 123–28, 130–33, 148–50, 154–55, 160–61, 166–68, 171–73, 192–93, 196–98, 202–3, 217, 220–25, 242–43
Sogbolisa, (name of God), 122
Soil, 20, 50, 68, 77, 92, 114, 130–31, 133–34, 173, 180–81, 188, 209–10, 217–18, 220, 222–23
Sojourn, earthly, 76, 79
Sokpoe, 48–50, 123–28, 130–31, 133–37, 146–47, 150–51, 153–60, 171–76, 178–91, 195–96, 199–201, 208–10, 215–19, 221–24, 241–44
  clan of, 151, 212
  -Bodzodife, 121, 133, 157, 211–12
  Christian (s), 12, 15, 64, 136, 199, 219, 222
  ecological area, 12, 54–55, 107, 115, 125, 138, 146, 150–51, 158, 167, 183–84, 195, 201, 205, 210, 222, 231–33
  ecological community, 139
  -Elavanyo, 129, 135–36, 144–48, 150–55, 157–59, 163, 172–74, 179–80, 186, 188, 196, 200, 206–9, 223, 242
  -Eve ix, xiii-xiv, xvi, 5–6, 10–11, 38–39, 72–73, 78–79, 119–20, 124–25, 140–43, 149–50, 154, 170, 178–79, 204–5, 210–11, 229
  Muslims, 139, 156, 166, 168
  primal religionists, 206, 221
  religious concept of death, 196
  religious Worldviews, 139
  -Vogɔme, 115, 190, 174, 176, 199–200
Sorely, Craig, 165
Soul, 68, 91, 123, 128, 133, 135–37, 141, 196, 199, 202, 204, 206, 218–19, 221–25, 246
  roaming, 200
Sources, 10, 52, 54, 61, 66, 81, 90–91, 100, 106

South and North Korea, demilitarized zone, 29
Space, 20, 27, 45–47, 49, 54, 61–62, 122–25, 127–28, 246
  dimensions of, 47–48
  earthly, 46–47, 49, 62
  earthly living, 140
Species, 24, 26–28, 30–31, 33, 37–38, 163
Spirit/breath, 131–33, 196–97
Spirit world, 45, 47, 49, 78, 201, 213, 230
Spiritual world, 51, 72, 195, 246
State, 27, 38, 55–56, 62, 74, 94, 132, 195, 199, 202, 211–12, 214–15, 217, 223
  spiritual, 141–42
Stewards, 57, 82, 101, 138–39
  of creation, 57, 139
Stewart, Mark, 23, 25, 235, 255
Structure, 13, 15, 43–45, 61, 72, 120, 123, 236
  phenomenological, 43, 45
Students, 2–4, 9, 19, 23, 25, 35, 107, 113–14, 235–36, 238
  non-science-major, 22
Study of African Culture, 41–42, 74
Subaltern deities, 43
Subterresphere, 125, 142, 215
Sun, 20, 26, 29, 45, 55, 85–86, 125, 172, 177–79, 182–85, 188–90, 232
(*Sunna*) works and (*hadith*) words of Mohammed, 52
Supreme Being, 43, 48, 73, 122
Surnames, 187, 190, 193
Sustainability, 10, 23, 26–29, 32–33, 104, 235
  environmental, 24–25
Sustainable human-Earth relationships, 5
Sustainer, 47, 53, 80, 91–92, 122
Swimme, Brian Thomas and Mary Evelyn Tucker, 20, 27, 29, 36–37, 54, 61, 67, 86, 129, 140
Systems,
  human, 32, 34
  religious, 41–42, 56, 182

Index

T

Taboos, 6, 61, 71, 73, 100, 104, 150, 155–56, 159–65, 201, 207, 209, 232
Tavewo (ponds), *tɔvuwo* (creeks, rivulets), *tagbawo* (lakes), 151
(*Taqwa*) (reverence for God), 80
(*Tawhīd*) (unity of reality), 81
Teach, 78, 87, 166, 182
Teachers, 3–4, 66, 191, 234
Teachings, 4, 8–9, 19, 26, 36, 81, 87, 91–92, 107, 165–66, 182, 188, 191, 234–35, 238
Technoscience, 113, 236
Telephone communication, personal, 192
Telephone interview, 50–51, 128, 137–39, 241
Temperature(s), 1–2
Temporality, 54, 67, 125, 179, 182, 184
Theocentrism, 91, 110
Theocology, 6, 8, 183, 234, 236
Theology, 7–8, 10, 13, 37, 58–59, 61, 165, 236, 250, 253, 256
Theomorphic, 57, 68, 95
This-worldly, 51, 125
Threat, 10, 23, 114
Toes, 152, 173, 212, 214–15, 223
Toklo, Bernice Peace Ama, v,
Transcript, 51, 108, 130–32, 137, 144, 147–48, 156, 159–60, 171, 176, 181, 183, 192
Transformation, 93, 249–50, 253–56
Transforming Higher Education, 23, 25, 235, 255
Translating, 11–12, 14, 38, 62, 93–94, 164, 253
Trees, 1, 46, 55, 66, 77, 85, 90, 97, 101, 104, 138, 144–49, 168, 178, 208
 coconut, 178
 imbued with spirits, 46
 last, 93
Trillions of degrees hot, 61
Trinitarian Theology of Religions, 14, 253
Trump, Donald, 23–24
Trust, 77, 82, 91, 101, 250–51

Trɔku (deity-caused death), 154, 196–97, 206–9, 233
Trɔve, (sacred forest), 154–55, 159,
Trɔwo, trɔnua, (deities, deity priests), 73, 122, 126, 155, 159, 162
Tucker, Evelyn Mary and John A. Grim, 8, 40, 103, 105, 110
Turner, Harold, 13
Tɔŋu ecological zone, 14
Tɔsisisewo, (river regulations), 162
Type, 85, 87, 166, 170, 196, 207, 212, 216–17, 224, 229

U

Ubiquitous malevolent and benevolent spirits, 72
(*Ulamā*) traditional Islamic teacher, 87, 109, 166
Umbilical cord, 92, 172, 175, 177–78, 180, 184, 192, 222
Unchallengeable creator, 49, 130
Unchristian, 183–84
Understanding of Environmental Ethics, 12, 52–56, 58, 71, 80–81, 83, 85–88, 90, 122
Units, 26–28
Unity, 68, 79, 81, 135, 137
Universe, 20, 26–27, 29, 34, 36–37, 51–52, 54–55, 60–61, 63, 66–68, 75–76, 85–86, 113, 129, 140
University, 9, 22–23, 25
Urinates, 92, 173, 180–81
Urine, 180–82

V

Vagaries, 2, 149, 174–75, 177
Valley View University (VVU), 24
Value trees, 148–49
Values, 13–14, 21, 33, 35, 41–42, 70–71, 77, 83, 91, 107, 113, 144, 147, 159, 209–10
 intrinsic, 146, 231
Vehicle, 221–22
 carrier, 221–22
Vicegerency, environmental, 91–92

Vicegerents, 57, 68, 82, 90, 95, 97–98, 101, 232
Victus, Solomon, 11, 58–60, 64–65, 67–68, 91, 93, 96–97, 99–100, 109–11, 255
Viɖeɖeɖego, (baby outdooring), 171–72, 183–85, 232–33
Village, 46, 202, 224
Vitsɔtsɔfiawo (showing baby to sun), 177–78, 183, 185, 232
Volta, 151–53, 160, 253
Vulnerability, 1
VVU (see Valley View University)

U

Uubɔ (bloody cemetery, ground for burying the dead from accidents), 213

W

Walls, Andrews F., 13, 39, 40–42, 44, 48, 151, 154, 211–13, 255
Water, 3, 20, 45, 50, 52, 55, 60, 66–67, 89, 92, 106, 150–52, 182, 188, 196–97
  cold, 77, 185, 212
  bodies, 1, 46, 114, 126, 150–52, 158, 160, 208, 223, 231
  table, 1
  taboos, 156, 158
WCC (World Council of Churches), 252
Weather, 2, 149, 174–75, 182, 184
Wenham, Gordon (early Western theology books never refer to ecocrisis), 111
West, 8, 58, 60–61, 63, 66, 92, 110–12, 165, 172, 178–79, 182, 184
West African Traditional Religion, 73–75, 254
Westermann, Claus, 60, 255
Westermann, Dietrich, 121–22, 123–24, 255
Western Christian, 111, 165, 193
Western Christian cosmology, 5–6
White, Lynn Jnr, 110

Wisdom, 34, 55, 65–66
  natural, 34
Woman, 50, 68, 130, 132, 184, 193, 207–8, 212
Women, 1, 113–14, 151, 157, 159, 212, 215, 224
Healing Earth, 49, 254
World, 8–9, 13, 22–24, 43, 51, 53–54, 60–65, 72, 81–84, 124, 128–30, 140–41, 177, 187, 250
  earthly, 64
  new, 62–63
  religions xv, 238, 255
Worldviews, 11–13, 15, 33, 39–43, 48, 58, 68, 71–73, 79, 92, 122, 136–37, 187, 201, 205–6
  Christian, 58, 67, 71, 90, 97
  durability of, 42,
  materialistic, 113
  phenomenological structure of, 43,
  theocentric, 73, 80, 90–91, 99, 101, 230
Wrath, 83, 204, 207–8, 221–22
Wright, Christopher J. A., 62–64, 110, 124, 127, 140, 256

X

Xexeme (creation), 54–55, 64, 119–29, 139–41, 171–72, 174, 179, 181, 187, 230, 247
  anyigba, (earthly), 64
  dzifo, (heavenly), 64
  origin of, 122
Xexemetɔwo, egodotɔwo, (worldly people; non-Christians), 64, 94
Xɔnudzɔgoe (Spirit-exorcising object), 175–76
Xɔmeku, Atsufe, 183,

Y

Yale University, 7–8, 251
Yame, gbadzaa (atmosphere, vast open), 123–24
Yɔdo, (grave), 196, 216, 217
Yɔhokpɔ Kɔwu, 172–73, 179, 181, 186, 188, 206, 243

Yɔme, or tsĩefe, (living-dead world, grave), 215, 217
Yɔfewɔwɔ (funerary celebration), 219
Yɔxɔme (funeral parlor), 209, 211, 215, 217
Young, Richard A. (Theocentric Eco-theologist), 91, 112

Z

(*Zamarama sarachi*), (see <u>Idrisu Ibrahim)</u>,, 86, 108, 148, 166

Zimbabwean earth-keepers, 6
Zizioulas, John of Pergamon, 97–98, 256
(*Zongo*), 87, 108, 148, 161, 166–67, 241
(*Zongo sarachi*), 108, 120, 126–27, 132–33, 160–61, 167, 171, 176–77, 192–93, 202
Zoocentrism, 146–48, 231

www.ingramcontent.com/pod-product-compliance
Lightning Source LLC
Chambersburg PA
CBHW070236230426
43664CB00014B/2325